LUFTWAFFE FIGHTERS AND BOMBERS

The Stackpole Military History Series

THE AMERICAN CIVIL WAR

Cavalry Raids of the Civil War
Ghost, Thunderbolt, and Wizard
Pickett's Charge
Witness to Gettysburg

WORLD WAR I

Doughboy War

WORLD WAR II

After D-Day
Airborne Combat
Armor Battles of the
    Waffen-SS, 1943–45
Armoured Guardsmen
Army of the West
Arnhem 1944
Australian Commandos
The B-24 in China
Backwater War
The Battle of Sicily
Battle of the Bulge, Vol. 1
Battle of the Bulge, Vol. 2
Beyond the Beachhead
Beyond Stalingrad
Blitzkrieg Unleashed
Blossoming Silk against the
    Rising Sun
Bodenplatte
The Brandenburger Commandos
The Brigade
Bringing the Thunder
The Canadian Army and the
    Normandy Campaign
Coast Watching in World War II
Colossal Cracks
Condor
A Dangerous Assignment
D-Day Bombers
D-Day Deception
D-Day to Berlin
Destination Normandy
Dive Bomber!
A Drop Too Many
Eagles of the Third Reich
The Early Battles of Eighth Army
Eastern Front Combat
Europe in Flames
Exit Rommel
Fist from the Sky
Flying American Combat Aircraft
    of World War II
For Europe
Forging the Thunderbolt
For the Homeland

Fortress France
The German Defeat in the East,
    1944–45
German Order of Battle, Vol. 1
German Order of Battle, Vol. 2
German Order of Battle, Vol. 3
The Germans in Normandy
Germany's Panzer Arm in
    World War II
GI Ingenuity
Goodwood
The Great Ships
Grenadiers
Hitler's Nemesis
Infantry Aces
In the Fire of the Eastern Front
Iron Arm
Iron Knights
Kampfgruppe Peiper at the Battle
    of the Bulge
The Key to the Bulge
Knight's Cross Panzers
Kursk
Luftwaffe Aces
Luftwaffe Fighter Ace
Luftwaffe Fighter-Bombers
    over Britain
Luftwaffe Fighters and Bombers
Massacre at Tobruk
Mechanized Juggernaut or
    Military Anachronism?
Messerschmitts over Sicily
Michael Wittmann, Vol. 1
Michael Wittmann, Vol. 2
Mountain Warriors
The Nazi Rocketeers
Night Flyer / Mosquito
    Pathfinder
No Holding Back
On the Canal
Operation Mercury
Packs On!
Panzer Aces
Panzer Aces II
Panzer Aces III
Panzer Commanders of the
    Western Front
Panzergrenadier Aces
Panzer Gunner
The Panzer Legions
Panzers in Normandy
Panzers in Winter
The Path to Blitzkrieg
Penalty Strike
Poland Betrayed
Red Road from Stalingrad

Red Star under the Baltic
Retreat to the Reich
Rommel's Desert Commanders
Rommel's Desert War
Rommel's Lieutenants
The Savage Sky
Ship-Busters
Siege of Küstrin, 1945
The Siegfried Line
A Soldier in the Cockpit
Soviet Blitzkrieg
Stalin's Keys to Victory
Surviving Bataan and Beyond
T-34 in Action
Tank Tactics
Tigers in the Mud
Triumphant Fox
The 12th SS, Vol. 1
The 12th SS, Vol. 2
Twilight of the Gods
Typhoon Attack
The War against Rommel's
    Supply Lines
War in the Aegean
Wolfpack Warriors
Zhukov at the Oder

THE COLD WAR / VIETNAM

Cyclops in the Jungle
Expendable Warriors
Fighting in Vietnam
Flying American Combat
    Aircraft: The Cold War
Here There Are Tigers
Land with No Sun
MiGs over North Vietnam
Phantom Reflections
Street without Joy
Through the Valley

WARS OF AFRICA AND THE MIDDLE EAST

Never-Ending Conflict
The Rhodesian War

GENERAL MILITARY HISTORY

Carriers in Combat
Cavalry from Hoof to Track
Desert Battles
Guerrilla Warfare
Ranger Dawn
Sieges

LUFTWAFFE FIGHTERS AND BOMBERS

The Battle of Britain

Chris Goss

STACKPOLE
BOOKS

Copyright © 2000 by Christopher H. Goss

Published in paperback in 2011 by
STACKPOLE BOOKS
5067 Ritter Road
Mechanicsburg, PA 17055
www.stackpolebooks.com

First published in Great Britain in 2000 by Crécy Publishing Limited as THE
LUFTWAFFE FIGHTERS' BATTLE OF BRITAIN and THE LUFTWAFFE
BOMBERS' BATTLE OF BRITAIN. This combined edition published by
arrangement with Crécy Publishing Limited. All rights reserved, including the
right to reproduce this book or portions thereof in any form or by any means,
electronic or mechanical, including photocopying, recording, or by any information storage and retrieval system, without permission in writing from the
publisher. All inquiries should be addressed to Crécy Publishing Limited, 1a
Ringway Trading Estate, Shadowmoss Road, Manchester, England, M22 5LH.

Cover design by Tracy Patterson

Printed in the United States of America

10 9 8 7 6 5 4 3 2 1

Library of Congress Cataloging-in-Publication Data

Goss, Chris, 1961–
    Luftwaffe fighters and bombers : the Battle of Britain / Chris Goss.
        p. cm. — (Stackpole military history series)
    Previously published as two seperate works: Luftwaffe fighters' Battle of
Britain and, Luftwaffe bombers' Battle of Britain. 2000.
    Includes bibliographical references and index.
    ISBN 978-0-8117-0749-7
    1. World War, 1939–1945—Aerial operations, German. 2. World War,
1939–1945—Campaigns—Great Britain. 3. Germany. Luftwaffe—History—
World War, 1939–1945. I. Goss, Chris, 1961– Luftwaffe fighters' Battle of Britain.
II. Goss, Chris, 1961– Luftwaffe bombers' Battle of Britain. III. Title.
    D787.G584 2011
    940.54'211—dc22
                                        2010032758

Contents

Introduction

L ike many others, I have always been fascinated by stories of the Battle of Britain and how the outnumbered RAF fought and defeated a far superior enemy, namely the fighter and bomber aircraft of the *Luftwaffe*. For obvious reasons, accounts of what happened during the summer of 1940 tended to be centred around the defenders, be they in the air or on the ground. However, what started to interest me was the story of the Battle of Britain from the other side. That story went largely untold—a fate always meted out to those who are on the losing side or team.

Twenty years ago, I started contacting those German aircrew who participated in the Battle of Britain, most of whom had been taken prisoners of war. At the same time, I attempted to trace where their aircraft crashed, who was responsible for their demise and, in some cases, put the victor and the vanquished in contact with each other. Over the years, a series of very personal, sometimes harrowing, sometimes heroic, sometimes tragic, stories have emerged which, when put in chronological order, give an interesting insight into the Battle of Britain from the antagonist's point of view. One must never lose sight of the fact that the *Luftwaffe* was an instrument of Adolf Hitler's evil designs for the world but, despite this, inside the German fighter and bomber aircraft were very ordinary people who had the misfortune to be born at the wrong time.

This book is the result of some twenty years of research, which will hopefully allow the reader to see the Battle of Britain from a different perspective. These are by no means comprehensive and definitive stories of the Battle of Britain but they will allow the reader to understand how it felt to be flying against a tenacious enemy who had nothing to lose and how it felt to be defeated when, for the previous year, all that the *Luftwaffe* had faced was, in the main, a combination of disorganised, technically and numerically inferior opponents.

Acknowledgments

I have been writing to, and collecting accounts of, German pilots and their RAF opponents for the last twenty years. Sadly, many who have written to me over those years and whose accounts are contained within this book are no longer with us. To all of them I owe a great debt of thanks and only hope that I have managed to portray their life and death struggles in a fitting manner.

As usual there are a number of friends and acquaintances whose help has been gratefully received. I would therefore like to single out for thanks the following: My good friends Mark Postlethwaite (for the proof reading, constructive criticism and encouragement), Bernd Rauchbach (for the translating and proof reading and continued help with research), Peter Cornwell, that mine of information on anything 'Battle of Britain', for his assistance with a number of photos and (Uncle) John Smith for giving me the original idea of this book.

The following all helped in one way or another—they are listed in no particular order: Hans Hoehler, John Foreman, Bill Norman, Ian Hutton, the late Horst Grahl, Robert Ciuraj, Ken Watkins, Chris Fright, the late Siegfried Rauher, Rosemarie Wolff, Squadron Leader Philip Camp DFM, Mrs M. Morgan, Richard Wittmann, Andy Saunders, Len Gosman, Wilhelm Rosenbaum, Alfred Kull, Alwin Machalett, Erwin Moll, Jean Dillen, Kurt Miethner, Herbert Schick, Otto Blumers, Wolfgang Falck, the late Air Cdre A. C. Deere, the late *Generalleutnant* Adolf Galland, Mrs Jennifer Dexter, Hans Hoeller, Cato Guhnfeld, Michael Payne, Bill Norman, Eberhard d'Elsa, Ray Stebbings, Geoff Rayner, the late Heinz Dudeck, the late Hans Ohly, the late Willi Morzinek, Dr Felix Sauer, Ernst-Albrecht Schulz, Rolf Pingel, Franz Fiby, Walter Rupp, the late Gp Capt Alec Ingle, Ludwig von Eimannsberger, Patrick Burgess, Peter May, *Generalleutnant* Herbert Wehnelt, Herbert Quehl, Josef Volk and Ian Hutton.

Finally, thanks again to my wife Sally and daughters Katherine, Megan and Alexandra. Time for a (well deserved?) break from book writing—at least for the time being!

Glossary and Abbreviations

AA	Anti-aircraft
Adj	Adjutant
Adler Angriff	Attack of Eagles (13 August 1940), also known as *Adler Tag*—Eagle Day
Aufklaerungsgruppe (Aufkl.Gr)	Reconnaissance Wing
Beobachter (B)	Observer
Besatzung	Crew
Bf	Bayerische Flugzeugwerke (Messerschmitt aircraft prefix used by Germans)
Bordfunker (BF)	Radio operator
Bordmechaniker (BM) (or Bordwart)	Flight engineer
Bordschuetz (BS)	Air gunner
CO	Commanding Officer
Cpl	Corporal
De Wilde	Tracer ammunition
Deckungsrotte	Lookout pair
Deflection	Aim off a weapon to allow for its target's velocity
DFC	Distinguished Flying Cross
DFM	Distinguished Flying Medal
Ditch	Force-land in the sea
Do	Dornier
DSO	Distinguished Service Order
Einzelmeldung	Detailed report listing air activities on a daily basis
Erprobungsgruppe	Experimental Wing
Experte	Ace
Feldwebel (Fw)	Flight Sergeant
Fern	Long Range
Fg Off	Flying Officer
Flak	Anti-aircraft fire

Flieger (Flg)	Aircraftman
Fliegerkorps	Air Corps, subordinate to *Luftflotte*
Flt Lt	Flight Lieutenant
Flt Sgt	Flight Sergeant
Flt	Flight
Flugzeugfuehrer (F)	Pilot
Freie Jagd	Free hunting fighter sweep
Fuehrer	Leader
Fuehrungsstab	Luftwaffe High Command Operations Staff
FW	Focke Wulf
Gefreiter (Gefr)	Leading Aircraftman
Generalfeldmarschall	Air Chief Marshal
Generalleutnant	Air Vice-Marshal
Geschwader (Gesch)	Group consisting of three *Gruppen*; commanded by a *Geschwader Kommodore (Gesch Komm)*
Gp Capt	Group Captain
Gp	Group
GRT	Gross registered tonnage
Gruppe (Gr)	Wing consisting of three Staffeln; commanded by a *Gruppen Kommandeur (Gr Kdr)*. *Gruppe* number denoted by Roman numerals (e.g., II)
Hauptmann (Hptm)	Flight Lieutenant
He	Heinkel
Heckschuetz (HS)	Waist gunner
Heer (H)	Army
Holzauge	Lookout
Hs	Henschel
Hund	Dog—slang for an aircraft flying as wingman to another (see *Kette*)
Ia	Operations Officer
Inj	Injured
Jabo	Fighter-bomber
Jafue	Fighter Leader or operational level of command
Jagdgeschwader (JG)	Fighter Group
Ju	Junkers
Kamerad	Friend

Kampfgeschwader (KG)	Bomber Group
Kampfgruppe	Bomber group or formation
Katchmarek	Wingman
Kette	Three aircraft tactical formation similar to a vic
Kph	Kilometres per hour
Kuestenfliegergruppe (Kue.Fl.Gr.)	Coastal Flying Wing
LAC	Leading Aircraftman
Lehrgeschwader (LG)	Technical Development Flying Group
Leutnant (Lt)	Pilot Officer
Leutnant zur See (Lt zS)	Sub Lieutenant
Lotfe	Optical bomb sight
Luftflotte	Air Fleet
Major (Maj)	Squadron Leader
Me	Messerschmitt (used by RAF)
Mit Eichenlaub	With Oakleaves (see *Ritterkreuz*)
Nachrichtenoffizier (NO)	Communications Officer
NCO	Non-commissioned Officer
NO	*Nachrichtenoffizier*—communications officer
Oberbefehlshaber der Luftwaffe (ObdL)	Commander in Chief of the Luftwaffe
Oberfeldwebel (Ofw)	Warrant Officer (WO)
Obergefreiter (Ogefr)	Senior Aircraftman
Oberleutnant (Oblt)	Flying Officer
Oberst	Group Captain
Oberstleutnant (Obstlt)	Wing Commander
Plt Off	Pilot Officer
POW	Prisoner of War
Regia Aeronautica	Italian Air Force
Reichsluftfahrt Ministerium	Air Ministry
Reichsmarschall	Marshal of the Air Force
Revi	Reflector gunsight
Ritterkreuz	Knight's Cross
Rotte	Two aircraft tactical formation; two Rotten made a Schwarm; commanded by a Rottenfuehrer
Rottenflieger	Wingman
RPM	Revolutions per minute

Schwarm	Four aircraft tactical formation; commanded by a *Schwarm Fuehrer*
Seeloewe	Sealion—German code name for the invasion of Great Britain
Seenotflugkommando	Air Sea Rescue Detachment
Seenotstaffel	Air Sea Rescue Squadron
Sgt	Sergeant
Sonderfuehrer (Sd Fhr)	Rank given to war reporters
Sonderstaffel	Special *Staffel*
Sqn Ldr	Squadron Leader
Sqn	Squadron
Stab	Staff or Headquarters; formation in which *Gr Kdr* and *Gesch Komm* flew
Stabsfeldwebel (Stfw)	Senior Warrant Officer
Staffel (St)	Squadron (twelve aircraft); commanded by a *Staffel Kapitaen (St Kap)*. *Staffel* number denoted by Arabic numerals (e.g., 2)
Stoerangriff	Nuisance attack
Stuka	Junkers 87
Sturzkampfgeschwader (StG)	Dive Bomber Group
Technischer Offizier (TO)	Technical Officer
TO	*Technischer Offizier*—Technical Officer
Uninj	Uninjured
Unteroffizier (Uffz)	Sergeant (Sgt)
Vector	A heading to fly
Vic	Three aircraft tactical formation used by the RAF
W	Wounded
Walther PPK	Small pistol carried by German aircrew that usual fit into a pocket
Werk Nummer (Wk Nr)	Serial number
Wg Cdr	Wing Commander
Zerstoerer (Z)	Destroyer
Zerstoerergeschwader (ZG)	Heavy fighter group
+	Killed

BOOK ONE

The Luftwaffe
Fighters' Battle of Britain,
July–October 1940

Prologue to the Battle

The fighter pilots of the *Luftwaffe* had experienced a relatively quiet war prior to spring 1940. During the invasion of Poland, they met a very tenacious opponent flying aircraft that were far inferior to their Messerschmitt 109s and 110s. Again, during the invasion of Scandinavia, their opponents were equally tenacious but were numerically inferior. The invasion of the Low Countries saw them pitted against a series of enemies who adopted different tactics to counter the German technical and numerical superiority and had to change and adapt these tactics whilst constantly retreating. Just eighteen days after the Germans launched their offensive in the west, Belgium capitulated and German forces were poised to crush the remnants of the British Expeditionary Force and their allies along the north-eastern coast of France. Meanwhile in Norway, British forces in the Narvik region, together with French and Polish troops, having recaptured the town from the German invasion force, were fighting a desperate rearguard action against a superior German force in that area.

Two *Luftwaffe* fighter pilots were about to experience first hand what the rest of the *Luftwaffe* would experience in the months to come. *Oblt* Hans Jaeger of 3/ZG 76 had scored his *Gruppe*'s second kill of the war when, on 2 September 1939, he had shot down a Polish PZL 24. In April 1940, prior to the German invasion of Norway, he had been moved to become the *Gruppen Adjutant* of I/ZG 76. However, on 11 May 1940, he was ordered to form a *Sonderstaffel* from the more experienced pilots within the *Gruppe*, its task being to provide fighter support for the Luftwaffe's bombers still attacking British forces in the Narvik area. To maximise their range and to increase the time on patrol, the Messerschmitt 110 D-1/R-1 was used, a sub-variant which used the 1,050 litre fuel tank known as the 'Dachshund belly' by its crews.

Flying from Trondheim, the *Staffel* commenced its first flight on 20 May 1940, the same day that the RAF re-established itself in northern Norway. Seven days later, on the first day that Allied troop reinforcements landed at Narvik, a *Schwarm* which was headed by Hans Jaeger escorting *Stukas* attacking Bodo, met RAF fighters for the first time:

Oblt *Hans Jaeger (right) with* Lt *Heinz Holborn (left) and* Hptm *Reinecke (centre),* Gr Kdr *of I/ZG 76.* (Kettling)

3

A long range tank being fitted to Ofw *Gerhard Herzog's Bf 110D-1 of 1/ZG 76.* (Kettling)

Flight Lieutenant Caesar Hull, 263 Squadron

Got the Gladiator going and shot off without helmet or waiting to do anything up. Circled the 'drome, climbing, and pinned an '87 at the bottom of its dive. It made off slowly over the sea and just as I was turning away, another '87 shot past me and shots went through my windscreen, knocking me out for a while. Came to and was thanking my lucky stars when I heard a rat-tat behind me and I felt my Gladiator hit. Went into a right-hand turn and dive but could not get out of it. Had given up hope at 200ft when she centralised and I gave her a burst of engine to clear some large rocks. Further rat-tats behind me so gave up hope and decided to get down. Held off, then crashed.

Hull had fallen victim to Jaeger's *Rottenflieger*, Lt Helmut Lent, whilst Jaeger claimed to have shot down another, believed to have been Lt Tony Lydekker RN who was wounded; it was his fourth and last kill. If the German crews thought that future meetings with RAF fighters would be this easy, they were soon to be proved wrong as they found out two days later when the whole *Staffel* flew to Bardufoss on an escort sortie:

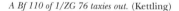

A Bf 110 of 1/ZG 76 taxies out. (Kettling)

Oberleutnant Hans Jaeger, I/ZG 76

On this sortie, *Hptm* Werner Restemeyer, our *Gruppen Kommandeur*, led the formation of eight aircraft; I flew as his *Rottenflieger*. We were attacked, to my great surprise, at an altitude of 5,000m by Hurricanes coming from above. I received several hits in both engines which were damaged and I had to dive away. I was forced to land in the sea 100m off the coast at Salanger. My *Bordfunker, Uffz* Helmut Feick, and I were not wounded but we were captured by Polish soldiers soon after we had swum to shore. The next day we were brought to Harstad and a few days later to London.

Hans Jaeger had never before encountered a 'modern' RAF fighter, 46 Squadron having landed at Bardufoss just two days before. In addition to Hans Jaeger being shot down, *Hauptmann* Restemeyer's fighter was badly hit and his *Bordfunker* badly wounded. They were probably victims of either Sgt Stanley Andrew, Flt Sgt Edward Shackley or Fg Off Phillip Frost.

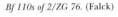

Bf 110s of 2/ZG 76. (Falck)

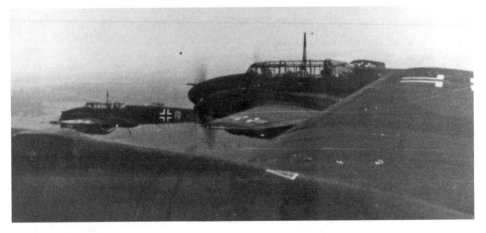

As Hans Jaeger was being marched away to captivity, over the beaches of north-eastern France, the *Luftwaffe* was now facing an RAF which was operating from established homeland bases and for the first time, its full arsenal of fighters – Spitfires, Hurricanes and Defiants – were being used. Just after dawn on 1 June 1940, a formation of about forty-eight Spitfires were patrolling the Belgian/French coast. For one German pilot, it was to be his first and last meeting with Spitfires:

Oberleutnant Juergen Moeller, *Staffelfuehrer* 2/ZG 1

My *Staffel Kapitaen, Oblt* Horst Lehrmann, was not flying this day and I was leading the *Staffel*. I was at the head of about twelve aircraft and we were flying over Dunkirk when we encountered some Spitfires. They flew directly opposite to our course. We had been told that it would be very unlikely that we would be involved in a frontal attack but if we ever were, we should never change course – whoever turns first or loses his nerve would die. So when I saw the Spitfires, I did exactly that, hoping that the RAF pilot would lose his nerve first. Either he was as stubborn as me or, this seems a strong possibility in retrospect, he was already dead. Witnesses noted that he did not fire in the last seconds. Both of us did not give an inch. He crashed into my right wing and tore it off. His 'plane exploded because I hit the centre of his aircraft. Both my *Bordfunker, Uffz* Karl Schieferstein, and myself parachuted to safety, landing amongst the thousands of soldiers on the beach.

Oblt *Juergen Moeller*. (Moeller)

Three Messerschmitt 110s of I/ZG 1 were shot down in this combat but, despite the superiority in numbers, it is believed that at least two Spitfires from 41 Squadron and four from 222 Squadron were lost when Messerschmitt 109s intervened. The aircraft that brought down *Oblt* Moeller is thought to have been flown either by Fg Off Gerald Massey-Sharpe or Sgt Leslie White of 222 Squadron, neither of whom survived. Nevertheless, it gave the RAF confidence when attacking the so-called Messerschmitt 110 'destroyer', despite the German belief that they would win any head on attack, as the following combat report, filed on 1 June 1940, shows:

Pilot Officer Timothy Vigors, 222 Squadron

A formation of twelve Me 110s were seen diving through the clouds. 19 Squadron attacked, driving a few back into the clouds. An Me 110 appeared through the cloud, 150 yards ahead and above me coming directly towards me. I opened fire at 100 yards and saw the enemy fly straight into my fire. One of the crew escaped by parachute…

By 4 June 1940, a total of 316,663 troops had been evacuated as part of Operation Dynamo; ten days later the Germans entered Paris. The French sued for peace on 22 June 1940, shortly after the final RAF elements withdrew to Great Britain. It was then left to the British Prime Minister and German *Fuehrer* to give an indication of what was to follow:

Winston Churchill

What General Weygand called the Battle of France is over. I expect that the Battle of Britain is about to begin. The whole fury and might of the enemy must very soon be turned on us. Hitler knows that he will have to break us in this island or lose the war…

Adolf Hitler

As England, despite her hopeless military situation, still shows no sign of willingness to come to terms, I have decided to and if necessary to carry out a landing operation against her… The aim of this operation is to eliminate the English motherland as a base from which war against Germany can be continued and if necessary, to occupy the Country completely.

In order to realise Hitler's aim, the *Luftwaffe* had firstly to achieve and maintain air superiority over the English Channel. They had not experienced the Channel during any previous invasions of the war. Their single seat fight-

A Bf 110C of I/ZG 1. (via Diener)

ers would be operating at maximum range. They had already seen shortfalls in the effectiveness of their twin-engined fighters and this time they would be facing an enemy with far superior fighters, operating from their own bases, over their own territory and possessing an effective early warning system. If the German aircrews thought that this time they might find things harder, they were soon to find out.

CHAPTER 1

The Battle Begins, July 1940

July 1940 started quietly for the German fighter pilots who must have been keen for a rest after their efforts during the previous two months. Initially, the *Luftwaffe* restricted its efforts to a series of reconnaissance flights and probing attacks on coastal targets along the length and breadth of Britain. The first co-ordinated major attack, with fighter escort, did not occur until the 4th of the month. From then on the tempo began to increase.

As well as escort flights, the German fighters enjoyed what were called *Freie Jagd*, literally free chases or fighter sweeps. Such missions soon inflicted a heavy price on unsuspecting RAF fighters over the Channel. However, the German fighter pilots soon began to dislike the regular flights escorting the much slower bomber and reconnaissance aircraft. For *Lt* Albert Striberny of 3/LG 2, such a mission would prove to be his downfall; he was destined to become the last German casualty before what would become officially known as the first day of the Battle of Britain:

Leutnant Albert Striberny, 3/LG 2

8 July – we were just about to leave the airfield at Ste Inglevert. It was rather late, about 2030 hrs, and we had our lodgings in Wissant, a little bathing resort between Cap Gris-Nez and Calais. Just then, a Dornier 17 landed on the airfield, the telephone rang and I was ordered to see our *Geschwader Kommodore*. I found him with a *Major* and his crew from the Do 17; he had to undertake a reconnaissance flight over Dover and the surroundings and my *Staffel* was ordered to escort them.

Not being very pleased after a long day's business and as it was evening, we agreed that we would fly at 4,500m altitude. Our *Staffel* had only five aircraft available for the task (normally twelve) so we started in a three and two aircraft formation, the latter *Rotte* to protect us. Having reached an altitude of 4,500m over the Channel we found ourselves in sunshine but saw that there were a lot of cumulus clouds over the English coast and Dover. The Do 17, contrary to our agreement, dived into the clouds and us three Bf 109s had to move together and follow him.

11

The remains of Striberny's Bf 109. (via Cornwell)

At about 1,700m, the clouds ended and together we flew over Dover. Besides photographing, the Dornier threw out some small bombs and then climbed back into cloud and we again joined up and followed. When the clouds ended, I quickly noticed the Do 17 near us but then, much higher, saw the sun shining on many aircraft – Spitfires!

Our situation was bad – low speed due to climbing through the cloud and so many aircraft coming down on us with the advantage of speed. I think now of the clear silhouette of our three aircraft against the white clouds.

In spite of our efforts to try and gain more speed, in no time they were on us and the battle was short. Whilst I was behind a Spitfire, another was behind me. I heard the sound as if one throws peas against a metal sheet and my cabin was full of dark smoke. I felt splashes of fuel on my face so I switched off the electrical system, dived back into cloud and threw off the cabin roof. The smoke disappeared and I could breathe freely and noticed that from the wings there came white streams of glycol. Whilst diving, I tried several times to start the engine, switching on the electrical system, but in vain. When I came out of cloud, I decided to bale out and undid the clasp of my seat belt and was about to climb onto the seat and jump when I thought of the high speed of the aircraft and I was afraid to be thrown against the tailplane so I pulled back the stick and slowed the aircraft down. This took a matter of seconds; I did a half roll and fell out.

As I was a bit afraid to mix up the handle for opening the parachute and the press-button that holds the parachute straps, I put my right hand on the handle and rolled the aircraft with the left. When falling, I didn't notice very much but, as we were told, counted to twenty-three then pulled the handle and after the drogue had opened over me, I felt a sudden jerk and hung under the opened parachute. There was no noise and I felt fixed to the sky. Then came the aircraft that shot me down – circling round me very close so I made a gesture with my hand that he should go away which he did and I was alone.

The wind from the west swept the parachute and me in a swinging motion and I drew with my weight and hands the lines of it to stop this movement as I didn't want to land in the sea. I had, of course, a life jacket but thought it better to land on a dry place.

By and by, but very slowly, I came nearer the earth. Below me on a road I noticed a bus and an ambulance. In the pocket of my trousers, I had an old silver pocket watch of my grandfather's. I took it out and opened the case and remember it was about 2130 hrs The feeling of falling down got stronger and when the horizon came up, I landed very softly in a gully in swampy land with a layer of moss. With a push, I freed myself from my parachute and waited for what was to come.

Albert Striberny had fallen victim to a patrolling Spitfire from 54 Squadron whose pilot filed a very comprehensive and conclusive report:

Flight Lieutenant Basil Way,
'B' Flight Commander, 54 Squadron

I was leading three sections of the Squadron with orders to patrol Dover at 3,000ft. Whilst orbiting over the coast, I was informed by RT that there were three Me 109s at 12,000ft in the vicinity. I was at 5,000ft and proceeded to climb. I saw two aircraft behind Green Section – I warned them that they might be enemy and former [sic] turned towards cloud. I continued to climb and immediately aircraft began to execute climbing spiral turns. I got right behind them (identified as Me 109s) – they were in vic formation and I attacked rear one, giving it a three second burst from astern at 200 yards. I don't think that enemy aircraft could have seen

'A' Flt 54 Sqn just before Dunkirk. Basil Way is sitting 2nd from the right. (Deere)

me until the moment of the attack. Glycol began to pour from its radiator with a certain amount of black smoke. I left this enemy aircraft and turned to attack the second. The second enemy aircraft dived straight down and I managed to get a long burst at 250 yards. Enemy aircraft continued to dive, skirting edge of cloud, 9,000ft over the coast. It came

Another 8 July 1940 victim – Lt Johann Boehm of 4/JG 51 was shot down by 74 Sqn.

The pilot that shot him down was Sgt Tony Mould. (May)

below and at 5,000ft, pilot baled out. I judged his position as five miles inland, north-west of Deal; parachute opened.

Sadly, Basil Way did not last the month. Shot down and killed off Dover on 25 July, his body was later washed ashore in France and buried near Dunkirk.

As the tempo increased, additional fighter *Geschwader* were moved from rest in Germany to bases all along France's northern coast. Further to the west, as targets were further away from France and as the range of the single seat fighters was limited, escorting the bombers was left in the main to Messerschmitt 110s. One of the first combats with these twin-engined fighters took place on 9 July when III/ZG 26 learned a painful lesson when they lost three aircraft to the Hurricanes of 56 Squadron with a further Messerschmitt limping home badly damaged. It would appear that the pain of the losses was tempered by what they claimed to have shot down – five Hurricanes and seven Spitfires. In fact, none were lost to German fighters.

Just as one Messerschmitt 110 unit suffered at the hands of the RAF, another, this time further west, was to undergo a similar fate. *Oblt* Gerhard Kadow, *Staffel Kapitaen* of 9/ZG 76, had already had an eventful war to date. On 8 June 1940, he and three other crews from the Messerschmitt 110 equipped II/ZG 1

Oblt Gerhard *Kadow (front centre) seen as a POW in Canada, Summer 1944. (Kadow)*

(which was later reformed as III/ZG 76) had been shot down by Swiss Messerschmitt 109s near Morteau. This had occurred because the Swiss Air Force had taken a tough stance against the frequent border incursions by German aircraft. Following a number of air battles, on 8 June the *Luftwaffe* attempted to provoke Swiss fighters into battle and then to inflict heavy losses on them. In fact the opposite occurred and this pointless tactic cost the lives of three men, one of whom was Gerhard Kadow's *Bordfunker*; Kadow himself was wounded.

With the Battle of France over, Gerhard Kadow's unit based itself at Laval in France where, recovered from his wounds, he was teamed up with a new *Bordfunker, Gefr* Helmut Scholz. On 11 July, it was his destiny to be shot down again:

Oberleutnant **Gerhard Kadow,** *Staffel Kapitaen* **9/ZG 76**

On 11 July 1940, we flew from Laval to Dinard to refuel and then towards England at 1200 hrs. My *Staffel* together with the other two from the *Gruppe* were ordered to protect *Stukas* which had targets in the Portland area.

Kadow's Bf 110. (via Cornwell)

Just before we took off, my *Geschwader Kommodore*, *Maj* Walter Grabmann, briefed us that it was imperative that no *Stuka* could be lost, even if it meant the loss of our fighters. On that day, my *Staffel* had only seven aircraft combat ready and I was briefed to protect the right flank at 4,000m altitude; the other two *Staffeln* had to protect the left flank at 6,000m altitude and provide close escort for the *Stukas* after they had dropped their bombs (the time at which *Stukas* were most vulnerable).

For much of the flight across the Channel, it was uneventful but as we approached the British coast, we were confronted by the enemy. I counted about twenty dark specks in the distance, somewhat higher than we were and when they came nearer, I was certain that they were British fighters but could not say whether they were Spitfires or Hurricanes.

I knew that my twin-engined fighter was not as manoeuvrable as a single-seat fighter so the chances of winning were reduced. The proportion of British fighters to my *Staffel* was about 3:1 but I had to follow our orders of protecting the *Stukas*. Relying on my two cannon and four forward facing guns, I carried out a head-on attack on the first fighter – I pressed all buttons and the bullets flew out like water out of a watering can. Our closing speed was very fast and both of us broke away in order not to collide. Whether I had any success I do not know, as in the next instant two other British fighters were behind me and opened fire. My engines stopped and I knew that getting home was impossible. My enemy saw his success and stopped shooting but followed me. I threw off the cabin roof (in the hope that it might hit one of the attacking fighters!) and I ordered Scholz to do the same. However, he reported that the mechanism to do this had been damaged by gunfire so because of this, I decided not to bale out or ditch in the Channel.

Because of all the above, I decided to make a crash-landing which I did so with success on Povington Heath near Wareham in Dorset at about 1245 hrs. After the crash-landing, I could not leave the aircraft immediately as a bullet had hit my seat and the damage that it had caused meant that the rough edges of the aluminium had snagged my parachute and flying suit. However, I managed to get out and helped out my *Bordfunker* who had suffered slight wounds from bullet splinters.

The first thing I decided to do was to destroy the aircraft. At this time we did not have an explosive charge to do this, so we opened the fuel tanks and then I tried to set the fuel on fire with my pistol. I used up eight bullets but without success. As this was going on, I heard impacts probably from bullets. I went to the other side of the aircraft to find out and immediately felt a blow to my heel – a bullet had entered the sole of my flying boot just as I was taking a step. The heel helped deflect the bullet which caused just a slight flesh wound. After this, we both left the aircraft alone and looked around us.

About twenty soldiers stood up and an officer ordered us to put our hands up – we did just that and became prisoners of war. I complained that it was unfair to shoot us fliers who had been shot down. He said that we had been trying to destroy our aircraft and he had tried to prevent us doing just that – be glad, he said, that we had not received a bullet in the belly!

During the air battle, two other aircraft from my *Staffel* had been shot down. One, piloted by *Oblt* Jochen Schroeder, had ditched and both he and his *Bordfunker* had got out. However, the *Bordfunker* had been badly wounded and soon died; Jochen was rescued by a boat. The other Messerschmitt was flown by *Oblt* Hans-Joachim Goering, nephew of *Generalfeldmarschall* Hermann Goering; he was probably mortally wounded and crashed still in the cockpit of his aircraft.

A further Messerschmitt 110 from 7/ZG 76 was lost to a tenacious RAF defence as well as just one of the *Stukas*. Gerhard Kadow's Messerschmitt was claimed by at least five RAF pilots from different squadrons. It is believed that the head-on attack that he reported was against Hurricanes of 238 Squadron but the credit for his demise went to another two pilots:

Sqn Ldr John Dewar.

Squadron Leader John Dewar, 87 Squadron

Having disposed of one Me 110, I went into a full turn to review the progress of the battle and to remove two other enemy aircraft trying to get onto my tail. I saw a bomb explode by some shipping in the harbour and two enemy aircraft diving for the ground. One enemy aircraft was still pursuing me. The Hurricane turned easily onto his tail – he was vertically banked. He then dived for ground going east. I followed but withheld fire as I was getting short of rounds. Enemy aircraft pulled out at about 1,000ft and continued 'S' turns. I gave him a burst from 100 yards and vapour came from both engines. I had to slam the throttle back to avoid overshooting. Vapour then ceased to come from the engines and he gathered way again. I was very close and saw no rear gun fire so I held my position and took careful non-deflection shots, using all ammunition. Enemy aircraft at once turned inland, going very slowly. Seeing me draw away, he turned seawards again. I went to head him off and he, apparently thinking I had more rounds, turned for land again, sinking slowly. At 200ft, another Hurricane came up and fired a short burst at him [Fg Off H K Riddle of 601 Sqn]. He immediately turned and landed on Grange Heath. Both crew got out wearing yellow life jackets. The Army were close by...

The scene was setting for the *Luftwaffe* for the remainder of the Battle of Britain but for the rest of the month of July 1940 fighter combats remained sporadic with no side emerging as the clear winner. For example, on 19 July the twin seat Boulton Paul Defiants of 141 Squadron were bounced by *Hptm* Hannes Trautloft's III/JG 51. Trautloft and the three other members of his *Stabschwarm, Oblt* Otto Kath, *Lt* Werner Pichon-Kalau and *Lt* Herbert Wehnelt, led the attack which resulted in the destruction of six Defiants and damaged a further one; in human terms, four pilots and six gunners were killed with a fur-

The victorious Stab *III/JG 51, St Omer/Clairmarais, Summer 1940. Left to Right* Oblt *Otto Kath (*Adj*), Lt* Werner *Pichon-Kalau (*TO*), Lt* Herbert Wehnelt *(*NO*), Hptm* Hannes Trautloft *(Gr Kdr). (Wehnelt)*

ther three pilots wounded. The Squadron was immediately withdrawn from the battle. For the *Luftwaffe*, the worst day for fighter losses was 24 July when JG 26 lost four aircraft. Of the four pilots, three were killed and one taken prisoner and of those, one pilot was a *Gruppen Kommandeur*, another the *Gruppe Technischer Offizier*. JG 52 fared no better, also losing four aircraft of which all four pilots were killed. Again, of those four, one was a *Gruppen Kommandeur* and two were *Staffel Kapitaene*. The losses of three *Gruppe* executives necessitated III/JG 52 being withdrawn from France. On this day, for one German pilot, this was his first combat over England. *Hptm* Adolf Galland was leading III/JG 26 and recalls clearly what happened:

Hauptmann Adolf Galland, *Gruppen Kommandeur* III/JG 26

On 24 July, I obtained my fifteenth victory. It was at about 1335 hrs, thirty kilometres north of Margate at an altitude of 2,200–3,000m. I could see the enemy pilot at the time he jumped out of his aircraft but unfortunately his parachute did not open. I did notice that the Spitfire crashed onto the water.

There was only one pilot fatality in this combat. Plt Off Johnny Allen of 54 Squadron was killed when his Spitfire crashed into an electricity sub-station at Margate. Galland's victim cannot be identified for sure on a day that reinforced Galland's belief that the RAF would be a difficult and tenacious opponent. During the same action, thirty year-old *Oblt* Lothar Ehrlich, *Staffel Kapitaen* of 8/JG 52 was seen by his comrades to have baled out in the middle of the Channel in between Dover and Calais following combat with a Spitfire. The victorious RAF pilot also noted the same:

Adolf Galland. (Galland)

Pilot Officer Colin Gray, 54 Squadron

I shot down an Me 109 some time after midday on 24 July 1940 and the pilot baled out into the sea. I saw him swimming for some object which I thought may have been a dinghy and passed details of his location to control but apparently he was not picked up. Whether or not this was *Oblt* Ehrlich, I do not know – the actual location as I remember was eight miles off Margate. If this was Ehrlich, I do not know how anyone else would know the location since I did not see any other aircraft in the vicinity. Nevertheless, it was the enemy aircraft I was after, not the pilot. In fact I was always pleased to see the pilot bale out and, in this case, I did my best to see that he was rescued although, unfortunately, to no avail.

Still the *Luftwaffe* tried to bomb shipping all along the Channel and as the end of the month approached, the weight and fury of their attacks increased. Nevertheless, the RAF managed to weather the storm, not realising that the storm to come would be even stronger. On the 29th of the month, it was decided that the daylight passage of ships through the Dover Straits would only occur during the hours of darkness. However, the day before that a combat took place which could have been an even greater blow to the *Luftwaffe* than the fighter losses that occurred on 24 July:

Oblt *Lothar Ehrlich, 8/JG 52, killed in action 24 July 1940.* (via Quehl)

Major Werner Moelders, *Geschwader Kommodore* JG 51

I flew on 28 July 1940 with my *Rottenflieger* and *Adjutant, Oblt* Erich Kircheis north of Dover. Suddenly I saw three British fighters, far behind them a lot of Spitfires in the haze. The three Spitfires were somewhat below us so I attacked this section. When I approached, both the outer Spitfires turned but the one in the middle flew straight on. I got behind it and opened fire from sixty metres. At once the wing caught fire, thick smoke and flame, and the Spitfire went down. I pulled up and saw eight to ten Spitfires behind me. I was frightened for a moment. There was only one chance – to go straight through the formation. I swept through the crowd. The first Spitfires were surprised but one of the rearmost was watchful. He fired with all guns and hit me! It rattled my aircraft, I had hits in the cooling system, wing and fuel tank. I broke away and dived with everything I had – 700kph towards the Channel. The engine was working well thank God! The Spitfires chased me and my flag of smoke but then *Oblt* Richard Leppla, who had seen the incident, rushed to my assistance. He shot at the Spitfire sitting behind me and, after a few seconds, it went down wrapped in a large cloud of smoke. When I reached the coast, the engine began to splutter and, during the crash-landing, the undercarriage collapsed and I made a perfect belly landing. When I tried to get out, my legs were strangely weak and I saw bloodstains. In hospital I discovered the reason why – three splinters in the thigh, one in the knee and one in the left foot; I had felt nothing in the heat of combat.

Moelders' initial attack wounded Fg Off Tony Lovell of 41 Squadron who managed to nurse his crippled Spitfire back to RAF Manston. It is believed that Flt Lt John Webster, also of 41 Squadron, was the pilot who managed to put a

Maj *Werner Moelders.* (via Moelders)

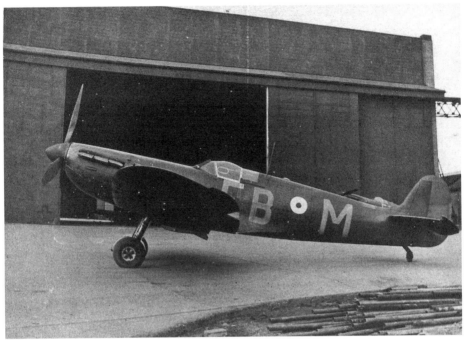

A Spitfire of 41 Sqn.

quick burst of fire into Moelders' fighter. As the German pilot tried to flee back to France, it was Plt Off Peter Stevenson who tried to finish him off only to be shot down by *Oblt* Leppla.

Despite poor weather conditions, attacks by German bombers continued on the last three days of the month but no German fighters were lost. However, they still managed to inflict losses on the RAF, one casualty being the pilot who wounded Werner Moelders, Flt Lt John Webster, who was hit in combat on 28 July but managed to return to RAF Manston with a damaged Spitfire. Activity on 31 July was severely curtailed by the weather, even if II/JG 51 managed to teach the RAF a final lesson by mauling 74 Squadron who lost two Spitfires and their pilots. The first month of the Battle of Britain then ended. The RAF had realised the effectiveness of the single-seat German fighters but had also realised the failings of the Messerschmitt 110. To the irritation of the German fighter pilots, they had increasingly been called upon to 'wet nurse' bomber and reconnaissance aircraft but when allowed to carry out *Freie Jagd,* could punish the RAF severely. Nevertheless, lessons had been learned on both sides and as July moved into August, both air forces were keen to put these lessons to good advantage.

CHAPTER 2

The Pace Quickens, August 1940

With air operations during July 1940 hampered in the main by poor weather, the same can be said of the first week of August 1940. Mist, low cloud and haze seemed to be the pattern for at least the first five days. When, on the 5th of the month, the first fighter combats occurred, neither side emerged the clear winner. However, one of the German injured, *Oblt* Reinhard Seiler, *Staffel Kapitaen* of 1/JG 54 was another casualty that the *Luftwaffe* could do without. A veteran of the Spanish Civil War where he had already claimed nine air combat victories and the Battle of France where he scored a further two, he was wounded in a combat with RAF fighters which meant he was off flying for the remainder of 1940[1].

Three days later, things took a dramatic turn for the worse for the RAF. Regarded by some as the first true day of the Battle of Britain, 8 August 1940 saw the might of the *Luftwaffe* thrown against Convoy CW9, codename PEE-WIT. Sailing from Southend in the late afternoon of 7 August, it passed through the Straits of Dover during the hours of darkness, apparently undetected. However, this was not the case for, as dawn started to break the next day, the convoy was attacked by German *E*-boats which scattered the convoy. As the ships approached the Isle of Wight, it was the turn of *Stukas* to finish what the *E*-boats had started.

Despite a heavy fighter escort, the first air attack of the day was successfully parried by Hurricanes of 145 Squadron even if they did lose three aircraft to I and III/JG 27. At lunchtime, with an even bigger escort of both Messerschmitt 109s and 110s, the *Stukas* returned. This time, more RAF fighters were thrown into battle. Plt Off David Crook of 609 Squadron noted in his book *Spitfire Pilot* that there was going to be a lot of trouble that day because the convoy was such a tempting target. His squadron had missed the earlier attack but as the convoy sailed further west and into their 'patch', it was not long before they were in action:

---

[1] *Oblt* Seiler would end the War having flown over 500 sorties and shot down 109 aircraft. He would also be awarded the Knight's Cross with Oakleaves.

25

Plt Off David Crook (centre with mug of tea).

Pilot Officer David Crook, 609 Squadron

We steered towards the convoy which was now about twelve miles south of Bournemouth. There was a small layer of cloud and while dodging in and out of this, Flt Lt McArthur and I got separated from the other three and a moment later, we also lost each other.

While looking around to try and find them, I glanced out towards the convoy and saw three balloons falling in flames. Obviously an attack was starting and I climbed above the cloud layer and went towards the convoy at full throttle, climbing all the time towards the sun so that I could deliver my attack with the sun behind me.

I was now about five miles from the convoy and could see a big number of enemy fighters circling above, looking exactly like a swarm of flies buzzing round a pot of jam. Below them, the dive-bombers were diving down on the ships and great fountains of white foam were springing up where their bombs had struck the water. I could see that one or two ships had already been hit and were on fire.

I was now at 16,000ft above the whole battle and turned round to look for a victim. At that moment, a Hurricane squadron appeared on the scene and attacked right into the middle of the enemy fighters which were split up immediately and a whole series of individual combats started covering a very big area of the sky...

A Spitfire of 609 Sqn. (Dexter)

Again, the battle above the convoy raged but the RAF fighters were not able to prevent damage being inflicted on the ships. German fighter kills were filed by I and III/JG 27 who claimed six RAF fighters and the Messerschmitt 110s of V(Z)/LG 1 which claimed a further eleven. These units also claimed eight barrage balloons, the same ones seen by David Crook going down in flames. As if this was not enough, a few hours later the Germans launched a further attack against the luckless convoy, the German fighters and bombers again being attacked tenaciously by RAF fighters. This final attack at about tea-time resulted in further claims for II and III/JG 27 and I/ZG 2 but this was to be the last assault on what was left of PEEWIT. Only four ships arrived unscathed at Swanage later than evening – seven had been sunk and another thirteen damaged. The RAF claimed to have shot down thirty-three German aircraft whilst the Germans claimed forty-seven. Actual losses were fourteen RAF fighters and twelve of their pilots killed whilst the *Luftwaffe* lost nine fighters and seven fighter aircrew killed in addition to eight *Stukas*. Although bloodied, the RAF had held its own against superior numbers of German fighters and had gained vital combat experience; the month, and for that matter the Battle of Britain, had only just started.

The following two days were quiet with little action for both sides, due in the main to the poor weather. However, the battles began again on 11 August with a series of raids ranging from Harwich in the east to Portland in the west.

The major attack of the day occurred mid-morning and was carried out by thirty-eight Junkers 88s of I and II/KG 54 against the harbour, fuel installations, ammunition depots and shipping at Portland. To ensure the bombers reached their target, a massive escort was provided by the whole of JG 2, JG 27, JG 53 and I and II/ZG 2. One of the escorting pilots was twenty-year-old *Lt* Wolf Muenchmeyer of 1/ZG 2. He had joined his *Staffel* on 14 May 1940 and had flown eight missions before France capitulated. Moving to Normandy, his *Gruppe* flew from a field flying strip at Ste Aubin where they carried out a few reconnaissance missions over the Channel with little reaction from the RAF. They then took part in the attack on the PEEWIT convoy before being tasked on 11 August:

Leutnant Wolf Muenchmeyer, 1/ZG 2

On 11 August, we went to Portland escorting Ju 88s, resulting in my first great air battle with hundreds of aircraft involved. Whilst I was guarding two Messerschmitt 110s ahead of me, suddenly a Spitfire approached from the side, pursued by an Me 109. I tried to avoid a burst of tracer bullets by lifting my port wing, this burst originating from the Spitfire aiming at me or from the Me 109 trying to get the Spitfire – I am not sure. In any case, I thought I had been lucky but then smoke poured from my port engine and I could not keep up with the rest and, looking around, I suddenly found myself surrounded by Spitfires left and right so I tried to escape by diving almost vertically at full engine power knowing that our Messerschmitts had a much higher wing loading than the Spitfires and therefore could get a much faster speed by diving. I calculated I reached 900–1,000kph, far greater than my instruments could tell me. Then, at sea level, I stopped my port engine and feathered the propeller. It took me an hour and a half to get back to France, my port engine having lost all of its oil and had seized. On that mission, we lost our *Gruppen Kommandeur, Maj* Ernst Ott.

It is hard to ascertain which RAF pilot was responsible for Wolf Muenchmeyer's early departure from the battle but one report is similar to what the German pilot experienced:

Lt Wolf Muenchmeyer, 1/ZG 2. (Muenchmeyer)

An unidentified Bf 110C of I/ZG 2 crash-landed somewhere in France. (Hoeller)

Pilot Officer David Crook, 609 Squadron

...Some Hurricanes were already attacking the Messerschmitts and the latter had formed their usual defensive circle, going round and round on each others' tails. This makes attack rather difficult as if you attack one, there is always another behind you. We were now about a 1,000ft above them at 25,000ft and the CO turned round and the whole of 609 went down to attack.

We came down right on top of the enemy formation, going at terrific speed, and as we approached them, we split up slightly, each pilot selecting his own target. I saw an Me 110 ahead of me going across in front. I fired a good burst at practically point-blank range. Some black smoke poured from his port engine and he turned to the right and stalled. I could not see what happened after this as I narrowly missed hitting his port wing. It flashed past so close that I instinctively ducked my head...

The RAF threw eight squadrons of fighters at the attacking Germans, claiming thirty-eight German aircraft destroyed for the loss of seventeen aircraft and fifteen pilots. German claims were exorbitant – fifty-seven RAF fighters for the loss of five bombers and seventeen fighters. Amongst those lost however were the *Gruppen Kommandeur* of II/KG 54, the *Geschwader Adjutant* of ZG 2, the *Gruppen Kommandeur* of I/ZG 2, the *Staffel Kapitaen* of 6/JG 2 and the *Gruppen Adjutant* of III/JG 2 – all experienced men who would be sorely missed over the coming weeks and months. Nevertheless, the German fighters succeeded in drawing their RAF opponents away from the bombers who successfully struck the oil tanks at Portland with numerous other hits on dockyard installations both at Portland and the secondary target of Weymouth.

The scene of battle then almost immediately shifted further east. The target this time was convoy BOOTY which, at midday, was just off the Essex coast. The bombers this time came from the specialist unit *Erprobungsgruppe* 210 which flew a mix of 30mm cannon-armed Messerschmitt 110s and Messerschmitt 109 and 110 fighter-bombers. This attack was undertaken purely by both types of Messerschmitt 110 with an escort from I/ZG 26:

Hauptmann Hans Kogler, *Staffel Kapitaen* 1/ZG 26

On 11 August, I/ZG 26 had to meet up with a fast bomber formation of Bf 110s over Gravelines and to escort them towards the Thames Estuary. Due to confusion during the planning (the *Gruppen Kommandeur, Hptm* Wilhelm Mackrocki was absent on this day and I was his deputy), we arrived three to four minutes late at the Gravelines assembly point where we found no aircraft to escort. I was of the opinion that the fighter bombers had already flown towards the target so I decided to head that way.

Somewhere west of Ipswich/Harwich, still without the fighter–bombers, we were attacked by Spitfires. My *Rottenflieger, Oblt* Wilhelm Spies, broke away and left me alone. Suddenly, I was attacked from behind by a Spitfire and was hit in both engines. I then glided from 1,500m to sea level and tried to fly east as I was not being followed. Soon both engines stopped and I was forced to ditch. The attack took place at about 1300 hrs and I ditched at about 1307–1310 hrs.

I lost consciousness and when I awoke, found the cockpit full of water and so I had to get out before I was dragged down. My *Bordfunker, Uffz* Adolf Bauer, had managed to release the dinghy from the fuselage so we both swam to it and got in. What followed was a hard time for both of us because we had nothing to eat and drink for the next four days.

All such things as cake, water, chocolate and cigarettes were lost that night when the dinghy was capsized by a wave and it was not until the afternoon of Wednesday 14 August at about 1600 hrs that we were picked up by two *E*-boats in the vicinity of Nieuport. By that time we were the best in our *Geschwader* at dinghy sailing!

Hptm *Hans Kogler (centre with cap) and* Uffz *Adolf Bauer (3rd from right) after their rescue, August* 1940. (Kogler)

Hans Kogler's injuries forced him to miss the remainder of the Battle of Britain but he continued to be associated with Messerschmitt 110s and ZG 26, eventually becoming that *Geschwader*'s *Kommodore* in the Summer of 1944 before it was redesignated JG 6 and the unit converted to the Focke Wulf 190. It was his fate to be shot down and taken prisoner on 1 January 1945 only to be killed in a freak hunting accident in the early 1980s.

As Hans Kogler and his *Bordfunker* tried as best they could to make themselves comfortable, the final attack of the day was taking place slightly to the west. However, despite heavy fighter involvement on both sides, the attack on the convoy came to very little and, as both sides returned to base, the weather put an end to any further assaults against convoys or maritime targets. In fact, a new phase of the Battle of Britain would start the following day which would turn out to be the day before the German's planned *Adler Angriff* major aerial assault.

The weather on Monday 12 August looked promising so the *Luftwaffe* commenced its pre-*Adler Angriff* missions by an early morning *Freie Jagd* by III/JG 26 designed to draw up RAF fighters so that *Erprobungsgruppe* 210 could attack unscathed. The targets for these fighter-bombers were the radar stations at Dover, Dunkirk, Pevensey and Rye and, for the loss of just one fighter, III/JG 26 seemed to achieve this as *Erprobungsgruppe* 210 succeeded in putting three sites temporarily out of action whilst at the same time suffering not a single loss.

The attacks on radar sites were a new venture for the *Luftwaffe* who by now had realised the importance of the early warning the RAF was getting from radar of their impending attacks. Added to this change in tactic were, a few hours

Maj *Kogler*, Gr Kdr *III/ZG 26, looks at one of his Gruppe's victims (a B-17), 11 April 1944.* (Kogler)

later, the attacks on the south Kent airfields at Lympne and Hawkinge with the sole aim of preventing them being used as fighter bases. Luckily for the RAF, these attacks did not achieve their aim.

As lunchtime approached, the scene of battle switched to the west as a massive formation of sixty-three Junkers 88s from KG 51 headed towards Portsmouth and the Isle of Wight. Their aim was twofold – firstly to attack the naval dockyard at Portsmouth and secondly to destroy the radar station at Ventnor on the Isle of Wight. The escort for this attack was even more massive being made up from the entire fighter elements of *Jafue* 2-JG 2, JG 27, JG 53, ZG 2, ZG 76 and V(Z)/LG 1.

One of the German fighter units new to the Battle was 1/JG 53, commanded by *Legion Condor* veteran *Hptm* Hans-Karl Mayer. Taking off from the forward airfield at Cherbourg-East, they stayed with the bombers until just off the Isle of Wight and witnessed the first of eight RAF fighter squadrons wading into the bombers and, if they got in the way, their fighter escorts which were holding off the Isle of Wight. *Hptm* Mayer spotted three Hurricanes attacking and setting on fire a single Messerschmitt 110 so he chose to exact retribution. Bouncing the jubilant RAF pilots, he set the right hand Hurricane on fire; shortly afterwards it plunged into the Channel. His *Rottenflieger, Uffz* Heinrich Ruehl, dispatched the left hand Hurricane in a similar fashion, even though the RAF pilot was aware of the attack and tried, unsuccessfully, to flee. The final Hurricane did put up a fight and managed to attack Mayer's aircraft before being mortally damaged by Mayer who saw it turn back, emitting smoke, for the Hampshire coast. Sadly, the smoke got

Hptm *Mayer sits astride his Bf 109 damaged 12 August 1940.*

thicker and, in a gradual shallow dive, the Hurricane hit the water and slipped beneath the waves.

As all of this was taking place, far above the *Deckungschwarm,* whose task was to protect the remainder of the *Staffel* from surprise attack, watched the drama unfold at the same time as they were scanning for any possible bounce:

Unteroffizier Heinrich Kopperschlaeger, 1/JG 53

After I saw *Hptm* Mayer shoot down a Hurricane, I noticed behind the *Staffel* a single machine. As I turned towards it, I saw that it was a Spitfire. He attempted to break away to escape; he then tried to dive away. At 40m range, I opened fire at him. He attempted to break away to port but suddenly I saw a white fuel trail and he crashed into the water. The pilot did not bale out.

The German bombers succeeded in their aims – Portsmouth Harbour was badly hit whilst Ventnor was off the air for three days. However, the RAF tactic of going for the bombers, albeit after they had attacked, paid off and, together with AA guns, accounted for ten bombers. One of those losses was the *Geschwader Kommodore* of KG 51. Five Messerschmitt 110s were destroyed (resulting in the deaths of the *Gruppen Kommandeur of* I/ZG 2 and the *Staffel Kapitaen* of 8/ZG 76) whilst the only single-engined fighter loss was that of *Hptm* Harro Harder, the *Gruppen Kommandeur* of III/JG 53. Again, German claims were high (thirty-six confirmed and a further seven possibles) whilst only eleven RAF fighters were actually lost.

As the day progressed, further incursions took place back over Kent but not with the intensity and ferocity of the earlier raids. Again, airfields were the targets and each attack was supported by heavy fighter escort:

Uffz *Heinrich Koepperschlager (right) with* Uffz *Heinrich Hoehnisch.* (Hoehnisch)

Oberleutnant Albrecht Dress, *Gruppen Technischer Offizier* III/JG 54

In the late afternoon of 12 August, my *Gruppe* was tasked to escort a bomber formation in its attack on the airfield at Canterbury[2]. However, at an altitude of 6,000m I attacked a Spitfire only to be attacked a short time later. I had luck that my aircraft did not catch fire just that my engine and propeller reduction gear were hit so I was forced to crash-land. I had suffered shrapnel wounds and was immediately taken to a nearby factory; shortly afterwards, I was taken to Margate General Hospital where I was treated and, after several days, I was then taken to the Royal Herbert Hospital in Woolwich after which I was sent to the prisoner of war camp at Grizedale Hall in the Lake District.

[2]The Germans did indeed report having bombed *Canterbury Airfield* at 1830hrs, scoring six direct hits on three hangars, four hits on taxyways and eight hits on miscellaneous buildings in addition to three aircraft. It is believed they were actually attacking Manston.

Oblt Dress' Bf 109 after its crash-landing. (Dress)

As usual with many German pilots, the only aircraft they encountered were Spitfires but it is believed that *Oblt* Dress was shot down by a Hurricane flown by Flt Lt Michael Crossley of 32 Squadron.

12 August had turned out to be a arduous day for both sides but the *Luftwaffe* must have been pleased with the results, especially against the radar stations. Bolstered by these attacks, *Adler Angriff* would commence the following day, but the German meteorologists forecast that the weather would perhaps have the last word on when exactly *Adler Angriff* could commence.

As dawn approached on 13 August, most of the airfields in northern France were hives of

THIS AND NEXT PAGE
Another fighter casualty on 12 August – the remains of Oblt *Friedrich Butterweck's Bf 109E-1 of 1/JG 26.*

An early morning casualty on 13 August – Oblt *Paul Temme,* Gr Adj *I/JG 2.*

activity and then, between 0550 hrs and 0610 hrs, the first bombers lifted off into a cloud-laden sky. However, the crews were not aware that, because of the inclement weather, the attack had been postponed and just after they were airborne, the message was passed. However, only the fighter escort heard that the attack was cancelled and returned to base whilst the bombers droned onwards unaware that they were unprotected.

Meanwhile, to the west another series of attacks was developing. Again, the Junkers 88s of KG 54 were the protagonists and were heading for the airfields of Odiham and Farnborough. A further formation of *Stukas from* StG 77 had their attack cancelled when they were half-way across the Channel. Again, as with previous assaults, there was a massive fighter escort but it failed to prevent the RAF from harrying the attackers, as one pilot remembers:

Leutnant Wolf Muenchmeyer, 1/ZG 2

> Early in the morning of 13 August, we went to the region of Aldershot escorting Ju 88s. We did not encounter any RAF defence because of cloudy skies and we landed back at base very short of fuel and just before it became fogged in.

At lunchtime, twenty-three Messerschmitt 110s of V(Z)/LG 1 were tasked for a *Freie Jagd* in the Portland area only to be severely mauled by two Hurricane squadrons which cost the Germans five of their fighters with a further five being seriously damaged. *Reichsmarschall* Hermann Goering got to hear of this débâcle and issued the following warning a few days later:

> The incident of V/LG 1 on 13 August shows that certain unit commanders have not yet learnt the importance of clear orders. I have repeatedly given orders that twin-engined fighters are only to be employed where the range of other fighters is inadequate or where it is for the purpose of assisting our single-engined aircraft to break off combat. Our stocks of twin-engined fighters are not great and we must use them as economically as possible.

Goering was a great supporter of the twin-engined 'Destroyer' but the RAF had quickly found its weaknesses, as had its crews. It was becoming evident that the Messerschmitt 110 was nowhere near as effective as it was thought and, as the day progressed, more of its pilots were to find this out the hard way.

Later that afternoon, another series of attacks developed in the west. Targets this time were the airfields of Boscombe Down, Warmwell, Yeovil, Worthy Down, Andover and Middle Wallop using a mix of Junkers 88s from LG 1 and *Stukas* from I/StG 1, II/StG 2 and StG 3. Again, the fighter escort was massive, made up from the Messerschmitt 109s of JG 2, JG 27 and JG 53 and the Messerschmitt 110s of ZG 2 and ZG 76. The RAF response was equally massive with ten squadrons being committed in one way or another. The attackers claimed thirty-five RAF fighters for the loss of seven bombers and seven fighters. Some of the bombers reached their targets but the results were poor. In any case, the majority of those airfields, like the majority of those attacked throughout the day, were not fighter bases and had little if no effect on Fighter Command's operations. This fact would have annoyed and upset one German pilot if he had known:

Leutnant Wolf Muenchmeyer, 1/ZG 2

In the afternoon again we were engaged escorting bombers even though they were diving into cloud and we could no longer see them. We were then free to look for possible adversaries and, by chance, we found them in the form of Hurricanes flying at a lower altitude. I was flying as rearguard to our formation of about eighteen aircraft and as I was diving down on them, getting faster, I was hit from beneath by a lone fighter which, unseen, made sport of this type of attack (diving from a great altitude, gathering speed, lifting his nose and shooting from beneath at the last aircraft before disappearing). Good luck for him and good luck for me (to have survived so far in the war). I was hit twice in the foot from beneath and another hit must have damaged the elevator controls. Unable to control the aircraft, we had to bale out and in doing so I hit the elevator with both legs and landed with both legs fractured and in a tree.

Muenchmeyer's *Bordfunker, Uffz* Fritz Labusch, also managed to bale out but fell to his death close to where the Messerschmitt 110 hit the ground. The aircraft made a twenty feet deep crater which burned for nearly 24 hours. The crash was witnessed by at least one person:

Wolf Muenchmeyer's Bf 110 before... (Muenchmeyer)

...and after. (via Cornwell)

Mr M E Vane

On 13 August 1940 I was haymaking at Manor Farm, Chilworth. We had not heard any warning and did not know that there was an air raid on until we heard machine gun fire overhead. The clouds were low and it was overcast and we could not see anything of what was going on. By this time, the farmer had stopped his tractor and we all took cover as best we could underneath the hayrick being built.

After a while, the dogfight above us seemed to have stopped so one of the farm workers said he was going back to the village so I went along with him. We had reached halfway between our hayrick and the village lane when it all started up again but with added intensity. After what seemed an extra long burst of machine gun fire, there was the scream of racing engines which made us look up at the low cloud wondering what was going to emerge. After what seemed like a lifetime but was in fact only a minute or less, a burning plane fell through the clouds to earth, its wings appeared to be folded back along the fuselage.

The crash itself was not witnessed by the victorious RAF pilot:

Sergeant Leonard Guy, 601 Squadron

I was Red 3, 'A' Flight. The flight intercepted twelve Me 110s at Botley at 1625 hrs at 12,500ft. I followed Red 1 into action but lost the section in the ensuing dogfight. I gave two Me 110s a short burst each, tracer bullets going into the second aircraft. No other effects were noted. I then attacked another Me 110 from astern underneath. I gave a four second burst at the port engine and I saw flames and black smoke pour from it. Enemy aircraft then started to dive steeply towards the ground...

Wolf Muenchmeyer's comment about luck for both himself and the RAF pilot was only partly true. Despite his injuries, the German pilot did survive the war whilst Leonard Guy was reported missing in action just five days later.

Adler Tag's daylight attacks then switched back to the east, ending with a devastating attack on the airfield at Detling in Kent. However, it was not used by Fighter Command and the material and personnel losses did not affect Fighter Command at all. As with nearly all of the day's attacks, *Adler Angriff* promised so much but achieved very little; the RAF had just about survived and waited for the next onslaught.

In comparison, 14 August was a much quieter day for the *Luftwaffe*'s fighter pilots even if their bomber counterparts ranged the length and breadth of the UK. It was also thought that Thursday 15 August would also be a quiet day because of anticipated bad weather over the UK. However, reconnaissance aircraft began to report that the weather was improving so at mid-morning it was decided to launch a synchronised series of attacks from as far north as Scotland down to the West Country. The day was to be the busiest day of the Battle of Britain so far for both the *Luftwaffe* and RAF and afterwards would become known as *Schwarzer Donnerstag* – Black Thursday.

The first raid materialised off the Kent coast at about 1200 hrs when *Stukas*, heavily escorted by a number of Messerschmitt 109 *Geschwader*, attacked the airfields at Lympne and Hawkinge. The escort managed to parry most of Fighter Command's attempts to thwart the attacks and both airfields were hit, Lympne being the worse off.

However, as this was taking place in the south bombers from the Denmark and Norway based *Luftflotte* 5 were nearing the Northumberland coast intending to attack RAF airfields in the north of England. Because the return distance from Norway to England was well beyond the range of the Messerschmitt 109, escort was provided by Messerschmitt 110s of I/ZG 76. Each aircraft was also fitted with an additional ventral fuel tank and two wing tanks to increase their range and to ensure that they stayed with the attacking Heinkel 111s of KG 26.

One of the pilots flying with 1/ZG 76 was 23-year-old *Oblt* Hans-Ulrich Kettling; behind him sat his *Bordfunker, Ogefr* Fritz Volk. Both had been crewed up just before the invasion of Norway in April 1940 but Kettling had flown operationally with I/ZG 76 since the invasion of Czechoslovakia and had two kills to his name. What happened to both crew this day is still very clear:

Oberleutnant Hans-Ulrich Kettling, 1/ZG 76

Our orders were to protect the He 111s of KG 26 which would attack airbases in northern England. Since our Bf 110s could not reach England and return with standard fuel tanks, we had one additional fuel tank under the belly and one under each wing. The idea was to use the fuel in the wing tanks first then to discard them over the sea and to reach England with the belly tank as the sole handicap. This ungainly blister was a handicap enough – it made the plane several kilometres per hour slower and the unused fuel sloshed around, making steering and aiming unstable and since the tank was made from plywood, it was highly flammable. We were all anything but happy to perform our first long-range raid with our mutilated planes.

The weather was fair and sunny with a slight haze over the sea – a very typical August day. We were told that special precautions had been taken to avoid premature detection but at about twenty miles from the English coast, the first of several waves of Spitfires came in for a fight.

Our altitude was about 15,000ft and our formation disintegrated into *Schwarm*, attacking the Spitfires and keeping them away from the bombers which had to continue on their course. All around dogfights developed rapidly and I followed my Number One, *Oblt* Helmut Lent [Later to become a highly successful and decorated night-fighter pilot] who went after two Spits to protect his rear. I heard *Ogefr* Volk working his machine gun and looking back, I stared into the flaming machine guns of four Spitfires in splendid formation...

Lt Hans-Ulrich Kettling, 1/ZG 76. (Kettling)

Volk's view in the Bf 110 looking forwards. (Volk via Guhnfeld)

Ogefr *Fritz Volk (2nd from right).* (Kettling)

Kettling's Rottenfuehrer
– Oblt *Helmut Lent.*
(Kettling)

Plt Off Ted Shipman. (Shipman)

Pilot Officer Ted Shipman, 41 Squadron

The weather on 15 August was fine but there was a fair amount of cloud between about 10,000 and 15,000ft. It was almost full cover inland of Newcastle. I was scrambled to 18,000ft over Durham at 1300 hrs – the raid was reported as 30-plus at first but this was later put up to 170 Me 110s and He 111s.

I was ordered to engage the Me 110s which were escorting the bombers. Turning in behind a flight of Messerschmitts, I ordered my chaps to form echelon port to do a 'Number Three' attack (which really meant three against three line astern). Before getting into firing range, the targets turned hard to port and came straight for us. I doubt if they had seen us for they didn't appear to fire at us which they could have done with four machine guns and two cannon in the nose. I fired at the first Messerschmitt head on at about 400 yards range with a short burst of two seconds. The target broke away at a very close range to my left and disappeared.

Ted Shipman sitting in his Spitfire in dispersal at Catterick. (Shipman)

Shipman's camera gun film shows Kettling's Bf 110. (Shipman)

Picking up another Me 110, I tried a series of deflection shots at various ranges with the target wading [sic] violently. No result and no return fire. Getting astern of the same target, I tried from about 200 yards. This was a long burst and the starboard engine was out of action with clouds of smoke. The Me 110 then made an erratic turn to port and disappeared into the cloud below, apparently out of control.

Oberleutnant Hans-Ulrich Kettling

...The plane was hit, not severely, but the right engine went dead, lost coolant and the oil temperature rose rapidly. I had to switch off the engine and feather the propeller and tried to reach the protection of the bombers which were overhead in close formation. I was not successful – the plane was slow and I could not gain height. Over the radio, I heard the boys in the bombers talking about my plane so I gave my 'mayday' because the Spits came in for the second attack and the kill...

Pilot Officer Ben Bennions, 41 Squadron

...I found myself about 300 yards astern of an Me 110 – I gave him a three second burst and the De Wilde appeared to be striking the fuse-lage. There was no reply from the rear gunner. The aircraft immediately dived for cloud cover on a south-westerly course. By this time, the recoil had put me about 400 yards astern but I dived after him, closing very slowly. He was travelling very fast indeed and getting closer to the clouds. I gave him another three second burst before entering the clouds.

When I came out of the clouds, I found myself midway between Piercebridge and Barnard Castle – about fifty miles from the point of interception. I reported to control that I thought I had just shot down an Me 110 in this area but didn't see him actually land...

Oberleutnant Hans-Ulrich Kettling

...This time they got the left engine, my *Bordfunker* and the front windscreen (the tracer bullets missing me by a fraction of inches). *Ogefr* Volk was lying on the floor, covered with blood and unconscious. I had no means of ascertaining whether he was alive or not. Since all flight controls were in perfect order (without the engines of course) and the belly tank empty, I decided to bring the plane down for a belly landing.

I dived away from the fighting, down and down, leaving the lethal Spitfires behind and looking for a suitable landing site. I eased the plane carefully down over a very large meadow but on touching down, I found the speed was still rather high. Finally, it crashed through a low stone wall which was hidden by a hedge, leaving the rear fuselage behind which broke just behind the cockpit. Looking back I saw the rubber dinghy, which was stowed in a partition under the fuselage and fixed with a long cable to the side of the cockpit, dangling behind along the meadow, inflating itself and following like a dog – a very grotesque sight.

The plane came to a halt at last. I jumped out, freed Volk and carried him to a safe distance, fearing fire and explosion. I disabled the radio with some shots from my pistol and I tried to set the plane on fire but the two incendiaries we carried for this purpose did not work as expected. One of them burned my right hand badly and that was the only honourable wound I had in the whole adventure.

After that, a lot of people (heaven knows where they all came from) came running armed with stick and stones, threatening and shouting from a distance until some red-capped Military Police took over and transported Volk, who had in some way recovered, and me to the police station of a nearby village where we were locked in two cells.

A doctor came and took care of Volk, who was after all not so very badly wounded, and he took care of my burnt hand too. We got an excellent dinner, with the compliments and good wishes from the local military big-shot. Several RAF officers came and asked questions and I think one of them was the pilot who shot me down. I went through these hours as in a trance – I only wanted to sleep...

THIS AND NEXT PAGE
Kettling's Bf 110 before...
(Volk via Guhnfeldt)

...and after.
(Norman and via Cornwell)

The attack was a disaster – I/ZG 76 lost seven aircraft whilst KG 26 lost eight bombers and failed to reach their targets. The RAF lost just one fighter – its pilot surviving. One of the luckier Messerschmitt 110 crews recalls what it was like to survive that day:

Unteroffizier Otto Dombrewski, 2/ZG 76

It was a black day for ZG 76 as we suffered such heavy losses. The *Schwarm* with *Hptm* Restemeyer, the *Gruppen Kommandeur,* flew at the rear in order to intervene wherever the trouble was greatest but they did not get a chance. Long before the coast, we were bounced by Spitfires and Hurricanes which attacked us in vastly superior numbers. We tried to form a circle but too late. The *Gruppenschwarm* was the first to be engaged in combat. We could see how they were broken up and *Hptm* Restemeyer shot down. We had to stay with the bombers and were in turn engaged in combat. Our circle of fighters was torn open and we were attacked from above and the left by a Hurricane. I asked my pilot, *Oblt* Uellenbeck, over the intercom to pull up to the left and we were able to open fire on the Hurricane as it turned out. She dropped away to the left in a steep dive, with a trail of fuel behind. When we got back to Aalborg in Denmark, we counted twenty-four hits – even the direction finding aerial had been completely shot away.

As this formation limped for home, the second and last ever major attack by *Luftflotte* 5 took place when unescorted Junkers 88s of KG 30 bombed the bomber airfield of Driffield, losing six of their number to a fresh formation of RAF fighters. The scene of battle then permanently moved back down to the south.

The first attack of the afternoon was by the fighter-bombers of *Erprobungsgruppe* 210 which successfully bombed the airfield of Martlesham Heath without loss. One of the escorting fighters holding back from the coast was lucky not to become a statistic:

Major Hans Truebenbach, *Gruppen Kommandeur* I/LG 2

Just off Ipswich, a British fighter pilot caught me at 8,000m altitude and put seven bullets into me from behind. Thank God all of them hit the inflatable dinghy which was stowed behind the armour plating behind me and so I did not spill a single drop of blood!

As this attack returned to France, Dornier 17s of KG 3 were heading for the airfields of Rochester and Eastchurch with a close escort of Messerschmitt 109s from three different *Geschwader* as well as a *Freie Jagd* by II and III/JG 26. The latter did particularly well:

Hauptmann Adolf Galland, *Gruppen Kommandeur* III/JG 26

The second aircraft I shot down on 15 August was at 1600 hrs, 15kms east of Folkestone–Dover at an altitude of 6,000m. Again, it was a Spitfire. Here our mission was a *Freie Jagd* west of Maidstone. When crossing the coast between Folkestone and Dover, we were bounced by twelve Spitfires coming from a higher altitude. Immediately, many individual dogfights started. I was able to get just behind one of the last Spitfires in this squadron without being discovered. From a distance of 100m to 300m, I fired with my cannon and machine guns until the Spitfire caught fire and big parts of it were flying all around, forcing me to evade. The Spitfire dived away and took a considerable time before it crashed.

The third aircraft I shot down on that day was again a Spitfire only seven minutes later at an altitude of 3,000m in the middle part of the Channel. I had assembled the *Gruppe* again just off the French coast. When flying back towards the British coast, at an altitude of 4,000m, I met some Spitfires beyond me. I attacked one and was able to approach him under the cover of his tail and shot directly into him from a distance of 100m. The aircraft made a half roll and remained on its back thus enabling me to continue firing. Sheet metal parts were suddenly all around and a thick grey-blue flame came out of the body and a white one out of the wings. After I broke away, the Spitfire was again fired at by *Oblt* Schoepfel; he followed the aircraft down and saw it ditch.

Another German pilot remembers this mission for another reason:

Leutnant Josef Buerschgens, 7/JG 26

After the dogfight during the *Freie Jagd*, Plt Off Ralph Roberts from Sheffield was forced to land near the beach at Wissant. Walter Blume, Gerhard Mueller-Duehe and I met him when we returned from the sweep over southern England. I was the first to run out of ammunition and was low on fuel and in the end, it was Gerhard who got Roberts. It was a hard fight and Roberts was very brave and an excellent pilot.

Lt *Josef Buerschgens and* Uffz *Luedewig, 7/JG 26.*
(Buerschgens)

Lt Gerhard Mueller-Duehe stands alongside Roberts' Spitfire

Unusually, the 64 Squadron pilot was the first of three RAF pilots to be captured that day; the next two occurring about an hour later as the scene of battle moved yet again to the west.

Again the targets were airfields and two separate attacks were intended to split the defences. Twelve Junkers 88s from I/LG 1 were briefed to attack Andover, a further fifteen Junkers 88s of II/LG 1 went after Worthy Down whilst twenty-seven *Stukas* from I/StG 1 and a further twenty from II/StG 2 attacked Portland (with Warmwell and Yeovil respectively being the secondary targets for the *Stukas*). Again, as with all previous attacks, the fighter escort was massive and made up from both Messerschmitt 109 and 110 *Geschwader*. The crews from II/ZG 76 had the task of escorting the Junkers 88s:

Unteroffizier Max Guschewski, 6/ZG 76

II/ZG 76 had been ordered to move to Guernsey and standby for further orders. Soon after lunch, the *Staffel Kapitaene* were ordered to the *Gruppen Kommandeur*, *Hptm* Groth, for briefing. The task for our 'Shark Gruppe' was to escort LG 1.

Take-off was ordered for 1400 hrs but half an hour before the scheduled time, it was postponed to 1600 hrs. At last the waiting came to an end and the Messerschmitts with the shark's jaws painted on their noses rumbled to the take-off positions. Due to the fact that the airfield was small (and completely surrounded by greenhouses!), only one *Staffel* at a time could take off. When all the planes of 4 and 5 *Staffel* were airborne, it was the *Staffel Kapitaen* of 6/ZG 76, *Hptm* Nacke with *Bordfunker Stfw* Kuehne, and his *Rottenflieger Fw* Jakob Birndorfer and my own turn to take off; after us the *Rotte* of *Lt* Jabs and finally the protection flight of three aircraft led by *Oblt* Herget. It was a beautiful, sunny mid-summer's day and the sky was the same blue as the waters of the Channel and there were no clouds at all. The *Haifischgeschwader* formed up in the typical shape of a wedge and climbing gradually it reached the ordered altitude of 4,000m. As we arrived over Cherbourg, in a huge formation LG 1 closed in from the south. Being one of its first sorties, LG 1 had the full number of aircraft whereas our unit had been properly fleeced during continuous operations in the French

Bf 110s in formation. (D'Elsa)

Hptm *Heinz Nacke's Bf 110C.* (Guschewski)

Fw *Jakob Birndorfer*. (Guschewski)

campaign and numerous sorties against England and consisted merely of sixteen planes.

After we had taken our positions to the left, right and behind the bombers, the whole armada moved across the Channel and crossed the English coast between Portland and the Isle of Wight. The crossing of the Channel lasted about thirty minutes during the course of which we had been followed by three Spitfires who kept a respectful distance, watching us from aloft. However, in my opinion, the attack on Salisbury Airport must have come as a great surprise for all the fighter planes were still on the ground when we approached the base[3]. Only when LG 1 had passed across from south to north, without dropping a single bomb, did the Spitfires start to take off in a most hectic manner, starting from all points of the compass! Whilst LG 1 was flying in a wide curve to the west in order to form up for an attack right from the centre of the sun, we were busy parrying enemy fighter attacks. The three Spitfires which had followed us came down in a nose dive, firing from all barrels. Meanwhile, the bombers went again over the airfield without dropping any bombs. We, the fighter escort, were all grinding our teeth because in the meantime, a great number of Spitfires had screwed their way up to our altitude and above and hurled down on us like swarms of wasps. The planes of 4 and 5/ZG 76 stuck to the heels of LG 1 who at last dropped their bombs and disappeared behind a huge cumulonimbus cloud in the south – Devil take the hindmost!

6/ZG 76 had no other choice but to get involved in air combat with an increasingly stronger growing enemy and I began to feel afraid that this might become our fateful day. First, *Fw* Birndorfer adhered faithfully to his task of shielding the *Staffel Kapitaen*. Only when three, soon after a fourth, Spitfires stuck to the tail of our Messerschmitt did he start to fight for our lives. Without speaking a single word, we both realised that only a miracle would allow us to escape our fate. While he tried all his tricks – tossing and turning sharply up and down and flying in narrow circles like a savage in an attempt to shake off the hunting pack – I emptied magazine after magazine through the barrel of the MG 15 without any perceptible results. We had lost sight of the *Staffel Kapitaen* and we could not see the *Rotte* of *Lt* Jabs or the protection flight of *Oblt* Herget. They must have been engaged in hand-to-hand combats and they all fought for their lives. I am unable to say

[3]The airfield was in fact Middle Wallop.

how long Birndorfer and I had been tossing about in the dogfight. It might have been minutes only but in my memory, it had lasted for hours. All of a sudden, I felt a fierce blow against my face – the thick rim of my sunglasses had been smashed by a shell splinter which then went into my left temple. Blood began to flow down my cheek and run over my life jacket. The same burst of fire blew out all the plexiglass panes in the cabin roof and the left engine was hit. Black and white smoke came out first and soon after flames spread quickly. The propeller of the blazing engine stopped and Jakob trimmed the plane and continued flying south towards the Channel. The pursuing Spitfires now followed us in single file and closed up to about five metres before opening fire. I could easily see the pilots and when they pressed the firing button, bullets from the eight machine guns hit our plane like a hailstorm – even today, after so many years, the terrible noise remains in my ears.

Soon the last of my ten magazines was expended. I could do no more than wait for the end. The plane in the meantime was so badly shredded that all the paint had come off and sheet metal of the wings looked more like a strainer but we were still flying. When we reached the Solent, my confidence that we might manage to escape grew bigger. But, alas, the ray of hope vanished with the change of tactics of the Spitfires. They now attacked us from the front. In the same instant, when Jakob had thrown off the cabin roof and both of us had loosened our belts in order to bale out, a full burst of fire hit the cockpit – we were both hit and I passed out.

Jakob Birndorfer had tried everything to get away, including flying through the Southampton balloon barrage but his two attackers, Plt Off Piotr Ostazewski of 609 Squadron and Plt Off Jan Zurakowski of 234 Squadron stuck with the Messerschmitt 110, firing when they could:

Pilot Officer Jan Zurakowski, 234 Squadron

After my first attack, there was no defensive fire so I attacked many times, firing short bursts. After every attack, I was breaking away hoping that the Me 110 would crash – the fuselage of the plane had a number of holes like somebody was sitting on the fuselage and attacking it with an axe. At one moment, I noticed another Spitfire attacking. We were approaching the Isle of Wight – the propellers of the Me 110 were rotating slowly. One warship in port on the north of the Isle of Wight opened fire and the Messerschmitt at fairly high speed crash-landed – some infantry soldiers were close to the crash site. Returning in formation with the other Spitfire, when the pilot removed his oxygen mask, I recognised the long nose of Plt Off Ostazewski.

Plt Off Janusz Zurakowski.

Sadly, Birndorfer was killed – Max Guschewski regained consciousness to stagger from the wreckage and then collapse. The other Messerschmitt 110s of II/ZG 76 had to fight their way back to the coast, losing seven of their number – another fighter was written off on its return; a further Messerschmitt 110 from *Stab*/ZG 76 was also lost. To the west, III/ZG 76 was also mauled, losing three aircraft including that of the *Gruppen Kommandeur*.

The day was by no means over. The Messerschmitt 109s of I/JG 53, who had also been escorting the Junkers 88s of LG 1, returned to their advance airstrip at Cherbourg-East and on landing, headed off for a debrief. It would appear

Oblt *Georg Claus, III/JG 53 (seen here with JG 51 on returning from his fourteenth kill, 12 October 1940).*

THIS AND NEXT PAGE *Funeral of Cecil Hight.* (via Stebbings)

that the Spitfires of 234 Sqn had fought a running battle with the returning German fighters. Plt Off Cecil Hight had been killed when his fighter crashed into housing in Bournemouth as he attempted to force-land in a non residential area whilst Plt Off Vincent Parker was shot down into the Channel and taken prisoner of war. However, Plt Off Richard Hardy found himself off Cherbourg and, it would appear, about to be shot down by *Oblt* Georg Claus of III/JG 53; Hardy was going to be the third RAF fighter pilot captured this day and the second to present the Germans with a Spitfire:

Unteroffizier Werner Karl, 1/JG 53

Somebody shouted "Spitfire!" and I looked up to see a Spitfire coming over the airfield. The anti-aircraft guns opened fire and the Spitfire banked around and landed. Having got over the shock, we crowded around the Spitfire. The pilot got out and surrendered to *Hptm* Rolf Pingel, *Staffel Kapitaen* of 2/JG 53.

The day was now coming to a close but not before the *Luftwaffe* launched two more attacks which cost them dearly. The fighter-bombers of *Erprobungsgruppe* 210 had been briefed to attack Kenley but in fact hit Croydon and the southern outskirts of London. They were then pounced upon by Hurricanes which shot down six Messerschmitt 110s and a Messerschmitt 109 with a further two Messerschmitt 110s returning home badly shot up. To add

234 Sqn, St Eval, July 1940 – Hight, Hardy and Parker are the first three sitting on the wing to the right. (Stebbings)

THIS AND NEXT PAGE
Hardy's Spitfire after its capture. (Broeker)

further insult to injury, Dornier 17s of KG 76 were briefed to attack the airfields at Redhill and Biggin Hill – the former was not a Fighter Command airfield whilst in respect of the latter, they bombed West Malling, an airfield still
under construction and not yet operational.

As night fell, the *Luftwaffe* worked out it had flown in excess of 2,000 sorties,
losing seventy-six aircraft against targets which were in the main not essential
to the defence of the UK. The RAF had lost just thirty-five fighters but only
eleven pilots had lost their lives – 128 German aircrew had failed to return.
This waste of effort could not be sustained, especially as now it was obvious that
there were no detectable weaknesses in the RAF's fighter defence around the
whole of the UK. Furthermore, the much vaunted Messerschmitt 110 had
received a severe mauling, losing twenty-seven shot down or written off on
their return. It was obvious that all types of fighter mission were better suited
to the Messerschmitt 109 but this aircraft did not have the range of the
Messerschmitt 110. In any case, there were not enough Messerschmitt 109
Geschwader to go around and thus more pressure was being put on the already
stretched single-seat fighter pilots.

If one thought that 16 August would be a day that the *Luftwaffe* would sit
back and lick its wounds, one would be much mistaken. In the late morning,
the attacks developed along the same lines as the previous day with airfields
being targeted from one end of England to the other. The German fighters
were heavily involved and lost seventeen Messerschmitt 109s and seven
Messerschmitt 110s, which cost the Germans two *Gruppen Kommandeure,* two
Staffel Kapitaene and one *Technischer Offizier.* The latter was *Lt* Richard
Marchfelder who had a very lucky escape. His *Gruppe* had been briefed to
escort a mixture of Junkers 88s and Heinkel 111s from various units which
were to go after such airfields as Hendon, Northolt, Redhill, Brooklands,
Gatwick and Croydon. He recalls that his main task was to look after the
'Croydon group':

Leutnant Richard Marchfelder, *Technischer Offizier* III/ZG 76

We started from Caen and I was on my way back to Lannion trying to
get above 10,000m to avoid the 'Cowboys' at Tangmere. I was asked to
look after two Ju 88s and it was a single Spitfire which did the damage. I
attacked him head on but at the last moment, we both turned towards
each other. Part of a wing or something hit my starboard engine; seconds
later the whole wing was on fire. I dived, feathered the engine and cut
the fuel to that engine and then set off the fire extinguisher. For ten to
fifteen minutes, I struggled to keep the aircraft flying before the heat
became unbearable and I told my *Bordfunker* Jentzch to bale out. He had
difficulties so I turned the plane on its back and he departed together
with the 'greenhouse'. I then had difficulties getting out and radioed
that I was trapped – for this reason, my comrades thought for many years

that I was missing and buried together with my plane! However, the next thing I remember, I was falling through the air but I did not open my parachute as I knew we were quite high up and had been on oxygen...

Both German crew survived the ordeal, even if Marchfelder did wrench his knee on landing. His *Gruppe* lost a further two aircraft with one crew being taken prisoner, the other being rescued from the Channel.

Earlier that afternoon, *Stukas* from three different *Geschwader* had taken off to attack airfields in and around Portsmouth. Met by a determined RAF defence, nine *Stukas* were shot down but not before they inflicted damage upon the airfields at Tangmere, Lee-On-Solent and Portsmouth as well as the unlucky radar station at Ventnor. 268 fighters escorted these raids and their claims were quite sensible – nine were claimed when in fact the RAF lost five. The German fighters had better luck when, in a one-sided fight, they shot down nineteen barrage balloons! Interestingly, during one of these attacks, three Hurricanes of 249 Squadron were bounced and shot down apparently by Messerschmitt 110s. No claims were made by any Messerschmitt 110 unit and one of the pilots, Flt Lt James Nicholson, was then awarded the Victoria Cross for staying in his burning fighter to press home an attack on a Messerschmitt 110; no loss of a Messerschmitt 110 can be matched to this incident.

Many of these fighters went back out again later in the afternoon, holding back off the coast waiting for the likes of *Lt* Marchfelder's *Geschwader* and the aircraft they were meant to be escorting. Some dogfights took place. 234 Squadron, who lost three aircraft and their pilots the day before, had the misfortune of meeting the same German unit again. *Hptm* Wolfgang Lippert of 3/JG 53, *Hptm* Guenther von Maltzahn, *Gruppen Kommandeur* of II/JG 53 and *Fw* Werner Kaufmann of 4/JG 53 each claimed a Spitfire. Fg Off Francis Connor baled out over the Solent, badly wounded. Fg Off Kenneth Dewhurst was more fortunate:

Hptm *von Maltzahn, II/JG 53.* (Schultz)

Oblt *Lippert, III/JG 53, 2nd from left.* (via Rupp)

Fw *Christian Hansen, 2/JG 53 crash-landed on the Isle of Wight on 16 August 1940.*

Flying Officer Kenneth Dewhurst, 234 Squadron

I was Blue Two patrolling with the Squadron over Southampton at 17,000ft. We met about fifty Me 109s. I turned to attack one enemy aircraft and gave two three-second bursts from dead astern at a range of 100 yards. Enemy aircraft dived steeply towards the sea. I was about to follow when I was attacked by another Me 109. A shell hit me. I turned towards the coast and then smoke started to come from the engine. After another two minutes, the aircraft was completely enveloped in smoke so I turned the aircraft onto its back and baled out. I landed safely and saw the aircraft crash in flames and blow up.

If the RAF was expecting a repeat performance of the previous two days, they were much mistaken and air activity over the UK was sporadic. However, 18 August would see the *Luftwaffe* renew its attacks with an added vehemence.

Apart from two interceptions against reconnaissance aircraft early in the morning, the main raids did not commence until early afternoon and can be divided into three distinct attacks. Firstly, a massive bomber formation thundered in over Kent heading for the airfields of Biggin Hill, West Malling, Croydon and Kenley. Accompanying the bombers was an equally massive fighter umbrella which was soon in action. The most impressive fighter action of this raid occurred near Canterbury when the *Staffel Kapitaen* of 9/JG 26, *Oblt* Gerhard Schoepfel, spotted Hurricanes of 501 Squadron trying to gain altitude to intercept them. Closing in behind and unseen, he shot down four Hurricanes in quick succession and only stopped his cull when oil from his last victim obscured his windscreen. During this raid and later that afternoon, on what would transpire to be the third and last raid of the day (targets again being the airfields of North Weald and Hornchurch), ZG 26 lost a total of fifteen Messerschmitt 110s with a further three returning damaged. In human terms, the day resulted in the deaths of nineteen men from this *Geschwader* and a further six being taken prisoner. Despite this, the following day *Reichsmarschall* Hermann Goering reiterated that there was still very much a use for the twin-engined fighter.

If 18 August saw another nail in the coffin of one German aircraft type in preference for another, following this day that aircraft was rarely seen again over the skies of southern England. The second major attack of the day was undertaken by *Stukas* against targets in the Solent area – I/StG 77's target was the airfield at Thorney Island, II/StG 77's the airfield at Ford whilst III/StG 77 attacked the radar station at Poling. Meanwhile, I/StG 3 was briefed to attack Gosport. As usual, there was a fighter escort but this time it was made up entirely of Messerschmitt 109s and of the fifteen such aircraft lost throughout this day, eight were lost on this attack:

Oblt Gerhard Schoepfel (2nd from left) with Lt Heinz Ebeling (9/JG 26), Lt Josef Haibock (Stab III/JG 26) and Lt Johannes Naumann (9/JG 26). (via Rayner)

Oberleutnant Rudolf Moellerfriedrich, 6/JG 2

By 18 August, I had only been with 6/JG 2 for fourteen days and had only flown one mission. That had been on 11 August when I saw my *Staffel Kapitaen, Oblt* Edgar Rempel, crash into the sea off Portland; all that we saw was the green marker dye in the sea and no trace of him was ever found.

On the morning of 18 August, we had moved from Beaumont-le-Roger to the airfield at Cherbourg where we refuelled. We were to escort *Stukas* in an attack on airfields near Portsmouth.

The crossing of the Channel was uneventful but worrying – we were all scared about running out of fuel on the way back. As we approached the Isle of Wight, we

Oblt Rudolf Moellerfriedrich, 6/JG 2. (Moellerfriedrich)

broke away. We saw three enemy aircraft – one at low altitude, another two higher up. Our *Staffel Fuehrer*, *Oblt* Gerlach, decided to attack. He went down with his *Rottenflieger* and attacked the lower aircraft. This aircraft did not crash so I attacked. My *Rottenflieger*, *Ofw* Wilhelm Laufer, and I followed and on breaking off my attack, I saw this aircraft was starting to smoke. As we had lost 1,000m in altitude, we started to climb back up. Then I saw a Spitfire – it was diving towards me and after separating me from *Ofw* Laufer, got onto my tail…

Flight Lieutenant Pat Hughes, 234 Squadron

As Blue One, 'B' Flight, I was on patrol when about twenty Me 109s appeared above me in the sun. I climbed towards them and my section was attacked individually. I fired a burst at one Messerschmitt with no effect and I then found myself attacked by two Me 109s, one of which fired at me at extreme range. I turned and set this aircraft on fire but was immediately attacked by the second Messerschmitt so I could not follow it down. He attacked and climbed away, then dived. I followed until he started to pull up and shot him with two bursts of two seconds each. This pilot immediately jumped out and landed on the Isle of Wight and his aircraft crashed there a few seconds later, on fire. When I had observed this crash, I saw a second cloud of smoke and fire just off the Isle of Wight which appeared to be the first 109.

The hunters in this case had become the hunted. 6/JG 2 lost two aircraft that afternoon – one is believed to be *Oblt* Moellerfriedrich's wingman who was later rescued wounded from the Channel. Rudolf Moellerfriedrich was not that lucky:

Oberleutnant Rudolf Moellerfriedrich

…I heard the sound of bullets hitting my aircraft and a volley of shots hit the left side of the cockpit. They smashed the throttle and wounded me in the left arm and smashed my left hand. They also managed to change the pitch of the aircraft's propellers. I knew that it was useless to try and get back to France so I turned towards the Isle of Wight and when over land, I baled out.

My parachute opened successfully and I proceeded to bandage my arm and hand with the first aid kit in my pocket. I did not see where my aircraft crashed but I was aware of the Spitfire that shot me down circling me.

I landed near a Youth Hostel I had visited earlier in the 'thirties and was captured by a Home Guardsman. I was taken to a hospital on the Island and later transferred to the mainland to another hospital.

Although the *Stukas* reached their targets, thirteen were shot down, three were written off on their return whilst numerous others were damaged. Coupled with the losses two days earlier, it was now decided that despite fighter cover, *Stukas* were not a viable weapon over the skies of southern England and were permanently withdrawn from the Battle of Britain.

Whether by luck or by divine intervention, the weather for the next five days restricted German air operations. The occasional fighter-against-fighter combat took place but kills and losses on both sides were infrequent. However, from a German fighter commander's viewpoint, these days were vital as *Reichsmarschall* Goering, infuriated by what he thought was a lack of aggressiveness by some of his fighter *Gruppen Kommandeure* and *Geschwader Kommodoren,* promoted many younger and successful pilots to take their places.

24 August saw an improvement in the weather and the start of the *Luftwaffe's* new aim to destroy the RAF fighters either in the air, on the ground or, for that matter, where they were being manufactured. This day also saw a new tactic in that the *Luftwaffe* tended to roll one attack into another so it is hard to differentiate between attacks unless the region over which the battle was being fought changed.

Just as 18 August saw the demise of the *Stuka*, 24 August was to see the beginning of the end for another aircraft type, this time from the RAF:

Pilot Officer Eric Barwell, 264 Squadron

The Squadron was sent on patrol and after an inconclusive engagement, landed at Manston to refuel and rearm. We had just completed that but were not ordered up again until we were scrambled in a hurry just as a number of Ju 88s were attacking Ramsgate and the edge of the airfield. We took off in twos and threes but had no time to form up as a Squadron. I had one new crew in my Section (Plt Offs Jones and Ponting) and we chased after the bombers as they headed for France. It was a long stern chase and before we were near enough to engage them, I spotted five enemy fighters. I at once called up Jones, "Bandits! Line astern – evasive action!" and turned as hard as possible as they attacked. Unfortunately, Jones did not turn hard enough and was hit and went down immediately. All five aircraft then concentrated on me and as each came in, I turned hard giving my gunner, Sgt Martin, a straight no deflection shot. I saw strikes on one or two of them and one went down into the sea. On one occasion, Martin did not fire – I do not think I swore at him but asked him why. "You blacked me out" was his answer. We were some miles out to sea and it meant I had to keep turning hard as each plane attacked and I began to think that we should never get back to the Kent coast but the attacks ceased. (I like to think that we had damaged the four other aircraft but probably they had run out of fuel or ammunition.) We landed back at Hornchurch with no damage but the squadron had suffered disastrously. We had lost our Commanding Officer, Sqn Ldr Philip Hunter, who had been so good at welding together the squadron and at developing Defiant tactics, and two other crews. In the afternoon we were at readiness again at Hornchurch, sitting in our aircraft as there was so much enemy activity. We learnt there were bombers aiming in our direction but we were kept on the ground until over the Tannoy came the order "264 Squadron scramble, scramble, scramble!". Personally I blame the panic in the voice for the serious damage to two Defiants – they collided on the ground when taxiing. As the rest of us took off, the bombs were falling on the airfield just about where we had been a moment before. A formation of Heinkels was overhead at 10,000–15,000ft. We did not have a chance to catch them. I believe that one or two of our machines were attacked by fighters and we lost one, the pilot being saved but the gunner dying of wounds.

A few hours later, during another raid, it was the turn of a German fighter pilot to be on the receiving end:

Pilots of 264 Sqn, 29 May 1940 – Sqn Ldr Philip Hunter is standing 3rd from left, Plt Off Eric Barwell is standing 3rd from right. (Barwell)

Feldwebel Herbert Bischoff, 1/JG 52

I joined JG 52 in February 1940 and flew about sixty to seventy operational flights of which twenty to twenty-five were over England. I had
just half a kill to my name – a Spitfire together with *Uffz* Ignatz
Schinabeck between Calais and Dover on 11 August 1940. On my last
flight of 24 August it was a Spitfire that got me – coming out of the sun
above me. He hit my engine which was then *kaput*. I was at 6,000m near
London at the time. I dived away but soon realised that it was impossible
to get back to my airfield at Coquelles as by then even my radiators were
kaput so I crash landed near Margate and became a prisoner of war for
the next seven years.

Pilots of 1/JG 52 – left to right Uffz Reinhard Neumann (+ 28 June 1940), *Fw* Herbert Bischoff *(POW 24 August 1940),*
Fw *Heinz Uerlings (POW 2 September 1940) and* Ofw *Oskar Strack (+ 26 October 1940).* (Bischoff)

A brand new 'Emil' for 1/JG 52 – Oblt *Carl Lommel, the* Staffel Kapitaen *(standing on the wing), is trying to get a pet cat off the exhaust stubs.* (Bischoff)

Herbert Bischoff's Bf 109 after its crash-landing.

As with many combats, the crash landing was not witnessed by the success-ful RAF pilot:

Flight Lieutenant George Gribble, 'B' Flight, 54 Squadron

I was leading 'B' Flight when the Squadron attacked about nine He 113s [sic] over Dover and itself was attacked by a large number of Me 109s. After a dogfight in which I engaged several enemy aircraft but was unable to see any results of my fire, I joined up with three other Spitfires over Manston and proceeded to Hornchurch. Between Manston and Herne Bay, I saw about fifty Me 109s in vics line astern. I dived onto the last section and fired the remainder of my ammunition (about ten seconds' worth) in bursts from 250 yards in astern attack. My last burst hit the starboard radiator and after that, the aircraft fell away out of control.

Pilots of 54 Sqn, July 1940. Flt Lt George Gribble is in the middle row far right. (Deere)

The crash-landing was not witnessed but the aircraft was heard and then seen by one teenager soon afterwards:

Richard Hambidge

My mother and I were in our air raid shelter in the back garden – we had been there for much of the day because it was quite hectic at that time. We were sitting and talking when all of a sudden 'zoom!' – it was so low, we never heard it coming. About half an hour later, our local air raid warden came into the garden and told us that it was a Messerschmitt that had just gone over and it had crashed out in the cornfields. He said he was one of the first to get to the scene of the crash and that the pilot was OK.

After that, I was off to see for myself. When I got out there, I was so surprised how close to home it had crashed and that it had caught one of its wings on the many concrete posts which had been put into open fields to hinder German gliders if they ever invaded us. The pilot must have been very lucky.

The final attack of the day appeared on Ventnor's radar screens, now just about working again, at about 1540 hrs when a formation of 100-plus aircraft were picked up north of the Somme Estuary and appeared to be heading towards Portsmouth. Forty-six Junkers 88s of I and III/KG 51 were briefed to attack the repair workshops and dry docks in Portsmouth Dockyard and to enable them to do that, a formation of 302 fighters, made up of both Messerschmitt 109s and 110s, escorted the bombers.

One of the escorting units was I/JG 53 whose task was to stay with the bombers, leaving the Messerschmitt 109s of II/JG 53 to go after the RAF fighters. The Spitfires and Hurricanes of No 10 Group were hurriedly scrambled and began to patrol, waiting for the arrival of the Germans. When they did arrive, the majority found themselves well below the German formation, helpless to prevent the bombers attacking Portsmouth.

As the bombers wheeled around and headed for home, 1/JG 53 broke away looking for prey. The Spitfires of 234 Squadron had been scrambled from the airfield at Middle Wallop and were in a good attacking position, or so they thought:

Pilot Officer Jan Zurakowski, 234 Squadron

I was Number Two in the last Section. My Section Leader was lagging too far behind the Squadron (probably because the Leader was using full power). I noticed slightly below us a formation of, I think, thirty-five-plus Me 110s or Ju 88s flying in seven vics of five aircraft each in the opposite direction. The position for a head on attack was excellent – I had good training in head-on attacks when in Poland so I decided to try.

I attacked straight ahead, slightly diving, at the last aircraft on the right side in the last vic. I reported later that I fired two bursts at approximately 400 and 150 yards. I could not see any results but think I was aiming correctly.

After the attack, I was trying to rejoin the Squadron in the hope that my Leader did not notice I was missing. I immediately heard a good bang and lost control of the elevator and rudder. My impression at the time was that the bombers had 20mm cannons installed for rear defence; later I thought it was more likely that Me 109s were hiding higher, in the sun, and were happy to attack a single aircraft hundreds of yards behind a squadron...

A lone Spitfire was spotted by the *Staffel Kapitaen* of 1/JG 53, *Hptm* Hans-Karl Mayer and it was he who chased after it. However, the credit for the kill went to another pilot:

Leutnant Alfred Zeis, 1/JG 53

We were on a *Freie Jagd* over Portsmouth and the Isle of Wight. I was flying as the mobile *Rotte* between the lead *Schwarm* and lookout *Schwarm*. *Hptm* Mayer attacked a Spitfire from behind and the aircraft curved left and *Hptm* Mayer was not outside of him. I came and was in a better position (above) to shoot. The aircraft went into a downwards spiral and crashed at a shallow angle on the eastern part of the Isle of Wight.

Pilots of 1/JG 53; Lt Alfred Zeis is 2nd from the left.

Although his report gave the impression it was over quickly, Zeis had to fire fifty-six 20mm rounds and a further 128 machine gun rounds to cause fatal damage to the Spitfire but he succeeded in his aim:

Pilot Officer Jan Zurakowski

...My Spitfire turned slowly, stalled and ended in a flat spin. I had to bale out. I was not sure which way I should jump – inside or outside the spin. It turned out later that I did it wrongly. I was descending faster than the aircraft and the Spitfire was spinning above my head and I was afraid to pull the ripcord. I was slowly gaining distance but the Spitfire was turning all the time exactly above my head. Looking down, I realised that the ground was approaching fast and when I could distinguish a man with a gun, I pulled the ripcord. My parachute opened fast, I heard a loud bang when the Spitfire hit the ground and a few seconds later, I landed close to this chap with a gun.

The old man (from the Home Guard) with a double-barrelled shotgun was shaken badly by an aircraft and a man dropping from the sky. I was not speaking English well so I was trying to show him my RAF identity card but his hands were shaking so much, he could not take it. A short time later, a British Army officer arrived and he cleared up the situation.

Despite the loss of two Messerschmitt 109s and a 110 as well as a Junkers 88 (which was a victim of AA fire), the raid was devastating and the loss of life was the highest in a single raid so far during the Battle of Britain. The German fighters appeared to have done their job well or perhaps the British Controller had put his fighters at the wrong altitude (probably expecting *Stukas*). Nevertheless, the bombers had done their job but at the same time had hit the city itself; later that night nocturnal bombers would accidentally do the same thing to parts of London. It was a grim taste of things to come for many civilians.

Despite good weather, 25 August saw little activity until the afternoon – the reason for this is unknown. Suffice it to say, apart from a few massed *Freie Jagd* off the Kent coast, it was not until late afternoon that signs of positive German action were seen as, yet again, another formation was detected to the west but instead of Portsmouth, seemed to be heading for a target in the Portland area.

Thirty-seven Junkers 88s from all three *Gruppen* of KG 51 were aiming to bomb the airfield of Warmwell and, to help them do this, they were escorted by 214 Messerschmitt 109s and a further 103 Messerschmitt 110s. One of the escorting pilots was 23-year-old *Gefr* Josef Broeker of 1/JG 53 who was on his second operational flight of the war and even that was not meant to have taken place that day:

Gefreiter Josef Broeker, 1/JG 53

In the morning, 1/JG 53 had flown from Rennes to the operational airfield near Cherbourg. I was not due to fly that day but because one pilot from our *Staffel* could not get his plane to start, I ended up flying. After receiving our orders, we went to our planes. I flew the one marked '15' and as I was the most inexperienced pilot (I had come to the front-line in early August), I had to fly as *Katschmarek* to my *Staffel Kapitaen*, *Hptm* Mayer. Behind me flew two experienced comrades.

Below us I could see the bombers (Ju 88s) and their escort. We had to fly a *Freie Jagd* mission. It was an emotional feeling to see, all of a sudden, the English coast beneath us. The sky was blue – no cloud to give us protection in case of emergency.

Gefr *Josef Broeker*. (Broeker)

Broeker's 'White 15' just before the 25 August 1940 mission. (Broeker)

Our *Staffel Kapitaen* had noticed enemy fighters and ordered us to attack. However, it was Spitfires that attacked us, coming out of the sun. Both near and far there were dogfights. We attacked the Spitfires by turning left and the *Staffel Kapitaen* fired the first bursts and I followed him. Both comrades behind me broke away and had their own dogfights.

Suddenly, I felt my plane being hit. It climbed for a moment, lost speed and, inverted, dived away. I got into a spin to the left and there was no feeling to the control column. I saw the view of England, France, England but I could not regain control...

Pilot Officer Walter Beaumont, 152 Squadron

I was Green Two and we were at 17,000ft when we met a large force of 109s and 110s. A dogfight started. I followed an Me 109 down onto the tail of a Spitfire. As he broke away, I kept on his tail and got in a burst as he stalled at the top of his climb. I followed him down and on my third burst, clouds of white smoke came from the starboard side of his engine. He immediately prepared to force-land as we were at about 500ft...

Gefreiter Josef Broeker

...there was another hit to my plane and I noticed some pressure on my control column. I tried and succeeded to get out of the spin. I pulled out of the dive towards the Channel and I noticed that I was at an altitude of 1,000m. I supposed the engine had been hit (the airscrew was just windmilling) and was then engaged by three (or possibly four) more British fighters which cut off my retreat. I lost more and more height and looked for a landing place. By this time, the British fighters were lining up behind me so there was no chance of escaping.

I landed in a field and after I had regained my calmness, I set fire to my plane. I had put my silk scarf into the fuel injection pump and lit it with a match. The plane exploded and I suffered burns to my hand and face. I also suffered spinal strain because of the force-landing...

Pilot Officer Roland Beamont, 87 Squadron

I now realise that I was not the only chap taking pot shots at him. Such is the fleeting nature of air combat. I did record seeing another Hurricane above and behind me as I pulled away as he [Broeker] made his final diving turn to port and belly-landed off it.

Mindful of the need to stop him setting fire to his plane, I turned in for a possible strafing run and then, with thumb on the button, decided I could not do that. As I flew over at about 50ft, the pilot was leaning into the cockpit and then, as I looked back, the plane was on fire.

Plt Off Roland Beamont, 87 Sqn.

Hurricane of 87 Sqn.

Gefreiter Josef Broeker

...Two men approached me and said "Good day, Sir; how are you?". At this moment I realised that I was a prisoner of war. They both took me to a house where I received first aid. Shortly afterwards, soldiers appeared who took me back to my plane which by now was almost completely burnt out. From there they brought me to an airfield which had obviously just been attacked by the Ju 88s. Little did I realise that from this time onwards I would stay in British and Canadian captivity until 7 January 1947 when I was released and could go home.

A total of eight Messerschmitt 109s fell victim to RAF fighters but only two pilots were lost, one being *Gefr* Broeker. However, the Messerschmitt 110s of the three participating *Geschwader* were, again, not so lucky. Nine Messerschmitt 110s were lost, one being discovered deep under farmland forty-one years later. The crew were identified by initials 'MD' found on a handkerchief – *Fw* Manfred Dahne of 8/ZG 76 had been one of those German pilots shot down by the Swiss on 8 June 1940. A total of nine aircrew lost their lives and a further five taken prisoner. One of these prisoners of war had a very exciting afternoon both during and after he was taken prisoner:

Unteroffizier Siegfried Becker, 1/ZG 2

The mission on the afternoon of 25 August 1940 was to escort a bomber formation in its attack on an airfield. I remember it was a Sunday afternoon with very good weather. The bombers overflew our airfield and we started after them and took position slanted away behind them. I flew as the lookout for the twelve aircraft from our *Staffel.*

The first I knew that we were under attack was when my *Bordfunker* started shooting and screamed "Break left!" and we were attacked from behind and the left. The attack was a complete surprise and had come out of the sun. The dogfight then lasted ten or fifteen minutes. I noted that I had lost my wingman – his *Bordfunker* was on his first operational flight so had probably not given him warning of the attack. The Spitfires were now behind me and I kept turning as if my life depended on it! I flew fast – first to the right and then to the left and then dived from 6,000m to 1,000m. I was by this time approaching the Channel and for the first time I was concerned that we would not get home. One engine was on fire and I could not get the fire out with the fire extinguisher. The other engine was loosing coolant and I noticed that the temperature was very high. There was no hope of me getting to the Channel so I gave the order to bale out. I jettisoned the cabin roof, rolled the aircraft on its back and we both fell out.

We both came down by parachute unwounded but my *Bordfunker* broke his ankle on landing. He was one side of a railway cutting and I the other. In the distance I saw a Home Guardsman so I tried getting away by running along the railway line. However, I soon saw British soldiers on a bridge over the line about 200–300m away. I was captured, disarmed and taken to a private house. I was later taken to Portland.

Becker had fallen victim to Blue Three and Blue Four of 609 Squadron – Plt Offs Geoffrey Gaunt and Noel Agazarian. The former's account of the action matches perfectly that of the German:

Pilot Officer Geoffrey Gaunt, 609 Squadron

...as I dived to attack the enemy formation, I saw an Me 110 climbing up about 800 yards in front of me, heading south. I dived towards him and he started diving. I followed him down firing short bursts, some of which appeared to hit the Me 110.

I continued firing until all of my ammunition was exhausted and followed him down to 3,000ft. I then did a steep turn to see if I was being followed. I lost sight of the Me 110 – during the dive I had experienced return fire from the rear gunner. I went down to about 500ft and while looking, saw smoke rising from the ground. I approached same and found it came from a crashed aircraft three to four miles south-west of Wareham. While flying around, I saw two parachutes land, one each side of a railway cutting in a field next to the crashed machine.

The Germans left having managed to bomb Warmwell and at the same time claiming to have shot down thirty-five RAF fighters. In reality, damage to Warmwell was not critical and only ten RAF fighters were lost costing the lives of six pilots with a further two being slightly wounded.

The day ended with a further raid, this time back over Kent. The Messerschmitt 109s of JG 26, on yet another *Freie Jagd* in support of the bombers, claimed seven RAF victims – in reality, 32 Squadron lost two Hurricanes to *Oblt* Ludwig Hafer and *Lt* Josef Buerschgens whilst the Spitfires of 610 and 616 Squadrons lost one and two respectively, Sgt Philip Waring of 616 Squadron being chased back across the Channel by *Oblt* Kurt Ruppert of 3/JG 26. Waring was then forced to land near Calais and was taken prisoner.

The next day, radar screens did not start showing signs of German air activity until midday when the first of two raids aimed against airfields in the east of England were detected. In both cases, the RAF fighters were dogged in their determination to thwart the attacks. The attacks on Biggin Hill and Hornchurch were effectively thwarted but the Dornier 17s attacking Debden succeeded in reaching and bombing their target. The RAF threw eleven squadrons at the attackers, including the Defiants of 264 Squadron. The twin seat fighters claimed seven enemy aircraft before Stab/JG 3 intervened and they then lost three aircraft. The claims by *Hptm* Guenther Luetzow, the *Geschwader Kommodore* of JG 3, and *Oblt* Friedrich Franz von Cramon, the *Geschwader Adjutant,* match the three Defiant losses.

Yet again, the scene of battle shifted back to the west on what would be the last major daylight attack in that part of the country for this phase of the Battle of Britain. For the first time in just over a month, Junkers 88s were replaced by Heinkel 111s when fifty-seven from I and II/KG 55 went for Portsmouth Dockyard. 277 fighters protected them, the vast majority being Messerschmitt 109s. Back on line, Ventnor's radar picked up the approaching formation and four squadrons successfully intercepted; again, accounts of the battle are vivid:

Oberleutnant Hans-Theodor Grisebach, *Staffel Fuehrer* 2/JG 2

It was a lovely summer's day when we took off on an escort mission over Portsmouth. It was so warm, all I was wearing was a shirt, blue trousers, flying boots with flares strapped to the top, a flying helmet and lifejacket. I also carried a pistol. I was leading the *Staffel* as *Oblt* Heinz Greisert was not flying this day. Shortly before I got it, I managed to attack and set on fire a Hurricane which was attacking an He 111; the poor pilot got his parachute caught behind the cockpit of his burning plane. If he had got out, his landing point could not be far from mine as immediately after, there was a bang and a smell of burning in the cockpit. I saw big holes in both wings and believe that I was attacked from below. I did not wait. I rolled my aircraft onto her back, removed the canopy and pushed the stick forward. I was then thrown out of the cockpit.

I pulled the ripcord when I reached a thin layer of cloud at about 600–800m (I had free fallen about 200m before opening my parachute) and I landed in a hedge. I saw many civilians running towards me from nearby houses – some of them even brought me cups of tea!

They thought, as I had no recognisable uniform, that I was Australian so I continued to act Australian! However, I then saw a military motorcycle coming towards me across the field. The rider knew that I was German so stood there and beckoned with his finger for me to come to him. I was then taken into captivity on the back of a motor cycle!

It is believed that Grisebach's victim was Plt Off Roy Lane of 43 Squadron who managed to bale out of his burning Hurricane both wounded and badly burnt; his Hurricane crashed about two miles from where Grisebach's

Oblt *Hans-Theodor Grisebach,* 2/JG 2. (Grisebach)

Hptm *Heinz Greisert, (right)* St Kap 2/JG 2, seen here as Gr Kdr II/JG 2 later in the war. *(Dudeck)*

Messerschmitt 109 came down. Grisebach was himself a victim of a Belgian pilot from Lane's Squadron:

Pilot Officer Albert van den Hove d'Ertsenrijk, 43 Squadron

I approached the enemy formation head-on and fired three bursts at the leading line of enemy aircraft and then at successive waves from below without result. I turned behind them but was attacked by an Me 109 which hit me twice through the fuselage and four times in the wing. I went into a spin and when I came out, saw an Me 109 following a Hurricane which was diving steeply. I got onto the tail of the Me 109, firing whenever possible, and white smoke poured from the engine. I lost the enemy aircraft into cloud somewhere north of Portsmouth and cannot say whether I shot him down.

As this was happening, another German pilot was notching up his fourth kill, having shot down an RAF fighter on each of the previous two days:

Leutnant Alfred Zeis, 1/JG 53

The *Staffel* had been given the order: *Freie Jagd* over Portsmouth. I was flying in *Oblt* Dittmar's lookout *Schwarm* as the last man. The *Staffel Kapitaen*, *Hptm* Mayer, spotted five enemy aircraft 1,000m under us and attacked them. *Oblt* Dittmar, *Hptm* Mayerweissflog and I immediately attacked two flying a little away from the five aircraft. I attacked the right aircraft from behind and above and saw a part of the plane fall away. Black smoke was seen and the aircraft dived away and was lost in cloud.

His victim cannot be ascertained for certain but one RAF pilot fell victim to a German fighter in the same location to the north-east of Portsmouth:

Pilot Officer Richard Gayner, 615 Squadron

Plt Off Richard Gayner (left) seen as a Sqn Ldr with 68 Sqn, 1943. (Williams)

I crash-landed in a mess – wheels up, covered in barbed wire (presumably erected to deter airborne landings). I was covered in glycol, perhaps with oil also. I think that I had to side-slip from side to side to get a forward view through the glycol stream. Apart from the shock from being shot up and from the crash-landing, I may have been half blinded by the glycol. I was bleeding from the mouth and feared an internal injury but this turned out to be merely my bitten or cut tongue. My wife says that I also had a bit of armour plate in me from the explosion of the shells. I would have been in a great hurry to get out of the aircraft for fear of fire. I have no memory of whether I managed to get out myself or people came and lifted me out of the cockpit.

As the Germans landed back in France, they reported that they had encountered heavy fighter and *flak* defences off Portsmouth and not one mention was made of the target being attacked. The RAF fighters had done their job, for the cost of five fighters but more importantly, no pilots lost their lives. The official German records at the time state that four Messerschmitt 109s and three

Heinkel 111s were lost. Post-war research indicates that KG 55 lost four Heinkel 111s whilst seven Messerschmitt 109s were lost costing the lives of six pilots. A further loss would occur a few hours later when a Heinkel 59 of *Seenotflugkommando* 2, whilst searching for survivors of the many ditchings south of the Isle of Wight, was shot down by Spitfires of 602 Squadron.

Over the next two days, the pattern of air operations would change. The fighters assigned to *Luftflotte* 3 to the west were reassigned to *Luftflotte* 2. The Messerschmitt 109s were re-based in airfields in and around the Pas de Calais. For the pilots of JG 2, JG 27 and JG 53, this meant that flights over the Channel were dramatically reduced, allowing the pilots greater time to operate and fight over England. These moves were staged over the next few days which, coupled with poor weather, explained why things were quiet on 27 August. However, *Luftflotte* 2 started targeting RAF airfields first thing on 28 August. One of the German fighter units had been rested from operations for the past two days and was keen for action. JG 26 had the task of escorting Dornier 17s and Heinkel 111s in their attacks on Eastchurch and Rochford airfields and had to fend off the attacks by four RAF squadrons. Unfortunately for one of these squadrons, after 28 August the survivors would take no further part in daylight operations during the Battle of Britain:

Pilot Officer Eric Barwell, 264 Squadron

> Due to losses and damage, we could only send off seven aircraft and we took off to be directed at once to a high altitude. The Leader climbed at full throttle – we were flying in two vics with one (me!) as tail-ender – and the blue sky above was streaked with vapour trails. I told Sgt Martin to keep looking into the sun as I was confident we would get bounced. In fact this happened without warning. I felt something hit us and I banked hard, only to see an Me 109 diving down well below us. I then saw one of the Defiants streaming petrol and saw where we had been hit – through the starboard wing. I was not flying my usual aircraft and as we were in the process of having self-sealing tanks fitted at that time, I did not know whether this aircraft had them or not. Having turned when hit, I was now well below and behind the remaining Defiants which were still climbing at full throttle. I called up Control to explain that I was away from the rest, to be told to patrol over Dover at 10,000ft. I explained that I was by myself but the order was repeated so I flew a one Defiant patrol over Dover (and its balloons) keeping a wary eye on the fuel gauge. Fortunately, I saw no other aircraft, the fuel was going down normally (I assumed therefore that self sealing tanks were fitted) and I landed at Hornchurch without further incident.

Barwell was one of the lucky Defiant aircrew. As the Defiants struggled to gain altitude, they had been spotted by *Stab* and III/JG 26 who needed little encouragement to bounce them:

Oberleutnant Walter Horten, *Technischer Offizier Stab*/JG 26

From the airbase at Wissant, we set out in a *Schwarm* on a *Freie Jagd*. Crossing the coast, our *Schwarm* then flew in battle formation – that is far apart from each other in a line to the left. *Maj* Adolf Galland and I formed the first pair, *Oblt* Georg Beyer and *Fw* Straub formed the second. We didn't see anything for a while until Galland's plane started to fly a bit erratically and I realised that he had seen something. I looked in the distance and saw far off and at the same height a single Defiant which we approached from behind and underneath. It flew straight on for a while until Galland got closer to a distance of 200m (pretty close!) and opened fire. So did the Defiant with its quadruple backwards facing machine guns. I can still see the 'corpse fingers' (British planes used tracer ammunition that left white streaks in the sky) between the two planes as if it was yesterday. The pilot pulled his plane up and turned left and came across the front of my plane from top right to bottom left. I fired my first 90 degree shot with both guns at a distance of about 300m. I went in, fired the first burst of 20mm too soon and watched the trail of bullets go behind the Defiant's tail. Quickly I corrected and I could hardly believe my eyes. The two sides of the Defiant lit up as if it had been struck by a match and it plunged down like a flaming torch. I did not see if the two crew got out – I hope that they escaped unhurt as I had hit the tanks in the wings and not the fuselage. This

Oblt *Walter Horten*. (Horten)

lasted just a few seconds during which Galland and I were pretty busy and I couldn't see the two other members of the *Schwarm*. *Oblt* Beyer must have been shot down at this moment by Hurricanes which were lying in wait, using the Defiants as bait.

JG 26 claimed a total of five Defiants – three were shot down and five crew killed, a further Defiant force-landed and was written off. At least three more Defiants were badly damaged, one of these did not have the luxury of self-sealing tanks:

Oblt Georg Beyer (seen with Lt Josef Buerschgens, right), one of the two III/JG 26 pilots shot down during the combat with 264 Sqn. (Buerschgens)

Sergeant John Lauder, 264 Squadron

We were ordered to intercept a gaggle of thirty to forty He 111s with masses of Me 109s as top escort. They were coming in over Dover and Folkestone heading north west and they had considerable height advantage over us. We were told to concentrate on the bombers whilst the Spitfires and Hurricanes took care of the Me 109s. We were endeavouring to climb up to the bombers when we were attacked by Me 109s diving vertically down onto us. I saw shells passing through my wings and it became evident that my petrol tanks must have been holed. The shells that had done the damage were obviously not of the incendiary type because there was no sign of fire. On checking the fuel situation on the fuel gauges, it was obvious we could take no further part in the action so I made for the nearest aerodrome which happened to be Rochford.

After landing, we heaved a sigh of relief and were examining the Defiant for further damage when we realised that Rochford was being attacked by several Heinkels and we made an ignominious retreat to a nearby slit trench. We spent an uncomfortable few minutes there until the all clear sounded and then reported to flying control.

It transpired that we lost so many crew and aircraft that day that the decision was taken to remove all Defiant squadrons from day fighting and transfer them to the night fighter role. The next day the remnants of 264 Squadron flew up to Kirton-in-Lindsey in Lincolnshire to lick their wounds, take on new crews and to train for the new role.

A further bombing raid occurred early that afternoon (the three remaining serviceable 264 Squadron Defiants being part of the force scrambled to intercept it) but the day ended with a number of massed *Freie Jagd* by a number of German units. This was the sort of combat that Fighter Command wanted to avoid – of the six squadrons scrambled to intercept, eight aircraft were shot down and although they claimed to have shot down fourteen Messerschmitt 109s, in reality German losses were less than this. One of the German pilots, himself a victim, managed to score his last victory just before he was shot down:

Oberfeldwebel Artur Dau, 7/JG 51

I shall certainly remember 28 August 1940 if I should ever live to be 100! That day, my *Staffel* was on a *Freie Jagd* over the Channel and southern England. Suddenly, I had two Hurricanes in my sights and, with my *Rottenflieger*, attacked them. I had opened fire on the second aircraft when I was hit by *flak* over Dover and had to bale out. After landing, I was taken into custody by Coastguards and then a Bobby arrived and took down my particulars. Then I was taken to Folkestone and locked up in a cell. Shortly after, an RAF officer with a bandaged head appeared in my cell. We shook hands and he asked me if I had been the pilot of a Bf 109 that had crashed near Folkestone. I said I was and he pointed to his head and said "You did that!" I answered him "I am sorry"; then he left.

Some hours later, I was driven to London and interrogated. That was the end of me as a pilot.

Dau was probably the pilot who shot down Sqn Ldr Don Finlay, 54 Squadron's Commanding Officer of just two days; he was bounced and baled out wounded at about the same time that Dau was shot down. Dau was not shot down by *flak* but probably by Sqn Ldr Peter Townsend, Commanding Officer of 85 Squadron.

The RAF fighters had been taught a lesson on 28 August and were not keen to go head-to-head with German fighters the following day. Despite one attempted bombing raid later that afternoon followed by another massed *Freie*

Ofw Artur Dau, 7/JG 51 is taken POW.

Jagd, the RAF fighters tried to avoid 'mixing' with the German fighters. Nevertheless, successes by pilots from JG 3, JG 26 and JG 51 were achieved but RAF losses were much less than the day before.

30 August saw an escalation of attacks which lasted virtually the whole day, one raid overlapping with the next in an attempt to swamp the RAF defences. The Messerschmitt 110 had been noticeable by its absence over England since 25 August but made an expensive reappearance on the 30th. The main raid of the day which involved them took place at about tea time when the designated target was the Vauxhall Factory at Luton. The Heinkel 111s briefed to carry out the attack were themselves escorted by II/ZG 2, II/ZG 26 and II/ZG 76 – the Messerschmitt 110s in turn appear to have had their own escort of Me 109s. Although the bombers managed to reach their target, inflicting heavy damage on the factory and its workforce, the Messerschmitt 110s were severely mauled by Hurricanes of 56 and 242 Squadrons. However, one claim was submitted by a pilot from another squadron who, by rights, should not have done so. 'B' Flight, 303 Squadron was on an interception exercise when, by luck, they ran into a formation of what they thought were sixty Dornier 17s and sixty Messerschmitt 110s. Against their orders, they broke away and in an action popularised by the post-war film *The Battle of Britain*, Fg Off Ludwik Paskiewicz latched on to what he thought was a Dornier 17 but was in fact a 4/ZG 76 Messerschmitt 110:

Unteroffizier Heinrich Nordmeier, 4/ZG 76

I joined II/ZG 76 just after the French Campaign as *Bordfunker* to *Hptm* Heinz Wagner, *Staffel Kapitaen* of 4/ZG 76. However, we did not get on well together so I became *Bordfunker* to *Ofw* Georg Anthony. We were escorting KG 1 in an attack on the Vauxhall Factory on the afternoon of 30 August 1940 when we were attacked by Hurricanes. They hit one engine which then caught fire. My pilot was also badly wounded – he had been shot in the stomach. Knowing that he could not control the plane much longer, he ordered me to bale out. I didn't want to – I was too frightened and still hoped that Georg could manage to fly home. However, he must have felt that he only had a few more seconds to live so he threw the cabin roof off, turned the Messerschmitt on its back and I fell out. The plane, still with the pilot on board, crashed about a mile further on. I came down on a farm with the farmer and farm hand waiting for me, shotguns in their hands. I sprained both ankles on landing and bruised my forehead.

Heinrich Nordmeier was luckier than the man that replaced him as *Hptm* Wagner's *Bordfunker*. In a fast and furious combat, Wagner and *Stfw* Heinrich Schmidt had the misfortune to be attacked by a Canadian pilot who had already accounted for two German aircraft that afternoon; they were about to be that pilot's thirteenth confirmed kill:

Pilot Officer Willie McKnight DFC, 242 Squadron

While patrolling with the Squadron over North Weald, enemy were sighted on the left at about 1705 hrs. The enemy aircraft were in a vic formation, stepped up from 12,000ft to 18,000ft. Attacked middle section of Me 110s and two enemy aircraft broke off to attack. Succeeded in getting behind one enemy and opened fire at approximately 100 yards. Enemy aircraft burst into flames and dived towards the ground. Next attacked He 111 formation and carried out a beam attack on nearest one, opening fire at approximately 150 to 200 yards. Port engine stopped and aircraft rolled over on back, finally starting to smoke, then burst into flames and crashed to earth. Lastly, was attacked by an Me 110 but succeeded in getting behind and followed him from 10,000ft to 1,000ft. Enemy aircraft used very steep turns for evasive action but finally straightened out. I opened fire from approximately thirty yards, enemy's starboard engine stopped and port engine burst into flame. Enemy crashed in flames alongside large reservoir. No return fire noticed from first two enemy but last machine used a large amount.

THIS AND NEXT PAGE
The remains of Hptm *Wagner's Bf 110.* (via Cornwell)

The day saw the RAF flying its largest number of sorties so far during the Battle – for the loss of twenty-one aircraft in combat and nine pilots killed. The *Luftwaffe*, in their biggest effort for two weeks, lost forty aircraft. Twelve of these were Messerschmitt 109s and a further seven were Messerschmitt 110s. The limitations of the Messerschmitt 110 were again evident and it would be another month before something was done for their long suffering crews. Until then, the suffering would continue, as many were to find out the following day.

The last day of August 1940 would see an even greater number of rolling attacks carried out by the *Luftwaffe* against such airfields as North Weald, Duxford, Debden, Eastchurch, Croydon and Hornchurch. The airfield at Biggin Hill was destined to be attacked twice that day – its ground crew had suffered one attack the previous day. This exerted an incredible pressure on the RAF fighter pilots who were now up against more German fighters than they had ever experienced before. Evidence of this is apparent by the claims filed by the various *Geschwader*. For example, JG 2 and JG 26 claimed eighteen fighters and twenty-two RAF fighters respectively on this date.

The day began early with Messerschmitt 109s trying to entice the RAF to battle by shooting down barrage balloons. It was the start of many raids and fierce air battles which cost the RAF dear. As these Messerschmitt 109s returned to France, two formations were plotted further to the east. These were Dornier 17s of KG 2 heading for the airfields of Debden and Duxford in East Anglia. Because of the distances involved, close escort was undertaken by Messerschmitt 110s of V(Z)/LG 1 and III/ZG 26. The Messerschmitt 109s of JG 26 were also involved but were flying to the limits of their range so any combat would have to be short and sweet.

The bombers succeeded in attacking Duxford and Debden but it was not until they were heading back that the German fighters were attacked:

Oberleutnant Erich von Bergen, 8/ZG 26

We were accompanying a unit of bombers attacking an airfield north of London the name of which I cannot recall. We had no contact with the RAF and in any case three of my *Schwarm* had turned back with engine trouble and I was on my own protecting the rear of the formation.

After the attack on the airfield and on the way home, I saw four Spitfires [sic] attacking us coming out of the sun. I was able to warn our formation and we turned to meet the attackers who overshot without causing any damage.

When we had reset our course for home, the Spitfires attacked again but this time from beneath. Although I saw them and warned the rest, they did not react. I turned towards the Spitfires and attacked the last one. Shortly after having shot down this one (the pilot baled out), the first one got me with a full salvo. The oxygen bottles in the rear of the fuselage exploded and the fuselage broke. The plane could not fly

Oblt *Erich von Bergen, 8/ZG 26.* (von Bergen)

any more so I gave the order to *Uffz* Becker to jump out and I followed immediately after. All of this happened at 7,000ft north of the Thames...

Von Bergen might have liked to have thought that he was attacked by Spitfires but his assailants were the Hurricanes of 257 Squadron. Three pilots claimed to have shot von Bergen down, the most vivid account being as follows:

Flying Officer Lance Mitchell, 257 Squadron

Green Three guarded my rear. I opened fire from 250 yards, deflection shot with short bursts at first until enemy aircraft more or less straightened out. Then I gave a four second burst. As I was doing my attack, Green Three informed me that the leading enemy aircraft were closing in on our rear. By this time, I had shot down the end of the Me 110. I saw the tail unit crumple and fall away and bits fly off the aircraft which went down in a spiral dive...

Plt Off Arthur Cochrane saw both crew bale out so it is beyond doubt that 257 Squadron got von Bergen. However, who von Bergen shot down is hard to say for certain. Plt Off Gerald Maffett was attacked from above and behind by a lone Messerschmitt 110 and his Hurricane fell away, the pilot baling out at 400ft but was killed. However, von Bergen saw the pilot of the Hurricane he attacked bale out and the two Germans and the RAF pilot were soon to meet face to face:

Flying Officer James Henderson, 257 Squadron

...All of a sudden, I saw two Me 110s coming directly at me, full throttle, line astern. Realising that I would present at easy target, I broke away. I flew straight at them and started firing at about 300 yards. I kept up the fire for five seconds. Both enemy aircraft broke away at point blank range, passing straight through my sights. First enemy aircraft must have shot at mine before breaking away as my instruments were shattered. A second or two later, the second Me 110 appeared and there was a great explosion in my aircraft as the fuel tank was hit, presumably by cannon fire. The cockpit immediately became a mass of flames and I baled out, falling into the sea three to four miles off Brightlingsea...

Oberleutnant Erich von Bergen

I was picked up by a Home Guardsman with a small boat. Though I was sour at my bad luck, I had to smile when he pointed his rifle at me, swimming helpless in the sea, and cried "Hands up!" Nevertheless, he took me on board. Later there came a boat that already had *Uffz* Becker on board. I came on board this boat which had a crew of two. They were looking for the British pilot I had shot down. When we found him, he could not get on board because he was badly wounded on one side. Becker and myself tried to get him on board...

Meanwhile, Hurricanes of 601 Squadron had managed to intercept the Messerschmitt 110s which had been escorting the bombers attacking Debden:

Leutnant Karl-Joachim Eichhorn, 14(Z)/LG 1

We had been transferred to a small airfield south of Boulogne from the airfield at Caen about a week before. On 31 August 1940, our *Gruppe* had to escort bombers attacking an airfield near Cambridge. Our *Staffel Kapitaen*, *Oblt* Michael Junge, was not flying this day so I had to lead the *Staffel*.

I can remember the *flak* from some cruisers in the Thames which was uncomfortable and the whole formation began 'swimming' from side to side. However, it was on our way back that my *Staffel* was attacked from behind by Hurricanes. We were flying at the rear of the *Gruppe* and my *Schwarm* (*Lt* Hugo Adametz and his *Rottenflieger*, *Fw* Jaeckel, as well as myself and my *Rottenflieger*, *Fw* Fritz) were at the back of the *Staffel*. The attack was a complete surprise and the first thing I recall was bullets smashing into my cabin and the aircraft. The right engine began to burn at once. My *Bordfunker*, *Uffz* Groewe, was shooting and crying at the same time. So to get away from my attackers, I dived from 6,000m to sea-level. There was some mist and nobody followed me. I now realised that Groewe had been hit by a whole volley and was lying dead in the rear of the cabin.

Lt *Karl Joachim Eichhorn (centre) with* Lt *Horst Werner (+ 13 August 1940) and* Oblt *Walter Fenske*. (Eichhorn)

I was now flying at twenty feet above the sea on one engine and after ten minutes, the other engine began losing power and I had to ditch. Before I did this, I threw off the cabin roof and took out my dinghy. After touching the sea, the plane sank like a stone and I had some trouble in getting out. After some swimming and many trials (my flying boots were dragging me down), I finally succeeded in getting into my dinghy. After two hours, a boat picked me up and landed me at Margate. There I received some medical attention and a local reporter took my picture. The Commanding Officer of the local Army unit also gave me a very warm welcome!

Lt *Eichhorn after being rescued and landed at Margate.* (via Eichhorn)

Eichhorn's *Rottenflieger* was also not destined to get home:

Obergefreiter Karl Doepfer, 14(Z)/LG 1

The attack by Hurricanes was a great surprise. I can remember that a Hurricane came out of the sun and fired. All I could do was warn the pilot "Attack from behind!" and I returned fire and the Hurricane pulled away. I was sure that I hit him. My pilot [*Fw* Fritz] swung the Bf 110 away to the left and, at that moment, another Hurricane attacked and I heard the bullets hitting our cabin. We were by now separated from the rest of the formation and had lost a lot of height. My pilot began to curse. "The left engine is burning. I am going into a dive, perhaps the flames will go out. Prepare to bale out!" I pulled the emergency handle to jettison the cabin roof but it must have been damaged during the attack and I could not do so. The port engine was still burning and the right motor was starting to splutter. We were at this time still over land and my pilot called "I am trying to reach the Channel and ditch – try to jettison the cabin roof!" Thank God, it suddenly flew away and soon after, we ditched. Our Bf 110 sank. We were unable to free our dinghy. It was about two hours before a fishing boat picked us up...

The tail of Fw *Fritz's Bf 110 just before it was shot down.* (Eichhorn)

It would appear that Doepfer and his pilot were shot down by Fg Off Carl Davis; Eichhorn was shot down by another pilot:

Pilot Officer Humphrey Gilbert, 601 Squadron

I attacked an Me 110 which was being attacked by another Hurricane. It went down about 5,000ft in a dive. I had the height advantage and was able to overtake the Me 110 at full power. I opened fire from 250ft and the starboard engine was hit almost immediately and glycol spurted out. The rear gunner was silenced. The Me 110 went down in a steep dive to the sea but I succeeded in overtaking it again and attacked while in the dive. I fired at the port engine from which came white and black smoke. The starboard engine then stopped and the Me 110 was only a few feet above the sea. I heard repeated calls for help in German and heard the position being relayed...

Help was at hand in the form of III/JG 26 but they had been in combat with 56 Squadron; the only German casualty was the *Staffel Kapitaen* of 9/JG 26, *Oblt* Heinz Ebeling. He managed to shoot down one Hurricane before being damaged by another. He ditched and was rescued quickly. Despite his soaking and a bump to his head, he was back in action that evening, claiming another two Hurricanes.

The last day of August 1940 had cost the RAF thirty-eight fighters and eight pilots; a further twenty-two pilots were wounded. The *Luftwaffe* also lost in the region of thirty-eight aircraft. The outlook was bleak. The RAF could not sustain such maulings from the *Luftwaffe* fighters and at the same time were allowing their bases to be bombed by the German bombers. Some historians have stated that 30 and 31 August 1940 saw the *Luftwaffe* fighters starting to get the air superiority they wanted. The RAF pilots were tired and many of their

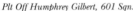

Plt Off Humphrey Gilbert, 601 Sqn.

airfields a mess and, if the Germans had wanted to, an invasion could possibly have been carried out. However, although the current German tactic would continue for a few more days, as we shall see, things would soon change – for the better for the RAF, for the worse for the *Luftwaffe*.

CHAPTER 3

Maximum Effort, September 1940

Despite the passing of the month, there was no change in the *Luftwaffe*'s tactics. The initial raid of the month materialised just before 1030 hrs on the 1st when a massed formation began to assemble over France and then, half an hour later, crossed the Kent coast and headed for Biggin Hill, Detling and Eastchurch airfields and London Docks. The massive fighter escort would cause problems for one fighter pilot that morning:

Oberleutnant Anton Stangl, *Staffel Kapitaen* 5/JG 54

At 1212 hrs on 1 September 1940 I collided at 7,600m with another Bf 109 during a dogfight. I remember the time exactly as I had looked at my watch just ten to fifteen seconds before the collision.

We were ordered to escort a *Kampfgruppe* which was attacking the harbour facilities of east London. We soon had contact with British fighters and my *Staffel* had been split up and each *Rotte* was having to fight by themselves. I noticed a Spitfire about 800m below me and I knew immediately that I had an excellent chance of shooting him down so I called up my *Rottenflieger* and told him to be ready to roll over and attack. Now I did what I always did before rolling over – I started looking back to the left and saw another Bf 109 of an unknown unit some fifty or sixty metres away with its airscrew shining in the sun approaching me at full speed. That look behind saved my life. I realised immediately that a collision was unavoidable, so I pushed my control column forward and to the right and felt a tremendous shock of the crash. My head was thrown forward and hit the gunsight (it bled very much afterwards but it was not serious) and I blacked out.

A few seconds later, I came to and I saw that my left wing had gone (giving me the best view I had ever had from an aircraft!) and a white fountain (either fuel or coolant) was shooting out of the engine cowling just a metre in front of me where the airscrew of the colliding Bf 109 had hit me. Now I reacted as I had been taught at least a hundred times during training. Waiting and thinking for a moment, throwing off the canopy and baling out (which was very easy from a plane in an inverted spin). I was thrown out with a terrible force and hit my left foot on the part of the canopy which was not jettisoned. I now fell through the air – a wonderful experience – and after waiting, opened my parachute. It opened at once at about 19,000ft and it took me half an hour to come down. The view was excellent – I could see much of the English Channel, Dungeness on one side and, on the other, Calais and the woods some kilometres to the east where our improvised airfield lay.

I landed in a barracks where British soldiers were exercising. I crashed into the top of a large pine tree and was brought down by a soldier who had the climbing ability of a most skilful ape. He looked at my blood-soaked face and asked if I was armed and in my schoolboy

Lt Anton Stangl after shooting down his fifth enemy aircraft, June 1940. (Stangl)

Anton Stangl in the cockpit of the Bf 109 from which he was forced to bale out of on 1 September 1940; ahead of him is the gunsight that cut open his head. (Stangl)

Bf 109s of II/JG 54. (Stangl)

The badge of II/JG 54 (formerly I/JG 134 and then I/JG 76).
(Stangl)

English answered that I had a pistol and handed it to him. He shouted down, "Oh, he speaks fluent English!" which pleased them all! So I became prisoner of war number 51816!

Immediately after lunch, another attack materialised when Dornier 17s of KG 76, heavily escorted by all of JG 26, II and III/ZG 76 and V(Z)/LG 1, yet again went after Biggin Hill and Kenley. Like Anton Stangl that morning, another fighter pilot would end up prisoner of war because of an accident:

Leutnant Josef Buerschgens, *Staffel Fuehrer* 7/JG 26

For some weeks, I had been leading 7/JG 26. At about 1300 hrs on 1 September we took off from Caffiers. As with many times before, I was hoping to return there in spite of the many wearying incidents I had already experienced over the Channel and southern England. This time, things were to turn out differently.

Our orders were to escort a *Gruppe* of bombers attacking Kenley. Flying at an altitude of about 6,000–7,000m, we reached the target without being attacked and only then were we engaged in aerial combat with British fighters which were more interested in the bombers and the Bf 110s. I had remained with the bombers when, immediately beneath me, a Bf 110 flying in a defensive circle was attacked from behind by a Spitfire. It took no effort on my part to place myself behind the attacker so there in a row were the Bf 110, the Spitfire and then the Bf 109 flown by me. The gunner opened fire on the Spitfire and the Spitfire in turn tried to knock out the gunner. It was relatively easy for me to lay into the Spitfire in a continuous attack. At once, smoke started to pour from the Spitfire who pulled away, diving steeply. During the attack, I had got rather close to the rear gunner of the Bf 110 who was still firing and I turned away to avoid ramming him. At this instant, I felt an impact by the side of my foot on the left of the cockpit, the engine cut out and the propeller began windmilling. My God! The gunner had taken me for an enemy fighter (coming as I was from an acute angle from behind, I must have looked like a Spitfire!) and had got me! My heart nearly stopped beating with shock for I knew only too well what that meant. Trailing fuel, I dipped my Bf 109 slightly and started gliding towards the French coast, hoping to perhaps reach the waters of the Channel where I might possibly be picked up by a German rescue plane. The sun shone warm and bright and the seconds seemed like hours.

I glided and glided whilst all around me furious battles were being fought. Some of our bombers which had been hit, fighters, enemies and friends fell, smoking, burning or disintegrating. Parachutes opened or didn't as the case might be. It was a gruesome yet thrilling spectacle. Never before had I been able to watch the fighting like now.

Lt *Josef Buerschgens.* (Buerschgens)

Gliding, I got nearer to the ground but could not reach the waters of the Channel. Near Rye, I finally disassembled my faithful Bf 109 into its many components. I regained consciousness in hospital, having suffered back and head injuries when I baled out.

Apart from another attack on Biggin Hill at tea time and an unopposed massed German fighter sweep over Kent, the RAF must have reflected that if the rest of September was going to be like the first day, the future looked grim.

They had lost twelve aircraft and three pilots whilst the Germans had lost just seven fighters and just one bomber. Added to this, Biggin Hill had been bombed three times that day and the last raid of the day which had gone unchallenged caused even more serious damage to the airfield.

However, flying escort missions sometimes three a day was starting to take its toll on the German fighter pilots and most started to suffer from what they called *Kanalkrankheit*, literally Channel sickness, as one pilot recalls:

Unteroffizier **Werner Karl, 1/JG 53**

There was no talk about fear of being killed or taken prisoner. At least, nobody admitted if he was scared. All around us, we saw heroes both in the newspapers and on the radio. I think that everybody thought that he was the only one who was afraid. For example, our briefings were always held outside in the open air. Immediately after it finished and before we went to our planes, we all ran to the latrines and sat on the toilet. At first we thought it was sabotage but in fact it was fear.

Uffz *Werner Karl in the cockpit of his fighter.* (Karl)

Werner Karl's part in the Battle of Britain was to come to a sudden ending on 2 September. The Germans were quick off the mark with the first signs of activity occurring at about 0715 hrs when two formations were plotted off Dover and a third off North Foreland. At 0740 hrs the first German aircraft crossed the coast and headed towards Biggin Hill, Eastchurch, North Weald and Rochford and were almost immediately engaged by the first of six RAF fighter squadrons:

Flying Officer Alec Trueman, 'B' Flight, 253 Squadron

I was in Green Section when we were attacked by fighters at 18,000ft just before we closed with the bombers they were escorting. I did a very steep diving turn to get them off my tail and had straightened out and was climbing again when an Me 109 dived in front of me. I got on his tail at once and fired two bursts of about two to three seconds each, opening fire at 250 yards and closing to 150 yards. I saw another Me 109 getting onto my tail and I dived away. Each time I fired, bits flew off his tailplane and rear end of fuselage. The attack was near Rochester aerodrome; I had no time to observe if enemy aircraft came down.

The escort for the attack was made up from I and II/ZG 26 and I/JG 51 and I/JG 53, all of which lost aircraft:

Unteroffizier Werner Karl, 1/JG 53

At about 0800 hrs, I went to the airfield at Neuville with the rest of the *Staffel*. This morning there was an unusually thick fog so we did not think that a combat mission was possible. To our surprise, the *Geschwader* command gave the combat order as, according to the meteorologists and reconnaissance aircraft, this ground fog was only ten metres high.

I think we took off at about 0830 hrs – we still could not see anything because of the fog and dust until after we had taken off when, as forecasted, we went through the thick fog into the most wonderful sunshine. At once we formed up – I was the *Katschmarek* of my highly decorated *Staffel Kapitaen Hptm* Hans-Karl Mayer in the first *Schwarm*. When we reached the middle of the Channel, Mayer had to turn back due to engine trouble and *Oblt* Ohly took command. So then positions changed and I had to fly at the rear of the formation with another comrade and had to protect the *Staffel* against attacks from behind.

Our mission was a *Freie Jagd* in between 4,000 and 5,000m as a cover for our bombers which were attacking a target north of London. We reached the southern outskirts of London without enemy contact but then, after we turned east, I heard the warning over the radio that enemy fighters were attacking from the west. Because I did not want to be caught by surprise from behind, I flew a turn to the left and so there was some distance between my *Staffel* and me. Just as I was turning, I saw three Spitfires [sic] rushing down on me. Simultaneously, we opened fired but, unfortunately, I received a concentrated burst of fire into the back of the fuselage which destroyed my radio. My *Staffel* did not see all of this and flew on. During the dogfight with the enemy fighters, I was outnumbered and without hope and I received many hits in the cockpit. One of these caused a superficial wound at the back of my head and I lost a lot of blood.

I tried to shake off my opponents (by now I counted only two of them) by going into a power dive. At first, I thought I had been successful. I could not see any pursuer so I made a kind of inventory of my plane. It looked quite bad so I headed for home. However, a quick look into my rear view mirror showed that there was an enemy fighter behind me in an ideal shooting position...

White 2 and White 10 of 1/JG 53 over England. (Tzschoppe)

It is thought that Werner Karl was initially damaged by Alec Trueman and if the German pilot thought that he was lucky to get away, his next assailant was not so obliging; for reasons that will become clear, that pilot had no reason to remember what was his twelfth of twenty-eight confirmed kills:

Sergeant James Lacey, 501 Squadron

According to my logbook, I had taken off at 0730 hrs and claimed an Me 109 destroyed in the Dungeness area which fits in well with Hythe where *Uffz* Karl crash-landed. I do remember that it did crash-land near a Do 17 at Newchurch. Later that day on my second sortie I again destroyed another 109 and also claimed a Do 215 damaged. My third trip of the day yielded nothing. This is the only time that I have ever had news of one of my ex-opponents!

Unteroffizier Werner Karl

...On instinct, I rolled over my right wing and dived again. I went down and tried to get rid of my pursuer by hedgehopping so it would not be possible for him to shoot at me. However, he was too clever. He flew about 200m higher and behind me so that he could get more hits when the situation was suitable. Apprehensive, I noticed that white and black smoke was coming out of my plane which meant hits in the engine and cooling system. There was a very strong smell of petrol in my bullet riddled cockpit – a fuel line had been hit. Now there was the danger of explosion the next time my cockpit was hit and my first thought was to bale out but that was absurd as I was too low. I looked back to my pursuer but could not see him but to my surprise, I noticed him to my right just above me. I do not know why he did not shoot me down – I was completely defenceless. Either he had no ammunition left or he thought it was not necessary any more. It was obvious that my flight was coming to an end and I only hoped that it would be possible to ditch in the Channel. This hope was in vain as after I had pulled my plane over rising ground, my engine stopped, perhaps due to over-heating. I could see the sea but could not reach it and had to make a forced-landing on the beach. My right wing was torn off by one of those obstacles to prevent airborne landings. I managed to get out of the cockpit before I fainted.

When I regained consciousness, I was lying on a bed in a hut. Soldiers had given me first aid as I had crash-landed near to their living quarters. Later they told me they thought that I was going to crash into

Werner Karl's White 14 – the aircraft in which he was shot down on 2 September 1940. (Karl)

their hut. After I got up and could stand on my own two feet, I was allowed to go down to the beach. At the water's edge, I sat down and looked across the Channel towards France. For the first time I now realised that I was a prisoner of war. A short time later, a young lieutenant came to me. In very good German he told me that I would be taken to a hospital in a short time. He tried to cheer me up and I said I should be happy being in captivity and still living – I would survive the war but he was not so sure about his fate.

Although Werner Karl could not see it, out in the Channel another one of his comrades was also in trouble:

Feldwebel Heinrich Hoehnisch, 1/JG 53

It was one of those days in the Summer of 1940 when we had to fly to England nearly every day. On this day, there was a thick yellow-brown haze in the sky and the horizon could not be seen. *Uffz* Heinrich Ruehl reported engine failure so he was flying back to France on his own. I then heard him saying "I can't stand it in my plane any longer," to which someone said "Throw off your canopy roof." I was also on my way back to France – I always looked around to make sure of enemy attacks. I did not want to be shot down by one of those British pilots which specialised in catching lonely German planes. We called them *Leichenfledderer* – one who robs corpses!

Fw *Heinrich Hoehnisch.* (Hoehnisch)

In the distance, I saw a small dot with a black line after it and when I came nearer, I realised that it was one of our fighters with black smoke coming out of the engine. The pilot sat in his open canopy – it was Ruehl. I then flew alongside him, waved my hand and waggled my wings. I flew above him to make sure that he was not attacked but we were now at 1,800m and he was still losing height. The engine of his plane was still running but very slowly. The French coast was visible in the haze but he was too low. His plane's shadow on the water came nearer and nearer and a fountain of spray appeared in the sea and the Messerschmitt could not longer be seen. Suddenly, the tail broke to the surface and I saw Ruehl in the water. Immediately, the water around him was coloured yellow. I flew around and over the spot to make sure that he was still alive and then headed for France. My red fuel warning light had been burning for about five minutes but nearer the coast, I saw a motor torpedo boat. In cases of emergency, we were told to fly over these ships and waggle our wings and then fly in the direction of the emergency. So I flew back to Ruehl and then back again and tried to correct the boat's course. Then I saw a Do 18 with Red Cross markings and I knew that it would get to Ruehl quicker than the boat so I showed the pilot the direction and could see him land near Ruehl before I had to turn back on the last drops of fuel.

Uffz *Heinrich Ruehl (right) with his* Staffel Kapitaen, Oblt *Hans Ohly.*

Another fighter *Staffel* suffered badly at the hands of 54 Squadron who carried out a very successful bounce on 1/JG 51. Commanded by *Oblt* Hermann-Friedrich Joppien, who achieved seventy kills by the time of his death just under a year later, in its ranks were *Fw* Heinz Baer, who by the end of the war achieved 221 kills, and *Uffz* Erwin Fleig, who had shot down sixty-six enemy aircraft by the time he was taken prisoner in May 1942. *Lt* Guenther Ruttkowski was the only pilot to die when he was shot down by Flt Lt George Gribble. The future ace *Fw* Heinz Baer's plane was so badly damaged that he was forced to ditch in the Channel but later rescued. Only one pilot was taken prisoner:

Leutnant Helmut Thoerl, 1/JG 51

The weather was clear as we headed back to France to our base at St Omer. Suddenly, I heard a noise as if you drop some peas on a plate and at the same moment, my cockpit filled with blue smoke. I looked into my mirror and saw a fighter directly behind me but I could not recognise whether it was a Spitfire or a 109. If it was a Spitfire, I only had one chance – push the stick forwards and give my plane full power. We knew that the engine of a Spitfire had a carburettor and caused the engine to stutter when you pushed the stick forwards. The Bf 109 had

fuel injection and the engine did not stutter in such manoeuvres. However, it was useless because my plane began to burn so I had to bale out at full speed as I could not close the throttle. After many efforts I succeeded and landed by parachute, with a burnt face and hands, in a meadow where many people were waiting for me. I was taken prisoner by Home Guards and taken to a nearby hospital.

Lt *Helmut Thoerl*. (Thoerl)

In a letter to Helmut Thoerl's father written later that same day, the *Staffel Kapitaen* tried to paint a rosy picture after having lost three aircraft:

Oberleutnant **Hermann-Friedrich Joppien,** *Staffel Kapitaen* **1/JG 51**

In this mission, which brought us the loss of your son, the *Staffel* was attacked from above and behind by Spitfires. Your son got left behind and we could not help him in time. I saw that his left wing was hit and pieces of it broke off because of the concentrated fire of the Spitfires. I saw him throw away the cabin roof and am sure he intended baling out. The Spitfire was then shot down in flames by *Uffz* Fleig. I hope that your son is unwounded and a prisoner.

No Spitfires were lost by 54 Squadron as the pilot who probably shot down Helmut Thoerl proves:

Oblt *Hermann-Friedrich Joppien,* Staffel Kapitaen *of 1/JG 51.*

Squadron Leader James Leathart, 54 Squadron

Enemy were sighted over Ashford when we were over Sheppey at 20,000ft. I climbed a further 5,000ft and attacked Number Five in a vic of five Me 109s. There was no result. I dived away, pulled up vertically under the second formation of five, firing at the flank aircraft with full deflection. He dropped vertically and exploded on hitting the ground.

In addition to the Messerschmitt 109s lost that morning, three Messerschmitt 110s were lost from I and II/ZG 26; during the next raid at lunchtime aimed at the airfields of Detling and Eastchurch, another two Messerschmitt 110s were lost and, by the end of the day, a total of seven Messerschmitt 110s were either lying in British fields, at the bottom of the Channel or wrecked in France. Messerschmitt 109 losses were also heavy with fifteen being lost. RAF casualties were about the same, many being lost in the furious dogfights that occurred over Kent during the afternoon. The Polish pilots of 303 Squadron, recently declared fully operational and on their second major combat, narrowly avoided disaster when they were bounced over Dover, the bounce being spotted by one of the 'weavers'. Aggressive to the end, they chased the Germans back to France and only turned away when shot at by German *flak*.

Attacks against airfields continued on 3 September. North Weald was heavily bombed but remained operational. Fierce dogfights took place over the Essex area with, surprisingly, the Messerschmitt 110s performing well enough to keep the RAF fighters away from the bombers. Together with JG 26, they inflicted heavy losses on the RAF that morning, the Messerschmitt 109s holding back off the coast and successfully bouncing a number of British fighters, albeit the claims were too high compared to what the RAF actually lost. Two claims that can be substantiated were made by the *Gruppen Kommandeur* of II/JG 26 *Hptm* Erich Bode who bounced 603 Squadron off Margate. One of the two pilots shot down was Plt Off Richard Hillary who, in his book *The Last Enemy*, recalls vividly what happened next:

Pilot Officer Richard Hillary, 603 Squadron

...I felt a terrific explosion which knocked the control column from my hand and the whole machine quivered like a stricken animal. In a second, the cockpit was a mass of flames; instinctively, I reached up to open the hood. It would not move. I tore off my straps and managed to force it back but this took time and when I dropped back in the seat and reached for the stick in an effort to turn the plane on its back, the heat was so intense I could feel myself going. I remember a second of sharp agony, remember thinking "This is it" and putting both hands to my eyes. Then I passed out.

Hillary managed to fall away from his Spitfire, very badly burned. By luck, all of this had been seen from the ground:

Chris Fright

On 3 September, a Spitfire was seen to crash into the sea off Margate. The pilot baled out. The Margate lifeboat was launched and after a long search, found the pilot badly burnt. My old friend Harry Sandwell held him in his arms all the way back to the coast; Harry was very proud of this until the day he [Harry] died.

Even though it was not obvious to both sides, the *Luftwaffe* was continuing to achieve and improve their air superiority over southern England. The RAF continued to inflict damage on *Luftwaffe* fighters and bombers but the Germans had many more replacements. The RAF was struggling to replace both aircraft and pilots. Their airfields and aircraft manufacturing works were also being bombed; time after time the German bombers were getting through. However, 4 September would give the exhausted RAF pilots a well-deserved morale boost.

Aerial activity on 4 September started in the mid-morning with fighter sweeps – the results of which were inevitable for those RAF squadrons tasked to intercept. Two Spitfires were shot down, with one pilot fatally wounded, as well as three Hurricanes with two pilots missing. German losses were just three Messerschmitt 109s with one pilot killed and one missing. Under cover of the German fighters, Dornier 17s went after the airfields of Rochford, Lympne and Eastchurch, dropped their bombs and returned without loss.

However, early in the afternoon, a massive formation of 300-plus aircraft was plotted, one group going after airfields and aircraft factories in the Kent region whilst another, consisting entirely of Messerschmitt 110 fighter-bombers of *Erprobungsgruppe* 210 and escorted by Messerschmitt 110s of ZG 2, ZG 76 and V(Z)/LG 1, headed for the Vickers Aircraft Factory at Brooklands in Surrey.

The attack did not start well. On seeing RAF fighters climbing towards them, the *Gruppen Kommandeur* of the fighter-bombers attempted a manoeuvre which had fatal consequences – his plane hit the Channel taking him and his *Bordfunker* to their deaths. Shortly afterwards, the RAF fighters pounced:

Unteroffizier Adolf Kaeser, 7/ZG 76

During the briefing on 4 September, the question arose as to who would fly with whom. I was assigned to fly with *Oblt* Muenich of 8 *Staffel.* Our instructions were this: take off at lunch time, climb to 3,000m. At this altitude, we were to wait for a formation of bomb-carrying Bf 110s. Together with them we were to fly as escort along the English coast to a target near London.

All was done as ordered but hardly had we crossed the coast, presumably in the area of Brighton, when I saw fighters climbing in the distance to the west. Either the *Kommandeur* had not seen them yet or, which is more likely, he had strict orders not to leave the bombers alone. However, the enemy was so quickly above us and soon Willy, my *Staffelkamerad*, had one on his tail. At once I told my pilot and told him of the Englishman's position because we were in a favourable position for an attack. He did not react but held his course, flew straight on and after a short while, I did not see either a friend or an enemy. I had a bad feeling because I could not see what was going on below. I was vigilant but soon it happened...

Unseen by the German crew, Plt Off Pat Horton and Sgt Zygmunt Klein of 234 Squadron succeeded in getting behind the Messerschmitt 110 and managed to hit the starboard engine. They then watched the rest of the drama unfold:

Unteroffizier Adolf Kaeser

...clouds of smoke were coming from the right engine. Now *Oblt* Muenich tried to extinguish the fire by going into a dive. As a result of this, the wing was covered in flames. The airspeed indicator registered a speed which was well over the warning line set at 760kph. Then, the left engine began to give off smoke. No doubt this was the end.

Muenich pulled the aircraft out of the dive and I told him that I was going to bale out so I pulled the cockpit hood jettisoning lever but nothing happened. Now I went forward to the radio equipment and pulled the lever that was there – the hood did not move. Then I got on the seat and pressed my back against the hood – nothing! Now I told Muenich that I was not able to get out of the plane so he stayed with the plane and headed for the coast. Suddenly, just before landing, the hood flew off but now it was too late to bale out.

Just before the aircraft landed, the pilot side-slipped to the left and the wing hit the ground and was compressed like an accordion. This way the force of the impact was reduced considerably. I only saw that the left engine was ripped out of its engine bearers and was rolling down the slope. Then I blacked out. When I came to my senses again, my head was throbbing – I had a scratch on my left temple. Then an old gentleman appeared next to me as if by magic as I had not seen any buildings from above and this area seemed to be deserted. I asked him how far it was to the coast. "Twelve miles," he replied. Then he left. I took the dinghy out of its stowage and together with *Oblt* Muenich quickly left the burning aircraft. We had hardly gone about 100m when there were explosions – the fire had reached the ammunition.

I could still not get the old man out of my mind – where did he come from and what was he doing here? I was soon to find out. We went through some bushes and after taking a few steps stopped – in the middle of a clearing there were some people on a blanket having a picnic. It was an idyllic sight but how could we pass them unseen? We had planned to make for the coast and to launch our dinghy under cover of darkness, hoping to be picked up by German air-sea rescue aircraft the next morning. Then I heard the sound of engines coming nearer. Soon we could see through a less dense part of the wood some military vehicles stopping not far from us. Now I was aware of the old man's role – I guess he was from the Observer Corps and had phoned and informed the military. That was a neat bit of work!

Because I still had my pistol, I put it under some moss and waited to see what would happen. We saw soldiers with rifles fanning out who, in an extended line, were heading towards us. So we went into captivity. After we had been captured, the commanding officer asked us if we wanted a souvenir from our aircraft. I thought that was a noble gesture.

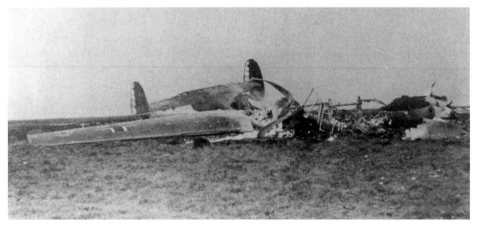

The remains of Adolf Kaeser's Bf 110. (Cornwell)

The German formation had to run the gauntlet of at least two lines of defence before the bombers reached their target. Despite all of this, however, they hit what they were after, causing 700 casualties of which 88 were killed. It took four days to clear the wreckage from the Vickers Factory and a number of days after that before full production was resumed.

However, as the Germans streaked for home additional RAF fighters were waiting for them and although the Messerschmitt 110 fighter-bombers returned unscathed, a total of seventeen Messerschmitt 110s failed to survive the day. The English countryside between Weybridge and Brighton was littered

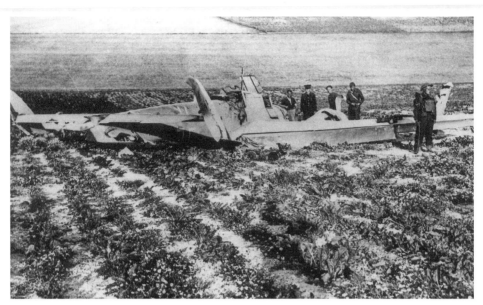

The only Bf 110 lost by ZG 2 on 4 September 1940 lies in a field near Shoreham; both crew were captured.

Another 4 September 1940 victim – M8+CP of 6/ZG 76 was seen to explode when attacked by Fg Off Ross Smither of 1 Sqn RCAF; both crew were killed. (Guschewski)

A pilot wounded in combat on 4 September 1940 was Hptm *Wilhelm Balthasar,* Gr Kdr *of III/JG 3. (Morzinek)*

with burning or battered wrecks of Hermann Goering's favourite but inadequate fighter.

5 September was a day of irritation for Fighter Command as, yet again, the *Luftwaffe* carried out a series of rolling attacks throughout the day against airfields in the south east. Bomber casualties were higher and the fighter-against-fighter combats vicious, as the following illustrates:

Pilot Officer Jan Zurakowski, 234 Squadron

I was diving from about 22,000ft to investigate two aircraft flying below when I noticed one Me 109 flying level and 'weaving'. I approached to about 150 yards and I fired about a two second burst. The Me 109 half rolled and dived close to the ground. At ground level and from thirty yards range, I opened fire until the guns stopped. Whilst firing, I had a problem in that due to the sudden descent to a low altitude, my front windscreen completely misted up and I was aiming using the wingtips of the Me 109 visible through the cockpit side panels. The Me 109 was flying very close to the ground but when some hills forced him a bit higher, I could see him better against the background of the sky so I started firing again until I ran out of ammunition and when I looked down, there was a town approaching. The Me 109 flew trailing smoke over Hastings, the canopy was jettisoned and the plane ditched about two miles from the shore and in a few minutes, the aircraft turned over and sank but the pilot was still in the water.

The misting up of Jan Zurakowski's cockpit which made it hard for him to see his victim also happened to his victim, so preventing the German pilot from seeing the approaching danger until too late:

Feldwebel Anton Ochsenkuehn, 9/JG 53

We took off from the airfield at Le Touquet at about 1500 hrs. Our task was a *Freie Jagd* in the London area. We were led by *Oblt* Jakob Stoll – I was *Rotte* Leader and, together with *Oblt* Herbert Seliger, we were flying the rear guard or *Deckungsrotte*.

As we were about to fly into the combat zone over the River Thames, we heard over the radio from our ground station, "Enemy planes over London." As far as I know, their altitude was given as 6,000m. Because we were nowhere near as high, we turned to the east and climbed to the necessary height. Then we changed our direction back to the combat zone. Very soon, we saw a Spitfire below us – *Oblt* Stoll attacked immediately and as far as I am aware, *Oblt* Josef Volk and *Uffz* Manfred Langer's attacks followed. However, all attacks were unsuccessful because the RAF

Bf 109s of JG 53 at Le Touquet.
(Sauer)

pilot had seen us and was obviously proficient. Then I went over to attack, the Spitfire descended in a spin and I stayed behind it without having the chance to shoot. After diving 2,000-3,000m, I was ordered to "break off pursuit and climb back up again." I let him know that I had understood and was about to climb back when my cockpit misted up so badly that I could not see a thing.

Now I did not want to put myself in danger of being surprised and shot down whilst in a slow climb so I put my nose down and waited until I had better visibility. I then looked back and I saw a plane behind me, far away and very small. I was not able to see if it was a friend or an enemy. Over the radio I tried to find out where my wingman was and the rest of the *Staffel.* I did not get a reply so I presumed that my radio was not working. So, for a while, we were flying one behind the other heading south but now I was having second thoughts. In this plane behind me there could be my wingman who in his efforts to catch up with me and looking too much in my direction could be surprised and shot down himself by an enemy fighter. Without hesitation, I turned and flew towards the plane but very quickly realised that it was a Spitfire which I recognised by the big radiator under its left wing. Instead of attacking, I turned back again hoping I could get away from the Spitfire but I was completely wrong. Because of the two turns, the Spitfire had got dangerously close to me so I flew at low level to get away. However, near the coast, I had to pull up over woodland and as this happened, I was hit in both radiators. The Messerschmitt slowed down alarmingly. I then flew over a town (probably Hastings) but over the water I had only an altitude of ten metres and an airspeed of 250kph. To be on the safe side, I threw off the canopy roof and, right after that, the engine broke

Anton Ochsenkuehn (far left) with Fw Klapdohr, Uffz Kurt Sauer (POW 16 July 1941) and Uffz Anders. (Volk)

down. I succeeded in ditching in such a way that I could get out of the cockpit quickly; the Spitfire which had been playing a waiting game and had followed me since the attack over the woodland circled round me and then flew back towards England.

One pilot who, despite being taken prisoner on 5 September 1940, managed to escape back to Germany was Lt Franz von Werra of II/JG 3. Seen here after his return, he was killed in a flying accident in October 1941.

6 September would be similar to the day before with the Germans yet again going after airfields and oil storage depots on the Thames in three distinct phases. One German pilot was destined to be his *Geschwader's* last casualty before, to the RAF's relief, the Germans made a gross error by changing tactics. No longer would airfields and aircraft manufacturers be the sole objects of their attention:

Leutnant Max Himmelheber, *Gruppen Adjutant* I/JG 2

On the 6th, my *Geschwader* flew on a routine flight over southern England. Until now, I had flown with *Stab*/JG 2 but today I was with I/JG 2 under the command of *Hptm* Hennig Struempel. We flew up to the southern outskirts of London and got involved in an air battle with British fighters. I received a hit in the radiator of my aircraft so that the engine was not able to work. I found myself at 10,000m and attempted to glide to one of our Red Cross boats in the Channel and then bale out. Approaching the coast, I flew over, at about 2,000m, a military airfield and was attacked by two Hurricanes which caused me to bale out. I landed in a meadow and as I was badly wounded, I was taken to a civilian hospital in the small town of Maidstone and there I was operated on. After a week, I was taken to a military hospital in Woolwich.

A Bf 109E of I/JG 2 over England. (Fiby)

Maj *Hennig Struempell (right)* with Oblt *Helmut Wick who was* to replace him as Gr Kdr *I/JG 2* on *7 September 1940.* (via Payne)

Another casualty on 6 September 1940 was this Bf 109E-4 of Uffz Hans Georg Schulte of 7/JG 53.

7 September 1940 dawned bright, clear and quiet – the RAF had no inkling at all that things were about to change. *Reichsmarschall* Goering had realised that the tactic of going for the fighter airfields was not having the desired result. He therefore decided that if the strategy changed to all-out attack on London, the RAF would commit every remaining fighter to the defence of the nation's capital. His belief was soon proved to be flawed.

There was little if no activity that morning and even then, the radar screens remained sinisterly clear until about 1600 hrs. The radars then picked up an ever increasing mass of enemy aircraft until in the region of 1,000 bombers and fighters clogged the screens, spread between altitudes of 14,000ft and 23,000ft. By 1630 hrs, more than twenty RAF fighter squadrons were either airborne or at readiness and the sight that greeted these RAF pilots must have been fearsome.

The RAF threw itself at the attackers but, against such odds, could do little to deter the Germans who, having dropped their bombs on London's dockland and setting much of it ablaze, turned for home. The attack had lasted just under an hour. However, the RAF succeeded in shooting down forty-one German aircraft that day, twenty-one of which were fighters that had tenaciously defended the bombers, allowing them to cause such devastation. Again,

Zerstoerers were mauled, in this case ZG 2 who lost eight aircraft and were withdrawn from the battle some two days later. The RAF lost twenty-two fighters but only ten pilots lost their lives.

That night the *Luftwaffe* visited the capital again, causing more death and destruction. But it must be said that, sad as these deaths were, the change of tactic from bombing military targets to bombing those of a political, commercial and civilian nature gave Fighter Command the slight relief they needed. Although it was not obvious then, the Germans had as good as lost the Battle of Britain. However, there was no respite for either side's aircrew who would continue to fight and in some cases die over the remaining month and a half of the campaign.

8 September was very much an anti-climax. The fear that a German invasion fleet had set sail was unfounded and Fighter Command was allowed to send some of its squadrons away from the fighting for well earned rest and recovery. Only two small raids took place but they were heavily escorted by Messerschmitt 109s of JG 3, JG 26, JG 27 and JG 53, the latter *Geschwader* claiming the lion's share of the four RAF fighters lost that day. However, they lost three themselves – one in combat and two in an accident:

Oberleutnant Heinz Wittmeyer, *Stab* I/JG 53

I had belonged to JG 53 since August 1940 and, on 8 September, I was attached to *Stab* I/JG 53 being introduced into the work of an *Adjutant*. It was about my thirtieth operational flight. The order for that day was to fly close air support for a *Gruppe* of He 111s into the area east of London. We flew in a *Gruppe* formation at about 20,000ft.

Before crossing the line Dungeness–Hastings, I spotted three fighters north-north-west and reported this to the *Gruppen Kommandeur*. As a consequence of this, he gave the order to the *Gruppe* to turn towards them. At this time, the smallest RAF formation was three aircraft whereas we had the two or four aircraft *Rotte* or *Schwarm* so we thought that these aircraft were RAF. Very soon, the three were identified as Bf 109s – they had exactly the same altitude as ourselves and came straight towards us. Normally, they should have given way to us – Numbers One and Two did so and dropped their Bf 109s beneath our *Schwarm*. However, the third didn't. I tried at the very last second to avoid disaster by pushing my stick forward but it was, at least for the other pilot, too late. Both Bf 109s disintegrated and I found, without doing anything, that I was in open air.

A little later, I opened the parachute. I was more or less blind in my right eye (later, in a field hospital, a specialist took more than twenty metal splinters out of it). I could, however, see a bit with my left eye (six splinters). On that day, there was a strong wind from the north west. It blew me towards the French coast. When I touched the sea, I tried to free myself from the parachute, initially without success. This was good because the parachute became a kite and I became one of the first windsurfers! The kite brought me nearer to the coast but on becoming wetter, the parachute collapsed. This time I got free and swam for nearly an hour after which I was helped ashore by soldiers near Cap Gris-Nez.

The other pilot, unfortunately, did not get out of his Messerschmitt. I was later told that the *Staffel* to which the three Bf 109s that crossed our course belonged had been in a fight with Spitfires near London and the *Staffel* had broken up. They were on their way back to their airfield and the pilot who had collided with me was probably looking backwards to be sure that they were not attacked again. It seems that during the collision, a propeller blade cut the cockpit just before my head and the next blade behind my head cutting my seat belts. Beside my eyes, I was injured with a cut on my right shoulder.

I was told by fellow pilots visiting me in the hospital that the pilot who collided with me was a newcomer and had no experience[4]. I had to stay some months in hospital, returning to the *Ergaenzungsgruppe* of JG

Oblt *Heinz Wittmeyer (2nd from right) with, L to R,* Lt *Guenther Hess (2/JG 53),* Oblt *Hans Ohly (1/JG 53),* Hptm *Rolf Pingel (*St Kap *2/JG 53) and* Hptm *Hans Karl Mayer (*St Kap *1/JG 53).* (Schultz)

[4]This was *Oblt* Heinz Kunert, *Staffel Kapitaen* of 8/JG 53. He was not inexperienced and had nine air combat victories, his last being on 5 September 1940.

53 in France and in Spring 1941 to I/JG 53 in Sicily. However, the eye-sight of my right eye had not recovered enough (whereas the left eye was good again) and I had to stop flying as a fighter pilot and was post-ed to II *Fliegerkorps* in Sicily.

Officers of III/JG 53, early 1940 – few were to survive that year. Oblt Heinz Kunert is back row, 2nd from left. Others are: front row L to R Lt Josef Volk, 9/JG 53 (POW 11 November 1940), Oblt Heinz Wittenberg, Stab, Hptm Werner Moelders, Gr Kdr (+22 November 1941), Lt Walter Radlick, Adj (+2 October 1940), Lt Georg Claus, TO (+11 November 1940). Middle row L to R Oblt Otto Boenigk, St Kap 9/JG 53, Dr Soestmann, Oblt Wolf-Dietrich Wilcke, St Kap 7/JG 53 (+23 March 1944), Lt Hans Riegel, 7/JG 53 (+ 6 September 1940), Lt Jakob Stoll, 8/JG 53 (+ 17 September 1940), Lt Horst Von Wegeman (+ 9 March 1941). Back row L to R Lt Ernst Panten, Kunert, Lt Hans Fleitz, 8/JG 53 (+ 3 June 1940), Oblt Hans von Hahn, St Kap 8/JG 53.

The following day saw the *Luftwaffe* launch the start of co-ordinated day and night destruction of London in preparation for the start of Operation *SEELOEWE*, the German invasion of Great Britain. The orders to launch the invasion would be issued on 11 September and the Germans anticipated that the landing assault would take place on 21 September. Nevertheless, daylight operations on 9 September did not start until late in the afternoon when many bombers, heavily escorted, made for various targets in and around London. The German fighters were greatly committed, losing twelve Messerschmitt 109s and four 110s. Two of the Messerschmitt 109 pilots had very different experiences that day:

Oberleutnant Erwin Daig, 5/JG 27

The mission took place late in the afternoon. Our unit had been detailed to fly as escort to a formation of bombers which was attacking London Docks. We took off from Fiennes in the Pas de Calais and before we reached our destination, we encountered rather lively opposition from British fighters. In the course of this, my aircraft must have been hit as from then on I was unable to accelerate properly. When the German formation turned for France, I was unable to follow. At that time, I must have been the only German aircraft in the area. Then I made a mistake which was to cost me my freedom. Instead of going into a glide, assisted by my engine and trying to reach the French coast at high speed, I maintained my course and height (6,000-7,000m). Immediately, I was attacked by two British fighters which came from an easterly direction from above and turned in behind me. They fired and my aircraft was hit. I stood the aircraft 'on its head' and attempted to reach a layer of cloud which was covering the French coast and southern England at a height of about 2,000-3,000m. I felt that I was succeeding as I received no more hits but just before I reached cloud cover, I was fired at again and I now thought that I had another pursuer behind me. I then went into a dive and tried to reach the Channel by hedge-hopping. However, it was useless. The aircraft started to smoke and I was unable to see so I threw off the cabin roof. I was also

losing speed. The last thing I saw was an area rising to the south with trees on top; in front of it was a large meadow covered in overturned lorries and other things to prevent gliders landing there. Then I must have hit the ground. That was it – the end of the chase, unfortunately!

Oblt *Erwin Daig.* (Daig)

Erwin Daig's fighter had been hit in the cooling system and he quickly jumped out of the plane, throwing down his gun and surrendering to troops from a nearby searchlight battery. This aircraft came in for close scrutiny by the RAF who noted that it carried a bomb rack. Although this was not the first time bomb racks had been discovered on Messerschmitt 109s, the full significance would not become clear until just under a month later when Messerschmitt 109s began to operate as *Jagdbombers* or *Jabos* – literally fighter-bombers.

Bf 109s of II/JG 27, early in the Battle of Britain. (via Moelders)

An unluckier pilot was *Feldwebel* Heinrich Hoehnisch of 1/JG 53. Now an experienced fighter pilot with six air combat victories, he had not increased his personal tally of kills since 13 August 1940. It was unlikely that he would shoot down anything else on 9 September – his unit had been 'chained' to the bomber formation and he was assigned to the lookout *Rotte:*

Feldwebel **Heinrich Hoehnisch, 1/JG 53**

On my last mission on 9 September 1940, our task was to give direct fighter cover to the rear of an He 111 bomber formation. One *Kette* of bombers got separated so our *Staffel* looked after them. We had only seven Bf 109s and I was the tail-end Charlie with *Ofw* Mueller.

Approaching London Docks, there was no contact with the enemy but I was sure that we could expect attacks out of the sun as soon as we turned 180 degrees for our return flight. To my surprise, I saw, when I was looking towards the rest of my *Staffel*, six Spitfires on a reciprocal course in a line about fifty metres above me. To avoid the inevitable attack, I tried to come up with my *Staffel* flying in front and below me. When I was level with my *Staffel Kapitaen*, I thought I had made it…

Heinrich Hoehnisch (left) just after he joined JG 53, early 1940. (Hoehnisch)

Combats on 9 September were confused. However, it would appear that the Duxford Wing, consisting of Spitfires of 19 Squadron and Hurricanes of 242 and 310 Squadrons were in the area south of London, close to Biggin Hill. 19 Squadron, led that day by Flt Lt Wilfrid Clouston, went after the fighters:

Flight Lieutenant Wilfrid Clouston, 19 Squadron

While on patrol leading the Squadron at 20,000ft, we encountered a large formation of enemy aircraft. We had been detailed by Wing Leader to attack fighters so I climbed and put the Squadron into position to attack seven Me 110s. Just as I was about to attack, two Me 109s crossed my sights so I turned on them. The rear one emitted glycol fumes after a short burst and then burst into flames. I then attacked the second Me 109 and fired the rest of the ammunition. I could see my shots hitting this aircraft and when my ammunition had finished, I saw him going down in a left hand gliding turn, looking rather the worse for wear...

Feldwebel **Heinrich Hoehnisch**

...There was a rattle like an explosion in my plane and, with the pressure of a blow torch, flames hit my face. With greatest difficulty, I got out of the plane. I landed with severe burns to my face and bullet wounds to my right calf. I stayed in hospital in Woolwich for two months.

THIS AND NEXT PAGE
Drawn by Heinrich Hoehnisch after his capture;
his sketches vividly portray his last flight.

9. September 1940

9. September 1940

Heinrich Hoehnisch was quickly captured, his aircraft crashing close to the fighter base at Biggin Hill. Interrogated by RAF officers and still in great pain from his burns, he gave away no information on his unit. In fact, he boasted that he knew all about the RAF airfields because British prisoners of war "gave away such a lot of information of this sort when interrogated." What particularly interested the RAF was found in the remains of his fighter. On the underside of one of the wings, towards the trailing edge, were two small discs about the size of a penny, painted like the RAF roundel with the date '13.8.40'. Today, Heinrich Hoehnisch can explain this unusual marking:

Feldwebel Heinrich Hoehnisch

On 13 August 1940, we had an escort mission for some Ju 88s near Portsmouth. I shared the shooting down of three Hurricanes flying in line. After that, we had a dogfight above a circling Bf 110 *Gruppe*. I hit a Spitfire between the fuselage and the wing with two 20mm shells. I was then hit in my right wing by a Hurricane which came up behind me. I escaped by rolling and diving. The Hurricane followed to sea-level but turned away when I climbed for home.

The days that followed 9 September were relatively quiet for the German fighter pilots. 10 September saw the return of bad weather and a corresponding reduction in German sorties. Bad weather again on 11 September prevented operations until mid-afternoon and then, because of apparent faulty routing for the bombers, the majority of the escorting Messerschmitt 109s returned early leaving much for the Messerschmitt 110s to do. Messerschmitt 109 losses were light – only three were lost in combat – but the Messerschmitt 110s lost seven in the attack on London and whilst escorting a smaller attack on Southampton by *Erprobungsgruppe* 210. Although the RAF wreaked havoc on the Heinkel 111s attacking London, thirty of their fighters were lost that day and eleven pilots were killed. Even two fighter Bristol Blenheims of 235 Squadron were lost escorting Fleet Air Arm aircraft attacking the German invasion barges. All in all, the Germans fared better that day and it was a relief to the RAF that the next two days saw the return, yet again, of bad weather which allowed the RAF light bombers to go on the offensive. Such daylight attacks were not without incident. For example, at 1545 hrs on 12 September, three Bristol Blenheims from Coastal Command's 59 Squadron took off to attack shipping off Le Havre. They picked up an escort of three Blenheims from 235 Squadron and then attacked a convoy, failing to hit a single ship, before a lone Messerschmitt 109 intervened:

Leutnant Alfred Zeis, 1/JG 53

I had been on a ferry flight from Rennes to Le Touquet and was flying along the coast. The weather was bad with almost total low-lying cloud cover. Just before I reached Le Havre, I saw some fountains on the edge of the harbour basin and saw three planes heading for the clouds, one after the other. At full throttle, I tried to intercept before they could reach the cloud and just before the last one disappeared, I expended all my 20mm ammunition against him without success – the range was too great. I followed the last plane into cloud, flying on instruments, and came up behind three Blenheims flying close together. I first shot at the engines of the left-hand Blenheim and then attacked the right one before they disappeared into cloud but not before my Messerschmitt had received some hits. Before they disappeared, I saw some effects of my fire – black smoke coming out of one plane. By now, I had to turn back and, using my compass, flew in the direction of Le Havre between two layers of cloud. Suddenly, another *Kette* of three Blenheims appeared in front of me – they climbed and fired at me. I was then hit again and it was high time I reached Le Havre airfield. When I arrived, the visibility was very poor and my plane totally covered in oil. Fortunately, I could land but the engine had to be changed and other repairs carried out. Two days later, I flew back to join the rest of the *Staffel.*

In my combat report, I said that at least one Blenheim had been damaged and when I was asked, I did not completely rule out a kill. However, it is probable that none of the Blenheims received severe damage because I did not have any cannon ammunition left. A victory was therefore questionable.

Lt *Alfred Zeis.* (Schultz)

Alfred Zeis's normal Bf 109 with his tenth victory tab, the Blenheim on 12 September 1940, visible on the rudder. (Sauer)

Unusually for the Germans, despite there being no positive evidence of a kill, Alfred Zeis was allowed to claim a Blenheim as his tenth kill. The 235 Squadron diary disagrees:

235 Squadron Diary Entry, 12 September 1940

Plt Off Wordsworth, Sgt Sutton and Flt Sgt Nelson provided bomber escort for three bomber aircraft to Le Havre. Four Me 109s were sighted. One attacked bombers but was driven off by Blenheims. Rear gunners concentrated fire on this aircraft and [it was] believed damaged.

Unusually, no record was made of the damage to Alfred Zeis's Messerschmitt 109.

Friday 13 September was again a quiet day for both sides whilst operations on the following day, again being hampered by bad weather, were restricted to a few small bombing attacks using clouds as cover. Unfortunately for Fighter Command, towards the end of the day the weather improved allowing many of the *Jagdgeschwader* to undertake *Freie Jagd* over much of southern England with some success, claiming twenty-five RAF fighters and allowing the German top scorers to increase their personal tallies. *Maj* Werner Moelders of JG 51 claimed his thirty-seventh kill, *Hptm* Adolf Galland of JG 26 his thirty-second, *Oblt* Joachim Muenchberg of 7/JG 26 his twentieth and *Hptm* Rolf Pingel of I/JG 26 his fifteenth. Twelve RAF fighters were lost in action and the RAF claimed to have shot down sixteen German aircraft. In reality, only three fighters and three bombers were lost that day.

If the results on 14 September left the RAF downbeat, the reduced attacks since the change in tactics on 7 September, particularly the German penchant for rolling attacks, had given Fighter Command a well needed breathing space. The attrition the RAF had suffered up to that date would, if it had continued, have seen Fighter Command on its knees prior to what the *Luftwaffe* was going to throw at them exactly half way through the month. However, with their backs against the wall, invasion imminent and with nothing else to lose, the RAF's fighter pilots were, surprisingly, relatively rested and in high spirits. The opposite could be said of the German bomber and fighter aircrew, some of whom had been in almost constant action since the start of the war. Despite all that they had done, there seemed to be no reduction in the numbers of Spitfires and Hurricanes that they kept on meeting over the skies of southern England. However, as a means of emasculating Fighter Command in order to carry out the invasion, the Germans had been planning an all out attack on the British capital and on Sunday 15 September, they decided to do just that.

The first attack was picked up on radar just after 1100 hrs as the Dornier 17s of KG 76 formed up just south of Calais. At the same time, Messerschmitt 109s of II/LG 2 carried out what was a relatively new concept – that of Messerschmitt 109s carrying bombs, much like the Messerschmitt 110s of *Erprobungsgruppe* 210. They attacked railway targets in south-eastern London but what they did was not regarded by the British as fair as one participating Austrian pilot recalls:

Hptm *Rolf Pingel of I/JG 26; the award of his Ritterkreuz was promulgated on 14 September 1940.* (Pingel)

Oberleutnant Viktor Krafft, *Kompaniechef Stab* **II/LG 2**

A British newspaper wrote when our *Gruppe* flew for the first time over Kent: 'Today flew a group of German fighters over Kent and London. Nobody had expected they were carrying bombs but they did so. It is not fair to fly like a fighter and then to drop bombs like a bomber.' I should say that we didn't do it because we were unfair. It was just a new development as is usual in war.

The unfair weapon – a 250kg bomb underneath a Bf 109. (Sauer)

However, it was the unfortunate Dornier 17s that suffered in that first attack. Spitfires went after the fighters whilst the bombers were initially engaged by the Hurricanes, attacking with such ferocity that the formation split up making it hard for the fighter escort to protect them. Later, Sqn Ldr Douglas Bader led his Duxford Wing consisting of two Spitfire and three Hurricane squadrons into the fray with the end result that, for once, the Germans were outnumbered and what followed was inevitable. One German pilot, *Oblt* Erwin Moll of 3/KG 76, later felt obliged to write alongside his log-book entry for that day, "Target London. Very heavy fighter defence" – the first and only time he had ever felt a need to write such a comment.

Even though the German bombers reached their intended target of the railway lines at Latchmere Junction, damage was slight but then the RAF fighters began to take their toll as the Dornier 17s headed back towards the safety of the Messerschmitt 109 escort in the Maidstone area. However, the German fighters were having their own problems:

Feldwebel Herbert Tzschoppe, 1/JG 53

On 15 September 1940 I, with *Uffz* Kopperschlaeger, was one of the last of the *Staffel* to take off – we had to fly as the *Deckungsrotte*. We flew at the back of the escort formation.

The *Staffel Kapitaen*, *Oblt* Ohly had to turn back with radio trouble and the lead was given to *Ofw* Mueller. We were flying at about 3,500m and had to fly with our flaps down so that we could stay close to the slower bombers. During a turn, we were attacked by Spitfires coming out of the sun – Mueller was hit in the arm and broke away and my plane was hit in both wings. I wanted to get back to France, thinking of my fiancée and forthcoming wedding at the end of September, and tried to hide in the clouds which were at about 1,500m. However, when I came out of the clouds, I was hit by a second burst so I threw off the cabin roof and undid my seat belt. I now think that the drills I learned in flying training then saved my life (we were often woken up at night and had to say what to do if we were hit – throw off the cabin roof, undo the seat belts, jump out and pull the rip cords). A third burst hit home – from the instrument panel there came flames like an oxyacetylene torch and my hands and face were severely burned. An explosion followed and I found myself hanging on a parachute...

Fw *Herbert Tzschoppe (2nd from left) with, L to R:* Uffz *Ghesla (POW 5 October 1940), Tzschoppe,* Fw *Hoehnisch (POW 9 September 1940),* Lt *Zeis (POW 5 October 1940),* Oblt *Ohly,* Hptm *Mayer (+ 17 October 1940),* Lt *Schultz,* Uffz *Karl (POW 2 September 1940) and* Uffz *Ruehl (+ 4 June 1941).*

Pilot Officer Tony Lovell, 'B' Flight, 41 Squadron

Flying as Blue Two, [we] broke up to attack Me 109s which were attacking us. [I] sighted my Me 109 turning east and diving. I dived after him and chased him for some fifteen miles in and out of cloud. After first burst, white fumes came from his port wing root but he carried on. I gave him two more bursts and he caught fire and I saw him bale out and being attended to on the ground.

Pilots of 41 Sqn prior to the Summer of 1940 – Plt Off Tony Lovell is in the middle row 3rd from right. (Shipman)

John Sampson

I was eighteen years of age and resident in Adisham near Canterbury in September 1940. On the morning of Sunday 15 September, a friend (the son of the local gamekeeper) and I were out shooting in the woods. We heard the sound of aerial combat and then saw someone descending by parachute. The pilot (I now know to be Tzschoppe) came to earth at the edge of a wood near to where we were standing. He surrendered to us (we both had 12-bore shotguns) and unloaded his pistol and handed it to us. We handed him over to a detachment of New Zealand soldiers who quickly appeared on the scene – this would have been about two to three miles from where the Me 109 crashed at Adisham Court. The victorious Spitfire overflew us after we had apprehended the German pilot.

Feldwebel Herbert Tzschoppe

...Two Spitfires circled me at full bank – the first pilot saluted and I did the same. I came down in a mixed forest and got hung up in a tree about five feet from the ground. I released myself from the parachute and landed heavily, hurting my knees. Two youths and shortly after that soldiers appeared and I was taken prisoner. I was taken by ambulance to a hospital where my burns were treated very well. The nursing was excellent, especially by the Irish nurses who I can remember very well! I was then taken to the Royal Herbert Hospital in London where I met *Ofw* Mueller and three other pilots from my *Staffel* who had been shot down before me.

It was a particularly bad mission for I/JG 53 who lost four more pilots, including two *Staffel Kapitaene*. The whole *Geschwader* claimed fourteen RAF fighters as means of retribution. It is thought that at least Messerschmitt Bf 109s were lost in the first major action of the day and if the *Jagdgeschwader* thought that they were in for a rest, they were gravely mistaken.

The two I/JG 53 Staffel Kapitaen *lost in the first attack on 15 September 1940:* Oblt *Rudi Schmidt of 2/JG 53 (centre) with (left)* Lt *Guenther Hess and (right)* Lt *Gebhardt Dittmar (+ 6 September 1940)...* (Schultz)

...and Oblt *Julius Haase of 3/JG 53 (second from right) with (L to R),* Uffz *Karl Kuhl,* Oblt *Wolfgang Lippert (+13 December 1941),* Ofw *Erich Kuhlmann (+ 2 September 1940).* (Rupp)

The pilots of JG 53 had barely enough time to land, refuel and rearm before they were sent off again; this was typical of many other *Jagdgeschwader* who were involved in the first attack of the day. This time the targets were the Royal Victoria, West India and Surrey Commercial Docks in eastern London and the attacking force was even bigger, made up of 114 Dornier 17s and Heinkel 111s flying in three parallel columns, three miles apart, the whole formation being some thirty miles wide.

Buzzing around all sides of this monstrous formation were the fighters including, on this occasion, Messerschmitt 110s from V(Z)/LG 1 and I/ZG 26. The RAF threw at least twenty-nine Spitfire and Hurricane squadrons at the formation coming from as far as Middle Wallop to the west and Duxford to the north. The RAF fighter pilots were tenacious, flying and fighting as if their lives depended on it. For some, this was not enough to ensure their survival:

Unteroffizier Heinrich Ruehl, 1/JG 53

We were flying in a *Schwarm* led by *Oblt* Ohly. I was his *Rottenflieger*. We were escorting a formation of Do 17s. Short of London, the bomber formation was suddenly attacked from the front by two enemy squadrons. The front-most squadron attacked through the bomber formation and pulled up. *Oblt* Ohly attacked the rearmost squadron. During this, I saw a Spitfire [sic] which flew through the bomber formation pulled up and turned. At this moment, I took aim and opened fire and saw in between the wing and fuselage a tongue of flame shoot out.

The fighter immediately caught fire and dived into the increasing cloud and, although the crash was not observed, both he and *Uffz* Kopperschlaeger were each credited with a Spitfire. It is likely that they had pounced on the Hurricanes of 303 Squadron which lost two aircraft – one pilot baling out, the other never to be seen again.

A Bf 109E of I/JG 53 is prepared for the next sortie. (Sauer)

As well as inflicting mortal damage on some of the bombers, the RAF succeeded in shooting down at least nine Messerschmitt 109s and three 110s of V(Z)/LG 1. Most of the aircrew shot down were not as fortunate as the two Messerschmitt 109s lost by I/LG 2 that afternoon. *Uffz* Herbert Streibing was shot down by one of the 303 Squadron Hurricanes that managed to avoid the attention of 1/JG 53, the German pilot crash-landing in Essex. The other LG 2 pilot had a similar experience:

Unteroffizier August Klik, 2/LG 2

Our operational airfield was Calais Marck on the Channel coast. The task of our *Staffel* was escorting bombers to England. Our losses were always very high because we flew on the furthest flank of the escort and so had no rear cover. Because of that, we were often pushed away to the east when attacked by British fighters so a fair number of pilots had to ditch because of lack of fuel and some of them drowned.

On 15 September, our order was: Victoria Docks, London; escort for I/KG 1, 5/KG 2, 6/KG 26 and KG 53. We were told good weather and not much opposition. However, things were very different.

Before we reached Tonbridge, heavy AA fire welcomed us and the sky began to cloud over (seven tenths cloud cover). Suddenly, the sky was full of British fighters. The first group of bombers was torn apart and disappeared into a protective cloud bank. During the subsequent air battle, we were pushed away to the east – again! The variable amounts of cloud and the tumult of battle made it difficult to tell the difference between friend and foe.

The cloud cover then broke up and just in front of me, a Hurricane approached from the right, in a steep turn. It was fifty metres and firing a broadside – nothing could go wrong for me! I was therefore so surprised that I made the mistake – like a beginner. I put my aircraft into a steep climb to see if my burst had hit home when there were hits in my starboard wing. Two planes were heading straight for me but the hits in my plane's wing must have come from another plane from behind and the left because the two aircraft did not show any muzzle flashes (perhaps they were as surprised as I was!).

500m below me on my right, there was a long cloud bank. It was the only protection against half a dozen British fighters...

August Klik (3rd from right) and other prisoners seen in Canada later in the war.

Flying Officer Leonard Haines, 19 Squadron

Whilst leading Green Section on a patrol south of London, I noticed AA fire just west of London and, on investigating, I noticed a force of some forty enemy aircraft which I could not identify. I put my section into line astern and made for the AA fire when two Me 109s appeared to my right. I accordingly turned and attacked them. I gave one a burst (deflection from above) and it half-rolled and dived vertically to 12,000ft where it straightened out. I had dived after it and as it finished its dive, I recommenced my attack. I was going faster than the enemy aircraft and I continued firing until I had to pull away to avoid collision. The enemy aircraft half-rolled and dived vertically with black smoke coming from underneath the pilot's seat, it seemed. I followed it down until it entered cloud at 6,000ft...

Unteroffizier August Klik

...I considered what had happened. All instruments showed normal readings, only the radiator temperature gauge was alarmingly high. It was getting hot in the cockpit and when I tried to put the safety pin of the cockpit hood into its second notch, the hood suddenly flew off.

The cloud bank had come to an end and below me there was the Thames Estuary. Because of the air combats around Maidstone and the bomber group having been pushed away, much fuel had been consumed – the red fuel warning lamp began to flicker.

There were three alternatives to be considered: baling out, a forced landing or the vague possibility of flying out to sea and being fished out by a German air sea rescue aircraft. Point number three was not worth the risk; point number one only in an emergency as a few days earlier we had been warned not to bale out as Polish pilots shot at every parachute over the coastal area! The engine was at only 880rpm so I turned towards dry land and made a smooth landing on an island in the Thames Estuary.

After five minutes, some Home Guards came and took away my sunglasses, watch and pistol. In return for these, they offered me a bottle of beer! I was taken to a cell in a fort at Sheerness by an army jeep and, together with some other prisoners, we went to Chatham. Later than evening, we were taken to a building in Hyde Park for interrogation. Just at this moment, London was receiving another bombing raid...

The cloud, a saviour for August Klik, was also a saviour for the intended targets that late Sunday afternoon. Another bomber formation arrived over London only to find their targets obscured by cloud and, in frustration, their

THIS AND NEXT PAGE
August Klik's Bf 109 comes in for some attention after it had been taken away to be recycled. (Cornwell)

bombs were dropped on the south-eastern outskirts of the capital as they turned for home, still being attacked mercilessly by the RAF fighters.

As the massive phalanx of German aircraft headed for home, another raid was developing to the west when unescorted Heinkel 111s attacked Portland and then, two hours later, the hard-worked *Erprobungsgruppe* 210 attacked the Supermarine Factory at Southampton. Both raids were ineffective (although the former raid lost one bomber) and it was left to the nocturnal German bombers to attack London, one of the six attacks before midnight being experienced first hand by August Klik.

The *Luftwaffe* had flown in excess of 1,000 sorties on that Sunday, losing fifty-six aircraft which in human terms was eighty-one aircrew killed or missing, sixty-three taken prisoner and thirty-one wounded. The cost in terms of fighters was three Messerschmitt 110s and six crew killed, twenty-three Messerschmitt 109s and nine pilots killed, eleven prisoners and two wounded. Twenty-eight RAF fighters were lost, twelve pilots killed, twelve wounded and, unusually, one prisoner (Sgt John Potter of 19 Squadron – a victim of JG 26). The Germans succeeded in causing damage to the railway lines (but rail traffic was only disrupted for three days) whilst the Docks had got away unscathed. Therefore, the day for the Germans was a failure – their bombers had not succeeded in any of their aims, the fighters, despite carrying out close escort, had failed to protect their charges and, notwithstanding all the German efforts, the RAF was still a potent force. Adding the cost in human terms and aircraft lost, it was a bitter pill for the German aircrew to swallow and as such, must have been their nadir. Now we recognise that it was the turning point in the Battle of Britain, although neither side had realised this yet.

Bad weather helped give both sides a rest on 16 September. A bomber formation turned back because of the conditions. The escort from JG 51, however, continued and although *Maj* Moelders claimed his thirty-eighth kill and *Oblt* Claus his thirteenth, the only unlucky victim was Plt Off Edward Watson of 605 Squadron who, wounded, managed to crash-land his Hurricane at Detling in Kent. 17 September saw the German bomber crews taking another day's rest, leaving the fighters, no longer chained to the bombers, to carry out a series of aggressive *Freie Jagd* in the evening. Three Messerschmitt 109s were lost and their pilots killed as opposed to four Hurricanes and two pilots.

18 September was a busier day with an early morning *Freie Jagd*, followed by an escorted bomber attack and then a lightly escorted bomber attack on oil installations at Gravesend. Fighter Command responded to each raid correctly – leaving the *Freie Jagd*, sending an adequate response to the escorted raid and then shooting down nine bombers in the last raid of the day, including one of the German fighters carrying out a simultaneous *Freie Jagd*:

Leutnant Erich Bodendiek, *Gruppen Technischer Offizier,* II/JG 53

I remember that the dogfight took place somewhere in the region of Tonbridge at 8,000m and happened on a remarkable afternoon. After three missions that day, those planes which were still serviceable, about eighteen in all, took off on a *Freie Jagd*. I was not flying my usual plane but, as I was the *Technischer Offizier*, I had to fly a plane with a new automatic propeller just to test it. That was my bad luck, having that bloody plane on that day for the first time because that 'automatic thing' turned the angle of the propeller so that an average speed was always maintained and not a kmh more! That meant trouble when starting and trouble at high altitude as the plane was nearly always unmanoeuvrable and swaggered through the air like a pregnant duck.

It was fine weather with clouds at an altitude of about 8,300m and out of this swung the RAF fighters when we were at 8,000m. They were obviously directed by radar but just missed us as they came out of clouds about a kilometre to the right of us. The *Gruppen Kommandeur*, *Hptm* von Maltzahn, did the best he could by climbing and trying to hide in the clouds. Everybody succeeded but me, thanks to my excellent propeller. My aircraft could not climb like the others had and therefore all the RAF fighters turned on me and I had no chance of escaping by diving as that wonderful propeller would ensure that I would travel at just 300 to 350kmh. Therefore I decided to fly straight ahead trying to gain altitude a metre at a time, perhaps reaching cloud without being shot down. I saw the Spitfires flying around me and shooting and my plane was hit several times. I heard the bullets hitting the armoured plate behind me but I was not hurt. Finally, one of them dived down, gaining speed and pulled up vertically and shot exactly when I flew over him. He then hit my fuel tank which caught fire immediately. Within a second, my cabin was full of smoke and fire and I had to get out...

Lt *Erich Bodendiek, October 1939.*
(Bodendiek)

Pilot Officer Bobby Oxspring, 66 Squadron

It appears that we had three patrols that day but it was only on the last one that we had a fight. It appears that we intercepted some Ju 88s with Me 109s covering, near Dover. I clobbered one which appeared to catch fire and the pilot baled out. My combat report says this happened a few miles north of Dover. I then fired at another from which I and my Number Two saw pieces fall off but in the ensuing melee, we didn't know the result and I claimed a damaged.

This all occurred over east Kent between 30,000ft and 20,000ft and the time was approximately 1700 hrs. The log also records that there was thick haze from 19,000ft to ground level and heavy cirrus around 30,000ft. So it was difficult to see any resulting crash either on the ground or in the Channel. We were accompanied by 92 Squadron that day and, as I say, the air was thick with aircraft. I, for one, never saw the Ju 88s for certain but from the initial contact, I was certainly concerned with the Me 109s in the same area.

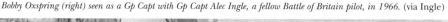

Bobby Oxspring (right) seen as a Gp Capt with Gp Capt Alec Ingle, a fellow Battle of Britain pilot, in 1966. (via Ingle)

Leutnant Erich Bodendiek

...I managed to get out and opened my parachute very quickly because I knew that there were high winds at that altitude and I calculated that it would take me thirty minutes or so to reach land. In the meantime, I would have covered nearly fifty kilometres and with the Channel being thirty-five kilometres wide, perhaps I had a chance to cross it!

Unfortunately, or should I say my good luck, the wind blew me the wrong direction so that I was driven along the coast and I finally dropped in the sea about two miles off Folkestone. I was collected by the Coastguards and overnight I was the guest of the Royal Artillery in Folkestone. They were rather suspicious because I did not wear a normal uniform, only breeches and white socks (I lost my fur-lined boots in the air) and a white pullover. I also had no identification, only my Iron Cross First Class which I had been awarded that afternoon and which I had put in my pocket. In my pocket, they also found some British money – the remains of the pounds I had when we were stationed on Guernsey. They must have thought I was a spy and must have been happy to hand me over to the RAF the next day. I was then taken to London – there they knew everything about me and my unit.

The final twelve days of September were to prove to be an anticlimax for both sides. On 19 September, Adolf Hitler postponed Operation *SEELOEWE* and the *Luftwaffe* began to change its tactics again, switching the emphasis of bombing attacks on London from day to night and increasing the use of Messerschmitt 109 *Jabos*. In addition to those units already designated for such attacks, each *Jagdgeschwader* had to designate one *Staffel* in each *Gruppe* as the *Jabostaffel*, a decision not at all popular with the pilots:

Gefreiter Heinz Zag, 8/JG 53

I had joined 8/JG 53 in early September 1940, expecting to be a fighter pilot. I flew one of the first Bf 109s in the *Staffel* which was modified to carry a bomb. However, the *Staffel* was not properly trained, which concerned me, I did not think it was a good idea – we had a short enough flying range before being weighed down by a bomb!

In twelve days time, Heinz Zag would experience the limitations of his *Staffel* and his Messerschmitt 109 *Jabo* first hand. In the mean time, *Jabo* training for the designated *Staffeln* increased, probably as a result of the success of the *Jabo* attack on London on 20 September which achieved its aim. Just one of the escorting fighters was lost whilst the RAF fighters, scrambled to intercept the *Jabos* too late, lost seven fighters to JG 2 and JG 26. Such an error on the part of the controllers would not be repeated.

Trying to emulate the success of 21 September, the Germans attempted the same tactic as the day before but the RAF was wise. Only *Maj* Adolf Galland managed to shoot at one of the RAF fighters – Plt Off Thomas Sherrington of 92 Squadron managing to force-land his damaged Spitfire successfully. Operations on the days that followed were similar if not sporadic but 23 September saw a sharp increase in combats and losses – eleven RAF fighters for the same number of Messerschmitt 109s. One of the losses was one twenty year-old *Faehnrich* Hans-Joachim Marseille of 1/LG 2 who managed to ditch in the Channel and was rescued; he would shoot down his seventh victim on 27 September before transferring to 4/JG 52 and then 3/JG 27. He would be dead in exactly two years and one week after his ditching but not before he had shot down a total of 158 aircraft.

The Jabo Staffel *of I/JG 53 – 3* Staffel. *L to R:* Gefr *Felix Sauer,* Uffz *Alexander Bleymueller (+ 14 May 1943),* Fhr *Walter Seiz,* Gefr *Alfred Baumer,* Oblt *Walter Rupp,* St Kap *(POW 17 October 1940).* Front: Lt *Wolfgang Tonne,* Lt *Karl Leonhard.* (Sauer)

The only JG 2 pilot to claim a victory on 20 September 1940 was Oblt *Hans Hahn (left),* St Kap *of 4/JG 2 seen here with* Lt *Julius Meimberg.* (Morzinek)

Preparing to load a 250 kg bomb to a Bf 109E-4/B. (Sauer)

24 September would have been another day of sporadic activity if it were not for two incidents. *Erprobungsgruppe* 210 carried out a lightning fast attack on the Supermarine works at Southampton, losing just one of their number to AA fire. Although production was not affected, forty-two workers were killed. Another attack later that afternoon was similarly unsuccessful but this time, two of the Messerschmitt 110 escorts were shot down. The second incident occurred a little earlier:

Major **Adolf Galland**, *Geschwader Kommodore* **JG 26**

> After a bombing raid on London, I attacked approximately thirty British fighters in the area of Southend but then got bounced during the approach by another squadron. The British formation broke up and then I attacked a single Hurricane which was at a higher altitude (about fifty metres) from behind climbing up and from sixty metres, and I saw it burst into flames. Thereupon, I saw the pilot bale out.

Fg Off Harold Bird-Wilson of 17 Squadron was Galland's fortieth kill for which Galland was awarded the Oakleaves to the Knight's Cross. Galland's 'rival', *Maj* Werner Moelders had achieved his fortieth kill on 20 September.

Maj *Werner Moelders in the cockpit of a Bf 109F. He first flew this variant operationally on 9 October 1940.*

The remainder of the month saw a series of attacks occurring to the west with the Bristol Aeroplane Company factory at Filton near Bristol being attacked on the 25th and the Supermarine factory, again, on 26 September. In the former attack, the RAF controllers got it wrong and misread the German intentions. The result was that the bombers reached their target almost unopposed, carpet bombing Filton. Ninety people were killed or fatally wounded and over 150 injured but the factory was not completely destroyed and full production was resumed a few months later. For the first time in a number of weeks, the escort was made up from Messerschmitt 110s of ZG 26 as well as Messerschmitt 109s from I and II/JG 2 and 5/JG 53. The twin-engined fighters did well and lost just three aircraft from III *Gruppe* and just two crew (one being taken prisoner and the other killed). The attack on the Supermarine factory the following day was also escorted by ZG 26 and, again, the attack was successful – only one bomber and two Messerschmitt 110s were lost and the factory was so badly damaged that construction of the Spitfire was dispersed away from Southampton.

However, perhaps the *Luftwaffe* had taken heart at these two successes and the appearance of the Messerschmitt 110 becoming effective again. 27 September was to prove them wrong and the death knell of the Messerschmitt 110 as a day fighter was sounded.

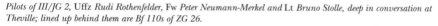

Pilots of III/JG 2, Uffz Rudi Rothenfelder, Fw Peter Neumann-Merkel and Lt Bruno Stolle, deep in conversation at Theville; lined up behind them are Bf 110s of ZG 26.

The day started with the old tactic of rolling attacks – the first clash occurring at 1000 hrs. Ten Messerschmitt 110s of what was left of V(Z)/LG 1 and thirteen Messerschmitt 110s of II and III/ZG 76 were tasked as an escort for Junkers 88s of I/KG 77. Messerschmitt 109 escort was undertaken by a number of units. The RAF was ready for all of them and ripped into the formation. Three Junkers 88s were lost as were eight of the escorting Messerschmitt 110s. V(Z)/LG 1 lost seven of their eleven aircraft including the *Gruppen* Kommandeur, *Hptm* Horst Liensberger and the *Staffel Kapitaen* of 15(Z)/LG 1, *Oblt* Ulrich Freiherr von Gravenreuth. With eleven aircrew dead and three prisoner, following their return to France the *Gruppe* was disbanded and its survivors withdrawn to southern Germany where they formed the nucleus of I/NJG 3. Only by making a break for home when the sky appeared to be clear of RAF fighters were twelve of the thirteen ZG 76 crews saved. The pilot of their only casualty was lucky to survive:

Hptm *Horst Liensberger,* Gr Kdr *of V(Z)/LG 1, killed in action 27 September 1940.* (Eimannsberger)

Oberleutnant Wilfried von Eichborn, *Geschwaderadjutant* ZG 76

27 September 1940 was an attack on an airfield north of London [sic]. Our *Geschwader* only had a third of its strength available and was quickly engaged by British fighters; we lost half of our number, the rest escaped to France. With one of my engines hit, I had to try to reach the coast by div-

Bf 110s of 5/ZG 26. (D'Elsa)

The wing of Hptm *Liensberger's Bf 110 coded L1+XB frames the orchestra – he was to meet his death in this aircraft.* (Eichhorn)

ing. I stupidly hoped to avoid more attacks but the British fighters followed me to the Channel, then a cable fire broke out in the fuselage and the aircraft burst into flames. With burns on my hands and to my head, I succeeded in setting down on the relatively calm sea and jumped into the water. However, my *Bordfunker* had baled out at high speed and was killed when he hit the sea. After drifting towards the Atlantic for several hours, kept afloat by my life jacket, later that afternoon I was picked up by a fishing boat and landed at Hastings. After a short time in a field hospital near Sevenoaks, I was brought to the Royal Herbert Hospital in Woolwich where I was put into a room with thirty German officers. I heard my neighbour in the next bed say to his neighbour the other side after looking at me, "Will that ever be a face again?" It did, the doctors attributing it to the long bath in sea water. The only annoying thing was that at Sevenoaks they had wrapped my face in cotton wool which now had to be laboriously picked off!

As this battered formation retreated, another raid, further to the west, would also see a further unit being decimated and, yet again, the losses would be just Messerschmitt 110s. It was *Erprobungsgruppe* 210's task to attack the Parnall Aircraft Factory at Yate near Bristol. Escort was provided by ZG 26 with elements of JG 2 and JG 53 covering the route to the coast and the return. This time a single unit, 504 Squadron, attacked the formation head-on, causing it to veer away, jettison its bombs and run for home. It was then that four more RAF

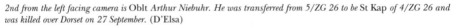

2nd from the left facing camera is Oblt *Arthur Niebuhr. He was transferred from 5/ZG 26 to be* St Kap *of 4/ZG 26 and was killed over Dorset on 27 September.* (D'Elsa)

fighter squadrons ripped into the survivors, chasing them back across the Channel. Six Messerschmitt 110s from ZG 26 were lost, including a *Staffel Kapitaen* and a *Gruppenadjutant*, whilst *Erprobungsgruppe* 210 lost four, including a very experienced *Gruppen Kommandeur* and *Staffel Kapitaen*, both of whom would be posthumously awarded the Knight's Cross.

The net result of these two attacks was that, apart from one more day in the Battle of Britain, Messerschmitt 110s were never seen in any great numbers. The reputation and effectiveness of the *Luftwaffe's* much vaunted 'Destroyer' had been well and truly destroyed. Furthermore, both attacks had been thwarted with the Germans suffering heavy losses.

As the second major offensive of the day was still fighting its way back home, the *Luftwaffe* switched back to attacking London, using Junkers 88s of KG 77 and Heinkel 111s of KG 53 in a series of rolling attacks interspersed with *Freie Jagd*. The day would be hard work for the German fighter pilots as the logbook of *Oblt* Jochen Schypek of 5/JG 54 shows – firstly escorting the early morning attack on London, then escorting Heinkel 111s attacking the same target around midday followed by another escort mission to London in the late afternoon. In between the second and third operational flight,

he also had to test fly another Messerschmitt 109, presumably so that it could be flown by another pilot later that afternoon. However, the cost to the Germans was eighteen fighters shot down or written off and even KG 77 lost eight of their number during the first afternoon attack in addition to the three lost that morning. RAF losses in action were a total of twenty-nine but, as high as they might seem, the *Luftwaffe's* losses and continued failures were much worse and harder to bear.

Hptm *Helmut Wick*, Gr Kdr *of I/JG 2 got his thirty-third and thirty-fourth kills on 30 September 1940.* (Morzinek)

The next two days were quieter, albeit German fighters managed to account for seventeen RAF fighters on 28 September for the loss of just two fighters in combat, proving that despite what the RAF thought, the Messerschmitt 109s could still teach the Spitfires and Hurricanes a lesson. However, the last lesson of the month for both sides, and what would later prove to be the last major daylight attack during the Battle of Britain, occurred on 30 September.

Throughout the day, the *Luftwaffe* adopted widespread rolling attacks starting with fighter sweeps over Kent at 0900 hrs, followed by another sweep at 1010 hrs. This second attack was probably the *Jabos* of II/LG 2 escorted by, amongst others, II/JG 54. As this plot was returning, another was appearing to the west of the Isle of Wight. This again was a *Freie Jagd* by Messerschmitt 109s and a few 110s which, whilst circling off the Needles, was bounced by 609 Squadron whose Spitfires were responsible for shooting down three Messerschmitt 109s; at the same time, *Hptm* Helmut Wick and *Oblt* Franz Fiby of *Stab* I/JG 2 were accounting for two 56 Squadron Hurricanes.

No real pattern to the attacks was evident until early in the afternoon when a much larger mixed formation was plotted heading for London. This was successfully intercepted and, although few German bombers were shot down, the remainder were turned back. What was thought to be the last attack in the east on that day occurred just before tea-time when a mixed formation of Ju 88s again headed for London together with a heavy escort of Messerschmitt 109s. The ensuing combats ranged from Kent almost into eastern Hampshire and saw many losses on both sides. For JG 26, it would be a particularly bad evening with their losing five fighters and four pilots, one of whom was just about to be given command of one of the *Gruppe* if the *Geschwader Kommodore* approved:

Hauptmann Walter Kienzle, *Stab*/JG 26

I was flying from Audembert with the *Stabschwarm* Maj Galland, *Oblt* Horten and one other whose name I cannot remember. We were supposed to be in formation with another fighter unit approaching southern England. From reports afterwards, I know that Galland attacked an RAF fighter and we were bounced – they must have got me. Galland told me afterwards that he saw my Messerschmitt fall like a fire ball and a parachute opened. I myself have no recollection of the event. I woke up two or three days later in a military hospital run by Canadians which specialised in pilots who had been shot down in flames. I was told that I landed almost in the hospital yard! As well as burns, my right leg had to be amputated just above the knee as it had been smashed when I baled out.

Hptm *Walter Kienzle.* (Kienzle)

Who shot Walter Kienzle down is not known for certain but one combat report comes close to the German pilot's recollections and the location where the remains of his fighter crashed:

Flight Lieutenant Gordon McGregor, 1 Squadron RCAF

...We sighted the bomber formation of about twenty-five with fighter escort above and behind of about forty Me 109s. About twelve dived down to attack. I held course through this attack and turned and engaged an Me 109 which was attacking a Hurricane. The Hurricane broke right and the Me 109 left where I opened fire. Towards the end of the full burst, he streamed smoke and spun down through clouds south of Brooklands.

The circumstances surrounding another German fighter lost in the same area at the same time were just as dramatic but, as it would later transpire, the unfortunate German pilot was a victim of friendly fire. A few years ago, the remains of a Messerschmitt 109 were discovered with evidence that the plane had been hit by 20mm cannon fire. No cannon-armed RAF aircraft were flying that day but one RAF pilot could have witnessed what happened:

Group Captain Stanley Vincent, RAF Northolt

...I climbed towards the sun and tried to attack an Me 109 but had to leave it owing to others coming down onto me from above but I saw three Me 109s chasing a Hurricane at right angles to me from left to right and when the Hurricane dived away (straightening out at 5,000ft below) and the Me 109s turned back on their course, I was able to get in a good position on the tail of the third one. Before I opened fire, I saw Number One burst into flames and the pilot jump out; he had obviously been shot down by the Number Two who was close astern of him...

Leutnant Herbert Schmidt, 6/JG 27

The last day of September 1940 – my last flight in the last war. Every year since that time I celebrate this day like a second birthday as it very much is.

In the afternoon, we had to protect bombers and got involved in heavy aerial combats with British fighters which caused our formation to break up. I remember that I pursued a Spitfire [sic]. It dived and I pulled back up for height. Looking around I was alone – a bad situation for a fighter. It was high time to fly back. Suddenly I saw tracer bullets exactly in my direction of flight and at the same time, my cockpit was full of flames. A terrible thought flashed through my brain – this is the end!

I tried to cast off the cockpit roof in order to get out. I lifted my left arm to do it but powerless, the arm fell down. I didn't know that it was smashed by bullets. I tried again and again and finally succeeded in getting rid of the roof. I couldn't see this but felt the fresh air penetrate the hell of flames and smoke I was sitting in. Now I tried to loosen the seat belts but couldn't manage it and lost consciousness.

When I recovered my senses, I was falling at high speed, turning somersaults. My first idea was open the parachute. It was very difficult to get the handle for my arm was following the turning movements of my body. With a great strain, I succeeded.

When the parachute opened, I thought I would be torn to pieces. Because of the high speed of the fall and the fact that nearly all of my clothing had been burnt away, so that the parachute harness did not sit close, the opening parachute caused a heavy blow to my body. Thereby my flying boots – plop! – fell away.

I floated in the air. Some things I still can see today. Three Spitfires roaming around and flying away. A look at the blackened tip of my nose and my black and bloody hands. No feeling of pain.

Suddenly a pain on my neck. Catching at it, I had a burning piece of my life jacket in my hand – my life jacket was still on fire. I tried to stub out the flames with my hands, always fearing that the parachute would catch fire and I would drop away like a stone.

Thank God it didn't happen. It took an eternity until I saw the ground. I made a safe landing near a road like a perfect parachutist, although I had never exercised this! I noticed two men standing by a truck. They came over to me. "Help!" I said and I heard one of them saying, "...badly burned..." Then blackout.

The following weeks were the worst of my life. I remember them like an awful dream. It is a wonder that I am alive but it would not be correct if I didn't mention the British and Canadian doctors and sisters who helped me when I thought I was at an end.

Lt Herbert Schmidt was flying this Bf 109 when he was shot down on 30 September 1940. (via Moelders)

As this German attack was disintegrating over the east, another was developing in the west when forty-three Heinkel 111s of KG 55 tried to attack the Westland Factory at Yeovil in Somerset whilst eleven Junkers 88s of KG 51 attacked Southampton. Yet again the formation, hampered by bad weather, was intercepted and turned back, the Heinkel 111s unknowingly dropping their bombs on the helpless town of Shaftesbury. The RAF fighters did lose six aircraft in combat with two being claimed by KG 51, eight by JG 2, two by JG 53 and, surprisingly, four by ZG 26. The latter unit suffered just one aircraft damaged but their success on this day did not influence the decision to continue withdrawing the Messerschmitt 110 from France. A further Messerschmitt 109 from II/JG 2 was lost in addition to four Heinkel 111s and a Junkers 88.

And so September 1940 finished – the *Luftwaffe* having lost thirty-one of its fighters in action that last day in addition to fourteen other aircraft. The RAF's debit sheet was just sixteen lost in action. It was an upbeat note on which Fighter Command could end the month. Despite its numerical superiority, the *Luftwaffe*, through the RAF's tenacity and German tactical errors and plain bad luck, had failed. It had almost achieved air superiority for the first six days of the month but with the change in tactics and emphasis, Fighter Command had won it back. Two aircraft types – the Junkers 87 and Messerschmitt 110 had been rendered impotent, the Dornier 17 was showing itself to be inadequate and the Heinkel 111 was starting to show its failings. These two aircraft would now be used more at night. The *Luftwaffe* hoped that the Junkers 88 would be the shining knight of its bombing fleets. However, without German air superiority, Fighter Command again and again broke up attacks by this aircraft type and inflicted heavy losses on the *Kampfgeschwader*. As to the effectiveness of the Messerschmitt 109 *Jabos*, they had so far been just an irritation to Fighter Command. But there was still one more month to go before the Battle of Britain was officially over – time for the Messerschmitt 109s, be they fighters or fighter-bombers, to try and regain air superiority.

CHAPTER 4

The Final Chapter, October 1940

The beginning of the new month was an anti-climax compared to the last day of the old one. The exact target of the aircraft that appeared off the Isle of Wight just before lunchtime was not clear but it appeared to fail in its objective, one of the escorting Messerschmitt 110s being shot down in the process. However, the Messerschmitt 109s of JG 2 were quick to punish the defending fighters, shooting down two each from 238 and 607 Squadrons and damaging another one from each Squadron; German claims matched exactly. Meanwhile, the first *Jabo* attack had already been launched against London, heavily escorted by various *Jagdgeschwader*. Only one single-engined fighter from each of the opponents was lost throughout the day.

A similar pattern followed the next day but on this occasion just heavily escorted *Jabo* attacks were carried out. This time, one of the new *Jabostaffeln* learned a valuable lesson:

Uffz *Kurt Buehligen of 4/JG 2 (seen here later during the war) shot down one of the Hurricanes off the Isle of Wight on 1 October 1940.* (Morzinek)

161

Gefreiter Heinz Zag, 8/JG 53

We were on our first *Jabo* mission on 2 October and our *Kette* was attacked from behind and three of us did not come home. Only my *Staffel Kapitaen* and myself were taken prisoner. The dogfight took place at 7,000–8,000m near London and my engine was hit and stopped – thank God it did not burn. I then glided down to land in a hop-field and during the crash-landing I was injured.

Oblt *Walter Radlick (far right) was the* Gr Adj *of III/JG 53 who was killed on 2 October 1940; he is seen here with other pilots from 2/JG 53. L to R:* Uffz *Hans Kornatz,* Lt *Rudi Schmidt (+ 15 September 1940),* Fw *Wilhelm Heidemeier (+ 11 July 1941),* Fw *Franz Kaiser (POW 21 April 1942),* Stfw *Ignatz Prestelle (+ 4 May 1942),* Oblt *Rolf Pingel (POW 4 July 1941),* Fw *Franz Gawlik,* Uffz *Josef Wurmheller (+22 June 1944), ?,* Lt *Walter Rupp (POW 17 October 1940).* (Rupp)

It was a bad start for III/JG 53 who not only lost three from 8/JG 53 including the *Staffel Kapitaen* but also the *Gruppen Adjutant.* 8/JG 53 was bounced by Spitfires of 603 Squadron who lost one Spitfire to a Messerschmitt 109 from 9/JG 53. The pilot who probably shot down Heinz Zag was luckier than that British pilot:

Sergeant George Bailey, 'A' Flight, 603 Squadron

> After meeting enemy aircraft at 26,000ft, I lost height and saw enemy aircraft in cloud. After coming through the cloud, I saw AA fire and then sighted enemy again and opened fire at it from astern. He then began to lose height with a stream of glycol coming from the machine. I then followed it to about fifty feet when I lost sight of it…

With just one Spitfire lost throughout the day compared to the four Messerschmitt 109s, the RAF was the clear winner. However, the winner the next two days was the weather as the UK was blanketed in low cloud and drizzle. But on 5 October, apart from another bombing raid in the Portsmouth/Southampton area (JG 2 claiming thirteen when in fact only one British fighter was lost and a further two badly damaged), it was a series of rolling *Freie Jagd* and *Jabo* attacks to the east that concentrated the minds of Fighter Command's pilots.

28 October 1940: Oblt *Karl-Heinz Krahl,* St Kap *3/JG 2 (5th from right) and* Ofw *Rudolf Taeschner, 1/JG 2 (far right) claimed four Hurricanes between them on 5 October 1940; the reality was considerably less. Other pilots are, R to L Taeschner,* Oblt *Ulrich Adrian, I/JG 2,* Oblt *Hermann Reifferscheidt,* St Kap *1/JG 2,* Lt *Franz Fiby,* Adj *I/JG 2, Krahl,* Oblt *Rudi Pflanz,* TO *JG 2,* Oblt *Erich Leie,* Adj *JG 2 and* Reichsmarschall *Goering.*

As the Messerschmitt 110s from *Erprobungsgruppe* 210 took off from their base at Calais just before lunch, heading for Becton Gasworks and the airfield at West Malling, they were destined to meet an already alert Fighter Command that had been scrambled to counter a *Jabo* attack on London by II/LG 2:

Flying Officer Bobby Oxspring, 66 Squadron

The Squadron was vectored onto a hostile raid near Maidstone at 20,000ft. Half a dozen spasmodic AA shell bursts drew our attention to a *Staffel* of Me 109s flying south-eastwards from London. They were about our height as we initiated a streaming attack on them. The enemy were flying in loose pairs which broke formation as we closed into firing range. One yellow-nosed Me 109 broke left to right across my front and I got a nice three seconds burst on it from behind and beneath. He turned through the hazy sun as I repeated the dose which resulted in a stream of grey smoke.

The aircraft dived down and I followed, firing from close range. The rudder flew off and almost immediately the aircraft burst into flames. Our hurtling descent carried us uncomfortably close to a squadron of Hurricanes concentrating on a climb out. I had to giggle when our sudden spectacular arrival from aloft split the Hurricane formation which cascaded in all directions. In striving to avoid ramming one of my startled friends, I managed to glimpse the Me 109 spinning down near Lympne; there was no sign of a parachute…

Fw *Wilhelm Pankratz (sitting, 2nd from right) as a POW in Canada; other Bf 109 pilots are* Uffz *Andreas Wallburger, 2/JG 27, POW 15 September 1940 (front, far left),* Fw *Werner Gottschalk, 6/LG 2, POW 6 September 1940 (front, far right),* Uffz *Emil von Stein, 4/JG 2, POW 2 September 1940 (back, far left),* Uffz *Werner Karl, 1/JG 53, POW 2 September 1940 (back, 3rd from right)* and Uffz *Valentin Blasyewski, 6/LG 2, POW 14 September 1940 (back, far right).* (Karl)

The *Jabo* pilot was luckier than Bobby Oxspring thought – *Fw* Wilhelm Pankratz of 6/LG 2 did manage to crash-land and was taken prisoner. However, it was the 'startled' Hurricanes that were to cause the carnage that followed:

Unteroffizier Willi Ghesla, 1/JG 53

The night before this flight, I was on guard duty and so was not assigned to what would become my last flight. However, as the mission was only escorting Bf 110s as far as Dover (because of low cloud), I agreed to fly with my *Staffel*. Near Dover, the cloud was higher and our *Staffel Kapitaen* ordered us to fly on to London at 7,000–8,000m altitude. A comrade and I flew as cover for the rest of the *Staffel* just under the clouds.

Suddenly, British fighters appeared out of the clouds and before being able to turn away, I received hits in the engine and oil cooler. I dived down to 4,000m, got my plane under control again and tried to make for Calais by gliding. But now I was fired at again and I lost consciousness for a short time. When I had a clear head again, I found myself near the ground and immediately looked for somewhere to land. I did not have a choice and I landed under difficult circumstances in a meadow. During this crash-landing (and because I had opened my seat belts instead of my parachute release), I hit my head on the *Revi* gunsight and got concussion. I quickly left my plane and walked to a nearby farmhouse where I was captured a few minutes later.

Uffz *Willi Ghesla*. (Ghesla)

Pilots of 1/JG 53 just before 5 October 1940. L to R: Uffz Ludwig Reibel (+20 December 1942), Lt Alfred Zeis (POW 5 October 1940), Uffz Heinrich Ruehl (+ 4 June 1941), Hptm Hans Karl Mayer (+ 17 October 1940), Uffz Willi Ghesla (POW 5 October 1940), Oblt Hans Ohly, Lt Ernst-Albrecht Schulz. (Ohly)

It would appear that Willi Ghesla had been bounced by Hurricanes of 1 Squadron RCAF and it is possible that two Hurricane pilots from this Squadron were responsible for the two 1/JG 53 losses that day – Willi Ghesla and his *Rottenfuehrer, Lt* Alfred Zeis:

Flying Officer Hartland Molson, 1 Squadron RCAF

My recollection of 5 October 1940 is that on our way south from Northolt, we were jumped by some Me 109s. I believe that we were flying as a Wing with 303 (Polish) Squadron and 229 Squadron vectored onto a bomber raid coming over the coast towards Canterbury.

When I returned to altitude, as so often happened, everybody seemed to be a long way off and I was alone but a few miles ahead was a terrific dogfight in sight. Heading to join, I saw a pair of Me 109s well above the party cruising around looking for a victim and I was conceited enough to think that I might score on them. At full bore, I tried to get closer to the rear one, opened fire too far away; he half rolled out of sight and I thought perhaps I had damaged him. I tried to close on the leader of the pair. I neglected to keep my eye on the first one who, of course, simply came up behind me and shot me down.

As well as being the pilot that possibly shot down Willi Ghesla, this Canadian pilot was likely the victim of the following:

Leutnant Alfred Zeis, 1/JG 53

During our mission on 5 October, we were surprised by Hurricanes and some Spitfires. Due to the fighting, our formation broke up and we were forced to fight individually. In the course of these engagements, I shot at a Hurricane which was flying below me and attacking another Bf 109. However, I was then attacked from behind and was hit in the engine, radiator and the aileron controls. I tried, as best as possible with my severely damaged plane, to disengage and subsequently got further hits during different evasive actions. Finally, after a turn, the plane got in a spin and because of the battle damage, I could not regain control so I was forced to bale out; I never could have made it back to France.

It is now thought that Zeis lost control of his fighter because the hydraulics had allowed the undercarriage to drop down and therefore, in his attempts to get away, had caused him to lose control of the plane. Again, accounts of the combat on this day are vague but one Canadian pilot could have been the one that shot him down:

Flying Officer Paul Pitcher, 1 Squadron RCAF

My Pilot's Flying Log Book reveals the following entry in relation to the sortie in question (which, incidentally, appears to have been the first of three that day): "5 Oct 40 – Hurricane YO-D – (Duty) Patrol Base and Dover – Me 109s and 110s engaged – (Duration of Flight) 1.05 – 1 Me 109 destroyed – engaged and damaged one Me 110 – Port fuel tank hit."

There is no mention of the hour of day we scrambled on that sortie so I cannot tie in the time of the sortie with that of the crash of Lt Zeis's aircraft. As you can gather from the records, it was an extremely busy hour and five minutes and positive recollection of details is difficult. However, as far as I can recall, the 109s undercarriage dropped down and if this is what I reported to the Intelligence Officer on landing, this was my impression at the time.

My most vivid impression of the sortie was the landing back at base. My aircraft was not equipped with self-sealing fuel tanks and my port fuel tank had been riddled with bullet holes and the cockpit was awash with fuel. The air turbulence on landing caused clouds of fuel to swirl over the engine cowling and hot exhaust stacks and, by some miracle, the whole aircraft failed to explode.

Suffice it to say, the attack by *Erprobungsgruppe* 210 failed in its objective, with the loss of the acting *Gruppen Kommandeur* and three other crewmen and two more crew wounded. The escort fared no better with a total of six Messerschmitt 109s being lost during this and other attacks during the day; the RAF lost just two fighters in combat.

The scene was set to stay the same for many of the days that followed – poor weather, *Freie Jagd* and *Jabo* attacks. The only exception was 7 October which saw an improvement in the weather and the appearance, for the first time in a week, of escorted Junkers 88s targeting London and the Westland Aircraft Factory at Yeovil. Mixed in with both formations were *Freie Jagd* and an audacious *Jabo* attack on London which cost the brother of the *Luftwaffe*'s top scoring fighter pilot his freedom:

Oberleutnant Victor Moelders, *Staffel Kapitaen* 2/JG 51

I joined JG 51 late in August 1940 as my brother wanted me to form a *Jabo Staffel*. I was given command of 2/JG 51.

Between 1000 hrs and 1030 hrs on the morning of Monday 7 October 1940, my brother tasked me to fly a mission. My *Staffel*, eight aircraft armed with 250kg bombs, were to take off from Pihen, climb to 6,000m, fly north to London and attack the Docks. We were then to fly back as quickly as possible. We were to be protected by the *Stab Schwarm* and eight aircraft.

As we approached the Thames Estuary, my brother informed me that he would remain at this altitude and return to Pihen as they were running low on fuel. I then dived with my *Staffel* and flew at rooftop height over the streets of London. It was funny to see the flak bursting above me! We dropped our bombs on the Docks and proceeded to return to France. Suddenly I heard the radio call "Indians behinds you!" and on looking saw about thirty aircraft at 6,000m diving towards us. I waited until they were close, then turned and flew towards them. All that I can remember after that is that I was hit in the radiator and I began to leak glycol and the engine temperature rose…

Maj *Werner Moelders (3rd from left)*, Lt *Erich Meyer (POW 7 October 1940) and* Oblt *Victor Moelders.* (Moelders)

The two Moelders brothers – Werner...

...and Victor. (Moelders)

Sergeant Eric Wright, 605 Squadron

Yellow Section was airborne at 0940 hrs and on patrol with 501 Squadron in the south London/Maidstone area. We sighted seven Me 109s flying east at 25,000ft and as we were 1,000ft above them, we dived down to attack.

Three Me 109s passed below me and I got in a two second burst at one from his stern quarter. He then dived and I gave chase and positioned myself underneath him where he couldn't see me. I got to 150 yards range then fired a seven second burst, seeing some smoke coming from the top of the engine cowling as he tried to climb away. I held my position and the smoke stopped. I then fired the rest of my ammunition at him and saw glycol coming from his wing radiator. I left him five miles south east of Maidstone, slowly losing height.

Oberleutnant Victor Moelders

...I decided to remain low as the engine was not capable of climbing. I got rid of the rear canopy and began switching the engine off and on. Looking behind I saw a lone RAF aircraft following me. I then went into cloud and when I emerged, I saw that this fighter was flying alongside me. He then broke away and I never saw him again.

The remains of Moelder's Bf 109E-4/B after its salvage. (via Payne)

I was too low to bale out so I began to look for a suitable field to land in. All the fields that I saw had old cars in them or other anti-glider obstacles. I eventually had to crash-land on top of an anti-tank ditch and did so too successfully – the aircraft showed no signs of burning. I tried to get out the flare pistol but couldn't and setting my map alight with my lighter and trying to start a fire also failed to destroy my aircraft.

Shortly after I was captured by some Home Guardsmen and put into a Rolls Royce and then taken for tea and cake in a house. Later I was taken to a police cell where I flushed my notes on the mission down the toilet and eventually handed my captors my pistol and other effects. The following day I was taken to London.

The results of these attacks were minimal – the damage at Westlands was slight and the Germans lost one bomber and, for the last time on a daylight mission over the UK, seven Messerschmitt 110s from II and III/ZG 26. The Messerschmitt 110s' last mission could have resulted in their total annihilation had the retreating formation not returned under the protection of the Messerschmitt 109s of JG 2.

As the month progressed, the weather worsened and the German bombers increasingly started to use the cover of darkness to achieve their aims. The RAF night fighter defence was very much in its infancy and it would be another month before they started to cause casualties amongst the *Kampfgeschwader*. Still, when the weather permitted, *Freie Jagd* and *Jabo* missions were flown but Fighter Command still had the upper hand. Casualties were still occurring on both sides but not on the same scale as the previous months. Fighter Command was still busy, now realising that it did have the superiority it wanted (as in fact it had for much of the Battle of Britain) and that *Jabo* attacks had to be countered. The final fighter actions of the Battle can best be illustrated by accounts from three different German pilots. The first relates to a combat on 12 October 1940:

Oberleutnant Guenter Buesgen, *Staffel Fuehrer* 1/JG 52

I had flown about eighty missions with 1/JG 52 and had eight victories – all British. I had taken over command of the *Staffel* from *Oblt* Carl Lommel who had been posted away. I had been *Staffel Fuehrer* for three days when between 1500 hrs and 1530 hrs on 12 October 1940 I was shot down.

We had taken off from Calais in the afternoon on an escort mission. We accompanied bombers to London and as we turned for home the RAF fighters, as usual, attacked. It was a confusing battle but my *Rottenflieger* stayed with me. Suddenly, I looked behind and glimpsed what I thought was a fighter. I immediately dived – our usual tactic – and levelled out at 1,000m. The engine was vibrating – I had been hit. I climbed back to 4,000m and throttled back as the engine temperature was rising. I put the propeller into gliding pitch and turned for home. However, it was no good. The temperature gauge was reading hot so I jettisoned the rear part of the canopy and rolled her onto her back but nothing happened so I rolled back. As I did this, I fell out of the aircraft and was not prepared for it. As a result, I hit the fuselage and was injured.

I came down safely by parachute and was welcomed by the Home Guard. They removed my gun (and my pilot's badge and Iron Cross) and I was taken to a local hospital. Later I was transferred to a hospital at Woolwich.

The victorious RAF pilot in this case is not known but is thought to have come from 92 Squadron. By way of contrast, the RAF was still suffering at the hands of the *Luftwaffe* as one inexperienced Spitfire pilot recalls:

Oblt *Guenter Buesgen on leave shortly before being shot down.* (Buesgen)

Sergeant Clive Hilken, 74 Squadron

Flying from Biggin Hill in Spitfire Mark II serial P7426 as Number Three in Yellow Section of 74 (Tiger) Squadron on an interception at Angels 20, I had my first and short experience of a dogfight on the afternoon of Sunday 20 October 1940.

I decided when we broke formation to follow [Flt Lt] Mungo-Park, my Section Leader, whose Number Two had left us. I followed his straight climb, weaving behind him and keeping a wary eye on our tails. He was obviously gaining height in order to come down out of the sun. I found, of course, that by weaving I was dropping behind so I tried watching our tails without weaving and tried to keep up. After what seemed to be a few seconds, my instrument panel seemed to explode at the right hand side and explosions shook the aircraft. From the bottom of the cockpit, smoke came up and the aircraft was uncontrollable. I baled out at what must have been 20,000ft; my flying boots, however, remained in the cockpit. Also, I hadn't unhitched my oxygen tube and the rubber stretched and gave way without pulling my mask off, giving me what turned out to be a beautiful black eye to add to the many bits of cannon shell shrapnel which I received in my left hand, right arm, face and body.

When my 'chute opened, I was left swinging wildly at first in that very cold rarefied air and not a sign of aircraft anywhere near! I was most uncomfortable in my harness and tried to adjust the straps only to find I was gasping for breath at the least exertion.

Out of habit, I glanced at my watch and remember that it was 3.00pm. I landed over a quarter of an hour later through and down the side of a tree in an orchard. I was helped up by two Land Army girls and was pulling the 'chute clear of the trees after releasing the harness when a bit of 'Dad's Army' occurred! The farmer came round the corner of a hedge with his double-barrelled shotgun trained on me, ordering me to put my hands up. I soon convinced him that I was one of 'us' and he then proceeded to lead me limping in stockinged feet across his smelly fold-yard so that he could phone Biggin Hill and report my arrival and get some medical assistance.

Soon the Medical Officer came in the ambulance and took me back to Biggin Hill and on to Orpington Hospital to have a larger piece of shrapnel removed from my right upper arm and to have X-rays which revealed many more tiny fragments, many of which came to the surface in subsequent years.

I had landed near Tonbridge but my aircraft broke into parts and came down at Cowden, east of Westerham – the main part and cockpit in the woods of Leighton Manor and the other part (as I found out a few years ago by enquiring in the village) came down behind the 'Sun

Sgt Clive Hilken (far right) with Sgts Rex Mallet and Jamie Dyke (left to right). (May)

Inn' just as the family was finishing their Sunday dinner. It pierced the brick pond behind the pub and the pond leaked and never regained its original level! I knew that the cockpit had been found because my black flying boots had been returned to me – the finders had found them in the wrecked aircraft and returned them to the nearest RAF station which was Biggin Hill!

This was the first of three times that this young pilot was to be on the receiving end. The last time, 27 June 1941, he was taken prisoner of war. It is not known for sure who got the novice pilot but *Stfw* Helmut Goedert of I/LG 2 claimed a Spitfire at exactly the same time noted by Clive Hilken – 1500hrs.

The final two German accounts for October 1940 come from two pilots from two different *Geschwader* who were lost on the same day when, on the 25th, the German fighters and fighter-bombers returned in force to the skies over south eastern England:

Oberleutnant Jochen Schypek, 5/JG 54

The last pages of my logbook confirm that I took off at 1010 hrs Central European Time on 25 October 1940 and did not return from a mission escorting Bf 109s carrying 250kg bombs to London.

We were attacked when the bombers had reached London Docks and I yelled an alarm "Indians at six o'clock!" The warning was received and the bombers released their bombs and started a 180 degree turn. Seconds later, I had an 'Indian' in my rear view mirror and guessed it was a Spitfire. With them, we had developed a standard and often successful escape procedure – our Daimler Benz engines were fuel injection ones whilst the Spitfires had carburettor engines. That meant once we put our noses down vertically and quick enough, our engines would continue to function without interruption whilst the Spitfires – and Hurricanes – attempting to stick to our tails would slow down long enough for us to put a safer distance between them and ourselves. The slowing down was the consequence of the float in the carburettor getting stuck due to the sudden change in position.

I had managed to break away at least a dozen times by means of this manoeuvre but lo and behold, it did not work this time! The 'Indian' was right on my tail in my steep dive and opened fire. I could see bullets hitting my wings and, from the white trails on both sides, I knew he had hit my radiator. It all started at a rather high altitude – we had been approaching London at some 25,000–26,000ft and when hit I was still at more than 20,000ft. I throttled back as I knew it would soon seize. My 'Indian' drew alongside and the aircraft appeared strange to me as I had never been so close to a live Spitfire before. I was rather relieved that he recognised I did not have any chance of getting home and that he did not insist he completed his kill…

Lt Jochen Schypek (right), August 1939. (Schypek)

Flying Officer Peter Brown, 'A' Flight, 41 Squadron

I followed Red Leader and attacked an Me 109 – no apparent results. Having lost the Squadron, I climbed to 25,000ft again and saw about nine Me 109s on my starboard beam. I turned to attack them and was involved in a dogfight. After two short bursts, glycol poured from out of one of the Me 109s. I gave it two more bursts, slight deflection. The enemy aircraft rolled over on its side and dived straight into cloud.

I then attacked another Me 109 – followed it over the sea but after one burst, my ammunition ran out. First enemy aircraft is believed to have crashed in the vicinity of Rye. Two of my guns did not fire due to the cold.

Oberleutnant Jochen Schypek

...First human reaction, after trying in vain to report my fate to my *Staffel* Kapitaen so I knew that my radio must have been shot up too, was a series of curses followed by deliberations of what to do next. I had levelled out of my steep dive, saw my engine temperature was rising quickly and felt the first shuddering sensations in my aircraft – the signal that the seizing was already in progress. Stopping my curses, I remembered instructions to the point that it was possible to glide from south of London beyond the coast, ditch and wait to be picked up by one of our very courageous air-sea-rescue planes – provided you found the appropriate gliding angle and speed!

During the glide through the clear blue sky, other more personal thoughts occupied my mind. If I could not make it, I meant reach the Channel waters and be picked up, my engagement party would have to be called off (I had a fiancée in Vienna and the party was scheduled for Christmas if I could get leave). Could I get a message through to Roloff von Aspern (my *Staffel Kapitaen* and best friend) to go and pick up the engagement ring I had ordered at a jewellers in Lille? How long would it take to inform my widowed mother in Berlin that I was alive? Only then did I worry about the water temperature in the Channel – would I stay conscious long enough to experience my rescue?

Meanwhile, I was losing altitude at a terrifying rate and Dungeness, my point of orientation, came dangerously close. I was too low already to reach my desired destination and was about three miles from the coast and therefore missed the only opportunity of ever using my parachute. When I was low enough to see soldiers working behind the beach with shovels I made my decision to turn around and belly land.

I eventually touched the ground, rather gently I remember, skidded a little to the right. I had thrown away my cabin roof and had turned off the ignition long ago. Anyhow, I was in a hurry to get away from the plane for how could I know that it would not blow up?

I heard soldiers shouting and running towards me with threatening shovels! "Hands Up!" I put them up and could see a Captain approaching me at a quick pace. I do not recall when and how we agreed to speak English – he seemed quite glad that I knew the language. Together we took a closer look at my 'Black 7'. The rear of the fuselage was perforated with bullet holes – thank God that during the discussions following the French surrender that the supporters of armour plating to protect the fuel tank and pilot won over those who did not wish to sacrifice an inch of altitude and speed – it certainly saved my life.

Jochen Schypek's 'Black 7'.

What followed was rather funny. The Captain pulled out a check list and registered my name and rank first and drew the automatic blanks when asking for unit, home base, etc. Next he wanted to have my pistol and was shocked that I only had my signal pistol to surrender. How could I enter enemy territory practically unarmed? I told him my 'arms' were in the aircraft wings and fuselage and in the narrow Messerschmitt cockpit a pistol holster was too much bother. I had to agree that by flying without a side arm, I had violated *Luftwaffe* regulations.

Next item: my map. When I said that I had none he was shocked again! A soldier in enemy territory without a map – how could I have ever dreamed of finding my way? I told him that the geography of southern England within the flying range of the Bf 109 was so easy to read that it did not require a map.

I was glad that I could co-operate when he wanted my parachute and life jacket. Meanwhile a vehicle, I think it was probably a weapons carrier, had pulled up and took me to Brigade HQ. I was introduced to a Colonel who rattled out some orders to the Captain which I did not catch. However, the result was I was turned over to a Lieutenant who marched me to the Officers' Mess.

I did have a watch but why I do not remember the hours when things occurred, I do not know. In a mess room I was served my first English tea – at home I never added milk – and some sandwiches. When it turned dark, I lay on a sofa and caught up on some sleep. Some noise at the door woke me up again. It was completely dark now with only an emergency light. In the darkness I recognised who had caused the noise and for seconds a terrific relief came over me – the person was my *Staffel* mate *Lt* Ernst Wagner. "Mensch, Ernst!" I cried. "Imagine what I had been dreaming just now: I was shot down and taken prisoner by the Tommies!" Ernst replied rather earnestly "That was no dream!" He had been caught during the second sortie of the day.

Gefr *Karl Raisinger's 'Yellow 13'*.
(via Cornwell)

There were many rolling attacks that day, Ernst Wagner crash-landing near Dungeness four and a half hours after Jochen Schypek. The experiences of another German pilot are very similar:

Gefreiter Karl Raisinger, 3/JG 77

On 25 October, we were flying to London – 1 and 2 *Staffeln* had bombs and 3 *Staffel* was escorting them. We were flying at about 10,000m and west on London, I saw many Spitfires and Hurricanes apparently waiting for us. Unfortunately, I had little experience as a fighter pilot and had to fly on the right flank of the formation (which was a fault) instead of the middle. When turning 180 degrees over London after the bombs were dropped, the British fighters attacked us and as I was without protection, they got me first.

I did not realise that I was hit. My plane was shaking but I thought because of the speed. But suddenly, there was smoke in my cockpit. I throttled back and tried to dive towards the Channel alone. To the south west I saw clouds and heard over the microphone that there was a lot of smoke coming from my plane. I disappeared into the clouds (I think it was raining) and came out and saw the coast. I was afraid to

The same 'Yellow 13' on display as an advertisement for National War Bonds. (via Cornwell)

Karl Raisinger (centre) on his way to captivity. (via Raisinger)

force-land in the sea and as the propeller had stopped, I removed the cockpit roof. I was by now at 100m over the sea so I turned back and force-landed in a field near Brighton.

The cost on this day was eleven German fighters with three pilots killed and seven taken prisoner; the RAF lost in the region of ten fighters but only two pilots were killed. In the wreckage of one of the aircraft, the RAF thought that they had found evidence that one of their pilots had shot down an ace. The rudder of the Messerschmitt 109 that crashed near Marden in Kent showed forty-eight kills, the aircraft of JG 51's *Maj* Werner Moelders. However, Moelders was now flying the Messerschmitt 109 F (achieving his first kill on this type on 22 October and a further two on 25 October). *Hptm* Hans Asmus had been using his *Kommodore*'s old 'Emil' and it was he, not Moelders, who had been shot down and taken prisoner.

With autumn turning to winter, the weather allowed more twin engined bombers to use the poor conditions as a means of defence. But still, when the weather permitted, the fighters and fighter-bombers came. The last day of the Battle of Britain on which major fighter-against-fighter action occurred was 29 October and it is therefore fitting that the last account should come from one of the victorious RAF pilots. Fifteen Messerschmitt 109s were lost on this day, amongst whose pilots were three *Staffel Kapitaen* and two *Gruppen Adjutant*. RAF losses were just four fighters:

Flying Officer Tadeusz Kumiega, 17 Squadron

I do remember that sortie on 29 October although I admit I remember more vividly other encounters when I fired my guns in anger.

We took off from Martlesham Heath on what I think was the second sortie of the day. Though one is not aware at the time of the overall picture, I believe that we were scrambled to intercept the tail end of an offensive sweep by a token number of bombers and a strong cover of fighters and to cover returning squadrons as they refuelled. We spotted a formation of Me 109s at about 25,000ft and went into attack in then fashionable tight formation with the motto 'Follow my lead.' We were at once attacked from above and behind and a general combat resulted from it. Although eyes are primarily engaged in seeking a target in front of your guns and one's safety behind, I remember the criss-cross of tracers as shots were fired in this melee.

An Me 109, which later turned out to be the victim, crossed my path from port to starboard in a shallow dive some 1,000ft or more in front of me. I abandoned my rear view mirror, dived after him on full power and found myself directly behind him, his tail some 100ft or more from the barrels of my guns. I knew that I could not gain on him in my Hurricane so I opened fire.

One can sometimes see the bullets hitting the target. I could not – the tracers appeared some distance in front of the target but with a second, longer burst, I could sense the Me 109 twitch. He immediately turned on his back, dived and then pulled out. I lost the distance in that move but, as I put my aircraft in a tight turning dive, I saw another Hurricane pounce on the enemy and fire. By then we were much lower, some 15,000ft. Sgt Hogg overshot and I too managed only one burst before I had to pull up. The Me 109 lost power and was in a gliding descent, a faint smudge of coolant trailing him. He was directly underneath me and as I prepared to deliver another attack, the pilot waved his wings – to me a sign of surrender. Sgt Hogg joined me and, well throttled back, we followed him. But as he headed for the open sea, I gave him a short burst. He continued for a while, still heading for the sea and slightly waving the wings. I felt he might try to ditch out in the sea in the hope of rescue and I decided to terminate it. I do remember a moment of pure human sorrow for the enemy who lost but I delivered a burst from some 300ft and Sgt Hogg followed the lead. The Me 109 turned immediately on his back and a canopy of parachute bellowed up against the grey texture of the land below. We watched the aircraft dive vertically, hit the ground and explode in a plume of black smoke. Did I imagine it or did I see two horses galloping away across the field? It might have been then or it might have been from some dream or film from the past.

We returned to base immediately afterwards, reviewed the combat, wrote reports and agreed to the share. We later heard that the pilot of the Me 109 [*Ofw* Konrad Jaeckel of 8/JG 26] was in hospital following his landing on a parachute. I had the chance to see him but I declined. It was not until almost a year later that I added to my score: one undivided Me 109.

Epilogue

The *Luftwaffe* had failed. For just under four months, their fighters and bombers had tried to gain the air superiority they wanted so that the German Army could invade the United Kingdom. They could easily have achieved this, having essentially attained it in the week that preceded 7 September. But then they changed tactics and gave the overworked and numerically inferior RAF fighter pilots the breathing space they wanted.

However, for August and much of September 1940, in the words of the Duke of Wellington after the Battle of Waterloo, 'It was a close run thing.' Some say Fighter Command was lucky, others say the Germans were unlucky. However, it was the dedication of a small force of men, some of whom suffered and died for their cause, that stopped Hitler in his tracks and made him and his generals think again. Unknowingly, they changed the course of World War Two.

A hero's funeral – as the war progressed, many more German fighter pilots would be killed but not afforded such a magnificent ceremony. (Bezner)

The period of the Battle of Britain is now celebrated from 10 July to 31 October 1940, with 'Battle of Britain Day' being 15 September. For the first time since 1940, today's RAF now celebrates it in the same way that the Royal Navy celebrates the Battle of Trafalgar. Nevertheless, it should be remembered that the first major *Luftwaffe* assault against the United Kingdom took place not during the Battle of Britain but on the night of 18/19 June 1940. Furthermore, following the official ending of the Battle of Britain on 31 October 1940, the months that followed saw no let up in the *Luftwaffe's* daylight tactics – in fact, for the first time since 18 August 1940, the *Stuka* appeared in the skies off the Kent Coast on 1 November, seeking shipping and losing one of their number. These daylight air battles were nowhere near as massive and furious and the night war now took precedence, forcing the RAF to develop and employ what would become a particularly effective weapon – the night fighter.

The German aircrew had suffered badly during the Battle of Britain and for many of those who had survived, they would either be killed or end up prisoners as many of their number had done during the summer/autumn of 1940. Likewise, many of the RAF fighter pilots would lose their lives. One such was Sgt John Glendinning. He had managed to shoot down five German aircraft before he too was shot down when, on 12 March 1941, it was his misfortune to become *Obstlt* Werner Moelder's sixty-first victim. By way of concluding this book on the German fighter pilot's Battle of Britain, John Glendinning's third kill on 15 November 1940 clearly shows that the 'Battle' was still being fought after its official close and would still be fought for another four and a half blood-stained years:

Sergeant John Glendinning, 'A' Flight 74 Squadron

I heard the shout "Snappers behind!" and broke away with my Section, weaving to the right and the left, and saw about twenty yellow-nosed Me 109s above me and on the port side. I immediately broke away to the right and turning steeply to both right and left saw four Me 109s going down in a vertical dive, attempting to catch a Spitfire. I tried to follow but could not get near. I again broke away and did climbing turns to 18,000ft. I was just levelling out when an Me 109 went past me on my port side. I deliv-

Sgt John Glendinning, killed in action 12 March 1941.

ered a beam attack and he flipped over onto his back for a few seconds, seeming to hang in the air. I closed again and gave another burst, pieces flew in all directions and it went down in a series of rolls. Still not being satisfied, I gave it another burst and something seemed to explode inside the aircraft and the tail came away. I remember seeing the tail but the next I saw it seemed to be all pieces going into the sea four miles east of Bognor.

The man responsible for John Glendinning's death – Obstlt *Werner Moelders. Glendinning is recorded as the sixty-first kill, fifth from the left on the bottom row of kill markings.* (Moelders)

Gefreiter Rudi Miese, 4/JG 2

We took off from Le Havre. 4 *Staffel* had six aircraft under the leadership of *Lt* Meimberg and was at the rear of the *Geschwader* acting as *Holzaugestaffel*. I flew at the rear of the *Staffel* with *Uffz* Dessoy as my *Rottenfuehrer*. Shortly before reaching the English coast, we spotted coming from the left and below a formation of twelve to fifteen Spitfires.

Dessoy and myself swung to the left and attacked them from the front and above. The machine I attacked, I do not know whether I hit it or not as it rolled and dived away. We were already below the sun when we pulled back to the left when from above and the left and behind the cockpit, I was hit by tracer.

Immediately, the aircraft burst into flames and dived. Simultaneously, I threw off the cockpit roof and undid my straps. Then I lost consciousness and must have fallen out and the parachute opened. As consciousness returned, I was hanging about 1,000–2,000m up, swinging on the parachute quite violently, without flying boots and socks and a hole in my life jacket. I was still over the water but not far from the coastline. My hands and face were burnt and my left arm smashed. Two British aircraft circled me and the pilots waved to me.

I was blown by the wind nearer the coast and landed on a road by the beach without injuring myself further. About twenty civilians and a bobby came running. The policeman rolled up the parachute and pulled it away from me. Then an RAF doctor came – he gave me first aid and bandaged my arm in the street. I was then rushed by ambulance to a hospital in Littlehampton. Here they operated on my arm three times.

Gefr *Rudi Miese*. (Miese)

Lt *Julius Meimberg of 4/JG 2. He would survive the war having shot down fifty-six aircraft; he shot down three times and badly wounded each time.* (Meimberg)

Uffz *Lorenz Dessoy of 4/JG 2. He was shot down and wounded at least twice during the war.* (Meimberg)

When I came round after the first operation in the evening after I was taken prisoner, by the side of my bed was an RAF officer who spoke good German and interrogated me. I did not answer him on questions about my unit but he reproached me for carrying my operational pilots pass, named my *Geschwader, Gruppe, Staffel* and the names of my *Kommodore, Kommandeur, Staffel Kapitaen* and all the pilots of 4/JG 2 as well as our airfield at Beaumont Le Roger and the operational airfields of Cherbourg and Le Havre. He also named the take off times from Le Havre (morning and afternoon) on the day I was shot down.

Dramatis Personae

#	Date	Unit	Aircraft	Personnel	Notes
1.	29 May 1940	I/ZG 76	Bf 110 D-1/R-1 M8+LL	*Oblt* Hans Jaeger (*F*) – POW, *Uffz* Helmut Feick (*BF*) – POW	Shot down by Hurricane of 46 Sqn and ditched off Salanger, Norway, 2000hrs
2.	1 June 1940	2/ZG 1	Bf 110 C	*Oblt* Juergen Moeller (*F, St Fhr*) – POW, *Uffz* Karl Schieferstein (*BF*) – POW	Collided in the morning with Spitfire off Dunkirk
3.	8 July 1940	3/LG 2	Bf 109 E-1 *Wk Nr* 2964	*Lt* Albert Striberny – POW	Shot down by Flt Lt B H Way, 54 Sqn and crashed at Buckland Farm, Sandwich, Kent 2000hrs
4.	11 July 1940	9/ZG 76	Bf 110 C-4 *Wk Nr* 3551 2N+EP	*Oblt* Gerhard Kadow (*St Kap, F*) – POW, *Gefr* Helmut Scholz (*BF*) – POW	Shot down by Sqn Ldr J S Dewar, 87 Sqn and Fg Off H K Riddle, 601 Sqn. Crash-landed Povington Heath, Lulworth, Dorset, 1210hrs
5.	28 July 1940	Stab/JG 51	Bf 109 E-3	*Maj* Werner Moelders (*Gesch Komm*) – W	Damaged in combat with Flt Lt J T Webster, 41 Sqn and crash-landed at Ste Inglevert, 1540hrs
6.	11 August 1940	1/ZG 2	Bf 110 C	*Lt* Wolf Muenchmeyer (*F*) – uninj, *Uffz* Fritz Labusch (*BF*) – uninj	Damaged in combat off Portland and crash-landed at Theville
7.	11 August 1940	1/ZG 26	Bf 110 D	*Hptm* Hans Kogler (*St Kap, F*) – W, *Uffz* Adolf Bauer (*BF*) – W	Damaged in combat off Harwich and ditched, 1310hrs; crew rescued 14 August 1940
8.	12 August 1940	Stab III/JG 54	Bf 109 E-4	*Oblt* Albrecht Dress (*TO*) – POW	Probably shot down by Flt Lt M N Crossley, 32 Sqn; <+ crash-landed Henmore, Margate, Kent, 1800hrs
9.	13 August 1940	1/ZG 2	Bf 110 C-4 *Wk Nr* 3201 3M+LH	*Lt* Wolf Muenchmeyer (*F*) – POW, *Uffz* Fritz Labusch (*BF*) – +	Shot down by Sgt L Guy, 601 Sqn and crashed at Knightwood Farm, Flexford, Hants 1600hrs
10.	15 August 1940	1/ZG 76	Bf 110 D-1/R-1 *Wk Nr* 3155 M8+CH	*Oblt* Hans-Ulrich Kettling (*F*) – POW, *Ogefr* Fritz Volk (*BF*) – POW	Shot down by Plt Off E A Shipman and Plt Off G H Bennions, 41 Sqn, and crash-landed at Streatlam near Barnard Castle, Co Durham, 1335hrs

Dramatis Personae continued

No.	Date	Unit	Aircraft	Crew	Notes
11.	15 August 1940	6/ZG 76	Bf 110 C M8+BP	*Fw* Jakob Birndorfer (*F*) – + / *Uffz* Max Guschewski (*Bf*) – POW	Shot down by Plt Off J Zurakowski, 234 Sqn and Plt Off P Ostazewski-Ostoja, 609 Sqn, and crash-landed at Ashey Down, Brading, Isle of Wight, 1806hrs
12.	16 August 1940	*Stab* III/ZG 76	Bf 110 C	*Lt* Richard Marchfelder (*TO, F*) – POW / *Ogefr* Herbert Jentzsch (*Bf*) – POW	Possibly damaged by 602 Sqn; crew baled out and aircraft crashed at Droke Cottages, East Dean, West Sussex, 1830hrs
13.	18 August 1940	6/JG 2	Bf 109 E-4	*Oblt* Rudolf Moellerfriedrich – POW	Shot down by Flt Lt P C Hughes, 234 Sqn and crashed at Tapnall Farm, Brookdown, Isle of Wight, 1440hrs
14.	24 August 1940	1/JG 52	Bf 109 E-1 White 9	*Fw* Herbert Bischoff – POW	Shot down by Flt Lt D G Gribble, 54 Sqn and crash-landed Minster Road, Westgate on Sea, Kent, 1545hrs
15.	25 August 1940	1/JG 53	Bf 109 E-1 White 15	*Gefr* Josef Broeker – POW	Shot down by Plt Off R P Beamont, 87 Sqn, Plt Off W Beaumont, 152 Sqn and Sgt R T Llewellyn, 213 Sqn; crash-landed Tatton House Farm, Buckland Ripers, Dorset, 1730hrs
16.	25 August 1940	1/ZG 2	Bf 110 C-4 Wk Nr 3208 3M+KH	*Uffz* Siegfried Becker (*F*) – POW / *Uffz* Walter Woetzel (*Bf*) – POW	Shot down by Plt Off N le C Agazarian and Plt Off G N Gaunt, 609 Sqn, and crashed at Priory Farm, East Holme, Dorset, 1800hrs
17.	26 August 1940	2/JG 2	Bf 109 E-4 Wk Nr 5383	*Oblt* Hans-Theodor Grisebach (*St Fhr*) – POW	Shot down by Plt Off A E A Van den Hove-d'Ertsenrijk, 43 Sqn and crashed at Newbarn Farm, Blendworth, Hants, 1725hrs
18.	28 August 1940	7/JG 51	Bf 109 E-4 Wk Nr 1523 White 14	*Ofw* Artur Dau – POW	Probably shot down by Sqn Ldr P W Townsend, 85 Sqn and crashed at Garden Wood, Poulton Farm, Houtham, Folkestone, Kent, 1655hrs

No.	Date	Unit	Aircraft	Crew	Fate
19.	30 August 1940	4./ZG 76	Bf 110 C, Wk Nr 3615, M8+MM	*Ofw* Georg Anthony (*F*) – +, *Uffz* Heinrich Nordmeier (*BF*) – POW	Shot down by Fg Off B J Wicks, 56 Sqn and Fg L W Paskiewicz, 303 Sqn; crashed at Barley Beans Off Farm, Kimpton, Herts, 1630hrs
20.	31 August 1940	8./ZG 26	Bf 110 D, Wk Nr 3396, 3U+HS	*Oblt* Erich Von Bergen (*F*) – POW, *Uffz* Hans Becker (*BF*) – POW	Shot down by 257 Sqn; crashed into sea between Colne Point and East Mersea off Essex Coast, 0830hrs
21.	31 August 1940	14(Z)./LG 1	Bf 110, Wk Nr 3617	*Lt* Karl-Joachim Eichhorn (*F*) – POW, *Uffz* Richard Growe (*BF*) – +	Shot down by Fg Off H T Gilbert, 601 Sqn and ditched off Foreness Point, 0905hrs
22.	31 August 1940	14(Z)./LG 1	Bf 110, Wk Nr 3805, L1+AK	*Fw* Gotlob Fritz (*F*) – POW, *Ogfr* Karl Doepfer (*BF*) – POW	Shot down by Fg Off C R Davis, 601 Sqn and ditched off Nore Light, Thames Estuary, 0910hrs
23.	1 September 1940	5./JG 54	Bf 109 E-4, Wk Nr 1277, Black 14	*Oblt* Anton Stangl (*St Kap*) – POW	Collided with another Bf 109 and crashed at Capel Farm, Bonnington, Ashford, Kent, 1115hrs
24.	1 September 1940	7./JG 26	Bf 109 E-1, Wk Nr 3892, White 11+I	*Lt* Josef Buerschgens (*St Flhr*) – POW	Shot down in error by Bf 110 and crashed at Newbridge Iden, Rye, East Sussex, 1403hrs
25.	2 September 1940	1./JG 53	Bf 109 E-4, Wk Nr 3584, White 14	*Uffz* Werner Karl – POW	Shot down by Fg Off A G Trueman, 253 Sqn and Sgt J H Lacey, 501 Sqn; crash-landed Hythe Ranges, 0817hrs
26.	2 September 1940	1./JG 51	Bf 109 E-1, Wk Nr 4850	*Lt* Helmut Thoerl – POW	Shot down by Sqn Ldr J A Leathart, 54 Sqn and crashed at Abbey Farm, South Poston, Kent at 0830hrs
27.	4 September 1940	8./ZG 76	Bf 110 C-4, Wk Nr 3101, 2N+CN	*Oblt* Hans Muenich (*F*) – POW, *Uffz* Adolf Kaeser (*BF*) – POW	Shot down by Plt Off P W Horton and Sgt Z Klein, 234 Sqn; crash-landed Black Patch Hill, Patching, West Sussex, 1345hrs
28.	5 September 1940	9./JG 53	Bf 109 E-1, Wk Nr 6252	*Fw* Anton Ochsenkuehn – POW	Shot down by Plt Off J Zurakowski, 234 Sqn and ditched south of Hastings, 1538hrs

Dramatis Personae continued

No.	Date	Unit	Aircraft	Crew	Notes
29.	6 September 1940	*Stab* I/JG 2	Bf 109 E-4, *Wk Nr* 5044	*Lt* Max Himmelheber (*Adj*) – POW	Possibly shot down by 601 Sqn; crashed Plumtree Farm, Headcorn, Kent, 0900hrs
30.	8 September 1940	*Stab* I/JG 53	Bf 109 E-1, *Wk Nr* 3478	*Oblt* Heinz Wittmeyer (*Gr Adj*)– Inj	Collided with Bf 109 E-7, *Wk Nr* 1171 flown by *Oblt* Heinz Kunert, *St Kap* 8./JG 53 and crashed off Cap Gris-Nez
31.	9 September 1940	5/JG 27	Bf 109 E-1, *Wk Nr* 3488, Black 13	*Oblt* Erwin Daig – POW	Damaged in combat and crash-landed at Chitty's Farm, Cootham, East Sussex, 1822hrs
32.	9 September 1940	1/JG 53	Bf 109 E-4, *Wk Nr* 1508, White 5	*Fw* Heinrich Hochnisch – POW	Probably shot down by Flt Lt W G Clouston, 19 Sqn and crashed at Cherry Lodge Farm, Old Jail Lane, Biggin Hill, Kent, 1800hrs
33.	15 September 1940	1/JG 53	Bf 109 E-4, *Wk Nr* 5194 <<+	*Fw* Herbert Tzschoppe – POW	Shot down by Plt Off A D J Lovell, 41 Sqn and crashed at Adisham Court, Canterbury, 1210hrs
34.	15 September 1940	2/LG 2	Bf 109 E-7, *Wk Nr* 2058, Red 2	*Uffz* August Klik – POW	Shot down by Fg Off L A Haines 19 Sqn and crash-landed at Shellness Point, Isle of Sheppey, 1450hrs
35.	18 September 1940	*Stab* II/JG 53	Bf 109 E-1, *Wk Nr* 4842, White 10	*Lt* Erich Bodendiek (*TO*) – POW	Shot down by Plt Off R W Oxspring, 66 Sqn and crashed at Guilton Ash, Sandwich, Kent, 1705hrs
36.	27 September 1940	*Stab*/ZG 76	Bf 110 D-3, *Wk Nr* 4215, M8+XE	*Oblt* Wilfried von Eichborn (*Adj, F*) – POW / *Uffz* Erich Bartmuss (*Bf*) – +	Probably shot down by Plt Off P A Worrall and Sgt G C Palliser, 249 Sqn and ditched off Hastings, 1000hrs
37.	30 September 1940	*Stab*/JG 26	Bf 109 E-4, *Wk Nr* 5818	*Hptm* Walter Kienzle – POW	Possibly shot down by Flt Lt G R McGregor, 1 Sqn (RCAF) and crashed at Roundhurst, Haslemere, Surrey, 1705hrs
38.	30 September 1940	6/JG 27	Bf 109 E-1, *Wk Nr* 3859, Yellow 3	*Lt* Herbert Schmidt – POW	Believed shot down in error by another Bf 109, and crashed at Holman's Grove, Grayswood, Surrey, 1640hrs

	Date	Unit	Aircraft	Pilot	Fate
39.	2 October 1940	8/JG 53	Bf 109 E-1, Wk Nr 6370, Black 3+I	*Gefr* Heinz Zag – POW	Probably shot down by Sgt G J Bailey, 603 Sqn and crash-landed at Forge Farm, Goudhurst, Kent, 1000hrs
40.	5 October 1940	1/JG 53	Bf 109 E-4, Wk Nr 1804, White 10	*Uffz* Willi Ghesla – POW	Probably shot down by Fg Off H de M Molson, 1 Sqn RCAF and crash-landed in between Frith Farm, Aldington and New Barn Farm, Bilsingdon, Kent, 1145hrs
41.	5 October 1940	1/JG 53	Bf 109 E-4, Wk Nr 1564, White 3	*Lt* Alfred Zeis – POW	Possibly shot down by Fg Off P B Pitcher, 1 Sqn RCAF and crashed at Sheerlands Farm, Pluckley, Kent, 1140hrs
42.	7 October 1940	2/JG 51	Bf 109 E-4/B, Wk Nr 4103, Black 1	*Oblt* Victor Moelders (*St Kap*) – POW	Probably shot down by Sgt E W Wright, 605 Sqn and crash-landed on Lidham Marshes, Doleham Farm, Guestling, East Sussex, 1115hrs
43.	12 October 1940	1/JG 52	Bf 109 E-3, Wk Nr 1966, White 11	*Oblt* Guenter Buesgen (*St Fhr*) – POW	Probably shot down by 92 Sqn and crashed at Bean's Hill, Harrietsham, Kent, 1530hrs
44.	20 October 1940	74 Sqn	Spitfire II P7426	Sgt C G Hilken – wounded	Possibly shot down by *Sfw* Helmut Goedert, I/LG 2; aircraft broke up in between Cowden and Leighton Manor, Kent, 1500hrs
45.	25 October 1940	5/JG 54	Bf 109 E-4, Wk Nr 1988, Black 7	*Oblt* Jochen Schypek – POW	Shot down by Fg Off M P Brown, 41 Sqn and crash-landed at Broom Hill, Lydd, Kent, 0930hrs
46.	25 October 1940	3/JG 77	Bf 109 E-4, Wk Nr 5104, Yellow 13	*Gefr* Karl Raisinger – POW	Damaged in combat and crash-landed at Harvey's Cross, Telscombe, Saltdean, Sussex, 1330hrs
47.	15 November 1940	4/JG 2	Bf 109 E-4, Wk Nr 5949, White 10	*Gefr* Rudi Miese – POW	Shot down by Sgt J N Glendinning, 74 Sqn and disintegrated off Felpham, West Sussex, 1615hrs

Select Bibliography

Caldwell, Donald, *The JG 26 War Diary, Volume 1, 1939-42*, Grub Street, London, 1996
Caldwell, Donald, *The JG 26 War Diary Volume 2, 1943-45*, Grub Street, London, 1998
Collier, Richard, *Eagle Day*, Pan Books, London, 1968
Eimannsberger, Ludwig Von, *Zerstoerergruppe*, Schiffer Military History, Atglen, 1998
Everson, Don, *The Reluctant Messerschmitt*, Portcullis Press, Redhill, 1978
Foreman, John, *Fighter Command War Diary, Part 1*, Air Research Publications, Walton on Thames, 1996
Foreman, John, *Fighter Command War Diary, Part 2*, Air Research Publications, Walton on Thames, 1998
Goss, Christopher, *Brothers in Arms*, Crécy Books, Bristol, 1994
Mason, Francis, *Battle over Britain*, McWhirter Twins, London, 1969
Obermaier, Ernst, *Die Ritterkreuztrager der Luftwaffe, Band 1*, Verlag Dieter Hoffmann, Mainz, 1989
Oxspring, Gp Capt Bobby, *Spitfire Command*, Grafton Books, London, 1987
Payne, Michael, *Messerschmitt Bf 109 Into the Battle*, Air Research Publications, Walton on Thames, 1987
Price, Dr Alfred, *Battle of Britain Day, 15 September 1940*, The RAF Air Power Review, Volume 2 No 2
Prien, Jochen, *Chronik Des JG 53 Pik As, Band 1*, Flugzeug Publikation, Illertissen
Prien, Jochen & Stemmler, Gerhard, *Messerschmitt Bf 109 im Einsatz bei Stab und I/JG 3*
Prien, Jochen & Stemmler, Gerhard, *Messerschmitt Bf 109 im Einsatz bei II/JG 3*
Prien, Jochen & Stemmler, Gerhard, *Messerschmitt Bf 109 im Einsatz bei III/JG 3*
Prien, Jochen, Rodeike, Peter & Stemmler, Gerhard, *Messerschmitt Bf 109 im Einsatz bei Stab und I/JG 27*
Prien, Jochen, Rodeike, Peter & Stemmler, Gerhard, *Messerschmitt Bf 109 im Einsatz bei II/JG 27*
Prien, Jochen, Rodeike, Peter & Stemmler, Gerhard, *Messerschmitt Bf 109 im Einsatz bei III/JG 27*
Ramsey, Winston (Ed.), *The Battle of Britain Then and Now, Mark III*, Battle of Britain Prints, London, 1985
Sarkar, Dilip, *Through Peril to the Stars*, Ramrod Publications, Malvern, 1993
Sarkar, Dilip, *Bader's Duxford Fighters*, Ramrod Publications, Worcester, 1997
Vasco, John, *Bombsights over England*, JAC Publications, Norwich, 1990
Vasco, John & Cornwell, Peter, *Zerstoerer*, JAC Publications, Norwich, 1995
Wynn, Kenneth, *Men of the Battle of Britain*, Gliddon Books, Norwich, 1989

BOOK TWO

The Luftwaffe Bombers' Battle of Britain, July–October 1940

Prologue to the Battle

The invasion of Poland on 1 September 1939 saw the might of the *Luftwaffe* being thrown against a far more technically inferior, albeit tenacious, country. The *Luftwaffe* proved itself very quickly when its Heinkel 111 and Dornier 17 twin-engined bombers and Junkers 87 and Henschel 123 close support bombers, escorted by German fighters, all but achieved total air superiority in twelve hours. The speed with which all German forces, both ground and air, achieved objective after objective was astounding and just twenty-seven days later, the campaign was over and Adolf Hitler's intentions turned to the west.

The He 111.

Jubilant crews from 7/KG 3
– the date on the bomb on the right is 10/9/39.

The Do 17Z (5K+KR of 7/KG 3, 1939).

197

The Ju 87 B. (Grahl)

The Hs 123. (Grahl)

On 3 September 1939, Great Britain's Prime Minister, Neville Chamberlain, had announced that, because of Germany's unjustified attack on Poland, Great Britain was at war with Germany. France followed Britain's lead almost immediately and both countries geared up for war. It was not until 16 October

1939 that the first German bombers were observed off the British coast and then, that afternoon, fifteen Junkers 88s of I/KG 30 attempted to attack warships in the Firth of Forth. The Junkers 88 was the latest hope of the *Luftwaffe*, being faster and more manoeuvrable than the other German twin-engined bombers. However, a sharp lesson was learned when Spitfires of 602 and 603 Squadron intercepted, shooting down two and damaging a third. Both sides' learning processes continued for the next seven months with frequent but relatively small scale incidents and combats taking place.

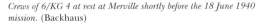

The Ju 88. (Ciuraj)

German air activity was initially limited to the waters around the east coast of Great Britain with the Germans not wishing to commit the error of dropping bombs on the mainland and risking casualties to the civilian population (something the RAF was also trying to avoid doing over Germany). However, all would change on 9 April 1940 when German forces invaded

Crews of 6/KG 4 at rest at Merville shortly before the 18 June 1940 mission. (Backhaus)

An early casualty – He 111 H-1 of 5/KG 26 was forced down by a Spitfire of 602 Sqn on 9 February 1940...

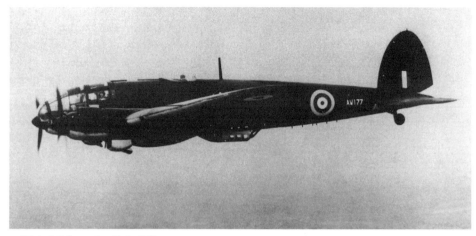

...Repaired, it flew again with the RAF.

Scandinavia and then, on 10 May, did the same to France and the Low Countries. In each campaign, the *Luftwaffe* played a crucial part and by 4 June 1940, it was all but over. France gave in to the Germans on 22 June 1940 and the world held its breath. The only remaining opposition to Germany's aims came from Great Britain. Unusually, the first major attack against targets on the British mainland took place not by day but by night when, during the hours of darkness on 18 and 19 June 1940, Heinkel 111s of KG 4 lifted off from their new airfields of Merville and Lille–Roubaix in France and headed for airfields and industrial targets in eastern England:

Leutnant Erich Simon, *Stab*/KG 4

I had been assigned to bomb oil dumps near Southend. My primary task was to mark the target area by dropping flares. The underside of the *Geschwader's* aircraft would be prepared by applying black paint so that we would be less discernible against the dark sky. Unfortunately, this paint did not arrive in time and was not available for this mission.

At approximately 2230 hrs, I took off first, followed by the other aircraft at short intervals between each. Initially we headed north-east over the North Sea until approaching Denmark when we altered course to the west towards the target area.

As soon as we coasted in near Hull, we were spotted and tracked by searchlights but there was no sign or evidence of night fighters. Besides, until then, we had been told the British did not have night fighters! As planned, I dropped my flares on target and, after my primary task was accomplished, I continued to bomb selected targets which then caught fire. Upon completion, I turned on an easterly heading to get away from the target area and this is the last thing I can remember that night...

The RAF had thrown a mix of Spitfires and Blenheim fighters to try and get at the attackers. Unfortunately for the Germans, many of the RAF pilots in the air that night had recent combat experience:

Flight Lieutenant Adolph 'Sailor' Malan, 'A' Flight, 74 Squadron

During an air raid in the locality of Southend, various enemy aircraft were observed and held by searchlights for prolonged periods. On request from the Squadron, I was allowed to take off with a Spitfire. I climbed towards an enemy aircraft which was making for the coast and held in a searchlight at 8,000ft. I positioned myself astern and opened fire at 200 yards and closed to 50 yards with one burst. I observed bullets entering the enemy aircraft and had my windscreen covered in oil, broke off to the left and immediately below as enemy aircraft spiralled out of beam.[1] I climbed to 12,000ft towards another enemy aircraft held by a searchlight on a northerly course. I opened fire at 250 yards taking care not to overshoot this time. I gave five 2-second bursts and observed bullets entering all over the enemy aircraft with slight deflection as he was turning to port. Enemy aircraft emitted heavy smoke and I observed one parachute open very close. Enemy aircraft went down in a spiral dive. The searchlights and I followed him right down until he crashed in flames near Chelmsford.

'Sailor' Malan (left) seen here handing over command of the Biggin Hill Wing to Michael Robinson, July 1941.

---

[1] This aircraft was probably that of *Hptm* Hermann Prochnow, *Staffel Kapitaen* of 4/KG 4. His aircraft was observed going down at a 45 degree angle and on fire near the coast. Prochnow's body was washed ashore in July 1940.

Leutnant Erich Simon

Evidently I did bail out although I cannot remember doing so. Apparently I hit the stabiliser of the aircraft after I left the cockpit. The proof of this assumption was several broken ribs and bruises near my spine. In addition to those injuries, I had a bullet wound in my left arm.

The remains of Lt *Simon's He 111 – bullet holes in the tail are just visible.* (via Watkins)

During the bailing out, I lost my flying boots. I was in a state of shock when I landed but followed what I had been taught to "immediately leave the crash site or wherever you come down with your parachute". I cannot recall the direction or for how long I walked but it must have been quite some distance because my socks had completely worn away.

I next remember coming to the gateway of a farm where I passed out. The people were, considering the situation, friendly and the farmer took me to the Chelmsford and Essex Hospital...

As Erich Simon was landing by parachute, further north another combat was taking place:

Oberleutnant Ulrich Jordan, *Stab* II/KG 4

Stationed at Merville, twenty miles south-west of Flanders, our *Gruppe* had orders to bomb the airfields of Honington and Mildenhall, both known to be the bases from which bombers attacked Germany every night. On account of the skies over England being well guarded by day fighters, we decided to attack by night – about twelve aircraft out of twenty-seven from our *Gruppe*, the remainder were under repair following an attack by Blenheims the day before or the crews lacked night experience.

An He 111 of Stab II/KG 4.

Responsible for planning our attack, I phoned the officer commanding the fighter units in Holland, Belgium and northern France and asked him whether British night fighters should be taken into account that night. His answer: "Definitely not! We have no night fighters ourselves and I'm sure the British haven't either. Don't worry about meeting British fighters at night!" This was a mistake which led to a catastrophe for II/KG 4 *General Wever*.

On account of British night fighters not being expected, we decided to fly singly – one plane following its predecessors at ten to fifteen minute intervals, my plane being the first.

All went well up to passing the Thames between London and its mouth. Then, all of a sudden, about ten or fifteen searchlights started to search for the plane, without *Flak* firing. This was a hint to expect night fighters in spite of the *Oberst*'s "Definitely not!" After a few minutes, three or four searchlights caught my plane. Nothing happened – no gunfire or fighters. We continued on to the targets to the north east of London with one group of searchlights handing our plane onto the next.

After a while, we saw far below, four points reflecting in the bright moonlight. A few minutes later, they were behind us – Blenheims. The fight lasted about ten to fifteen minutes. The fighters attacked continuously from the rear, one after the other causing a lot of damage to the fuselage, engines and the tail. The seats being protected by armoured plating are the reason for me being able to write this account even though they were not liked by the pilots, including myself, because of the extra weight. About a fifth of our Heinkel 111s had armoured seats and the plane I usually flew hadn't. By luck, I had to change to this plane because of the damage done to mine by the bombing attack by Blenheims.

Left to right Oblt *Ernst Dieter von Tellmann,* Oblt *Joachim von Arnim,* Maj *Erdmann (*Gr Kdr*),* Oblt *Ulrich Jordan.*

Blenheim night fighter (seen here from 29 Sqn). (via Earnshaw)

During the fight, the *Bordmechaniker* was hit twice – once in the belly and once in the leg so he was not able to use his machine gun in the lower part of the plane. The fighters, two of which had disappeared in the meantime (I don't know whether they were shot down or not[2]) now started to attack only from behind and below and finally managed to stop one of the engines at a height of 15,000ft about thirty-five miles from the coast. I then ordered the bombs to be dropped to make the plane lighter and to try and reach an airfield on the Continent. The fight continued until, eventually, the other engine stopped, apparently due to damage to the cooling system which happened just after the last of the fighters had disappeared, probably due to lack of fuel and ammunition…

Flight Lieutenant Raymond Duke-Wooley, Blue Section, 23 Squadron

Whilst flying at 5,000ft, three miles north of Kings Lynn, I observed an aircraft, subsequently identified as an He 111, held in a searchlight beam at 8,000ft. Time 0045 hrs. I observed a ball of fire which I took to be a Blenheim in flames breaking away from behind the tail of the enemy aircraft. I climbed to engage enemy aircraft and attacked from below the tail after the searchlight was no longer holding. Range 50 yards. Enemy aircraft returned fire and appeared to throttle back suddenly. Our own speed was 130 to 140 miles per hour and I estimated enemy aircraft slowing to 110 miles per hour. I delivered five attacks. Air Gunner [AC Derek Bell] fired seven short bursts at varying ranges. After a front attack, Air Gunner reported that the port engine of the enemy aircraft was on fire. I returned to base and landed as my starboard engine was unserviceable. Several bullets had holed the wings and fuselage of aircraft including hits in the starboard wing and the rear of the fuselage by cannon.

Oberleutnant Ulrich Jordan

…Now came the most important decision of the mission – to leave the plane by parachute or to try and reach the sea and land on its surface (landing on unknown land at night could have fatal consequences). Because my *Bordmechaniker* was severely wounded, it was impossible for him to bale out. Gliding, meanwhile, led to the decision

[2] Blenheim L1458/YP-S of 23 Squadron was hit by return fire and crashed at Terrington St Clement, Norfolk; the pilot Sgt Alan Close was killed but the gunner, LAC Lawrence Karasek, baled out uninjured.

to land in the sea close to land – I knew that a plane normally floats for a few minutes at least.

We ditched and left the floating plane, helping the *Bordmechaniker* out, and swam to the shore where we found a fishing boat which we used for protection against the cold, our clothes being soaked. After a while, men in civilian clothes with rifles, wearing a red badge on their sleeves, appeared. I went to them with my pistol in my hand and asked them in an urgent voice to get a doctor as soon as possible. They went away, probably glad that they hadn't any trouble, and after an hour, small groups of soldiers arrived, led by a First Lieutenant. They had a stretcher on which we carried our wounded crew member to a field station about two miles from the shore...

THIS AND PREVIOUS PAGE Oblt *Jordan's He111 lies just off the Norfolk coast.* (Humphreys)

As the two aircraft of 23 Squadron were battling with *Oblt* Jordan's Heinkel, further north, closer to the intended targets of Honington and Mildenhall, another Heinkel was receiving the attention of two different fighters:

Oberleutnant Joachim von Arnim, 4/KG 4

Oblt *Joachim von Arnim and* Fw *Willi Maier.* (von Arnim)

It was a full moon that night and, as far as I remember, no clouds whatsoever. Before crossing the coast en route to Mildenhall, we were easily found by many searchlights and unable to evade. On approaching our target, the rear gunner [*Fw* Karl] Hauck reported night fighters in sight. They immediately attacked us, hundreds of bullets hit our aircraft from the rear – it sounded like somebody hitting a thousand drums. Fortunately for us we had installed, just a day before, armour plating in the cockpit and for the two in the rear of the plane. The Spitfire made several attacks on us – it was funny to see the tracer going down in front of us. Both my boys in the rear answered the attacks with their machine guns. As far as I can remember, one of the

Spitfires was hit and shot down by my rear gunner at about the same time our Heinkel 111 went out of control – I always wondered if we did in fact shoot one of the Spitfires down...

There was more than one night fighter chasing after *Oblt* von Arnim and his crew:

Squadron Leader Joseph O'Brien, 'A' Flight Commander, 23 Squadron

...Intercepted one He 111 at 12,000ft in the vicinity of Newmarket. I opened fire at enemy aircraft with rear gun from a position below and in front. Enemy aircraft turned to port and slowed and I then gave him several long bursts with the front guns from 50 to 100 yards and saw clouds of smoke from his port engine. I then overshot enemy aircraft and passed very close below and in front of him. Air Gunner put a burst in at close range into the cockpit. Enemy aircraft disappeared, apparently out of control. Suddenly, I lost control of my aircraft which spun violently to the left. Failing to recover from the spin, I ordered my crew to bail out and I followed the Navigator out through the top hatch...

Sadly, Sqn Ldr O'Brien's Navigator and Air Gunner, Plt Off Cuthbert King-Clark and Cpl David Little, were both killed. Although the Blenheim crew were not aware of it, another night fighter was attacking the Heinkel and its pilot suffered at the hands of the Heinkel's gunners. Fg Off Petre was not able to file a combat report at the time but dictated the following to his Station Commander, Wg Cdr Woodhall:

Flying Officer G W 'John' Petre, 19 Squadron

Whilst on patrol between Ely and Newmarket, an enemy aircraft was sighted in the vicinity of Newmarket. Fg Off Petre shadowed it and was just about to open fire when he saw a Blenheim in the way. He then sheered off to one side and came in on the quarter of the enemy aircraft, firing a burst in a deflection shot. He saw his tracer going into the enemy and, immediately after, one engine poured out volumes of black smoke where the tracer was going into it. At this moment, our searchlights caught and held Fg Off Petre with the result that the enemy gunner had an illuminated target and opened fire. The Spitfire was hit by what was thought to be an explosive bullet and caught fire. The enemy aircraft immediately caught fire after and came down in flames near the Duxford–Newmarket road about one mile east of Six Mile Bottom. Fg Off Petre jumped by parachute after being badly burned around the face and hands...

Oberleutnant Joachim von Arnim

...Everything happened very quickly. [*Fw* Willi] Maier was unable to hold the plane on course and in a few seconds we all jumped out. In the moonlight, I could see I was hanging 200m above Maier. I saw the aircraft exploding on the ground and Maier and myself landed smoothly in a potato field. A couple of hours later we were taken prisoner by Home Guardsmen under the command of a Major Evans. He took us to

his farm and then British soldiers took us to barracks at Bury St Edmunds. The next day, RAF officers ferried us to Duxford. They were all extremely polite, nice and friendly. Fine type of sportsmen. I was then told that Hauck had been found close to Duxford and had been wounded and taken to hospital. [*Fw*] Paul Gersch had sadly been killed when his parachute had failed to open.

Fw *Paul Gersch (left, with* Fw *Willi Maier), the only fatality in the von Arnim crew.* (von Arnim)

The remains of Oblt *von Arnim's He 111.* (via Watkins)

The remaining crew member Fw *Karl Hauck was wounded.* (Hauck)

This was not destined to be the last combat that night:

Unteroffizier Theo Kuehn, 6/KG 4

We were flying at 5,000m altitude and had crossed the British coast south of Harwich. On the way home, the *Flak* stopped firing and a short time afterwards, I felt that our plane had been hit. The attack was a complete surprise – none of us saw the Spitfire. On the second and third attacks, both engines were damaged. I returned fire but without any result but to this day am thankful that we had armour plating. We flew lower and lower and when we were over Margate, the pilot started the right engine again so that we could ditch in the sea. At that moment Fw Alfred Reitzig, the *Beobachter,* baled out but got his parachute caught on the tail the same instant that we ditched.

We all managed to get out quickly and into our lifeboat. Of Reitzig, there was no sign…

Uffz *Theo Kuehn.* (Kuehn)

Again, it was a Spitfire pilot that shot this Heinkel down:

Flying Officer Eric Ball, Green Section, 'B' Flight, 19 Squadron

At 0135 hrs, I had been detailed to intercept a bandit over Mildenhall at 12,000ft. At approximately 0150 hrs, I sighted the enemy aircraft which was held in a searchlight beam. As I was manoeuvring into position for the attack, it burst into flames and two occupants left the machine by parachute. I saw one machine crash about eight miles east of Duxford. I was then instructed to intercept a raid on Newmarket. I turned and spotted four searchlights concentrated on one spot roughly in that direction. After flying for five minutes, I saw the enemy aircraft which by that time had set a south-easterly course. It took me some time to overtake him and manoeuvre into position before I finally opened fire at a range of 200 yards, firing all the way up to 50 yards. I duly broke away and attacked him once more, experiencing no return fire and very little evasive tactics. By this time, the He 111 was enveloped in clouds of smoke and seemed to be losing height. As I broke away, the searchlights lost him and I consequently failed to pick him up again.

The crash of the Heinkel just off Margate would be one of many during the coming months and years but being one of the first, memories of its arrival are vivid:

Colin Cuthbert

We were on the cliff top looking out to sea when with a rush of wind, the He 111 came almost over our heads, missing a very large flagpole, over the cliffs and flopped into the water. We ran down a gap, split up by some 25 yards and very quickly dug two holes and pointed our .303s in the right direction.

A searchlight about a mile away clicked on and for the first time we saw the plane with water up to its wings with a big swastika on the tail. We really thought this was it! The Germans inflated their dinghy and paddled in silence to about 10 yards from the water's edge where they all put their hands up (still in silence) and sat there bobbing up and down.

I decided to show myself and shouted to Roy Ovenden to cover me. I waded in and pulled them to the shore. They got out and we searched them for weapons. They were all young and very cool, obviously thinking that they would only be prisoners for a short time. One of them combed his hair and a lot of jabbering went on – we couldn't understand German and they couldn't understand English.

One of them, after a time, put his hand on an under arm holster and handed in another gun. They then let us know that there was another crew member who had parachuted out. I then swam to the plane and found the missing crew member (dead) whose parachute had gone one side of the tail fin and he had gone the other. He had been strangled by the parachute cords.

And so ended the first major attack on mainland Britain during World War Two and what transpired to have been the first night combat of the war. The cost on the German side was six bombers (*Oblt* Falk Willis and his crew of *Stab* I/KG 4 crash-landed on the beach ten kilometres east of Calais after being damaged by a night fighter), nine experienced aircrew killed and eleven prisoners of war. Amongst those losses were one *Gruppen Kom-*

Lt *Hansjuergen Backhaus, pilot of the He 111 that ditched off Margate.* (Backhaus)

Fw *Alfred Reitzig was killed when his parachute became entangled in the Heinkel's tail...* (Kuehn)

...he still lies buried in Margate's Cemetery. (via Fright)

Uffz *Fritz Boeck, another survivor from the Backhaus crew.* (Kuehn)

mandeur, one *Staffel Kapitaen,* a *Geschwader Adjutant* and a *Gruppe Technischer Offizier.* RAF losses were four aircraft with five aircrew killed.

The days that followed were quiet – a lull before the storm. Aircrew on both sides of the Channel needed a well earned rest to prepare for the coming onslaught. The combats fought on the night of 18/19 June 1940 taught both sides a salutary lesson. Even more lessons would be learned from the first day of the next month, a month which would see the start of the Battle of Britain.

The tail of Lt *Backhaus' He 111 is hauled ashore – the parachute of* Fw *Reitzig is seen near the base of the tail.* (via Watkins)

Officers of I/KG 4 just before the invasion of Poland – Maj *von Massenbach (second row, sixth from left) would be taken POW on 19 June 1940;* Hptm *Prochnow (back row, fourth from left) would be killed; most of the others would not survive the war.* (Koch)

The luckier officers of KG 4, all prisoners in Canada. Oblt *Jordan (front, second from left),* Maj *von Massenbach (front row, centre),* Lt *Backhaus (back row, far left),* Oblt *von Arnim (back row, third from left) and* Lt *Simon (back row, centre), all taken prisoner on 19 June 1940.* (Koch)

CHAPTER 1

The Battle Begins, July 1940

If the RAF was expecting an onslaught to coincide with the start of the month, they were wrong. Even though the Battle of Britain officially started on 10 July 1940, the month saw regular combats and incidents taking place off or over the British coast with each day seeing an increase in the ferocity and frequency of such actions. It was therefore ironic that the first *Luftwaffe* loss of July 1940 resulted in bitter recriminations:

The He 59, similar to that operated by Seenotflugkommando 3. (Rauher)

Leutnant Hans-Joachim Fehske, *Seenotflugkommando* 3

Being a reserve officer, I initially belonged to *Kuestenfliegergruppe* 106 based at Norderney. After the Scandinavian Campaign, I was transferred at short notice to *Seenotflugkommando* 3, together with my crew, and we were posted to Amsterdam–Schiphol.

During the night of 30 June/1 July 1940, some German seaplanes laid mines in the shipping lanes around Middlesborough. One aircraft commanded by *LtzS* Schroeder had to carry out an emergency landing in a British minefield off the east coast.

Our *Gruppenkommandeur* ordered us to fly to the area in question and to look for this aircraft. The sea is large, a plane small, the speed of the current very high because of the strong turn of the tide off the east coast. My pilot had not been trained in instrument flying and that was why we had to wait until first light for take off. Consequently, another loss of time was unavoidable.

According to our dead reckonings, we arrived at the correct latitude shortly before 0600 hrs. There we changed course and headed towards the British east coast. My intention was to orientate myself by finding a clear landmark. By doing this I would be able to correct my position and improve the chances of a successful search.

During our approach, we were flying in low stratus/haze. Immediately after changing course direction west, the fog lifted. The visibility was excellent and we were flying between the coast and a convoy headed south. One can understand that the RAF did not like that. Consequently, there were two British fighters behind us a few minutes later and very quickly we were shot down. Our plane was painted white with big red crosses. According to international agreements, we carried no armament on our search and rescue plane.

One engine and the light metal floats had been hit. The radio equipment failed and our *Bordwart* received two gunshot wounds (the bullets had passed right through). The floats failed to keep the plane afloat so we took to our dinghy and tried to row towards England. A short time after, we were fished out of the sea by the escort vessel *Black Swan* and were taken prisoners of war. In retrospect, I have to remark that we were treated remarkably correctly and politely on board the *Black Swan*.

This was probably the first incident where an unarmed German aircraft clearly on a mission of mercy had been attacked and shot down – the Red Cross markings must have been clearly visible to the three 72 Squadron pilots responsible even though one of the combat reports makes little mention:

Flight Sergeant Harry Steere, Blue 3, 72 Squadron

Blue 1 [Flt Lt Ted Graham] ordered Number One attack. Blue 1 and 2 [Fg Off Edgar Wilcox] fired, I closed to 250 yards and the machine turned right. I had a simple deflection shot. The machine touched the water and I broke off the attack. The machine jettisoned several articles after Blue 2 finished his attack.

Despite German complaints, the three RAF pilots' actions were vindicated when an order was issued that any German plane, armed or otherwise, found in the vicinity of a British convoy did so at their own risk.

Sporadic combats and incidents continued throughout the day but, just before tea-time, the RAF fighters in the north claimed another victim:

Pilots of 72 Sqn at readiness at Acklington, July 1940. (Pocock)

Oberleutnant Friedrich-Wilhelm Koch, 3/KG 4

On 1 July 1940, my *Gruppe* was for the first time ordered to perform a daylight attack against an industrial target. Each of the three *Staffel* had to nominate one crew – in my *Staffel*, I volunteered and was lucky to get the last serviceable aircraft. However, that aircraft, unfortunately, also became unserviceable during pre-take off checks but the indefatigable groundcrew managed to allow me to take off two hours later.

Oblt *Friedrich-Wilhelm Koch, Copenhagen, April 1940.* (Koch)

We were to undertake a high level attack against a chemical works at Middlesborough with a secondary target being the oil tanks at Hull. So, with the Juist Beacon as a navigational aid, the course was set for Flamborough Head. The weather conditions for the attack (attack was to be broken off if the cloud cover 100 kilometres from the coast was less than 5/10ths) did not suit. However, after hearing that both the other aircraft had broken off their attacks, I felt obliged to press home my attack. Just short of 100 kilometres from the coast, a thin stratus layer indicated that cloud cover could be expected. At about 1630 hrs (German Summer Time), we descended, and broke through clouds exactly where we wanted to be – just south of Flamborough Head. However, I decided not to fly to Middlesborough but to turn south where the cloud cover seemed to be thicker.

He 111 of 3/KG 4, Langenau, September 1939. (Koch)

Just north of the Humber Estuary, the cloud broke up and the town of Hull lay in front of us under a nearly spotless blue sky. Shortly afterwards having left the cloud cover, my *Bordfunker* [*Fw* Alfred Weber] reported three Spitfires. In order not to be spotted by them, I turned back into cloud and headed towards Middlesborough. After twenty minutes, the cloud broke up and became thin and hazy. Whilst I was pondering on what to do, again Spitfires were reported in sight. Six of them flying at the same altitude but apparently not having sighted us. It seemed to me that it was more than mere chance that these fighters were there and only afterwards did I learn about radar. My ignorance of radar resulted in me deciding to fly eastwards for ten minutes then, at a safe distance parallel to the coast up to Hull.

I intended remaining in cloud and then to break cloud to orientate myself for the subsequent attack. This was our last chance as apart from being low on fuel, my pilot [*Ofw* Hermann Draisbach] had only twenty minutes oxygen remaining due to a defect in the oxygen system. Navigation was exact as when leaving cloud, we hit the coastline. Suddenly I saw an airfield with a number of light coloured planes. In a sudden impulse, I felt tempted to attack this dream target. However, the lack of the usual camouflage led me to think that it was a mock airfield and I resisted the temptation.

Ofw *Hermann Draisbach (right) and* Ofw *Rudolf Ernst.* (Koch)

We were now in cloud at about 18,000ft. Some scattered clouds at about 12,000ft obscured my view so we descended. Shortly before reaching the town, I turned in for the final run when my *Bordfunker* again reported three Spitfires in sight. I had to make a quick decision – either to return into the cloud or to continue the target run. Since it was doubtful that we would make it home, I decided to do what I was here for – to bomb the oil tanks. For the whole time we were in the target area, we were subjected to *Flak* which was extremely unpleasant during the final approach because for best results, I had to keep altitude, speed and course constant thus giving the gunners an easy target. In fact, one of the shell fragments entered the cockpit and damaged part of the instrument panel.

In spite of these irritations, we continued the target run up to the moment I dropped the bombs. I must say I have praise for the outstanding performance of my pilot who executed my corrections with calmness and coolness. After I dropped my bombs, I ordered the pilot to perform a steep turn and to dive at full speed. I noticed that the twelve 50 kilogram bombs had straddled the target with several hits, causing explosions and fire. I tried to set up a coded mission report because I doubted very much that we could do it later.

Oblt *Koch in position in the He 111.* (Koch)

Still several thousand feet up, we reached the Humber Estuary when the Spitfires circled in for their first attack. For the time we flew in the *Flak* zone, they had waited a safe distance but now they closed for the kill. Although lying in the front part of the plane, manning the forward gun, I was able to follow the events over the intercom...

Pilot Officer John Brewster, Yellow 3, 616 Squadron

I followed Number 2 [Plt Off John Bell] into the attack. On going into the attack, I noticed that the port engine was on fire and a little smoke appeared from the starboard engine. Fire was opened at about 220 yards and tracer bullets were seen to go into the fuselage and wings. A lot of debris fell off from the enemy aircraft approximately halfway up the fuselage on the top port side. Range was now about 100 yards. Oil then appeared on my windscreen and when closing to about 50 yards, enemy aircraft was completely enveloped in a circular cloud of black smoke. My windscreen was now completely covered in oil and it was impossible to distinguish enemy aircraft in the smoke. I broke right because I was very near the enemy aircraft and it seemed better to break right than left where Number 2 had broken. I then turned east at about 4,000ft and saw enemy aircraft below me diving down to the sea on fire. I manoeuvred to attack again and on turning dead astern of the enemy aircraft in a diving turn, I lost sight of it due to the oil on my windscreen. I had dived to 2,000ft and then turned to starboard and circled for enemy aircraft but failed to locate it. I then returned to base and landed.

Tracer ammunition was most useful and enabled me to see where my bullets were hitting enemy aircraft. No enemy fire was encountered. On landing, I found that there were three dents in my wing caused by flying debris from enemy aircraft. Also, the leading edge of my mainplane, especially the port, spinner, wireless aerial mast, tailplane leading edge and fin were covered with a film of oil in addition to the windscreen through which it was impossible to see for landing, necessitating looking over the side.

Oberleutnant Friedrich-Wilhelm Koch

...Already after the first machine gun bursts of my *Bordfunker* in the upper rear position, the gun had suffered a malfunction. From this moment on, the Spitfires could perform their attacks unhindered and from close range. One after the other made his run. Each time a Spitfire launched his attack, a noisy stream of bullets rushed through our aircraft. At first the instrument panel was shot to pieces, then one engine put out of action. Next, the landing gear came down and the flaps flew off. After the second engine was also put out of action and the starboard ailerons had been shot away, the Spitfires left their crippled victim and returned to their base. The pilot, without instruments, flaps and ailerons, a damaged rudder and propellers that could not be feathered, struggled with the controls, miraculously keeping the aircraft flying. Now after the continuous rattling noise of the bullets had stopped, it became dead and quiet in the aircraft. My pilot asked me to guess the speed and altitude since he had no instruments and was fully occupied in struggling with the controls.

I called the *Bordmechaniker* [*Ofw* Rudolf Ernst] who answered that the *Bordfunker* had been hit several times and it seemed likely that he was dead. He himself had been hit in the leg and buttocks and was joking about an inglorious end! I

The exposed pilot's instrument panel in the He 111. (Backhaus)

went back, noticed that we could not get out the dinghy there because the dead *Bordfunker* blocked the upper exit so I pulled the dinghy into the cockpit, followed by the *Bordmechaniker*. Back in the cockpit I realised that we were very low over the surface of the sea and I could assist the pilot by calling out the distance to the surface until we hit. Due to the undercarriage being down, we flipped over and started sinking. Because

Oblt *Koch (right) and his crew practice inflating the dinghy – this practice helped on 1 July 1940.* (Koch)

of the impact, I was thrown forward and lost consciousness. Then, when I had recovered, I noticed that we were under the water and that water was streaming through many openings. However, we all floated upwards and broke surface, floating silently. We brought our dinghy over, inflated it and our lifebelts and got on board the dinghy. At this moment, we saw the *Bordfunker* move so we got the dinghy to him and pulled our badly wounded comrade on board. At the same moment, the Heinkel sank.

Now for the first time we were in a position to analyse our new situation. In view of the critical state of the *Bordfunker* who had been shot through the eye, head, an arm and chest, we decided to use signal flares and markers to signal our position to a Short Sunderland flying boat which had been circling over the convoy we had seen from the air. Since we were about 25 miles off the British coast, we could not hope for rescue by German vessels, at least not during the night to come. About half an hour later, a ship came in sight (the *Black Swan*) and we were taken on board...

After such a frantic start to the month, the poor weather hampered air operations on 2 July with just one combat resulting in one German loss (a reconnaissance aircraft) on that day. The return of the good weather saw the air activity increase over the following days but with no real obvious pattern. However, the appearance of the much feared *Stuka* over Portland Naval base on the morning of 4 July was a portent of things to come, or was it?

Experienced pilot Fw Richard Saft and his crew of 2/KG 77 were lost on 3 July 1940; briefed to strafe the area in between Dover and Hawkinge, it is thought they were shot down by ground fire and crashed into the Channel. (Bohn)

The absence of RAF fighters over the German's target allowed them to get away scot-free (and resulted in the award of the Victoria Cross to anti-aircraft gunner Jack Mantle). The same day also saw the first concerted attack on shipping when eighteen Dornier 17s of II/KG 2 attacked a small convoy off the straits of Dover in the mid-afternoon. The escort of thirty Messerschmitt 109s kept two squadrons of RAF fighters away and just two of the German bombers returned with lightly wounded crew members.

It was not until 7 July that there was a marked increase along the length and breadth of Great Britain but with the main effort again being against a convoy sailing from west to east along the Channel. It must have been clear to the RAF that convoys were the *Luftwaffe's* chosen prey and on this day RAF casualties had been high (seven fighters lost and four pilots

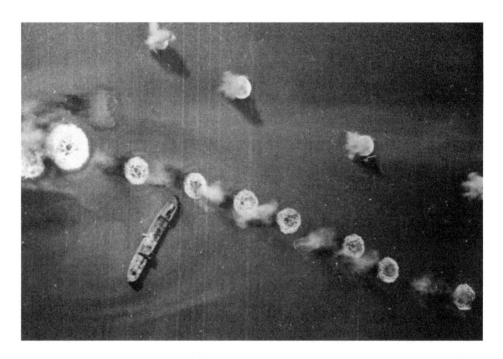

Another success – what is believed to be the sinking of the Kolga *by Uffz Robert Ciuraj, 4/KG 51 on 4 July 1940.* (Ciuraj)

Uffz Ciuraj and his crew of 4/KG 51. (Ciuraj)

The Do 17 of Ofw Hans Wolff of KG 2 (second from right, seen as a POW in Canada later in the war) was damaged in combat off Dover on 4 July 1940; coincidentally the officer to his right, Hptm Alfred Kindler, collected him by car from where he landed later that day. (Wolff)

killed) whilst no bombers had been lost in the convoy attack. The day after was not much better with the *Kanalkampffuehrer* (literally Channel Bomber Leader) *Oberst* Johannes Fink's Dornier 17s having another go at another convoy. The scene was setting fast.

The Dornier 17s of III/KG 2 continued where they had left off by attacking convoy BREAD on the afternoon of 10 July 1940. The day after, it was the turn of yet another convoy and the harbours of Portland and Portsmouth (the former receiving the attention of *Stukas*, the latter Heinkel 111s). The latter attack could have been partly responsible for what happened the following afternoon. The Heinkel 111s of KG 55 had been tasked on this daylight raid and were also to attack Cardiff by night on 12 July and one of the *Geschwader's* Heinkels had been sent out to have a look:

Feldwebel **Heinz Kalina,** *Stab*/**KG 55**

We started around midday from Villacoublay near Paris for a reconnaissance flight over southern England. The weather was fine. Suddenly, near Portsmouth at about 6,000m altitude, we were attacked by about a dozen Hurricanes and we were badly hit. The starboard engine cut out and we had to land. Badly wounded, we were taken prisoner.

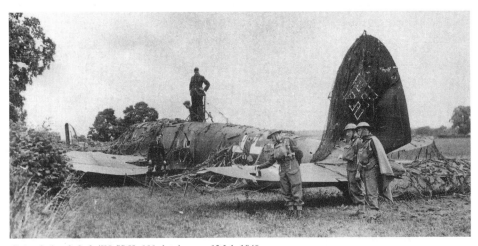

Sitting duck – the Stab/KG 55 *He 111 shot down on 12 July 1940.*

Heinz Kalina's account does not reveal the carnage that the Hurricanes of 43 Squadron must have inflicted on this lone, relatively undefended German bomber. For those RAF pilots involved, it must have been a simple 'kill'. However, an eyewitness on the ground gives a better idea as to what happened:

Alexander McKee

With one engine spluttering and banging, it came towards a field near the village of Southwick; wheels up, it passed over a hedge and went skidding and bumping wildly across a ploughed field coming to a stop 50 yards from a public house... The observer, shot through the head, lay dead across the bombsight. A subaltern from one of the forts on Portsdown Hill took the surrender of the crew about an hour after they had come down – owing to the winding country lanes, it took some time to find the crash[1]

The Heinkel was painted grey and green on top, light greenish blue below; the *Geschwader* crest was a red griffon with blue wings on a shield...

I crawled in through a small hatch on the port side and walked up to the nose... I settled down in the pilot's seat and tried out the controls and then had a look at the instrument panel: a gyro, larger than ours, artificial horizon, Lorenz indicator for blind flying with kicker and one neon light only and most interesting of all, a vertical compass with no grid wires or north seeking needle. Instead a miniature aeroplane pointing the bearing...

I got into the front gunner's position – the nose was entirely perspex, now rather blood-spattered. There was a trap door in the floor where he lay when firing the gun. I slid back the trap door revealing a blood-drenched bombsight and compass. The blood must have pumped out – every cranny was thickly saturated with it...

Convoy attacks continued on 13 and 14 July when the RAF suffered at the hands of the escorting German single-engined fighters. It was a different matter when the German bombers were escorted by just the twin-engined Messerschmitt 110s.

Poor weather had again made itself felt on 14 July and for the next four days German bombers did stray over and around Great Britain but for a number of crews, the bad weather did not protect them:

Oberleutnant Ottmar Hollman, 2/KG 26

On 15 July 1940, I started out on my mission at about 1000 hrs from Kristiansand, Norway. The sky was blue until I reached the middle of the North Sea. Then there was an unbroken layer of cloud beneath me. I was flying at about 2,000m; the wind was from the south-west.

---

[1] The dazed German crew were captured by 37 year-old Samuel Brown and the landlord of the 'Horse and Jockey' public house with the aid of a toy pistol. Interest in the crash and the exploits of the captors resulted in many visitors and "a fortnight's supply of beer [was] sold in just one night".

I had calculated that shortly before the British coast, I should descend through the cloud and orientate myself. I came out of the cloud at 200m or 300m and at first saw only the sea below me. After a short time, however, I reached the coast. Here the cloud was solid and was only 100m up. It was very difficult to fix one's position. My *Beobachter* [*Uffz* Erich Walz] made out that we were north of our target. The target was an airfield just north of the Firth of Forth where night fighters were reported to have been based[2]. So, I flew southwards and the cloud base got lower and lower and I was just above sea level. I can still remember quite clearly that there was a lighthouse on my right

The North Sea as seen from the cockpit of a KG 26 He 111. (Zimmer)

Oblt *Hollmann (front centre)*. (Hollmann)

hand side and I felt that I could reach out and touch it. Soon, however, we could see absolutely nothing as the clouds came down to sea level. I was forced to abandon this approach. I pulled up into the clouds and took a course for the secondary target – Aberdeen Harbour. But here too, I saw nothing because of the covering clouds and mist. I began to consider whether I should at once return to Kristiansand or to try once again to reach the airfield. I took the latter course and flew south into the clouds, hoping for better visibility as the wind was coming from the south west and that I could get a visual fix and reach the target that way.

At the time, I was well aware that my flight was being tracked by British ground stations and that with an improvement in the weather, I would have to reckon with Spitfires. The weather gave me a feeling of security – after an attack, I could vanish back into the clouds.

[2] With an increase in night missions, the *Luftwaffe* had already learned what effect a potent night fighter force could have. However, their intelligence was not good – no night fighter base existed.

Then, suddenly, the clouds became a little thinner and the cloud base rose to about 100m. I climbed in order to fly immediately below the clouds so that if in danger of attack, I could vanish. However, it was already too late because the next second, two Spitfires attacked...

Pilot Officer James Morton, Yellow Section, 'A' Flight, 603 Squadron

I think that he was very unlucky to get downed as we only had quite a short burst each with quite a lot of deflection. I think that it was almost certainly Dudley [Plt Off Dudley Stewart-Clarke] who did the damage though it could have possibly been me who hit his port engine as I remember thinking at the time that I had made rather a cock of it and missed him to port. I take it that it was the rear gunner who was killed – they seemed to have very little protection which was just as well as some of them were very good shots. I got a lot of bullet holes a few days later from another Heinkel 111 and was extremely lucky to get home.

Oberleutnant Ottmar Hollman

...My starboard engine was hit and the starboard wing was riddled with hundreds of holes, one man dead and another wounded in the upper part of the thigh. The radio was wrecked. My immediate and instinctive reaction was a sharp turn to port in order to vanish into the clouds again. I then saw two Spitfires fly past.

This all happened in a few seconds and then I was back into the clouds. First we jettisoned our bombs. I switched off the starboard engine and successfully feathered the propeller. Thick plumes of smoke came out of the engine and the oil temperature rose to the point of the engine seizing.

My port engine was running quite normally and all instrument indications were normal. I was flying on instruments on just the port engine and intended to return to Kristiansand. I had all the dead weight such as the guns thrown out and tried to gain height. After twenty minutes I succeeded in getting to 800m. Even I was convinced I could reach Norway. Then it happened – the port engine failed! I immediately put the nose down to gain speed – over the intercom, I told the crew we were ditching. I came out of the cloud at 100m and saw below me the white caps of the restless sea. I then landed wheels up in the water. I tried to touch down tail first – I succeeded and set the aircraft down with a great deal of noise. For a split second, I could see nothing but the water around me and I thought this was the end. The cockpit and I then surfaced again. I opened the upper window and climbed out. I ran back over the fuselage in order to help my crew out. I got them and the dinghy out at the rear – there were four of us as the dead man [*Ogefr* Walter Reinhardt] remained in the plane. The dinghy was successfully inflated by a compressed air bottle – fortunately it was undamaged (even today, I'm still grateful to the two British pilots for that!).

We had barely got into the dinghy when the He 111 put its nose down and vanished into the sea, the tail nearly taking us with it. It was suddenly very quiet. We bobbed up and down in isolation on the waves, up to our navels in water. We had three paddles at our disposal and I told my crew that I didn't think we could reach Norway but we could reach the British coast if we put all our strength into it.

We finally landed two or three days later. I cannot remember where exactly. We had sighted land then were picked up in a state of total exhaustion by two friendly Scottish fishermen about a mile off shore. I calculated that we had crashed into the sea 50 to 80 kilometres off the coast. By our own efforts, but also I suspect as a result of a particularly favourable current, we were driven far to the north. The days spent in the dinghy, the spiritual, mental and physical events and experiences are a different story...

The RAF Dyce Station Record Book noted they were landed at Fraserburgh on 17 July and had spent fifty hours at sea, attributing their survival to regular dinghy and ditching practice back in Norway!

The bad weather continued for the next two days with only isolated or sporadic attacks occurring. An improvement on 18 July allowed the *Luftwaffe* to increase the number of reconnaissance flights and incursions by lone bombers. However, on 19 July the weather improved sufficiently for an attack by *Stukas* against Portland and Dover and, curiously, Heinkel 115 seaplanes to lay mines in the Thames Estuary. RAF losses outweighed *Luftwaffe* losses on this day, not helped by the massacre of 141 Squadron's Boulton Paul Defiants by Messerschmitt 109s of III/JG 51.

On the night of 19/20 July, an unusual loss occurred when a Focke Wulf 200 *Condor* was shot down by anti-aircraft guns off Hartlepool. The *Luftwaffe* had felt confident enough to commit one of its four-engined bombers to mine-laying tasks close to the British Coast but this loss and another, lost a few days later, would cause them to change their tactics and to commit the vulnerable *Condor* to missions further away from enemy territory.

20 July saw a number of combats and German incursions which included the shooting down of two more Heinkel 59 seaplanes and an attack on another convoy which resulted in the RAF fighters successfully bouncing the German formation from out of the sun. For the RAF, the day was a vast improvement on the previous days and must have been a considerable morale boost for the RAF fighter pilots.

Sunday 21 July was a much quieter day and German bombers were committed against a convoy sailing west. However, for two German reconnaissance crews, this particular Sunday was memorable:

Oberleutnant Friedrich Karl Runde, 4(F)/14

On 21 July 1940, myself and [*Fw*] Willi Baden, my *Bordfunker*, took off from Villacoublay airfield near Paris. According to the weather forecast, we could expect clear skies and were ordered to fly a high altitude reconnaissance (at about 8,000m) and had some heavy photographic equipment installed in our plane. Before crossing the Channel, we landed at Cherbourg to refuel and then headed for the British Isles flying extremely low, between 10m and 50m, so as to avoid radar, and finally climbed to altitude only shortly before the British Coast. However, we found that there were clouds at 2,000m so we couldn't use our high-altitude photographic equipment so decided to undertake reconnaissance just using our eyes. However, it seemed useless and we returned to Cherbourg. We noticed just one enemy aircraft...

Flying Officer John Wray, No 1 Flying Training School

I was an instructor on the Advanced Training Squadron and on 21 July 1940, I was detailed to give an Instrument Flying Test to a pupil who, I think, was a Royal Marine [Lt Churchill]. For instrument flying, the pupil sat in the back cockpit of the Fairey Battle under what we called a Blind Flying Hood which covered the cockpit. This allowed the instructor to have a better all round view from the front where, apart from his instructional duties, he was also acting as a safety pilot avoiding collision or near misses with other aircraft.

We took off and headed towards Southampton, though I would be giving my pupil an instruction to turn 90° to avoid setting off the Southampton air raid sirens. I was allowing him to settle down before turning and we were at about 2,000ft. Suddenly, an Me 110 slid past us on the starboard side at about 100 to 200 yards. I had never seen an Me 110 up until this moment and had it not had a big black cross on the fuselage, I might have thought it was one of the many strange aircraft that flew out of Boscombe Down at that time.

He was overtaking us on a parallel course. I did a double take, not expecting to see German fighters so far west. In fact, the thought of encountering them at all was never in my mind so it is perhaps not surprising that I did nothing initially.

When he had got to about two o'clock to me, the rear gunner opened fire and there was a loud bang on my Battle. Fortunately, there was a lot of fluffy cloud above me and so I slammed open the throttle, entered the cloud and headed north west on the supposition that his range would preclude him following me for long.

Having reached some degree of safety, my two priorities were firstly to escape and secondly to try and find out what damage had been done to my aircraft. The pupil was quite unaware of what was happening as he was under the hood. Communication was by Gosport Tube which, on the Battle, was obviously quite long and therefore required one to shout a bit. Informing him was low on my priorities though it did not occur to me at the time that he might have been what the bullet(s) hit!

Very soon, my first priority was overtaken by the second because my engine started to run very rough. Looking at the oil pressure gauge, I noticed the pressure dropping and the coolant gauge showed a rapid rise in temperature. It was clear that my engine was not going to keep going for much longer.

I decided to leave the cloud and hoped that the Me 110 had given up the chase. We came out just west of Warminster where I informed my pupil of what had occurred. My engine was now close to stopping altogether so it was clear that I would not make one of the five airfields that stretched north from Salisbury.

Although from the air Salisbury Plain looks fairly benign and flat, it does of course comprise large humps and hollows, shell holes and wooded areas, all a deterrent to a successful landing. When night flying, we on the Advanced Training Squadron had to teach landing on a dummy deck. This required a flare path comprising pillar lights and other equipment found on an aircraft carrier which gave quite a bright display on the airfield at night so against the threat of bombing, we transferred our night flying to a field at Shrewton on Salisbury Plain. It was in this field that I decided to attempt a landing.

I made my approach wheels down and then my engine stopped and it was clear that I wasn't going to make Shrewton so I raised the undercarriage and crash-landed on the side of a hill just short of

A crash-landed Fairey Battle. (Camp)

Shrewton. We skidded along and my port wing hit a grain silo. My head jerked forward and banged against the windscreen. I was not knocked out but was rather dazed.

The pupil, who was unhurt, came round and helped me out and sat me on a wing. He then ran to a nearby farmhouse where, after a few minutes, a woman appeared carrying a pot of tea. She and others looked after me until the ambulance and fire tender arrived about thirty minutes later. I was taken to Sick Quarters where I was examined by the Medical Officer. A few days later I was admitted to the RAF Hospital at Torquay.

The two German aircrew returned thinking nothing more of this incident but for them, the day was still not over:

Oberleutnant Friedrich Karl Runde

...At Cherbourg, the weather turned really fine and, after refuelling, we thought we would make another try despite having no orders telling us to do this. Coming back to the 'Other Side', the situation seemed not to have changed and as we didn't want to come back again without a result, we penetrated deeper. We then ran into a training aircraft and shot it down. Both of us felt very sad when we noticed the parachute of the young fellow didn't open.[3]

Oblt *Runde's Bf 110 after its repair...*

...and repaint. (via Wray)

We turned back and then Willi Baden noticed fighters heading for us. I thought we would be able to escape into the clouds but these turned out to be some kind of summer fog which was dissipating with the sun rising higher. So that is how they got us. Both engines hit and despite managing to get away from them, I had to make a belly landing as both engines had seized.

---

[3] This was Acting Leading Airman J A Seed Royal Navy who, whilst flying solo in a Hawker Hart serial K6485 of No 1 Flying Training School, was sadly killed near Old Sarum airfield.

Pilot Officer Charles Davis, Red 2, 'A' Flight, 238 Squadron

Red Section was detailed to Raid X48 and took off at 1005 hrs, landed at 1035 hrs. I was Red 2 and we were ordered into line astern when enemy aircraft was seen at 6,000ft, ten miles south-east of base [Middle Wallop in Hampshire]. Enemy aircraft turned sharply east and Red Leader [Flt Lt Donald Turner] ordered Red 3 [Plt Off John Wigglesworth] and myself into cloud. I went other side of the cloud and got in a half attack when enemy aircraft came out. It was a running engagement with the enemy aircraft adopting most peculiar tactics. I fired short bursts whenever enemy aircraft came out of cloud. Finally it disappeared into a large cloud with smoke pouring from the starboard engine. Accuracy of aim was difficult owing to the bumpy conditions. Enemy aircraft did the most unusual manoeuvres – stall turns, half rolls etc.

Oblt Runde succeeded in crash-landing his Messerschmitt 110 so well that it was recovered by the RAF and by using parts from other captured Messerschmitt 110s, flew again. Curiously, John Wray inspected this aircraft later in the war not knowing until fifty-two years after the event that this aircraft was the one that had shot him down!

Nearly four hours later, the same three Hurricane pilots were in action again against another German aircraft from the same reconnaissance unit:

Leutnant Georg Thiel, 4(F)/14

4(F)/14 served as tactical reconnaissance under the VIth Army (von Kluge) during the Battle of France. From the beginning of July 1940, we were out at the disposal of V *Fliegerkorps* (*Generalleutnant* Robert Ritter von Griem).

On 21 July 1940, we started from the airport of Villacoublay, refuelled at Cherbourg and crossed the Channel at a height of between 5,500m and 6,500m. This was the absolute ceiling of our (worn out) Do 17.

After crossing the coast, I began filming as ordered. However, somewhere north of Southampton we got our first Spitfire [sic]/Hurricane salvo and dived down to hide in clouds. However, the oxygen system had been hit and the port engine had stopped and was burning.

The 'worn out Do 17 M' similar to that operated by 4(F)/14.

Georg Thiel's Do 17 in flames after the crash-landing. (via Cornwell)

Fw Bohnen about to be taken away to hospital. (via Cornwell)

We lost height, tumbling down out of the clouds and then got hit again. *Uffz* Werner, the rear gunner, was clearly not able to ward off the RAF fighters with a single MG 15 machine gun. The pilot, *Fw* Bohnen, was unconscious for some time but anyhow we managed a crash landing and to get out of our 'bird' which was by then in flames.

It was two Sections of Hurricanes from 238 Squadron that had pounced on this unfortunate reconnaissance aircraft and shared its destruction:

Sergeant Leslie Batt, Yellow 3, 'A' Flight, 238 Squadron

First attack was carried out by Red Section [the same pilots that had shot down the Messerschmitt 110 from the same German unit earlier that day], line astern. Enemy then dived into cloud. I went south and under cloud and sighted enemy and attacked astern. Port engine was stopped and my fire concentrated on the starboard engine and enemy lost height rapidly. I broke away once and Red 1 attacked. I attacked again and stopped the starboard engine and then watched enemy crash-land without wheels. It then caught fire.

This quiet phase continued until 24 July. However, during the hours of darkness, the *Luftwaffe* was increasing its night missions, mainly mine laying in order to seal off ports and harbours in preparation for Operation *SEELOEWE,* the invasion of Great Britain. Such nocturnal forays were a nuisance for the embryonic RAF night fighter force. Nevertheless, on the night of 23/24 July 1940, Fg Off Glynn Ashfield of the Fighter Interception Unit with Plt Off Geoff Morris and Sgt Reg Leyland carried out the first ground radar assisted interception, claiming to have shot down a Dornier 17 into the Channel five miles south of Bognor Regis. The RAF would have to wait until 19 November 1940 for the first airborne radar assisted kill. The same night, another German bomber was lost but not to the guns of the RAF:

Hauptmann Volkmar Zenker, 2/KG 40

I was flying a Focke Wulf 200 *Condor* and we had started at Lueneburg in Germany on 23 July 1940. We refuelled at Brest and there we were loaded with two tons of magnetic mines. Our orders were to drop these in the shipping lanes at Belfast Harbour. We only managed to drop three mines before disaster struck.

I had descended from 1,800m over the Irish Sea. The engines were idling as I was hoping not to be detected. During the first part of the

An FW 200 of I/KG 40. (Wachtel)

A Condor of I/KG 40 over the Irish Sea – the low altitude left little room for error. (Hintze)

mission, I was flying at 100m but then I opened the throttles very slowly hoping to lose more height and to get rid of the last mine which was stuck in its holder. I succeeded but by now we were at 15m altitude. When I opened the throttles further, the two port engines stopped and the plane banked suddenly. In order to avoid the wingtip hitting the water, I stopped the starboard engines and ditched. The plane had not run out of fuel, by the way, but there had been an air blockage in the fuel lines caused by the long glide with idled engines.

After the ditching, the plane sank pretty fast. The *Bordfunker* [*Uffz* Heinz Hoecker] and *Bordschuetz* [*Gefr* Leo Hohmann] were able to leave by the main door and got out the dinghy…

Unteroffizier Heinz Hoecker, 2/KG 40

Because of the impact, the plane was full of water very quickly. In the cockpit I saw my comrades in the water looking for an exit. As a result of this, I swam to the exit at the back, called my comrade Hohmann and told him to get the dinghy ready. I pushed open the door and got out. In the pitch dark, I called to the others. All that I had in the dinghy was a distress signal in a tin and the dinghy was not fully inflated…

Hauptmann Volkmar Zenker

...My co-pilot [*Fw* Willi Andreas], *Bordmechaniker* [*Uffz* Rudolf Wagner] and myself were caught in the cockpit because the escape door jammed. I tried to send them aft but we were already under water. I dived through the aircraft and managed to get to where the water had risen close to the door. I waited for the other two for a moment and then joined the two who were swimming with the inflated dinghy. We expected the missing crew members, who were uninjured and able to swim, to join us but I think that they had panicked and had tried to leave by the hatch at the top of the cockpit or through windows which were too small. Because we did not know how long the Condor would float, we did not dare go back in. In any case, after a few minutes it sank.

The dinghy proved to be our next problem. The self-inflating mechanism did not work and the CO_2 bottle was empty. We had to pump the dinghy up by using bellows which took us nearly three quarters of an hour. One oar was lost during the hubbub so we could not reach the coast under cover of darkness although we tried hard, knowing that we were not too far from the Southern Ireland border...

Unteroffizier Heinz Hoecker

...In the morning, we noticed a ship on the horizon which was heading towards us. I realised that *Hptm* Zenker had exhausted himself and so I took command. In case of capture, I reminded them that we had been told that we should say we had been on a reconnaissance flight with a Do 17. Then I searched *Hptm* Zenker's pockets and threw overboard everything that could be useful to the British. The ship came towards us – the crew stood on deck with rifles loaded; the officer had a pistol. We were ordered "Hands up!" – I had already fired off two signal flares and thrown the pistol and the rest of the flares overboard. One at a time we climbed up the ladder and after we had been searched, the sailors gave us some rum – I was grateful for that because by then, I had had enough.

On our way into Belfast, I saw a ship at the bottom of the harbour. When I asked how it had sunk, I was told it had caught fire[4]...

The Germans, when interrogated, stuck to their story as proved by the diary entry for Flag Officer Belfast:

On the morning of 24 July, three German airmen were rescued from a rubber float by the anti-submarine trawler HMS *Paynter* close to Blackhead

[4] The SS *Troutpool* had sunk on 20 July, the victim of a magnetic mine dropped by the *Luftwaffe* the night before.

and were landed at Larne. When interrogated, they stated that their machine, an He 111, had crashed in the early hours of the morning during a reconnaissance flight over the area with the loss of two lives.

For the remainder of the month, the pattern was the same – attacks on convoys and coastal targets, interspersed with fighter sweeps, both of which were keenly opposed by the RAF. At this time, the much feared *Stuka* was still making its presence felt, albeit on a smaller scale than in the Battle of France:

Oberleutnant Klaus Ostmann, 8/StG 1

I was posted to StG1 in Bretagne in July 1940. Coming from Koeln, I flew over the first traces of the battles in France. Having seen the destruction, I can understand what our *Stukas* could achieve and had to achieve. I phoned my new *Geschwader* from the airfield at Compiègne and asked them to pick me up. The phone line was excellent – a direct line from Compiègne to the Channel coast! Later that day, a liaison aircraft took me to StG1 – on our way, we circled over destroyed traffic junctions, bridges and buildings.

The *Geschwader* had its HQ in a château near Caen. There I reported to the *Kommodore*, *Maj* Walter Hagen – the first holder of the *Ritterkreuz* I have ever faced. I am posted to 8/StG1 – the *Gruppen Kommandeur* was *Hptm* Helmut Mahlke, my *Staffelkapitaen* was *Oblt* Guenter Skambraks. We were billeted in a villa in Falaise – in our opinion a little bit dilapidated.

Oblt *Klaus Ostmann – the nautical flavour of the badge is because III/StG 1 was originally designated I(Stuka)/186 and destined to operate from an aircraft carrier.* (Ostmann)

The airfield is only a narrow strip, completely surrounded by bushes – well camouflaged but aeronautically very difficult. I am assigned Ju 87 'Gustav' – J9+GK.

For missions, we moved to the forward airfield of Theville near Cherbourg. My first mission was from there on 25 July. The *Gruppe* crossed the Channel, climbing to 4,500m. Below us the shimmering sea. It was difficult to estimate your own height and very often you thought that you would plunge into the water when you pointed the aircraft's nose down. Then in the distance a dark line appears – the English coast. Flying over the water had strained our nerves and this feeling was now intensifying.

Stukas *of* Stab/*StG1 over the Channel.* (Grahl)

Very often we were able to listen to the enemy's radio traffic which tells us that their fighters have already taken off. Well, we saw them high above us before we attacked. They looked like birds of prey waiting to pounce. It was an uneasy feeling. For good reasons, our own radio traffic had been kept to essentials. Our target was a convoy near Portland Bill. I had not seen anything – it is difficult to spot a ship at sea level – but the formation had already started to dive. After all the tension, a feeling of relief comes over you. You are determined to get the target and there was only one aim – to hit the target. One does not notice the *Flak* which shoots by and bursts either side. Now I have picked the target, dropped the bombs and by taking wild evasive action, I follow the formation which is already joining up again. But now our machine guns are hammering and I can see the eight trails of a Spitfire's tracer bullets trying to reach me again and again, like ghostly fingers. A few times, you can hear a crack but the plane's fuselage is wide and if nothing vital has been hit, the faithful *Stuka* can take a lot of hits like that. I have succeeded in shaking off the last attacker and without any problems, I landed on the advanced airfield. All of us have come under heavy fire. The *Staffelkapitaen*'s aircraft has received a hit in the oil tank and only with great difficulty could he find his way home. Everything was smeared with oil and so he had to make an emergency landing at a small airfield near Cherbourg. I led the formation back.

However, for the last six days of July 1940 the weather yet again continued to play its part in limiting German air operations. Of interest were the attacks undertaken by the specialised fighter-bomber unit *Erprobungsgruppe* 210. This unit had flown its first mission on 13 July 1940 and during the weeks that followed, had flown a number of missions for the loss of just two Messerschmitt 110s and their crews. One pilot kept a diary of his time with the unit only for it to fall into the RAF's hands when he was shot down and killed on 15 August 1940. Still in existence today in the RAF's Air Historical Branch, the diary entry for 29 July 1940 gives a clear idea of what it was like flying fighter-bomber missions against convoys and how the writer almost became the unit's third combat loss of the war:

Leutnant Erich Beudel, 1/*ErprGr* 210

My second war flight. A Dornier 17 has reported an English convoy of sixty ships sailing northwards from the Thames Estuary. *ErprGr* 210 takes off from St Omer at 1635 hrs; eight Bf 110 bombers of 2 *Staffel* and three Bf 110 C-6s of 1 *Staffel* fly over Dunkirk and meet thirty Bf 110 C-2s of ZG 26 who are acting as fighter escort on account of probable clear skies. Thirty minutes flying northwards at sea level, then ten minutes climbing towards the clouds at 4,500ft. The bombers attack at 1715 hrs just off Orfordness... At the same time two Hurricane squadrons approach from the left, one below us and one above. The Chief makes a tight climbing turn and I fall back a bit, then it is a flat out climb. I have to abandon the idea of getting on the tail of one of the lower Englishmen because the upper formation comes at me from above and the right. Straightening up for a moment, I fire a short burst at a singleton who comes past me but he doesn't fall. The next moment my gunner shouts something unintelligible and a hail of fire rips through my whole aircraft from the right. The intercom packs up completely but in another two seconds, I am in the clouds. I circle to take stock and decide to beat it. Above the clouds I come across three Bf 110s, the Chief and two aircraft of ZG 26 who want to attack again. I feel inclined to join them but my gunner calls out "I am wounded; let's go home!" So I head for the Dutch Coast. My trim tabs are shot away and oil spurts from the starboard engine. At last at 1805 hrs I land at St Omer with tyres shot through. My aircraft has suffered about thirty hits; one shot struck an ammunition drum and exploded all the cartridges. Other hits in engines, cockpit, wings and landing flaps. Result of the attack – one hit on a 1,000 ton ship and one hit on an 8,000 ton ship. ZG 26 bagged four Hurricanes without loss.[5]

Very little changed for the last two days of the month and it appeared that the RAF had survived the first month of the Battle of Britain even though, as yet, it had not received the undivided and unwelcome attention of the

---

[5] The attack was against Convoy CAT which was defended by just one RAF squadron. 151 Squadron attacked in two separate flights (hence Beudel thought two squadrons) and suffered just two Hurricanes damaged.

Luftwaffe. For the *Luftwaffe*, its bombers had little chance so far to attack en masse, targets being more suitable to attacks by smaller formations or by *Stukas*, easily defended by its fighters. Nevertheless, German bomber and reconnaissance aircraft had roamed the length and breadth of the United Kingdom and its surrounding waters, normally with impunity, and at the same time had found that there was no sign of any major weakness in the RAF's defences either by day or, it now seemed, by night. However, August 1940 would see changes to the German battle plan and the RAF fighter pilots being severely tested.

CHAPTER 2

The Pace Quickens,
August 1940

From the viewpoint of German bomber crews, the first seven days of August
1940 were, because of poor weather conditions, an anti-climax. What effort
was expended was done so against convoys or harbours but of note was an
attack against the Boulton Paul Aircraft Factory at Norwich on the afternoon
of 1 August. Four 250 kilogram bombs slightly damaged the factory and nearby
railway yard, setting fire to a timber yard and injuring in excess of forty
civilians. Despite the close proximity of the fighter airfield at Coltishall, the
attacker got away unscathed.

Mine laying and attacks on harbour installations took place that night and
on the nights that followed. Of particular interest was that the *Luftwaffe*
reported dropping 300 kilograms of leaflets in and around London detailing
the *Fuehrer*'s latest speech on the night of 2/3 August – other major cities
received similar deliveries on subsequent nights. Also, despite the weather,
German reconnaissance aircraft were very active and in addition to maritime
targets were also making particular notes of airfields and the RAF aircraft
observed there – perhaps the *Luftwaffe* was considering a change in target?
By the middle of the month, it would be clear as to what the *Luftwaffe*'s
targets were.

8 August would see a dramatic change in the level of air activity. At 1930 hrs
on 7 August, German sources had reported a large convoy of an unknown
number of ships 10 kilometres south of Dungeness headed west. Early the next
morning, this convoy, now totalling in the region of eighteen ships, was
reported south east of the Isle of Wight. Convoy CW9, code named PEEWIT,
was about to receive the undivided attention of the *Luftwaffe*'s bombers.

Oberleutnant Klaus Ostmann, 8/StG 1

Another flight to the forward airfield was not in vain. There we were,
standing by, lying on our deck chairs. On the radio, you could hear the
popular hit song *Auf dem Dach Welt* [On Top of the World]. Even today I
can still hear this catchy tune. Suddenly there was the order *Grosseinsatz* –
big attack. We were briefed to attack a well protected convoy 10 miles
south-west of the Isle of Wight which had been attacked by E-boats at
night. Take off time from Theville was 0930 hrs.

243

Again, the long flight over the water was quite nerve-racking but the complete *Geschwader* was in action and the sky was full of *Stukas*. This gave you a reassuring feeling. This time I saw more than I did on my first mission – the smoke trails were the characteristic mark of our target, the convoy. We are the last *Staffel* and so our job was the hardest. We would be longer in the range of fire, we would be the last to fly back and a tempting target for the enemy fighters – the Devil takes the hindmost!

Now we are over the target. Down we go from a high altitude. I had to correct the bomb run the whole time because the ships are spreading out – zigzagging wildly.

I think I stayed over the target too long and was separated from the rest of the *Staffel*. Flying wild evasive manoeuvres, I tried to catch up with the formation. There was a big cumulus cloud ahead. I flew into the cloud and think myself safe but hardly have I left it than enemy fighters attacked from above. They knew that something had to come out of this cloud and so they were able to pick me off. There was a loud bang in my plane. An indescribable blow hit my right arm and knee. The aircraft nose dived but then I regained consciousness. Using my left arm, I pulled the plane out of the dive just above sea level. Spasmodically, a stream of blood came out of my knee. As good as I can, I applied a tourniquet to my right leg with the laces of my map board. Now *Oblt* Karl Lion, *Ia* of III/StG 1 was flying next to me and encouraged me to hold on. The way back takes about fifty minutes – an eternity. I was really in a bad way. As soon as I see the French coast, all my energies came back. At full speed I approached the airfield. I brought the plane down, it bounced a few times and then skidded to the left – the undercarriage had also been hit. Then I lost consciousness – when I came to, I was on my way to a field hospital at Valognes near Cherbourg. I did not return to StG 1 until August 1941.

The sole RAF squadron to intercept this attack was the Hurricane-equipped 145 Squadron. Claiming two destroyed, nine probably destroyed and five damaged, to tie down who for certain damaged *Oblt* Ostmann's *Stuka* is difficult but the following RAF pilot could be considered as the likely protagonist:

Oblt *Klaus Ostmann returns to the front,*
exactly a year after being wounded.
(Ostmann)

Squadron Leader John Peel, 'A' Flight, 145 Squadron

...I attacked another Ju 87 some distance behind with a beam attack but guns stopped after a two second burst. Enemy aircraft dropped to sea level and flew off in a right-hand turn, unsteady and probably badly damaged.

Stukas *of I/StG 1 off the English south coast.* (Grahl)

Heavily escorted, the attack was not in fact carried out by all of StG 1 but twenty-nine *Stukas* of I/StG 3 together with twenty-eight from III/StG 1. After losing just one *Stuka* from III/StG 1, it was the turn of forty-nine *Stukas* from I and III/StG 2 to attack the convoy again just after lunch time – this time no *Stukas* were lost. Still, the convoy sailed on so it was attacked a third time by twenty-two *Stukas* from *Hptm* Paul Werner Hozzel's I/StG 1 and an undisclosed number of *Stukas* from *Hptm* Walter Sigel's I/StG 3 and *Hptm* Waldemar Plewig's II/StG 77. It was hoped that this time, the *Stukas* would annihilate the convoy:

Hauptmann Waldemar Plewig, *Gruppen Kommandeur* II/StG 77

In the area around Caen, several *Geschwader* were ready for action on 8 August 1940. The results of reconnaissance flights reported a very large convoy near the Isle of Wight but because of apparent bad weather, the *Oberbefehlshaber der Luftwaffe* did not give the okay for action. With the permission of the *Geschwader* I went up in my *Gruppe's* Do 17 to make my own reconnaissance and found that an attack against clearly recognisable shipping targets was certainly possible. So, after midday, we finally received clearance for three *Gruppen* of *Stukas* to go into action. Besides the *Gruppen* commanded by *Hptms* Hozzel and Sigel, my *Gruppe* was to assemble at 1600 hrs over Cherbourg and to carry out a large scale attack.

My *Gruppe* started as ordered but noticed that one of the other *Gruppen* was not ready for take off. Climbing steadily, we proceeded to the gathering point. As we approached the coast, I realised that the third *Gruppe* was already hanging over the Channel above us, long before the stated time. Our own fighters must have split up as only a few Bf 109s and Bf 110s were to be seen. The majority of the fighter escort must have flown to the target area with the *Gruppe* of early starters. Only this could explain why my *Gruppe*, when approaching the convoy, flew right into the arms of the RAF fighters which had been lured up by the first *Gruppe*; our escort then split up, the first *Gruppe* already returning with the escort whilst my far weaker escort had to fight against overwhelming odds.

Under the circumstances, there was no turning back and I ordered the three *Staffeln* to attack. I, with the reinforced *Stabs Kette*, waited until the end. As we could see more and more

Hptm *Waldemar Plewig – he was awarded the* Ritterkreuz *whilst in captivity.* (Plewig)

enemy fighters appearing above us, I decided not to climb up to the usual altitude and started the attack from about 4,000m. After the three *Staffeln* had attacked their targets, I chose mine and went into a dive and released my bombs from about 600m. The Spitfires and Hurricanes dived with us but we were able to observe some near misses. It did not matter so much about direct hits as our bombs were fitted with delayed fuses so that they didn't explode on impact but after penetrating the water, thus causing a strong pressure wave.

Now I attempted to throw off my adversaries by irregular flying at sea level – we always flew off that way as it gave fighters less of a chance to hit us. However, during the descent, I was repeatedly shot at. My gunner, *Fw* Schauer, fired until he was hit, presumably in the neck and thigh as I noticed a jet of blood. In the meantime, I was hit in the right arm and right calf and had to fly with my left hand. At the same time, the oxygen supply was hit as was a box of ammunition by tracer bullets. When the plane started to show signs of burning on the right side, I decided to bale out. My gunner did not reply over the intercom and I could see him hanging lifelessly in the harness. As he did not react to my order to throw off the canopy and I had levelled off above the water and the plane was well alight, I decided to jump at the last moment. I had failed in my efforts to throw out the gunner – he was certainly dead and I hoped that his body might be washed up somewhere. So, I said goodbye to my companion and friend Schauer.

I must have been low when I jumped and got caught up in the lines. Although it was summer, the sea was rough and I had great difficulty in freeing myself from the harness, being constantly pushed under by the water. My knife was strapped to my right leg and I had to get it with my left hand. When I finally cut myself free of the lines, my parachute was still inflated and I did not know which way I was drifting – either towards France, England or the Atlantic. I managed to get rid of the parachute. Still, I might be lucky and washed up against one of the 'Udet' lifeboats.

The kapok life jacket favoured by Hptm *Plewig and other bomber crews, here worn by* Fw *Robert Ciuraj and* Lt *Bernhard Sartor of 4/KG 51.* (Ciuraj)

For the moment, I was glad that I was wearing a kapok lifejacket which originated from the Merchant Navy and was fitted with a 'Stuart' collar which kept my head well out of the water. It is difficult to describe what happened after. I can only say that during the minutes and hours that I drifted in the water, all my past life passed before me like a kaleidoscope. However, I certainly had the will to live.

When it got dark, I noticed a small ship pass me. My yellow marker dye was still working but who could see this in the heavy swell? Again and again, British and German fighters flew over me and I tried to make myself seen. After four or five hours, a corvette passed close to me. She disappeared but came back and I saw that they were lowering a small boat and I think that two sailors were trying to reach me. After many attempts, they succeeded and threw me a rope which I gripped with my left hand and they heaved me into the boat. Now started a far more difficult phase, namely to get the boat back to the corvette. Several attempts were made and finally they succeeded and a rope was lowered which they thought I could grip. One of the sailors had to tie me to the rope and I was heaved onto the deck. There I had a great reception – to this day, I remember they wanted to feed me on rum and white bread. However, all the sea water I had swallowed had filled me up and when I asked for a bowl, they offered me more rum – I couldn't speak enough English! Anyway, I was very sick and I then felt better and was taken below.

I was admitted to a naval hospital in Portsmouth in the late evening. Here too I was well treated. One of the nurses found a Walther PPK in the back pocket of my trousers – she kept it and asked me not to say anything about it as she wanted it as a souvenir. Later a military chaplain came to see me and then I remember waking up in a small ward surrounded by doctors and nurses. The surgeon was very worried about me – he reminded me of my uncle who was also a doctor. Unfortunately, I was later transferred to a hospital at Woolwich but I shall never forget the Naval Hospital, most of all the people there.

The aim by the *Luftwaffe* to annihilate the convoy almost succeeded – only four ships arrived unscathed at Swanage later that evening, the *Stukas* having sunk seven and damaged another thirteen. The air battle over the convoy had been particularly fierce which enabled the *Stukas* to achieve their success. Despite the RAF claiming to have shot down thirty-three German aircraft, the *Luftwaffe* lost eight *Stukas* with a further seven damaged – the human cost was thirteen aircrew killed, three prisoners of war and seven wounded. Three executive officers were lost – in addition to the *Gruppen Kommandeur* of II/StG 77, *Hptm* Horst-Hennig Schmack, the *Staffel Kapitaen* of 4/StG 77 was killed and *Oblt* Martin Mueller, *Adjutant* of I/StG 3 was taken prisoner. A further nine fighters and seven fighter aircrew were killed. For the RAF, it had been a hard battle – despite the Germans claiming to have shot down forty-seven fighters, only fourteen RAF fighters were lost but, more crucially, twelve pilots were killed.

For the RAF, this had been an ominous start to the month's fighting. The next two days were quiet – in the words of the writer of the *Luftwaffe*

Fuehrungsstab diary: "nothing of particular importance to report." Sporadic attacks were carried out against various minor targets and then, on 11 August, it was the turn of the Junkers 88 to enter the battle en masse.

This time, the target was the harbour and associated installations at Portland. Thirty-eight Junkers 88s from I and II/KG 54 (with two Heinkel 111s as air sea rescue support – obviously a lesson learnt from the 8 August battles) took off at 0935 hrs and reported hits on the oil pipeline, mole, floating dock, loading bridges and railway lines. A fuel storage tank was set on fire and at least two freighters and a destroyer damaged as well as a small ship being sunk in Weymouth harbour. Again, the German fighter escort was massive, forcing the RAF to commit eight fighter squadrons. The German tactics succeeded in drawing many of the RAF fighters away, thus allowing the bombers to reach their target but it did not prevent the loss of four bombers, including that flown by the *Gruppen Kommandeur* of II/KG 54, *Maj* Kurt Leonhardy. Meanwhile, the last actions of this phase of the Battle of Britain were being fought further to the east with attacks against shipping and convoys by a number of *Kampfgeschwadern* and *Erprobungsgruppe* 210.

Overnight, Heinkel 111s of a number of units were in action against harbours, aircraft factories and shipping. A rare nocturnal success was when the *Gruppen Kommandeur* of II/KG 27's Heinkel 111 was hit by anti-aircraft fire and crashed in Dorset – *Maj* Friedrich-Karl Schlichting and his crew, which also included *Maj* Hans-Juergen Brehmer, were all captured. However, it soon became clear as 12 August 1940 progressed that airfields and radar stations were now on the target list.

The first objectives for the day were the radar stations at Dover, Dunkirk, Pevensey and Rye – heavily escorted, *Erprobungsgruppe* 210 succeeded in putting three sites temporarily out of action for no loss to themselves. Shortly afterwards, attacks were carried out by II/KG 2 and another Dornier 17 unit against the airfields of Lympne and Hawkinge with the sole aim of preventing these airfields being used as a fighter base. Lympne was, according to the *Luftwaffe* crews involved, heavily bombed but this did not affect the operational effectiveness of the airfield. Hawkinge, attacked later during the day as well, was operational again within twenty-four hours.

The next major raid appeared on the radar screens further west just before lunchtime. Sixty-three Junkers 88s from all three *Gruppe* of KG 51 lifted off from the airfields of Melun, Orly and Etampes–Montdesir at about 1130 hrs Central European Time. Their targets were Portsmouth Harbour and the radar station at Ventnor on the Isle of Wight. Again, the escort was massive, made up from three different Messerschmitt 110 *Geschwader* and three Messerschmitt 109 *Geschwader*. The RAF response was to throw eight fighter squadrons at the approaching armada and what followed was memorable for many of the German crews involved:

Oberleutnant Werner Luederitz, *Stab*/KG 51

The aircraft of the *Geschwader Stab* were stationed at Orly near Paris, along with II/KG 51. On 11 August 1940, the weather forecast (obtained from the special meteorological units and KG 40) was for good weather for an attack against the British Isles the following day, mainly because of high pressure over the Azores.

On the morning of 12 August, the *Kommodore, Oberst Dr* Hans Fisser, received by telephone from the Chief of *Luftflotte* 3 in Paris, *Generalfeldmarschall* Hugo Sperrle, the order to carry out an attack by all serviceable aircraft against the radar station at Ventnor (south-east Isle of Wight) and the harbour at Portsmouth. The aim was to knock out the radar station and to destroy the harbour facilities, yards, fuel dumps and ships at Portsmouth. The secondary objective was to lure out the British fighters which would be destroyed by our escorting fighters allowing us to establish air superiority over southern England.

The *Kommodore* decided that the *Geschwader Kette* would take part in the attack on the radar station. The bomb load for the attack was either two SC 1,000 kilogram bombs or four 250 kilogram bombs – my aircraft coded 9K+AA was loaded with two 1,000 kilogram bombs.[1]

Werner Luederitz (seen here as a Leutnant*).* (Luederitz)

We rendezvoused over Le Havre at 5,000m altitude and headed for England. After overflying the western half of the Isle of Wight, we turned eastward and split up – *Geschwader Kette* and II *Gruppe* towards Ventnor from the north, whilst I and III *Gruppen* turned towards Portsmouth. We came down at a 70° angle in a loose formation from 4,000m, released the bombs at 1,200m and intended to climb from 800m to transit level and fly home. However, the port engine quickly lost power and stopped – during our dive, we had taken a lot of *Flak* and shrapnel had hit the port engine and interrupted the fuel supply. We remained far behind the formation which was climbing and I took the necessary steps for asymmetric flight (feathering the propeller, trimming

---

[1] The total number of bombs to be dropped by KG 51 were briefed as eight SC 1,000, thirty-six SC 500 and thirty-six SC 250 (SC were thin cased high explosive bombs) in addition to six PC 500 bombs (PC bombs were armour-piercing and used against warships) and four Flam 250 bombs (flammable oil bombs).

Generalfeldmarschall *Hugo Sperrle*. (Wittmann)

Ventnor and its radar station above it as seen by a German aircraft in 1943. (Wenger)

The cockpit armament of a KG 51 Ju 88. (Ciuraj)

and dumping all unnecessary fuel and equipment, except for parachutes and machine guns). We found ourselves alone over the Isle of Wight at about 1,000m flying south and still trying to gain height. There was no sign of our escort – they were in dogfights further north.

Shortly after crossing the coast, we were attacked by three Hurricanes [sic], one after another and all from behind. We could see the bullets hitting our control surfaces – a few shots even went through the cockpit without doing any great damage. However, our impaired flying performance was further affected by damage to the flying controls. The Hurricanes were, of course, much faster and on each attack let off a short burst. 9K+AA was fitted with side machine guns in the cockpit so that we were able to fire at the departing fighters which exposed their undersides. I do not know if we had any success. As a result of evasive manoeuvres, we had lost height very quickly and were, after five or six attacks, about 50m above sea level and expected to ditch.

However, as we had been told that coastal waters around the United Kingdom had been mined in expectation of an invasion, we turned towards land. After further attacks whilst we were very low, I put the aircraft down wheels up. We crashed through hedges and the aircraft burst into flames...

Claims for Junkers 88s by the RAF were many and confused. However, it is likely that Spitfires of 152 Squadron intercepted the Ventnor attackers and one combat report does seem to match with *Oblt* Luederitz's account of the battle:

Sergeant Edmund Shepperd, White 2, 152 Squadron

I was on patrol at 15,000ft when I met a formation of about twelve Junkers 88s. 'A' Flight formed into line astern and did a dive attack onto the formation which split up. I did an astern attack on one Ju 88 with a burst of eight seconds and Plt Off Bayles confirms that the port engine burst into flames... I then attacked another Ju 88 at 4,000ft with full deflection, closing to 100 yards with a burst of four seconds. I did a second attack with a range of 200 yards and finished my ammunition. I followed the aircraft down until it force-landed in a field and burst into flames.

Oberleutnant Werner Luederitz

...Surrounded by flames, I felt that the plane had stopped. I undid my harness, fell out the port side and clawed my way out of the sea of flames. My clothes, parachute and life jacket were burning so I rolled in the grass. I saw the other two crew members – Franz Schad and Adam Nothelfer who had escaped to starboard. Schad had also extinguished his burning clothes but Nothelfer, still in a state of shock, was sitting on the grass, his parachute still burning. I shouted at him to roll in the grass but there was no reaction but Schad, who was nearby, knocked him over and put the flames out. Nothing was to be seen of the *Kommodore*. We moved about 50m away from the burning aircraft and were surrounded by civilians wearing armbands and carrying rifles and

Oberst Dr *Hans Fisser (right)*, Kommodore *of KG 51, killed in action 12 August 1940; the pilot being awarded the Iron Cross,* Oblt *Eberhard Wildermuth of 8/KG 51, was also shot down on 12 August 1940.* (Wildermuth)

a few unarmed men in uniform and members of the public. The aircraft was by now enveloped in flames and we could hear the remaining ammunition exploding.

Schad and myself had second and third degree burns on our faces, hands and throat whilst Nothelfer was also burnt on his back and legs. A little grey haired lady first quietened a hysterical young Army officer who was shouting at us (he wore a beret with a red pom-pom) then tried to dress our wounds. We were taken by ambulance to a small hospital and then, because of the severity of our burns, to a large military hospital near Cowes [Osborne House].

The attack on Ventnor was a success but the radar station was back on line by 15 August 1940. In addition to the loss of the *Geschwader Kommodore* and his crew, *Oblt* Hans-Joachim Flegel and his crew from 6/KG 51 were shot down into the sea off the Isle of Wight. However, as one air battle was taking place over the Isle of Wight, another more bloody battle was taking place over Portsmouth Harbour:

Unteroffizier Karl Zimmermann, 3/KG 51

We were based at Melun – 12 August was a nice sunny day but we were destined not to enjoy it. We got into our aircraft, started our engines and warmed them up for a short while. One 3 *Staffel* aircraft after another took off with a heavy bomb load intended for Portsmouth. Flying between 4,000m and 5,000m, it was quiet – no ship or fighter aircraft were seen. When we got closer to the Isle of Wight, *Flak* bursts appeared below us. However, the closer we got to the target, more and more RAF fighters were seen. Around us – above, below and next to us, things were in turmoil. We had almost arrived at the target when – oh my goodness! – a Spitfire was behind us and there was a bang and the instrument panel was shattered. I have trouble with the controls, the port engine seizes up and the crew is screaming. The *Bordfunker* [*Ogefr* Oskar Hansmann] bleeds from his hand, the *Beobachter* [*Gefr* Theo Dickel] has been hit seriously whilst I have a bullet and some splinters in my left leg. Only the *Bordmechaniker* [*Ogefr* Karl-Heinz Fahrenheim] in the gondola had not been hit. I then lost control of the aircraft and shouted "Get out! Bale out!" The *Bordfunker* threw off the canopy roof and with great difficulty, we struggled out of the plane. Wriggling, we all hang on our parachutes – we could hear bullets hissing past us and saw other planes going down in flames. I landed in a vegetable patch at Haslar, spraining my legs. Hardly had I touched the ground when four men came up to me armed with rifles and pistols. I was frisked and taken to a car. Afterwards, I had lunch, was interrogated and then taken to a hospital at Netley. By the way, my comrade Dickel lost his life.

Uffz Karl Zimmermann's capture was related in the 13 August 1940 edition of the local newspaper, their account appearing far more dramatic than the German pilot remembers:

> ...One of the crew of a German aeroplane who landed by parachute during an air raid in Southern England yesterday was held up with a gun by a farm groom and afterwards handed over to the police and military authorities.
>
> The German, who was wounded in the left leg and was given first aid treatment, was seen by a doctor on arrival at a local police station and was given a meal and made comfortable. It is understood that another of the occupants of the plane landed in the sea and was drowned.
>
> The injured aviator who is between 25 and 35 years of age was dressed in a grey zip-fastener flying suit. He landed by parachute in a farm garden only a few yards away from where the groom, William Reid, was standing. Seizing a double-barrelled gun, Mr Reid rushed to the spot and at the same time Mr W S Jeffreys, who had been in his mother's house nearby and saw the airman descending, arrived at the scene carrying a revolver.
>
> The wounded German was covered by Mr Reid whilst Mr Jeffreys, with assistance, searched him. First aid was rendered by Mr Jeffreys who took the German to his house and gave him brandy...

Meanwhile, over the Harbour itself, the destruction of another Junkers 88 was witnessed by many onlookers, one of whom recorded the attack in great detail:

Alexander McKee

> ...a Junkers plunged headlong, twisting and jerking...like a dead thing it dropped out of sight like a falling leaf... The Ju 88 which we saw come down had its tail blown off by the gunners of the *Courbet* [a French battleship which was serving as a depot ship for the Free French Navy] which explains the falling leaf act...

Three out of the four crew from this aircraft were lucky to survive such a traumatic shooting down:

Oberleutnant Eberhard Wildermuth, 8/KG 51

> In the morning of 12 August 1940, III/KG 51, then stationed at Etampes–Montdesir, received orders to attack shipping in Portsmouth Harbour. With my *Kette* (*Oblt* Wilhelm Noelken in 9K+AS and *Uffz* Richard Metschuldt in 9K+ES) I was also to provide cover to the rest of

The view from the cockpit of a 8/KG 51 Ju 88 during a practice dive attack, August 1940. (Wildermuth)

Oblt *Eberhard Wildermuth, June 1940.* (Wildermuth)

the *Gruppe* against enemy fighters. At the time the order was given, some technical modifications were being carried out on my plane and I was therefore unable to start immediately. However, I succeeded to fly after the others and catch them up over the Channel.

There was not a cloud in the sky when at midday, we approached Portsmouth across the Isle of Wight. Over the Isle of Wight, there was a thick layer of smoke caused by the *Flak* – incredibly, we flew at an altitude of 4,000m right through a witch's cauldron of exploding shells.

We had orders to dive down on targets in the harbour and not to level out higher than 1,200m, which meant that we had to dive in between the barrage balloons at 2,000m, keep the target in our sights and at 1,200m press the button which pulled us out of the dive and released the bombs at the same time. The plane then carried on falling to about 700m – during the dive, the plane was under heavy attack from the *Flak* and shaken by the explosions all around.

I had dropped the bombs and pulled back the plane to about 1,500m when suddenly, I lost all feeling in the stick – the controls had gone and the plane went into a dreaded spin. Through the throat microphone I yelled "I can't hold the plane – get out!" and threw off the cockpit roof and unclipped my seat belt. The *Beobachter* sitting alongside me [*Oblt* Otto Staerk] did the same. The centrifugal forces created by the spin pressed me into the perspex dome of the front of the cockpit – the force was so strong that I was unable to move my arms. From where I was, I could see the altimeter – 1,400m, 1,300m, 1,200m... I looked at the *Beobachter* who was pressed into the cockpit next to me and I was sure that now the 'stove had gone out'.

Then, suddenly, a rush of air dragged both of us out. After the roar of the engines racing at super speed, everything went deathly quiet. I saw the left wing whizzing past my head and shortly afterwards, heard the air hissing into my parachute. I had released the parachute quite automatically and was now gradually floating towards the waters of the harbour. Looking up, I noticed that my *Beobachter*, dangling above me on his parachute, was taking photos of me – he was a real photo fan and never went on a flight without his camera dangling around his neck. I waved to him and wondered if I would be able to swim to the French coast! With interest, I watched tracer bullets being fired from the ground and ten seconds later, I splashed into the water and was engulfed by my parachute.

Luckily, the water was not deep so I was able to get a breath of air now and then if I stood on tiptoe. At last, I managed to get out of the straps and in the meantime, my *Beobachter* had also freed himself from his parachute and, 50m away, I saw my *Bordfunker* [*Uffz* Droese] who had also parachuted down. Of the *Bordmechaniker* [*Uffz* Roesch] there was no sign.

For another half an hour, we stayed in the water whilst the planes who followed us dropped their bombs. Some of them exploded right next to us and sent up fountains of water all around us. Finally, the raid finished and a group of perhaps ten British soldiers who had previously manned the *Flak* guns fished us out of the water and brought us ashore.

I remember taking off my soaking wet flying suit and putting it in the sun to dry. I never saw it again – presumably a soldier took it as a souvenir. One of them seeing my unhappy face said "You're lucky – for you the war is over" – all I could say was "S**t!"

We were then taken to a nearby Naval Officers' Mess and were given something to eat. By now, I was so tired (we had spent the previous night sightseeing in Paris and had not returned to Etampes until early in the morning!). Then, after taking off my wet clothes, I lay down on a bed and slept like the dead...

Oblt *Wildermuth and* Uffz *Droese; behind them is* Ju 88 A-1, Werk Nummer *4078 coded 9K+BS which crashed into Portsmouth Harbour on 12 August 1940.* (Wildermuth)

French sailors from the battleship Courbet *after having recovered items from the crashed Ju 88 which, sadly, include tatters of uniform belonging to* Uffz Roesch. (via Saunders)

Portsmouth had been badly hit but the RAF tactic of targeting the bombers worked, even if they did so after most had attacked. Together with anti-aircraft guns, the RAF shot down a further eight bombers in addition to the two that were lost in the attack on Ventnor. In human terms, twenty-nine bomber aircrew were killed, seven taken prisoner and a further two wounded. Despite the bombing success, the loss of sixteen percent of the attacking force was sobering and the RAF's success against such overwhelming numbers must have been encouraging, as one Spitfire pilot noted:

Pilot Officer David Crook, 609 Squadron

"My God," I muttered to myself, "What a party." I was not the only person to be impressed. Several other people (not only in 609) who were also in this fight told me afterwards that their main impression had been one of blank astonishment at the numbers of aircraft involved. As somebody remarked "There was the whole German Air Force, bar Goering." Later in the summer, we got used to seeing these enormous formations but this first occasion certainly made us think a bit.

Despite the massive effort by *Luftflotte* 3, it was left to *Luftflotte* 2 to continue the day's fighting targeting the airfields of Manston, Hawkinge and Lympne, stretching the defences to the full. The day had seen the most intensive day's fighting so far in the Battle of Britain and, alarmingly, the RAF had seen a switch in the *Luftwaffe*'s aims to targets specifically involved with the air defence of the United Kingdom. If the RAF pilots had found 12 August 1940 hard work, many of the days that followed would be similarly hard.

At first light on 13 August, most of the German airfields commanded by *Luftflotte* 2 were hives of activity and then, between 0550 hrs and 0610 hrs, the first bombers lifted off into a cloud-laden sky. *Adlerangriff* had begun – a systematic attack against what the Germans thought were fighter airfields. However, the crews were not aware that because of the inclement weather, the attack had been postponed and just after they were airborne, the message was passed. However, only the fighter escort heard that the attack was cancelled and returned to base whilst the bombers droned onwards unaware that they were unprotected. To add further insult, a number of the airfields briefed to be attacked on this day did not belong to Fighter Command and, as a result, aircraft and lives would be lost and crews taken prisoner unnecessarily:

Oberleutnant Heinz Schlegel, *Stab*/KG 2

13 August 1940 was declared *Adlertag*. All of the *Luftwaffe* was to pounce on the RAF and destroy it on the ground as far as it was possible. KG 2 had been briefed to attack the RAF airfield at Eastchurch near the Thames Estuary. A *Zerstoerergeschwader* was to escort us and ensure our protection. As far as I remember, all three *Staffeln* of III *Gruppe* and the *Stabstaffel* took off from Arras at about 0600 hrs.

The *Geschwaderkommodore* was *Oberst* Johannes Fink. He was a conscientious officer – no daredevil. Before commanding KG 2, he had been responsible for the investigation of flying accidents at the *Reichsluftfahrtministerium*. There, he had very often seen accidents caused by ignoring flying orders (such as visiting relatives) and therefore he always fulfilled the orders given to him. He had the order to go to Eastchurch and so he went to Eastchurch.

The *Stabstaffel* was on its way with three aircraft: in the centre the *Kommodore*, my aircraft on his left, a little but higher and behind him.[2] If I can remember, this *Kette* was flying behind the rest of the *Geschwader*. Anyhow, in the very first plane was a *Staffelkapitaen* who was in radio contact with the *Kommodore* to receive further orders. The whole unit had switched to this wavelength which was the reason that nobody heard the attack had been cancelled because of bad weather. It was only possible to recall I *Gruppe*.

Different to normal missions, the *Staffelkapitaen Oblt* Osswald flew with us. He was always scared and only flew when it was unavoidable – like this day. Because he was convinced that nothing could happen to

---

[2] The third aircraft in the *Stabstaffel* was flown by *Oblt* Hans Langer.

Oblt *Heinz Schlegel (left)*. *To his left are unidentified,* Ofw *Ernst Holz and* Ofw *Gustav Babbe.* (Schlegel)

Oblt *Gerhard Osswald*, Staffelkapitaen *of*
Stabstaffel/*KG 2*. (Schlegel)

me (I had been shot down in France during a low level reconnaissance flight), he climbed into my aircraft.

And so KG 2 (less I *Gruppe*) flew towards the Thames Estuary longing to see a *Zerstoerer* escort. After reaching the Channel, the formation flew into a thick layer of cloud. A single *Zerstoerer*, which presumably was there to draw our attention to the fact that the mission had been cancelled, circled us and disappeared again. It was obviously mistaken for our escort. When in our estimation we had reached the target, the clouds became thinner but the target could still not be seen so the formation flew in a wide turn towards London where we turned around again. Now the formation was on an easterly course. The airfield was spotted through a hole in the cloud which was at 800m height – we were flying at 1,500m.

After flying another 180° turn, we attacked descending through this hole and dropped our bombs quite accurately. But then, the British fighters came from the east from the direction of the sea where the rising sun prevented us from seeing them. So, it came as a complete surprise when their salvoes hit us. Neither the *Bordfunker* nor the *Bordmechaniker* had a chance to shoot. Both were wounded, especially in their forearms. The aircraft was hit in the fuselage and in the engines. I succeeded in pulling the plane into the thin layer of cloud but soon the left then right engine seized.

Stab/*KG 2 on an operational flight during the Battle of France.* (Schlegel)

Damage to the 142 Sqn hangar at Eastchurch, 13 August 1940. (Gosman)

I realised that we could not fly back over the Channel again and I did not know if the wounded crew members could operate their parachutes so the only thing to do was to make a force landing. An open meadow appeared, or it seemed to be open, so was the obvious place. But, everywhere in southern Britain, the inhabitants had done things to prevent these meadows from being used by aircraft – ditches had been dug, earth piled up in ramparts and poles had been rammed into the ground so this friendly meadow turned out to be quite bumpy. The aircraft landed heavily and came to a standstill at a big tree. After we had got out and had a look around, some unarmed soldiers appeared. They asked for our pistols – there was no way we could have conquered England with those pistols anyway!

All across southern England, *Luftwaffe* bombers roamed looking for targets – to the west, twenty Junkers 88s of I/KG 54 and a further eighteen from II/KG 54 headed for the airfields of Farnborough and Odiham; a further eighty-eight *Stukas from* StG 77 had their attack cancelled when they were half-way across the Channel. Again, as with previous attacks mounted by *Luftflotte* 3, there was a massive fighter escort but, again, it failed to prevent the RAF from harrying the bombers. The Germans did report attacking the two airfields but it would appear that little damage, if any, was caused. The cost to these attackers was four Junkers 88s shot down and a further nine returning to France with varying

THIS AND NEXT PAGE Oblt *Schlegel's Do 17 after its enforced landing.* (via Cornwell)

Oblt *Heinz Rose* of Stab *II/KG 54 is helped to captivity – his Ju 88 crashed into a lake near Arundel early in the morning of 13 August 1940.* (via Hutton)

degrees of damage. Again, the human cost was high – thirteen killed, six prisoners of war and four wounded. Added to the losses suffered by KG 2 – five bombers destroyed and seven damaged with eleven killed, nine prisoners of war and seven wounded – *Adlerangriff*'s false start had cost the German bomber crews dearly.

To make matters worse, later that afternoon another confusing series of attacks developed to the west. Targets this time were the airfields of Boscombe Down, Warmwell, Yeovil, Worthy Down, Andover and Middle Wallop using a mix of thirty-nine Junkers 88s from I and II/LG 1 and fifty-two *Stukas* from I/StG 1 and II/StG 2. A further sixty-one Junkers 88s and fifty-two *Stukas* of StG 3 were also briefed to attack airfields in the Portland area and Portland itself slightly later but, because of deteriorating weather, this was not carried out. Nevertheless, the two raids cost the *Luftwaffe* six *Stukas* from II/StG 2 and two Junkers 88s from III/LG 1 and again, despite reporting to have badly damaged Andover and Middle Wallop airfields and military and maritime targets in between and including Southampton and Bournemouth, very little damage was inflicted and what damage was done had no adverse impact on Fighter Command.

Adlertag's daylight attacks then switched back to the east, the daylight attacks ending with an unopposed attack on the airfield at Detling in Kent by twenty-six *Stukas* believed to be from IV/LG 1. In addition to the destruction of buildings, hangars and aircraft, in excess of sixty military and civilian personnel were killed, including the Station Commander. However, Detling did not figure in Fighter Command's order of battle and despite the personnel losses and severe damage to the airfield itself, the attack did not affect the RAF's ability to counter German air attacks.

So ended *Adlerangriff* – a day riddled with errors, miscalculations and misinformation from the German point of view. Following the Detling attack, a few *Luftwaffe* aircraft strayed over the United Kingdom and for the first time in a number of nights, nocturnal attacks were few and far between even though Heinkel 111s of KG 27 and KGr 100 attacked industrial targets as far north as Glasgow. The RAF could have done better throughout 13 August 1940 but the weather, earlier attacks on radar stations and the size and depth of attacks made things difficult, whilst what successes they achieved were further assisted by the *Luftwaffe*'s errors.

In comparison, 14 August 1940 was a much quieter day. At about lunchtime, *Erprobungsgruppe* 210 carried out an attack against the hard-hit Manston airfield, losing two Messerschmitt 110s to light anti-aircraft fire. Soon after that, a heavily escorted formation of *Stukas* from IV/LG 1 unsuccessfully attacked Hawkinge airfield and sank the Goodwin Lightship. The attacks that then occurred for the remainder of the day were undertaken by a number of units against a number of targets using the poor weather as a means of defence. The attacks were numerous and ranged far and wide. Seventeen Junkers 88s of I/LG 1 carried out an armed reconnaissance in the Bristol area and attacked a number of airfields in the south west of England; III/KG 55 carried out seven separate attacks against the airfields at Abingdon, Upavon, Bicester, Worthy Down, Netheravon and Brize Norton and the Rolls Royce factory at Crewe whilst I/KG 27 sent eighteen Heinkel 111s to attack the airfields at Little Rissington, Hullavington, Upavon, Netheravon, Boscombe Down and 'Minchinhampton' (presumably Aston Down). The final unit in action that afternoon was III/KG 27 which sent

Bomb damage to a hangar at Middle Wallop on 14 August 1940.

The remains of the aircraft that did it – Oblt Wilhelm Heinrici's Ju 88 from 1/LG 1.

twenty-five Heinkel 111s to attack the airfields at Blandford Forum, Yeovilton, Filton and Sealand near Chester. For the defenders, it was a confusing series of attacks to defend against. However, I/LG 1 lost a Junkers 88 to a Spitfire of 234 Squadron and another from 609 Squadron whilst another of that unit's Junkers 88s was shot down by four Hurricanes from 43 Squadron. III/KG 27 lost five bombers to Spitfires from 92 Squadron and three Spitfires flown by instructors from Number 7 Operational Training Unit. The final loss was more serious for the *Luftwaffe* when the *Geschwaderkommodore* of KG 55, *Oberst* Alois Stoeckl, the Chief of Staff for V *Fliegerkorps*, *Oberst* Walter Frank and KG 55's navigation officer, *Oblt* Bruno Brossler were all killed when their Heinkel 111 was shot down by two Spitfires from 609 Squadron.

German air attacks that night were much reduced and it was anticipated that Thursday 15 August 1940 would see air operations over the United Kingdom hampered again by bad weather. Apparently, the bad weather prompted *Reichsmarschall* Goering to summon his senior officers to Germany; these officers were destined not to witness first hand a day that the surviving German aircrew would call *Schwarzer Donnerstag* – Black Thursday.

One of the successful No. 7 OTU pilots that shot down a He 111 of 8/KG 27 on 14 August 1940 was Fg Off Peter Ayerst.

Heinkel 115 (seen here from 1/706). (Rosenbaum)

German losses began early. A number of German aircraft, predominantly Heinkel 115 seaplanes, carried out mine-laying and attacks against airfields in north eastern Scotland. One of their number was dazzled by searchlights and flew into the ground near Arbroath at 0430 hrs.

As dawn broke, numerous German reconnaissance aircraft scurried along the south coast, *Oblt* Hans Horn's Dornier 17 P of 3(F)/31 having the misfortune to be shot down off the Isle of Wight at about 0800 hrs. However, the first full scale raid did not materialise until just before lunchtime when the airfields of Lympne and Hawkinge were attacked by *Stukas* from IV/LG 1. Both airfields were bombed but the intervention of RAF fighters managed to thwart much of the attack on Hawkinge (a fact confirmed by returning German crews) but Lympne was badly hit and was non-operational for the next two days. The German fighters inflicted casualties on the RAF fighters but did not prevent the loss of two *Stukas* – one was chased into high tension cables at Folkestone whilst the other came down off the coast:

Hauptmann Rolf Muenchenhagen, 10 *(Stuka)*/ LG 1

We took off from Tramecourt under the lead of the *Gruppen Kommandeur*, *Hptm* Roeder. I was not the *Staffel Kapitaen* but was being trained as one; as a result, I had only been with the *Geschwader* for three days. About five miles from the English coast between Dover and Folkestone, we were attacked by Hurricanes. One Hurricane attacked me from behind (I was the last one in the *Staffel*) and he hit my *Stuka*. I was forced to bale out but on the way out, I myself was hit. As I went down, the Hurricane circled me. Just before I hit the water, I released myself

from the parachute and I landed in the sea without any trouble. As I
floated in the water, the Hurricane dived at me at intervals as if to show
my position. Shortly afterwards, a patrol boat picked me up – the crew
were very fair and they gave me cigarettes and covered me with a blanket.
I was then landed at Dover and taken to a military hospital. I later found
out that I had lost an eye and a number of teeth.

Hptm Muenchenhagen was a victim of a Hurricane of 501 Squadron. Who
shot him down for certain cannot be said for sure but one pilot's combat
report gives a good idea of what it was like shooting down a 10/LG 1 aircraft
and could have been the pilot who circled the German pilot floating in the
Channel:

Flying Officer Robert Dafforn, Green 2, 'B' Flight, 501 Squadron

Enemy aircraft were first sighted five miles south of Folkestone (twenty
Ju 87s and six Me 109s[3]) heading towards Hawkinge. I singled out a Ju 87
and did a Number One attack from rather below (five seconds burst).
Enemy aircraft started to smoke and dived away and I broke away. I was
unable to see what happened to the enemy aircraft.

I then singled out another Ju 87 and did a Number One attack from
dead astern. Eleven second burst from 300 yards gradually closing.
Enemy aircraft started smoking and diving. I broke away but was unable
to see what happened to the enemy aircraft. My ammunition was now
exhausted but I noticed two pilots in the sea three miles south of
Folkestone so I attracted the attention of a boat in Folkestone Harbour
and then circled the two pilots. They were eventually picked up by
Motor Torpedo Boats from Dover...[4]

As this raid was taking place in the south, the scene of battle was about to
shift much further to the north. For the first time in the Battle of Britain,
Luftflotte 5 was carrying out its first major attack. The targets were the airfields
of Dishforth and Linton-on-Ouse in Yorkshire (both bomber airfields) with
secondary targets being harbours along the north eastern coast. The dubious
honour of carrying out this attack went to the Heinkel 111s of I and III/KG 26
based in Norway:

---

[3] There were considerably more than six Messerschmitt 109s as the escort was made
up from various *Gruppen* from JG 26 and JG 51.
[4] There were at least three RAF pilots in the water at that time – Sgt Norman Lawrence
of 54 Sqn and Flt Lt Alan Putt and Fg Off John Gibson of 501 Sqn.

Oberleutnant Hermann Riedel, 8/KG 26

Tension began to build before 14 August 1940 indicating that we were in for some action. Then the order arrived to prepare for an attack on Britain. It was said that the British fighter defences were reduced to about thirty or forty aircraft. Therefore a simultaneous attack on airfields in the south and the north would have a crippling effect.

KG 26 was briefed to meet over Stavanger and attack in close formation. Up to a certain point escort would be undertaken by Bf 109s from II/JG 77 and in the middle of the North Sea, I/ZG 76 would take over. I/ZG 76 was equipped with the Bf 110 with additional tanks. All preparations were made and then the attack was changed from 14 to 15 August.

The airfield at Stavanger was very busy. By 1100 hrs, everything was ready – crews in their aircraft, engines running. Slowly the *Ketten* and *Staffeln* taxied to the take off position. In the lead was the *Gruppen Kommandeur Maj* Guenther Wolfien. The *Ketten* took off in swift succession – *Staffel Kapitaen Hptm* Josef Stefan was in the lead *Kette* of 8/KG 26 – the leader of the port *Kette* was *Oblt* Horst von Besser; I was the leader of the starboard one. Climbing very slowly, we all closed up in tight formation.

Oblt *Hermann Riedel (right) with* Fw *Willi Scholl.* (Riedel)

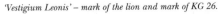

'Vestigium Leonis' – mark of the lion and mark of KG 26.

Off the coast, I/KG 26 from Kristiansand appeared. We climbed slowly to 6,000m altitude. All around, the fighters from II/JG 77 capered reassuringly. After a while, the *Zerstoerers* appeared on both sides of the formation and the Bf 109s left for home. As the final *Kette* on the starboard side, I had a splendid view up and down the vast formation. The Bf 110s held a steady course – some times they came closer, went on ahead or dropped back.

Radio silence was ordered for the duration of the flight. We had a Signals Officer who, it was said, could identify British pilots by their voices. He kept monitoring British radio traffic throughout the flight. However, about 100 kilometres from the coast, unintelligible warnings came over the radio and in no time, the formation became nervous. Over the radio and from my crew came warnings of enemy fighters and I observed several on reciprocal courses to ourselves. In a wide curve, they came in to the rear of the *Zerstoerers* and a glimpse to the right saw two Bf 110s falling in flames. The attack was swift but I did not see any of the bombers being attacked.

We followed our course undisturbed and crossed the coastline. A damaged *Zerstoerer*, so I was informed from the lower gun position, was trying to find protection from us but it soon disappeared. After crossing the coast, we should have changed course but we continued. Eventually, we turned south but clouds covered the airfields and in a wide turn, the

Two other crew members, Ofw Kalle Mueller (left) and Ofw Paul Suessenbach (right), inspect damage to their He 111 received over Narvik with another unidentified crew member. (Riedel)

Gruppe turned north east towards Newcastle where the city and harbour was clearly visible.[5] The harbour was our alternative target so we unloaded our bombs there. Reaching the sea, the *Gruppe* inexplicably turned left back towards the city and now, without warning, enemy fighters closed on the formation and attacked.

My aircraft was immediately under heavy fire. The bullets, like rain, passed my head left and right and into the instrument panel. We were just about able to keep formation when, over the city, we were attacked again. The starboard engine broke down with a jolt and began to burn. A Spitfire then flew alongside – the pilot waved his hand and then disappeared. He was obviously out of ammunition and wished us good luck!

As I was not able to keep formation and had to extinguish the engine fire, I dropped away from our disintegrating formation and headed east. The clouds were now broken but I managed to level off in a cloud bank and set course for Holland. The aircraft was

[5] It is believed that Sunderland not Newcastle was the city seen as it was the former that was bombed.

in a shambles both inside and out. The fire had gone out and the port engine seemed to be running normally but nearly all the instruments were destroyed. Amazingly, all the crew were uninjured but there was quite a tension in the aircraft. We were determined to reach safety. My *Beobachter Fw* Willi Scholl calculated the straightest course whilst the *Bordfunker, Ofw* Paul Suessenbach, tried to contact a ground station. He was lucky and managed to transmit a distress message despite much confusion over the radio frequency.

We checked all parts of the aircraft very carefully especially the still running engine. Our height by now was only some 1,000m above the sea and after some time had passed, we were startled by rough noises coming from the port engine. One of the still working instruments showed that the oil temperature was rising and I had to throttle back. We slowed right down and started losing height. Keeping the aircraft in a shallow glide, I tried to keep going but then the oil temperature suddenly shot up, the engine began to smoke and with a shudder, it broke down. Height was now just 200–300m, enough time to prepare for ditching. The dinghy was ready and everybody tightened their seat belts and gliding down, with the flaps slightly down, we touched the waves.

All of a sudden, water was all around – dark and tasting very salty! Then slowly, it got quieter and we saw some light – we were afloat. We threw off the roof hatch, left the aircraft and got into the dinghy. To save weight, we only took the emergency rations pack. Boarding the dinghy last, I remembered my cine camera. With a jump, Kalle Mueller [*Ofw* Kalle Mueller, the *Bordmechaniker*] returned to the cockpit and came back with it – quite a feat in the rough sea! Unfortunately, all the flight documents and exposed films had to be left in the cockpit.

It was all quiet in the dinghy. We drifted fast, moving away from the pitching aircraft. The dinghy drifted like a leaf on the wind and it was impossible to steer by paddles or sail. Minutes later, the starboard wing and nose of the Heinkel dipped forwards and the plane disappeared, the tail being the last to say goodbye...

For *Oblt* Riedel and his crew, rescue was on its way but their adventures that day

Oblt *Riedel's He 111 slips beneath the waves.* (Riedel)

He 111s of I/KG 26 during the Narvik Campaign. (Kull)

were not destined to end there as the reader will see later.

III/KG 26 had suffered badly – 8/KG 26 had lost five aircraft whilst 9/KG 26 had the misfortune of running into three Bristol Blenheims from 235 Sqn who were on a sweep of the Danish coast. Two He 111s were immediately shot down – one by Plt Off Norman Jackson-Smith, the other being shared between Jackson-Smith, Plt Off John Laughlin and Sgt P. F. Hall. I/KG 26 was lucky to lose just one bomber:

Flieger Ernst Henrichsen, 1/KG 26

About 60 miles from the coast, we were joined by Bf 110s. Shortly afterwards, the warning 'enemy fighters' was given. The Bf 110s were engaged at once and I could see how one Hurricane attacked by a Bf 110 exploded into an orange fireball. The Bf 110 was at once attacked by a Hurricane and went down with smoking engines. Seconds later, this Hurricane exploded, just like the first.[6] After that, the dogfights went further away. I could see planes going down but could not see if they were friend or foe.

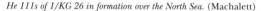

He 111s of 1/KG 26 in formation over the North Sea. (Machalett)

[6] Only one Hurricane was lost during the whole combat.

It all became quiet again and we reached the coast where we were welcomed by anti-aircraft fire. The shells exploded quite near and I could see the clouds of the explosions touch the wings of our plane. After crossing the coast, we flew on westwards for quite a time. I could hear some comments on the network like "What is going on?" and "Has the old man lost his way?" and so on. This suspicion was confirmed when I saw that we were over the sea again, apparently the Irish Sea and I saw what I thought was the Isle of Man. Then we turned around and crossed England a second time.

Nothing happened until we reached the coast again where we got the order to attack port facilities and warehouses. In order to do this, we had to break up our tight formation and during the following bomb run, we became dispersed. After our bombs had gone (I did not see if we had hit anything), I heard *Oblt* Roch telling the pilot *Uffz* Zimmermann "Flieg schneller! Den letzten beissen die Hunde!" ("Fly faster! The last [one] gets bitten by the dog!") He was right about that, for at the same time I saw Hurricanes were coming. There being no fighter escort any more, we were now attacked. They used a very prudent tactic. They attacked right from behind and shot at us from a distance of 1,500ft. At this distance, our single machine gun and inferior aiming were no match for the combined fire power of the Hurricane.

Soon both engines were out of commission having been hit in the cooling system. Moreover, the three rear gunners were wounded – the upper rear gunner (*Gefr* Kulick) in the head, the lower rear gunner (*Gefr* Machalett) in the knee (with a broken leg) and I was hit by shrapnel in the upper and right side of the head. I had the feeling that someone had hit me over the head with a big stick! Then I could not see anything – I tried to wipe my eyes, could see again and saw that my hands were full of blood. For the first time, I realised that I had been wounded. This fighter attack took some time and we were by then back out to sea so the pilot turned back towards the coast and glided towards it.

At this time, the Hurricane stopped shooting at us. We were escorted up until the time the pilot ditched the plane. When we hit the water, the lower hatch opened and the sea entered the plane. In seconds, we were half full of water. I went back to

Gefr *Alwin Machalett in front of the He 111 in which he was shot down on 15 August 1940.* (Machalett)

help the lower rear gunner and while doing this I had a look at the newly installed armour plating – it was criss-crossed by rows of impacts by bullets just where I had been standing during the attack. However, we left the plane, inflated the dinghy and just about got away from the plane before it sank. About two hours later, we were taken aboard a trawler and made prisoners of war...

The RAF claimed forty-four Heinkel 111s and Messerschmitt 110s destroyed and it is difficult to tie RAF claims to German losses although it is believed that Australian Plt Off William Millington of 79 Squadron, who claimed three Heinkel 111s destroyed in this action, was responsible for shooting down the 1/KG 26 bomber.

As an example, the following report gives an idea of what many of the RAF pilots experienced on that day:

Plt Off William Millington in the cockpit of his Hurricane after he had joined 249 Sqn; he was reported missing in action on 30 October 1940.

Flight Lieutenant Forgave Smith, 72 Squadron

We started that day with our take off at about 1230 hrs with the Squadron of eleven Spitfires in three sections led by Flt Lt Ted Graham. As 'A' Flt Commander, I led one of those sections consisting Plt Offs Holland and Deacon-Elliott and, I think, Sgt Douthwaite. It was very unusual at that time for more than a flight to be at readiness. We flew due east, out to sea and at about 40 miles from the coast encountered a large formation of enemy bombers flying in close formation, escorted by Me 110s. At the time, due to our inexperience, we thought that the bombers were Ju 88s but they were in fact He 111s.

Upon sighting the enemy aircraft, Ted Graham gave the order to attack and I put my Section into echelon port. As it was not possible to turn into the attack quickly enough in that formation, I ordered a change to echelon starboard. As Deacon-Elliott crossed behind 'Dutch' Holland, it was thought by 'Dutch' that he was being attacked by Me 110s and he and Deacon engaged in a lively private battle!

I selected one of the bombers and attacked it from astern, firing at the starboard engine from which large pieces broke away. I turned away and attacked another He 111 causing smoke to stream from the port engine. I then attacked a third He 111 and could see the explosive 'De Wilde' ammunition flashing on contact. I pressed the attack very closely, firing directly into the fuselage. Presumably a bomb detonated and the aircraft exploded in a huge ball of flame which I narrowly avoided flying into. Breaking away, an Me 110 was approaching head on and I gave him a quick burst before running out of ammunition. During the engagement, the Me 110s flew in defensive circles.

On the day of the attack, there was a thin layer of unbroken cloud at about 10,000–12,000ft. This was very fortunate for Newcastle as the bombers which penetrated inland were unable to see the densely populated cities along the Tyne which probably saved them from serious damage.

After landing at Acklington, I quickly refuelled and rearmed and reported and then took off again alone and flew south along the coast to try and make contact but was not successful and returned to base.

If he had continued further south, he would have found himself intercepting another raid. This was an attack on another bomber airfield, that of Driffield near Bridlington in Yorkshire, by Junkers 88s from KG 30:

Unteroffizier Werner Evers, 7/KG 30

We had been at Aalborg in Denmark for about two months. It was a very quiet time with some flights to Great Britain such as the Rolls Royce factory. On 15 August 1940, the whole *Geschwader* took off from Aalborg for Great Britain. I do not remember the target but at that time targets were only military places or factories. We had the newest Ju 88 which was the fastest so we started last. As we reached the British coast, the Spitfires [sic] were waiting and they came in from behind, attacking the last aircraft. So, they started on us with success. One engine had no oil, the other no oil or coolant but we were still airborne. Our *Bordfunker* was dead (we did not know this but he had stopped shooting). The pilot, *Oblt* Bachmann, and myself tried to figure out what to do next and best. We could either try flying along the coast southwards for France but thought that we couldn't make it and so decided to fly over Britain to try and reach Eire, not to become prisoners of war but to be interned. However, after we returned from the sea to the land, another Spitfire was on our tail and started shooting immediately. We had no chance to escape and I tried to throw off the cockpit roof to jump out by parachute. The roof came off immediately and all papers, cards etc flew out. When we were in

a prisoner of war camp, we were visited by the Spitfire pilot who shot us down and learned from him that he thought after we lost our roof and he saw all the flying papers, that we had surrendered and he stopped shooting.

As we had lost height, we decided to crash-land. Bachmann already had experience of crash-landing. We looked for a wheat field but before that we jettisoned our bombs. The landing was successful and the aircraft didn't catch fire. We thought that the gunner *Flg* Walther must have been killed as he was in the belly of the aircraft and was lying there when we touched down. Anyone who knows the Ju 88 wouldn't believe that he survived. We noticed that *Fw*

Uffz *Werner Evers a few days before he was shot down.* (Evers)

Werner Evers' Ju 88 on show somewhere in the UK in November 1940. (via Cornwell)

Henneske was dead (shot in the head). Bachmann and myself had to pull him out of his seat as it was stopping Walther from getting out. We had orders to set the Ju 88 on fire but we couldn't as we were soon taken prisoner. As we still had our pistols, we were scared that we might get shot but I spoke some English and handed them over...

The two RAF Squadrons that intercepted this attack managed to shoot down eight Junkers 88s and badly damaged a further three. The German bombers did manage to drop 169 bombs on the airfield, killing thirteen personnel, wounding countless others and causing extensive damage to the airfield. Numerous building were damaged and destroyed including all five hangars. The attack also resulted in the destruction of eleven Armstrong Whitworth Whitley bombers but yet again, this airfield and those aircraft were not part of the air defence of Great Britain.

Luftflotte 5 had been taught a painful lesson and never again attempted such a major daylight attack. For the *Luftwaffe*, it clearly proved that there was no detectable weakness to the RAF's defences and, contrary to what propaganda was saying, the RAF was not down to its last forty fighters.

Now the scene of battle shifted back to the south with *Erprobungsgruppe* 210 carrying out its first attack of the day against the airfield of Martlesham Heath closely followed by attacks on the airfields at Eastchurch, Hornchurch, Rochester and Gravesend by Dornier 17s of KG 2 and KG 3. Milling about this massive formation was an equally massive formation of escorting fighters which allowed the attackers to successfully bomb Rochester and Eastchurch but KG 3 lost two bombers in the process with a further six returning with varying degrees of damage and wounded crew members.

Sgt Alexander McNay, Flt Lt Reg Lovett and Sgt John Brimble of 73 Sqn show off trophies from the Ju 88 of 3/KG 30 shot down near Bridlington; all three pilots would be dead within a month.

Again, as this raid turned for home, another was appearing to the west. Twelve Junkers 88s of I/LG 1 were heading for the airfield of Andover whilst a further fifteen from II/LG 1 were heading for Worthy Down. Simultaneously to the west, twenty-seven *Stukas* from I/StG 1 and twenty from II/StG 2 would attack Portland, hopefully splitting the fighter defences. Unfortunately for many of those Germans involved, this ruse did not work and in any case the two airfields were, yet again, not Fighter Command airfields. Almost immediately after sweeping in over Selsey Bill, the Junkers 88s were attacked by Hurricanes of 32, 43, 111 and 601 Squadrons:

Unteroffizier Otto Rezeppa, 4/LG 1

We took off from Orléans–Bricy on the evening of 15 August 1940 and orbited waiting to form up. Our target was an airfield north of Winchester. Over St Omer, we picked up our escort of Bf 109s and in the distance to the west we could see the Bf 110s.

I flew in the aircraft that was the furthest right in the formation. Another aircraft in our *Kette* was flown by *Uffz* Erwin Poggensee. After we crossed the coast, I was the first to spot the enemy. I shouted and fired in the direction of the fighters as they swept in from the right. In what seemed a few seconds but was probably ten minutes, everything happened. We shot at a Hurricane on the tail of *Oblt* Hans-Joachim Helbig's aircraft (he was our *Staffel Kapitaen*). Suddenly, the *Beobachter*, *Uffz* Willi Rimek, panicked and jettisoned the cockpit roof and my gun. He then collapsed and lay on the cockpit floor with his mouth wide open – he had been shot in the back of the head and killed instantly. I then waved my handkerchief at the attacking Hurricane and *Uffz* Fritz Dieter decided to crash-land which he did at very high speed in a corn field. As the aircraft stopped, we all got out. I was limping – I had been shot in the right leg. We dragged out Willi's body just as British soldiers arrived and we all stood there, covered in dust. They took my camera, gun and knife and took me away from the aircraft on a stretcher. We were then taken to a hospital in Chichester where I met an RAF pilot who had a wound in his shoulder. He said I was lucky as I would survive the war – he was not sure he would.

Uffz *Otto Rezeppa.* (Rezeppa)

Uffz *Willi Rimek and* Uffz *Fritz Dieter in front of the Ju 88 that they were flying on 15 August 1940.* (Rezeppa)

The RAF pilot who shot down *Uffz* Rezeppa's aircraft did not witness any of the dramatic events in the aircraft as his very terse combat report shows:

Flight Lieutenant Stanley Connors, Green 1, 111 Squadron

An initial attack was blocked by twelve Me 109s. I then selected another Ju 88 and carried out a quarter and astern attack. Bits fell off the port engine and the starboard smoked badly. Aircraft glided down and force-landed. I watched the crew surrender to farm workers who ran up to the machine.

Otto Rezeppa's Ju 88 lying in a West Sussex field. (via Cornwell)

Flt Lt Stanley Connors of 111 Sqn.
(Morgan)

Meanwhile, other Junkers 88s from II/LG 1 had managed to get further inland but for another five crews their destiny was not to return to France, as one of them recalls:

Fw *Willi Lueder (left) and two unidentified personnel of III/KG 3.*

Feldwebel Willi Lueder, *Stab* II/LG 1

We could see the Isle of Wight when the circus started and the fighters were engaged in fights with Spitfires [sic]. Anyway, everything happened very quickly – there were losses on both sides and we saw many aircraft going down in flames. Suddenly, Hurricanes descended on us and hit us in the starboard engine. We left the formation – the smoke made breathing in the cockpit impossible and we could not hold the aircraft any longer. We jettisoned the bombs as we wanted to crash-land. Suddenly, the pilot gave us the order to bale out. I was the first to go, *Ofw* Heinz Grund followed. As we were dangling on our parachutes, we were circled by a welcoming committee of two Hurricanes…

Sergeant Leonard Guy, Red 3, 'A' Flight, 601 Squadron

I followed Red Leader [Flt Lt Archibald Hope] into the engagement but broke away after one short burst at an enemy aircraft from the beam. I then saw a Ju 88 being attacked by a Hurricane. I dived to join the attack and delivered several short bursts from astern and one from underneath. Black smoke was pouring from the starboard engine. During these attacks, enemy aircraft had lost height from about 15,000ft to 5,000ft. Then one airman jumped and landed safely and about a minute later, a second landed by parachute. Enemy aircraft continued to lose height very slowly and crash-landed in a field north-west of Petersfield. Flt Lt Hope was in the other Hurricane attacking enemy aircraft and witnessed its destruction. It crash-landed 200 yards from a second enemy aircraft which was on fire; Fg Off Davis (Yellow 1, 'A' Flt) was circling this blazing machine.[7]

Flight Lieutenant Archibald Hope, 'A' Flight, 601 Squadron

My logbook shows that we took off from Tangmere at 1705 hrs which presumably would have been local time because the rule that all flying times were recorded in GMT was not introduced until 1944. I was leading eleven aircraft of 601 Sqn flying in my usual Hurricane coded UP-P. We

---

[7] The burning Ju 88 was probably from 5/LG 1 – *Fw* Herbert Pauck and his crew remain missing to this day.

were ordered to patrol base and then I see that I recorded the height as 19,000ft. I think that this was the maximum height reached during the flight which lasted an hour. My logbook then reads "Found twelve Ju 88s and attacked them over Bishops Waltham. Beam and two stern attacks on main formation. One damaged then forced down with Sgt Guy near West Meon after firing at engines. Three parachutes. John McGrath and Mouse Cleaver wounded."

After circling around for what seemed a long time, because I was out of ammunition, the parachutes emerged and then the Ju 88 seemed to make a semi-controlled landing in a field just west or just south of quite a major road. It hit the near side of a hedge and then slid on its belly for about 25–50 yards. There was no fire.

Willi Lueder's Ju 88 creating much interest amongst the local populace. (via Hutton)

At the time, responsibility for the crashed aircraft was with Tangmere and I asked the Adjutant, Flt Lt Thompson, to see if he could get me the pilot's Mauser pistol. He could not get the pistol but he did give me the pilot's throat microphone.

Feldwebel Willi Lueder

...We landed in a meadow about 400m apart. My first thought was "There goes my leave!" because two days later I was to have gone on eight days leave. Instead I got myself six and a half years as a prisoner of war!

After about ten minutes, four Home Guard turned up and called from far away "Hands Up!" I didn't because I had landed rather heavily on my backside and had got myself a lot of bruises. I thought how I could make contact so I called "You have a cigarette for me?" "Yes, yes!" – the shotgun was pointed downwards and the question as to whether I was wounded were the signs between us. I handed them my pistol and gravity knife as a souvenir for what good would they have been to me? For me, the war was over.

All but one of these II/LG 1 were taken prisoner on 15 August 1940; a further eleven aircrew were killed. Back (l to r): Ofw *Willi Lueder (*Stab *II),* Fw *Horst Burkhardt (4/LG 1),* Ofw *Heinz Dittmann (4/LG 1),* Oblt *Pit Stuetzel (*Stab *II, POW 17 September 1940),* Ofw *Heinz Grund (*Stab *II),* Fw *Otto Rezeppa (4/LG 1),* Fw *Fritz Dieter (4/LG 1). Front:* Fw *Erwin Kusche (4/LG 1),* Ofw *Willi Richter (4/LG 1),* Fw *Willi Mueller (4/LG 1),* Fw *Erwin Poggensee (4/LG 1) (missing* Fw *Kurt Weigang and* Oblt *Stephan Suin de Boutemard (*Stab *II).*

Both I and II/LG 1 made it to their targets, even if I/LG 1 bombed Middle Wallop instead of Andover (Middle Wallop being a fighter airfield but the Germans appear not to have known that). One of the fleeing II/LG 1 aircraft also managed to bomb Tangmere but without any detriment to the airfield.

Meanwhile, to the west, the RAF fighters were mauling the *Stukas* and their escort, accounting for four dive bombers; damage to Portland was reported as being negligible.

Luckily for the *Luftwaffe*, the day was coming to a close but before night fell, more bombers and lives would be lost. Dornier 17s of I/KG 76 were to attack Kenley but confused Croydon, Biggin Hill and Redhill airfields, ending up bombing what they thought was Biggin Hill but was in fact West Malling! At the same time, III/KG 76 was

A Do 17 Z of KG 76. (Moll)

briefed to attack Redhill, the Messerschmitt 110 fighter-bombers of *Erprobungsgruppe* 210 carried out what has become one of the most well known if not controversial raids of the Battle of Britain. Briefed to attack Kenley, they in fact bombed Croydon airfield a few more miles further north. Although they succeeded in hitting the airfield (and, by mistake, civilian housing just outside the perimeter), they were pounced upon by at least three Hurricane squadrons.

Six Messerschmitt 110s were shot down fleeing for the coast as well as an escorting Messerschmitt 109 from 3/*Erprobungsgruppe* 210. The *Gruppen Kommandeur*, *Hptm* Walter Rubensdorfer, was one of those who failed to

Two of the ErprGr *210 fighter-bombers landed intact on 15 August 1940 – this one was flown by* Oblt *Karl-Heinz Koch.* (via Saunders)

return. If he had, perhaps he would have had to incur the wrath of his senior officers for bombing the wrong target and, more importantly, the London suburbs. Instead, he and his *Bordfunker* were killed; four days later he was posthumously awarded the *Ritterkreuz*. All of this was of little interest to the RAF pilot responsible for shooting him down; for him, it was just another incident at the end of a very busy day:

Pilot Officer Ron Duckenfield, 501 Squadron

On 15 August 1940, we were operating from Gravesend. In the afternoon, we were sent up to intercept a raid of about twenty Do 17s of which I claimed one damaged (over Detling). Then at about tea-time, just after we had refuelled, there was a much larger raid. This headed for Croydon and inflicted severe damage not only on the airfield but also on the town itself.

The scramble was given a little late so it was not until the enemy had actually finished his attack that we began to close. In the subsequent mêlée, the enemy formation having been broken by attacks from other RAF fighters, I suddenly found a Do 215 [sic] heading south in a long shallow dive towards the coast which gave him such a turn of speed that it took me some minutes before I could come near enough to open fire. I fired several bursts with no apparent effect (he was weaving pretty violently) but then, we were both down to about 4,000ft, I managed to hit him with the last of my ammunition. One engine caught fire and there must have also been a casualty in the cockpit because he rolled over and dived into the ground somewhere just west of Tunbridge Wells. I had no time to check exactly where because I was already very low on petrol.

Darkness now fell and the *Luftwaffe*'s nocturnal bombers set forth. The RAF had survived its first major test and had taught the *Luftwaffe* not to underestimate its strengths wherever they might attack in Great Britain. For those crews fortunate to make it back to their bases on the Continent, the loss of so many aircraft and personnel must have been sobering. However, for one German crew the day was by no means over and their misfortune was set to continue. Shot down during the *Luftflotte* 5 attack on the north of England, one German bomber crew was still adrift in the North Sea:

Oberleutnant Hermann Riedel, 8/KG 26

To soothe our nerves, we calculated our position and how long it would take to cross the North Sea. We thought that we were close to the British coast so refrained from shooting off flares – we were not set to become prisoners of war. The high waves gave us no end of trouble and

after a while, some of us were affected by sea sickness. Conversation was
sparse and as the day turned into evening, we began to lose hope of
being rescued – Paul's [*Ofw* Paul Suessenbach] nerves gave way and he
got the blues.

Then, from the south, in spite of the slapping of the waves, we heard
the sound of an aircraft engine. A speck appeared to the south east
which turned out to be a seaplane. We waited to be sure of the type and,
when we clearly identified a Heinkel 59 [from *Seenotstaffel* IV,
Norderney], we promptly shot off our distress flares. We had to wait a few
anxious minutes before we saw the plane had spotted us. In a wide curve,
it returned, crossed over us and prepared to land. I could hardly believe
that the plane would be able to land on those waves and after several
attempts, it touched down near to our dinghy. Again and again, the
Heinkel disappeared behind mountains of water until at last the crew
could throw us a hook. I still cannot remember how we managed to get
on board the seaplane. We were dragged through an open hatch in the
rear, brought forward and sat down. The dinghy was taken in and left in
the back. At once the pilot tried to take off – this seemed to me to be the
most difficult and longest take-off of my life.

The seaplane rocked like mad, increased its speed, slapped back into
the water and just would not gain height. It seemed to be burying itself
into the waves. In the cockpit, I could see the legs of the pilot, water and
froth and how the pilot was struggling with his aircraft. After a long
time, the banging in the plane and the rumbling engines quietened
down – we were obviously in the air. This was an even greater relief to us
than the end of the fighter attack.

Once in the air, my crew were dried and taken care of. We received
dry underwear, track suits and blankets. My men then made themselves
comfortable in the cabin. I introduced myself to the commander (the
Beobachter) and the pilot. The pilot was busy but informed me that we
were headed for Heligoland. The commander was a *Leutnant zur See*
[Siegfried Boerner] and had only recently trained to be a *Beobachter*. He
told me that there had been many distress calls during the afternoon
and was not sure how close he was to the British coast as he had lost his
bearings.

In the meantime, it was now night. I lingered a while with the pilot
(he was an old hand). The *Beobachter* was in the open forward
observation position. I joined him later – we had a clear night sky, flying
above the clouds. Back in the cockpit, I noticed the *Bordfunker* operating
his Morse lamp so I went to find out what he was signalling to. On
arriving at where he was standing, a look to the rear made my blood
freeze. Not more than 50m above and behind hung a Wellington [sic]
and it was following us.

I yelled to the *Beobachter* "That is a British aircraft!" and hurried as
fast as I could into the cockpit. "Down into the clouds! It's an enemy

bomber!" I shouted to the pilot. "Oh no…" he replied "…It is a German long range night fighter patrolling around here." "Down into the clouds!" I yelled again "They are going to attack immediately!" I couldn't get him to change height and then the bullets rattled into our aircraft. I jumped down and shouted to my crew to take cover behind boxes and bundles. Meanwhile, the Wellington, swinging from one side to the other, covered us with sustained fire – the bullets came from everywhere. I noticed at once that the starboard engine was beginning to stutter and a look through the window showed the engine sprouting flames.

At long last, the pilot went down and with roll dived into the clouds, then levelling the aircraft. Slowly the plane lost height and soon force-landed on the sea. A few moments later, the enemy aircraft came in from behind and opened fire again. I ordered the dinghies be prepared and to get them in the water as I feared we would be bombed. The *Beobachter* then cried out and collapsed – he had been hit in the belly and was in great pain. The *Bordmechaniker* and I took care of him. After some time, the shooting stopped and an eerie stillness came over the aircraft…

The German seaplane had been detected by a Lockheed Hudson of 206 Squadron, not a Wellington as Hermann Riedel had thought. The following report was submitted on its return to base:

Aircraft 'V' of 206 Sqn sighted a He 59 on the surface of the sea with engines running at 2155 hrs. Enemy aircraft fired recognition signals of orange and red turning to green and then took off. 'V' began attack with starboard 'K' gun and continued with front gun and finished with side gun. Enemy aircraft was brought down onto the sea and was last seen on fire at 2230 hrs. Combat fought at 0–500ft and 1,700 rounds fired. Enemy aircraft reported as having good manoeuvrability and top speed was considered to be 125-knot.

Meanwhile, back on the surface of the North Sea, the two German crews had further problems:

Oberleutnant **Hermann Riedel**

…We were busy with the casualty. We wiped the wound and dressed it as best we could but couldn't do any more for him. We had no injections in the First Aid kit and in any case did not know how to use them.

The wounded man soon became semi-conscious. The aircraft wobbled in the high seas and tilted more and more to starboard. The *Bordfunker* tried to contact a coastal station but soon gave up – the radio was dead.

I then looked at my men and saw that they had bravely attacked the emergency rum rations. They were quite drunk. I had strictly rationed our rum after our first ditching and then handed it out after we had been picked up. I didn't know that our rescuers had also handed out some rum. Paul Suessenbach wanted to show off to his colleague and pottered about with the radio. "I'll show you how to raise the whole world!" he boasted. He too had no luck – the radio stayed dead.

The seaplane tilted more and more dangerously to starboard. We were convinced that it would capsize so I ordered my crew and the *Bordfunker* to get into the dinghies and to be ready to get away from the plane if it capsized. Three of us stayed on board. We secured a dinghy to the port float and clambered onto the port wing tip. We were convinced that we would be rescued at daybreak. The waves were still very high but the *Bordmechaniker* and I carried the now deceased *Leutnant* from the cockpit to the port float, securing him safely to ensure that we took him with us in case we had to get into the dinghy.

The night passed slowly and the weather got worse. During the night, the dinghies with the rest of the crew drifted away and despite working hard were not able to return to the seaplane. Very soon they were far away…

The nightmare for Hermann Riedel and the two crews was set to continue despite them surviving the night on the freezing North Sea. Meanwhile, as dawn broke on 16 August 1940, if the two Air Forces thought that there would be a let up in German attacks, they were sorely mistaken. The day would see yet more action but this time it would be confined to the southern part of Great Britain.

The first attacks manifested themselves mid to late morning when a series of 'rolling' raids took place against a number of airfields in Kent and Essex. However, just after lunchtime another German formation was again plotted approaching the Isle of Wight and this attack would prove the vulnerability of one of the *Luftwaffe's* hitherto terrifying bombers.

Twenty-nine *Stukas* of I/StG 1 were briefed to attack Tangmere together with twenty-five from III/StG 2. Simultaneously, *Stab* and III/StG 1 would attack the Fleet Air Arm airfield of Lee-on-Solent and Ventnor radar station whilst twenty-two *Stukas* from I/StG 3 would attack Gosport airfield. The fighter escort was equally massive with a mix of 268 Messerschmitt 109s and Messerschmitt 110s. However, despite all this effort, only one of the three airfields, Tangmere, housed fighters and the *Luftwaffe* would, yet again, end up spending considerable nugatory effort against targets not related to air defence.

The RAF response had been to match the threat but was not able to prevent serious damage being inflicted on Tangmere. Every hangar was hit, as were most other buildings and a number of aircraft destroyed or damaged. Personnel casualties were inevitable – in the region of twenty killed and nearly fifty wounded. The *Stukas* also succeeded in bombing Lee on Solent and

Portsmouth airfields but not as badly as Tangmere, and yet again Ventnor radar was put out of action for nearly a week. Destruction and damage could have been worse had not III/StG 2 been mauled to such an extent that four *Stukas* were shot down (all from 7/StG 2) and a further four returning with dead or wounded crew (one of the wounded being the *Gruppen Kommandeur, Hptm* Heinrich Bruecker) and their part in the attack was called off. I/StG 1 also suffered, losing five aircraft with five crew men killed and four being taken prisoner:

Unteroffizier Erich Koenig, 3/StG 2

At the end of June 1940, I joined the *Staffel*. The attack on Tangmere was my only one against the British mainland – all others were against convoys or patrol flights. On this day, *Fw* Rocktaeschel and I were flying in the *Kette* of *Oblt* Goetzpeter Vollmer, our *Staffel Kapitaen*. After dropping our bombs on Tangmere, I tried to get away from the attacking fighters by flying very low. Two fighters pursued me and attacked constantly. During the course of this chase, we received several hits. East of the Isle of Wight, our engine seized up. Before that, I had tried to gain height for a parachute jump but now we were too low to bale out and my badly wounded *Bordfunker* would not have managed it. There was not too much time to think. I shouted for him to unbuckle, then threw off the roof, unbuckled as well and was only just able to level the plane when we hit the water. Our aircraft turned over and we were hurled out.

The two British fighter aircraft had stayed with us to the end. They circled the spot where we had hit the sea and I can remember that one of the pilots waved when he saw us swimming in the water and then flew away towards the coast. I think he notified the British rescue service or the Royal Navy.

Lying on its back, the aircraft stayed afloat for a few minutes and then it sank. After I had resurfaced, I swam to the aircraft, opened the compressed air bottle in my life jacket and looked for my *Bordfunker*. He had surfaced near the plane as well. It could have been a great deal worse for me. My life jacket had been damaged and did not hold air but I had an airbed with me which I had always put on my parachute, filled with a little bit of air. The parachute and airbed had also been thrown out of the plane so I was able to use it like a life jacket. I tied myself to my *Bordfunker* so that we would not drift apart and after we had been in the water for some time, a British sea plane arrived, leading a speedboat to us. The boat's crew pulled us aboard and when they saw that we were both wounded, they waved the sea plane to land. We were then transferred to this aircraft, flown to an airfield and from there taken by ambulance to a hospital in Chichester.

A few times a Squadron Leader visited me in the hospital. From him, I learned that *Fw* Rocktaeschel and *Ofw* Witt had been killed during the attack on Tangmere. He also told me that from the logbooks which were found in *Ofw* Witt's briefcase, he knew that both had been old hands with many missions in Poland and France. *Ofw* Witt was responsible for keeping the logbooks in accordance with the rules. He had collected all the logbooks to check and sign them and he had taken his briefcase on this mission!

The battered remains of Fw Rocktaeschel's *Stuka – mortally wounded, he managed to land the aircraft.* (via Watkins)

The series of attacks, although achieving some success, had resulted in many lives lost and, in the case of III/StG 2, they had not even made it to the target. If the *Stuka* crews thought that 16 August 1940 was a bad day, worse would come in two days time.

Later in the afternoon of 16 August, a series of attacks, all against airfields from Benson in Oxfordshire in the west to Hornchurch in Essex in the east, stretched Fighter Command's resources to the limit. The major attack was by seventy-five Heinkel 111s from all three *Gruppe* of KG 55 against airfields at Heathrow, Heston and Feltham. Even this attack was not directed against fighter airfields and the Germans suffered four bombers destroyed, a further one damaged, ten crew killed, three taken prisoner and four wounded. However, one attack, again against a non-fighter airfield, had spectacular results when two Junkers 88s from an unknown unit carried out an audacious attack on Brize Norton in Oxfordshire. The result was that nearly fifty training aircraft were destroyed and countless others damaged.

Meanwhile, back in the North Sea, the two German crews, shot down over twenty-four hours before, were still struggling to survive:

Oberleutnant Hermann Riedel, 8/KG 26

Around noon on 16 August 1940, a seaplane appeared. It was an air sea rescue seaplane like ours – white with red crosses. It was a three engined Dornier 24[8]. It circled round us and prepared to land. With red signal flares and by waving our arms, we tried to make the pilot to go towards the drifting dinghies. The crew understood this and flew off north-east. We did not see anything of this plane for the rest of the day. We waited in vain.

The Do 24 arrives overhead. (Riedel)

In the afternoon, a ship appeared but remained at a certain distance. Nothing further happened that day – we were stiff from the cold, hungry and thirsty. We had some emergency rations but most of them were in the dinghies that had drifted away.

Early in the afternoon of the next day, we had drifted nearer to the ship. It had to be a German mine sweeper. Then a motor launch left the ship and crept nearer and with great difficulty tied up to the starboard

[8] This was a Dornier 24 coded D-APDA of *Seenotflugkommando* 1 flown by *Oblt* Karl Born.

float to take us on board. We had to stay on the wing tip until our dead comrade was taken on board. This was difficult and the boat was damaged so much that the naval ratings went back to the ship with great difficulty. Once there, the motor launch sank!

It took a long time before a rowing boat left the ship and reached our seaplane. This one came to the port float and we jumped on board. The oarsmen pulled away and relieved of our weight, the seaplane tilted to starboard and sank.

The minesweeper and help arrives. (Riedel)

The He 59 capsizes. (Riedel)

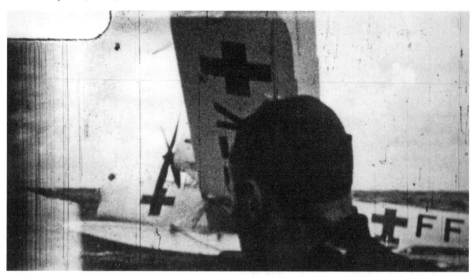

Once on board the ship, we received a hearty reception. We promptly had a medical check up, a hot bath and dry clothes before being given a bunk. I got up and made my way to the bridge and questioned the Captain. From what I told him, he was able to make towards the other dinghies and seaplane. The seaplane and the ship made radio contact and we knew that all were safe and sound. As we neared the Do 24, we could see all three engines hanging down from the wings.

The launch went out to bring the crews to the ship – thank God all were well. The day before, the Do 24 had found the dinghies but on landing in the rough seas, the three engines had broken from their mountings but the plane itself had remained seaworthy. I also learned from the Captain of the minesweeper that they had spotted us the day before but as we were in a minefield, they had not dared to come any closer!

The ship took the Do 24 in tow but near the entrance to Norderney Harbour, the seaplane, rocking dangerously, had to be cast off and sunk by gunfire. Once in the harbour, our dead *LtzS* was carried ashore and we were taken to hospital. The next day I was able to fly a borrowed aircraft to KG 26's home airfield of Schwerin where I reported back. It was no surprise to learn that we were still reported as missing in action.

Despite the above dramatic events, German air operations for 17 August 1940 were almost non-existent and many might have hoped that 18 August 1940 would be similar. Apart from the usual reconnaissance flights, the first of three massive attacks on this day did not materialise until early in the afternoon. The first was aimed against the airfields at Biggin Hill, West Malling and Kenley

The Do 24 under tow. (Riedel)

The burnt out remains of the only loss of KG 1 – Lt Rudolf Ahrens of I/KG 1 successfully crash-landed and then managed to destroy his He 111.

by Heinkel 111s of KG 1 and Dornier 17s and Junkers 88s of KG 76. The attack
on Kenley was a complex one consisting of high level attacks by all three
Gruppe of KG 76 with 9/KG 76 finishing off with a low level attack. However,
because of a delay over France and already alerted defences, the attack was not
as successful as hoped. The same can be said about the attack by KG 1 which
failed to cause any major damage to the airfield. The Germans lost nine
bombers with a further ten damaged.

To add insult to injury, many of the bombers on this attack were carrying
war reporters and cameramen (about eight in total) as well as a number of
officers to gain experience. The most senior officer along for the attack, *Oberst
Dr* Otto Sommer, was killed whilst one war reporter, *Sonderfuehrer* Walter Surk
was killed and another captured:

Sonderfuehrer Willi Perchemeier

On a magnificent day, we took off from our airfield at Creil. The target
was Kenley aerodrome, the date 18 August 1940. It was intended that our
Staffel would lure away the British fighters and *Flak* attention from another
Staffel which would attack at low level. In addition, we would then dive-
bomb the target. We flew at an altitude of 4,000m. A short time after the
Flak stopped, the fighters appeared. One of them hit our port engine
which immediately burst into flames. The fighter pilot had luck in so far
as our gunner's machine gun jammed.

There was no alternative other than to drop the bombs from high
level rather than dive bombing and there was enough time afterwards to
bale out. Unfortunately, our pilot could not get out of the plane in time
and died an airman's death. Fear? Not at all – there hadn't been
enough time; you just acted like a robot.

Near the ground, hanging on my parachute, I tried to get past a
threshing and harvesting machine but failed, landing between the tow
bars and hurting my spine. I then dragged myself, limping, along the
meadow until somebody from the Home Guard spotted and then
arrested me. I was then taken away to a cell by car.

Much worse was about to occur to the west. The whole of StG 77 together
with I/StG 3 were briefed to attack airfields in the Solent area. Twenty-eight
Stukas from I *Gruppe* went for the Coastal Command airfield of Thorney Island,
the same number of *Stukas* from II *Gruppe* targeted the Fleet Air Arm airfield at
Ford whilst III *Gruppe*'s target was the radar station at Poling. Gosport airfield
(which housed a torpedo development unit) was the target of I/StG 3. Again,
the only target which had any relevance to the air defence of the United
Kingdom was Poling. Although damage was inflicted on the airfields, especially
Ford which was non-operational until September 1940, and Poling radar station
which was put out of action for nearly a week, *Stuka* losses were nearly

catastrophic. Ten *Stukas* from I/StG 77 were shot down and a further one written off on its return – seventeen aircrew, including the *Gruppen Kommandeur Hptm* Herbert Meisel were killed, five captured and six wounded. II *Gruppe* lost three aircraft, five men killed and one captured whilst III *Gruppe* lost one aircraft and one written off on its return and four men killed. Added to this, eight of the *Stuka's* escort were shot down whilst Fighter Command lost just five aircraft with two pilots killed and three wounded.

One more major attack would take place before dark. Dornier 17s of KG 2 aimed to attack Hornchurch airfield whilst the Heinkel 111s of KG 53 went for the airfield of North Weald. Eight RAF squadrons were scrambled to intercept both raids and their massive escort. However, both targets were obscured by cloud and the German bombers turned for home, dropping their bombs on coastal targets but not before four Heinkel 111s from KG 53, including one flown by the II *Gruppe Kommandeur, Maj* Reinhold Tamm, were shot down.

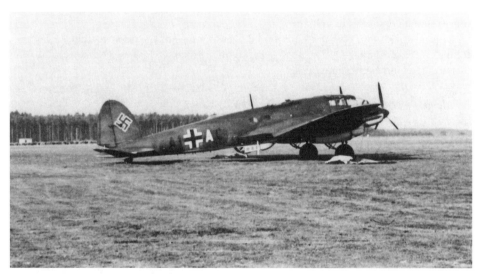

The Gruppen Kommandeur's *He 111 of II/KG 53, probably the same one flown by* Maj *Tamm on 18 August 1940.* (Hoehler)

Again, as night fell, the nocturnal bombers took to the air again, their crews probably relieved that they did not have to face Spitfires and Hurricanes. As for 18 August 1940, it stands out as the day in the Battle of Britain which saw the greatest number of aircraft destroyed or damaged on both sides. The *Luftwaffe* suffered sixty-nine aircraft damaged beyond repair or destroyed as opposed to the RAF's thirty-nine. However, the British lost a further twenty-nine, which were written off after being attacked on the ground. Furthermore, added to the losses suffered by the *Stukas* two days before, 18 August 1940 saw the end of Junkers 87 operations in the Battle of Britain. Yet again, thanks to correct tactics, courage and tenacity, Fighter Command had survived another test. For the *Luftwaffe*, criticism was heaped on the fighter *Geschwader* with the result that many of the *Geschwader* executive officers were replaced by younger, more aggressive men with specific orders to protect the bombers even closer. This was a blow to the Messerschmitt 109 and 110 pilots, especially the former, because on their *Freie Jagd* they were having greater successes over Fighter Command.

The next two days were virtually incident free. The only noteworthy incident being on 19 August when *Fw* Johann Moser of 7/KG 51 carried out another one of those audacious attacks against an airfield. This time it was the grass strip at Bibury in Gloucestershire, temporary home of 92 Squadron. One Spitfire was destroyed, another three damaged and one ground crew member killed. Two 92 Squadron Spitfires gave chase and shot the Junkers 88 into the sea but not before the Spitfire of Plt Off Trevor Wade had been damaged by return fire. He crash landed and managed to get clear of the Spitfire before it exploded; the four German crew were all killed.

21 August, however, saw the *Luftwaffe* taking advantage of the poor weather to undertake a number of *Stoerangriffe* or nuisance attacks. The first German loss occurred just before lunchtime:

Sonderfuehrer Kurt Rasche, attached to 2/KG 2

On 21 August, we had breakfast at our Officers' Mess – the mess being nothing more than an ordinary living room in a farmhouse. We were looking forward to our next trip into the town of Arras and as the cloud base was only as high as 300m, we didn't expect any flying. Nevertheless, we were ordered to take off – one aircraft only. We were to cause a little 'storm' on the other side – causing air raid alarms and, consequently, forcing people to hurry to the air raid shelters (especially, of course, the working population). The aircraft chosen was coded 'F' for 'Fritz', that is to say the one I regularly flew in.

Having taken off, we broke through the cloud but then reached another [layer]1,000m above the first one and broke through that one too and flew above the white cloudy sky in the sunshine. In the distance, we saw a British plane on a reciprocal course, possibly entrusted with orders similar to ours. Soon we guessed we were above

Sd Fhr *Kurt Rasche*. (Rasche)

England – a good reason to break back through the clouds. Finding ourselves still over water, we continued at that altitude and after a while we could see the land below us. Flying across woodland, we suddenly noticed a vast clearance and, under the trees near its edge, a big hangar. There was no question that this was a good object for our bombs. For this purpose, we turned back towards the hangar and dropped our bombs.[9]

A Do 17 Z of I/KG 2 practices an airfield attack.

Having not seen a single burst, we repeated our attack, flying towards the hangar. A second attack and we noticed nothing so we went into a dive. All at once, on the other side of the clearing, we discovered a number of military huts. At this moment we were certain that this was an airfield so we turned back to scrutinise in closer but this turned out to be once too much as suddenly one of the crew shouted "Spitfire!" They then attacked us from the flank – three Hurricanes…

[9] This was possibly Pulham airfield.

Sub-Lieutenant Richard Gardner, 'B' Flight, 242 Squadron

At 1200 hrs, 'Blue' Section [Flt Lt George Powell-Sheddon, Gardner and Plt Off John Latta] scrambled off its patrol line of Norwich. At 1210 hrs, we were given a vector of 190° followed by another of 240°. Enemy aircraft was sighted by the whole Section just off our port bow flying on a course of 270° magnetic. We were flying between two layers of intermittent cloud 8/10ths at 3,000ft. Enemy aircraft on sighting us dived in a left hand spiral showing the white crosses on his fuselage. Blue 1 got in a burst before enemy aircraft reached the cloud. Blue 2 and myself dived through the cloud after him. As I came out of the cloud, I found Blue 1 attacking again. I was unable to open fire. The enemy aircraft opened very heavy fire at Blue 1 as he closed in and broke away to the right.

I opened fire at 250 yards and concentrated on his port engine which caught alight. I then transferred my fire to his fuselage which also burst into flames after two seconds of fire. I closed to 20 yards. I stopped firing and followed enemy aircraft until he crashed in a wood.

Unteroffizier Heinz Hermsen, 2/KG 2

...As I was the *Bordfunker*, I was sitting with my back to the direction of flight and my duty was to pay attention to the rear. I did not realise what was going on at the front – I only noticed that something was wrong in the cockpit. When I turned my head, I saw fire and smoke. Now it was obvious – fighter attack! Then, three fighters appeared and attacked from behind. Over the intercom, I reported that we were under attack from behind but did not get an answer. Now, I had to repel the attacks and I think that one of the fighters had been hit because it showed a trail of smoke and turned to port. Because there was a short break in the attacks, I asked again what was going on but as before, there was no reply. Our entry hatch had gone and I couldn't see anyone...

Uffz *Heinz Hermsen*. (Hermsen)

Sonderfuehrer Kurt Rasche

...The long threads of their tracer approached our plane – immediately the port engine caught fire. I tried to defend ourselves by using the left hand machine gun. Ridiculous – what could I do with only one ammunition drum!

I felt that something had hit my legs. At that moment, the cockpit burst into flames. I couldn't see my comrades in the cockpit or the rear gunner and all at once, I was getting uneasy. I have no reason to be ashamed of admitting I was thoroughly frightened.

I tried to pull the red lever in the floor of the cabin for the door to drop away but I couldn't find the lever in the sea of flames. In fact, it was impossible to see anything at all. Suddenly, I realised that the cockpit roof had flown off and I tried to extricate myself upwards but in vain. The plane climbed and pressed me back but then it dived and I shot out quite by myself. I opened my parachute and landed in a meadow.

From afar, I heard dogs barking and a female voice getting closer and calling in German "Remain lying – we'll help you." Later a jeep arrived and took me to the camp we had just bombed. I was given immediate medical assistance and friendly attention. The Commanding Officer lent me his own pyjamas and later even his wife and child came to see me. In that camp, by the way, I came to know that our bombs had not exploded – our *Beobachter* had failed to arm them!

Unteroffizier Heinz Hermsen

...The plane was diving very fast and steeply towards the ground. Then there were critical moments. A new fighter attack. It was not possible for me to climb over my seat and bale out of the hatch. I had no choice but to pull the emergency lever and jettison the cockpit roof. Within seconds, the airstream blew the roof away which pulled me out of the aircraft. In my hand was the roof but not the ripcord. I had to feel for it and somehow I managed it. Looking back, I must say that I had been lucky because a few seconds after my parachute opened, I touched the ground. My watch said it was a few minutes to midday.

I met the *Beobachter* some time later – his hands were badly burnt. He told me that the pilot had been killed in the first attack and that his burns had been caused by an incendiary bomb and signal flares which exploded after this attack.

Dropping its cockpit together with the guns, the bomber continued flying northwards, missing a town hall clock by 50 feet. It then clipped a tree, crash-landed and careered across the ground at speed through a garden, killing two ponies, before it hit another tree and burst into flames. The charred remains of *Lt* Heinz Ermecke were buried five days later in the town into which the Dornier had almost crashed.

Less than an hour later, the next incident took place:

Sergeant Andrew Darling, Yellow 3, 'A' Flight, 611 Squadron

Yellow Section sighted the Do 17s flying inland at 4,000–5,000ft, speed 230–250 and in a tight 'V'. No evasive action taken by enemy aircraft before first attack. Yellow Leader [Sqn Ldr James McComb] ordered Number 3 attack and when in position to fire, I only got one burst at number three enemy aircraft as formation entered cloud. Immediately on picking up enemy aircraft for the second time, they again went into cloud. Before going in, I saw that number two enemy aircraft was pouring out smoke from starboard engine. I followed enemy aircraft, who were still in tight formation, into cloud and knowing I was close behind (because of the slipstream), gave another burst. Still in cloud, thick black smoke covered my windscreen and on coming out, I saw enemy aircraft hit ground and burst into flames. As enemy aircraft hit, I observed six or seven enemy descending by parachute.

Oberleutnant Herbert Schwartz, *Staffel Kapitaen* 6/KG 3

On 21 August, I had just returned from a training flight with two of the new aircrew when I learned that three planes each from 4 and 5 *Staffeln* had taken off for a mission. I got permission from the *Geschwader Kommodore* for a mission as well and decided to take the two new crews with me, thinking that this might be a good opportunity to get them acquainted with the real thing. In fact, both behaved very well flying out in cloud. Before we reached the British coast, we got word that we had been detected by radar. Still, this was no reason to abandon the mission.

Unfortunately, leaving cloud to prepare for the attack, we found the Spitfires directly behind us and they had the good luck to silence my port engine. This meant abandoning the mission and returning home. As

Left to right Oblt *Herbert Schwartz,* Lt *Guenther Zein (+29 August 1940) and* Oblt *Ulrich Matschoss, Brussels, July/August 1940.* (Dillen)

both the radio and intercom were out of action, I could only hope that the other crews would understand my change of course for Antwerp and disappearing into cloud again. Unfortunately, one of the aircraft [flown by *Uffz* Georg Pollmann] lost me in this manoeuvre and tried to find me again in the clouds which in fact he did but tearing off about two metres of the left wing and cutting deep into my fuselage, beheading the *Bordfunker* in the process.

The remains of Oblt *Schwartz's Do 17, 21 August 1940.* (via Cornwell)

My plane went into spin and we were fast spiralling down. None of the usual manoeuvres could get the plane out of the spin and I decided to try the last resort – putting the plane onto its back. I didn't have to worry because the plane then broke up. As I gathered, the tail broke off, letting the fuselage flip upside down. My *Beobachter* broke through the cockpit roof and I must have got out the same way after my seat belt had broken. How the *Bordmechaniker* got out I do not know.

I only had to open my parachute and it was nice to hear the birds singing after all the noise of a few seconds before. In the distance, I counted four parachutes from the other aircraft and I still saw our adversaries flying around. I guess I came out at an altitude of about 400m because I landed very quickly. All of us were then rounded up by the personnel of a searchlight battery.

Oberleutnant Ulrich Matschoss, 6/KG 3

There is not much to add to the report of my pilot. I only remember that when we collided, I was pressed into the corner of the cockpit, unable to reach the handle for the emergency exit even though it was only a few inches from my extended arm. A movement of the plane threw me to the other side and I was then thrown forwards. I lost consciousness for a few seconds, woke up, saw my legs above me, then the earth, then my legs again and I thought it was high time to pull the handle of my parachute. I did so, it opened and I was then on the ground. Apparently the hole made by me when I was thrown out was also used by the rest of the crew.

Incidentally, that day I had caught a rather bad cold and was going to the medical station on the airfield when I met Herbert Schwartz who asked me to come with him on the mission. I said "I'm rather ill, I want to go to bed" and he said "You can lie down in two hours' time – we'll be back by then." It was seven years until we were back!

The foray by II/KG 3 was quite costly – in addition to the two Dornier 17s lost by 6 *Staffel*, Red Section of 611 Squadron also shot down two Dornier 17s from 4 *Staffel* flown by *Lt* Hellmut Krueger and *Fw* Max Zimmermann. This 'quiet' day had so far cost the *Luftwaffe* five Dornier 17s with ten aircrew killed and ten prisoners of war. The only RAF casualties were five Spitfires from 611 Squadron damaged in combat with II/KG 3.

Things then went quiet for a few hours before the *Luftwaffe* appeared over the now sporadically cloud laden British skies. This time, I and II/KG 54 took off to attack the airfields of Brize Norton and Abingdon and the Supermarine Factory at Southampton. The weather was both a blessing and a curse for the German crews as in addition to giving them protection, the targets were also to an extent protected. However, it didn't stop Red Section of 234 Squadron from shooting down *Ogefr* Gerhard Freude and his crew from 1/KG 54 – the aircraft crashed and exploded near Winchester: its crew are still listed as missing. Exactly two hours later, two of the II *Gruppe* aircraft briefed to attack the Supermarine Factory were intercepted by Hurricanes of 17 Squadron:

Oberfeldwebel Heinz Apollony, 4/KG 54

Briefing was at 1330 hrs, take off time about 1400 hrs. Fly singly from St André to Cherbourg, cross the Channel to Brighton, change course to London, from there change course to Bristol, change course to Southampton to drop high explosive incendiaries onto the Spitfire factory. Weather was supposed to be 8/10ths at 15,000ft. This would have been ideal weather for our mission but the moment we crossed the British coast, there were clear blue skies.

We decided not to fly the full course but to dive into Southampton and to get out as fast as possible. However, my *Bordfunker* must have been asleep because I saw the Hurricanes before he did and they were already diving towards us. All I could do was dump fuel which

Ofw *Heinz Apollony*. (Apollony)

Uffz *Kurt Miethner,* Bordfunker *in*
Ofw *Apollony's crew.* (Miethner)

momentarily stopped the attack and gave me time to release the bombs which fell into fields. Now I tried to outmanoeuvre the Hurricanes and to get back into the clouds over the Channel which I did successfully but the damage to the plane was too severe (both engines were overheating and losing power quickly whilst the dinghy was hanging in shreds behind the tail). It was therefore impossible to reach France.

I dropped out of clouds again – I knew that the Hurricanes would be waiting so the moment we came out, I released the canopy to show the pilots I was helpless and wanted to give up. This they accepted and stopped firing. Seeing a big enough field for an emergency landing, I came in for a good belly landing. Three minutes later we were taken prisoner.

Two Sections from 17 Squadron were scrambled to orbit their base at Tangmere. The first interception was by Blue Section from 'B' Flight:

Squadron Leader Cedric Williams, 17 Squadron

I was leading Blue Section [with Plt Off Harold Bird-Wilson and Plt Off Jack Ross] and was ordered to orbit base at 5,000ft at 1545 hrs. After being vectored to Worthing and return, an enemy aircraft was sighted 5 miles north-west of Tangmere just above cloud at 7,000ft. Enemy aircraft was then turning south. When the Section was about a mile away, enemy aircraft saw us and jettisoned bombs. I made a beam attack before

THIS AND NEXT PAGE *Blue Section of 17 Sqn were quick to visit the scene of their kill, 21 August 1940.* (Bird-Wilson)

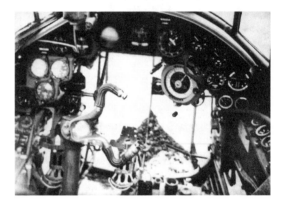

enemy aircraft could reach cloud and he received some hits. On emerging, I did a second attack from slightly above and astern. Enemy aircraft then disappeared. On re-emerging, I saw Blue Two sitting behind it and firing. I waited a few seconds and made another beam to quarter attack. Spurts of flame were then seen to come from enemy aircraft which disappeared into cloud. It later crashed at East Wittering.

An hour later, Red Section accounted for the 4/KG 54 Junkers 88 of *Lt* Alfred Kiefer:

Flying Officer Count Manfred Czernin, 'A' Flight, 17 Squadron

Red Section [Czernin, Sgt Cliff Chew and Sgt Leonard Bartlett] was ordered to patrol base below clouds at 1645 hrs. Cloud was 8/10ths at 5,000ft. We were given three vectors before going above cloud. We were then over Beachy Head. On going above, I saw enemy aircraft at about 8,000ft and 3 miles away. I ordered Section into line astern and gave chase. Section delivered a stern attack and put rear gunner out of action. Enemy aircraft's speed at first seemed 250mph but after attack slowed down to 160mph. We then delivered three beam attacks; enemy aircraft took no avoiding action but was going down slowly. After fourth attack, enemy aircraft's starboard engine, which had then been smoking, burst into flames. Two crew thereupon jumped with their parachutes which opened and they landed in the sea. I then approached enemy aircraft which was still on an even keel although losing height. I saw behind the cross a red snake-like crest and in front the number 'B3' or '33'.[10] As we were then 20 miles south over the sea, I did not think it wise to follow enemy aircraft which was obviously going down.

The pain for the *Luftwaffe* did not finish there. Just before the above combat, Plt Off Ted Shipman leading Green Section of 41 Squadron (Plt Off Gerald Langley and Sgt Frank Usmar) shot down the Heinkel 111 flown by *Fw* Otto Henkel of 9/KG 53 into the sea 15 miles east of Scarborough – the crew of five (which included *Hptm* Georg Pfeiffer, *Staffel Kapitaen* of 9/KG 53) all perished. Then 238 Squadron shot down two Junkers 88s flown by *Uffz* Kurt Conrad and *Uffz* Jochen Hartmann of 2/KGr 806 following an attack on the airfield at St Eval in Cornwall. This unit, ostensibly trained to attack coastal targets and as such normally carried *Kriegsmarine Beobachters*, was apparently making its first appearance over the United Kingdom and lost eight aircrew for its troubles. Two more German bombers would be lost before midnight – *Lt* Konrad Ksienzyk and his crew from 8/KG 2 were shot down near Ipswich whilst on another nuisance raid and a 9/KG 30 Junkers 88 suffered engine failure during a nocturnal attack on the north of England and ditched just before midnight. The crews from these last two aircraft were taken prisoner.

21 August 1940 appeared a quiet day but proved the effectiveness of Fighter Command. Only one fighter was lost (catching fire and burning out after crash-landing) and that pilot slightly injured. The Germans lost thirteen bombers – in human terms, thirty-one men died and twenty-two were taken prisoner. If the days before 21 August had seen heavy losses resulting from considerable effort, this day saw even heavier losses resulting from a considerably reduced *Luftwaffe* effort.

The days that followed saw sporadic German bomber activity, not helped by the weather. On 22 August *Erprobungsgruppe* 210 put in two appearances, attacking a convoy code named TOTEM off Dover and then Manston airfield. 23 August was even quieter than the days before and only one German bomber was lost over the United Kingdom that day:

Oberleutnant Johann-Heinrich Hellmers, *Staffel Kapitaen* Stab/KG 2

Because the weather forecast for 23 August was not favourable, no sorties were planned for KG 2. However, the *Stabstaffel* was to carry out a reconnaissance flight and *Stoerangriffe* on the engine factory at Coventry if the weather conditions permitted. According to the weather station, it seemed possible to carry out this mission. I took off from St Leger near Cambrai first, the other crews would follow at thirty minute intervals.

[10] B3 was the code for KG 54.

However, as we approached the Straits of Dover I noticed that the weather conditions were worse than forecast. We crossed the coast near Cap Gris Nez, entered cloud and flew around to the east of London. I wanted both to ascertain where I was and to get the wind strength and direction to get my bearings for Coventry. The clouds were now at 800m and we were flying just underneath them with the aircraft on auto-pilot. Whilst I was occupied with reckoning the course, the *Bordmechaniker* reported an aerodrome with bomb craters below us to the left. I could not see it from my seat on the right of the cockpit but a moment later, the airfield's anti-aircraft defences opened fire and a few seconds later, our aircraft was hit in the port engine which then caught fire. The tail was also hit.

Immediately, the pilot turned into clouds and to try and extinguish the fire, we side-

Oblt *Johann-Heinrich Hellmers*, Stab/KG 2. (Hellmers)

Do 17Z coded U5+BA of Stab/KG 2 *on a training flight.* (Schlegel)

slipped. Doing this, we lost a lot of height but we managed to put the fire out at an altitude of 150–200m. To try and reduce the plane's weight, we dropped the bombs blind in a field but the anti-aircraft fire had also affected the starboard engine, the engine speed reduced by about 100rpm and numerous instruments and the radio failed. The attempt to fly back on one engine (we had succeeded doing this a few days before) failed because we were descending at a rate of 1.5 metres per second. It was too low to bale out so the only thing to do was to force-land.

After we had stopped, we tried to set the plane on fire with incendiary bombs. Mine did not ignite and although the *Bordmechaniker* managed to put his bomb into a hole he had made in the wing, when he left the aircraft, the bomb slipped out. By then, Home Guard had hurried over and we were taken prisoner.

All were very friendly and there was an amusing event. The leader of the unit had taken away my flying suit, camera, money and cigarettes but he forgot to take my pistol. Only when I asked him what to do with it in captivity did he tell me to hand it over. Well the Sergeant standing next to us had a lot of fun – it was probably his first capture of prisoners of war! Kept under guard, I was taken to a big oak tree and whilst I was thinking about my situation, two soldiers brought me a packet of cigarettes and a mug of tea. We were then taken by bus to the airfield which had shot us down.[11]

The report which appeared in the local paper a week later was similarly amusing:

Bury Free Press and Post, 31 August 1940

Another Dornier crashed in a field of clover in an isolated parish a few miles away on Friday, apparently damaged by both British anti-aircraft guns and fighters. The four occupants, who were unhurt, climbed out and surrendered to a gamekeeper, Mr Lewis Frith, who was armed with a pitchfork and was accompanied by his two gun dogs. Mr Frith's first action was to tap the pocket of the first German he came to for his revolver which was at once handed over to him. The others handed their automatics to an Army officer who came up.

All four Germans spoke English. The Germans were equipped with little cases containing their personal belongings and from these, they produced peppermints and chocolate which they insisted in offering to their captors. Some mention was made of the war whereupon one of them exclaimed "One year September!" Another of the crew was anxious to know whether he would be allowed to write home and naturally received assurances on this point. The military then took charge. One interesting point was a little red, white and blue ring painted on one wing and bearing a date. This was a hole where repair had obviously been made to the fabric and was possibly a memento of a previous clash with British fighters.

---

[11] Believed to be Stradishall in Suffolk.

24 August saw the *Luftwaffe* increasing its efforts to annihilate Fighter Command both in the air and on the ground – the third and, for the RAF, most critical phase of the Battle of Britain had begun. The day wasn't made easier for the RAF when a series of problems with the reporting system allowed early morning German aircraft to meander over southern England with relative impunity. The new German tactic of 'rolling' one attack into another made it difficult to separate one attack from another but in the east, targets were the airfields of Hornchurch, North Weald and Manston whilst to the west, I and III/KG 51 attacked Portsmouth Harbour. The latter attack clearly illustrated the nightmare that RAF controllers were experiencing that day when the majority of the defending fighters were sent to patrol at a much lower altitude. The result was that the German formation was some 5,000ft above the Spitfires and Hurricanes and able to attack almost unmolested. Over 100 civilians were killed and well over 200 injured in addition to around fifty Royal Navy personnel. 200 bombs landed both in the Dockyard and City and the resulting fires raged for over twenty-four hours. The Germans lost one bomber to *Flak* and three fighters. The raid was a total success.

The first day of Phase Three of the Battle of Britain was in general a success for the Germans. It also saw the RAF's turret-armed Boulton Paul Defiant being badly mauled by German fighters (a similar mauling four days later resulted in the Defiant, like the *Stuka*, being withdrawn from the front line). The Germans lost eleven bombers in combat throughout the day and a number of those aircraft contained Executive Officers. *Maj* Friedrich Moericke, *Gruppen Kommandeur* of II/KG 76 was killed in the attack on Manston whilst the attack on Hornchurch by KG 53 resulted in the *Staffel Kapitaen* of 9/KG 53 of just three days, *Hptm* Heinz Loncier, being taken prisoner whilst *Maj* Kurt Ritscherle from *Stab* III/KG 53 had the misfortune of being shot down by one of the Defiants which hadn't been damaged in combat earlier in the day:

Pilot Officer Michael Young, 264 Squadron

I have rather vague memories of the action on 24 August 1940. However, I do remember flying as Number 2 to Sqn Ldr Hunter and that twenty Ju 88s were attacking Manston airfield. I remember following Philip Hunter seawards when we were attacked by Me 109s and became separated in the ensuing dogfight. Sqn Ldr Hunter failed to return from that patrol.

The next entry in my logbook was for a second patrol during which I recall finding a lone He 111 flying north towards Colchester. We used the classic Defiant attack approaching from under his port side and LAC Russell, my gunner, fired up into his belly. I don't recall any return fire and after what seemed a long time and without the German taking much avoiding action, he eventually crashed near a reservoir somewhere south of Colchester. I vaguely recall seeing a parachute.

That night, German bombers continued their attacks and were virtually unopposed. The RAF did try to intercept some of these attackers – Plt Off Bob Braham flying a Bristol Blenheim of 29 Squadron claimed to have probably destroyed a Heinkel 111 near the Humber Estuary whilst Flt Lt James Sanders flying a 615 Squadron Hurricane claimed to have destroyed a Junkers 88 and damaged a Heinkel 111. The only loss that can be matched to these three claims is *Fw* Alois Schmaderer's Heinkel 111 of 9/KG 55 which was shot down into the Channel south of Hastings (by Sanders) after attacking Harwell airfield.

During daylight on 25 August 1940, the *Luftwaffe* did not put in an appearance in strength until late in the afternoon. Simultaneously, the Junkers 88s of KG 51 attacked the airfield of Warmwell in Dorset whilst Dornier 17s of KG 76 attacked Hawkinge in Kent. The former attack was broken up by the RAF fighters, even though seven Junkers 88s managed to attack the airfield, and two bombers were shot down. The attack on Hawkinge was turned back for the loss of one Dornier 17.

That night, as the German bombers headed for British targets, RAF bombers headed for the German capital in a reprisal for the bombs that had been inadvertently dropped by the *Luftwaffe* on London the previous night. The damage caused was slight but the effect on German civilian morale was considerable. The night war was starting to escalate.

Three separate raids took place on 26 August 1940. First of all, the airfields at Biggin Hill, West Malling and Kenley were targeted by Dornier 17s of KG 3 and, it is believed, Heinkel 111s of KG 53. The RAF succeeded in preventing the German bombers from attacking their intended targets. A few hours later, the Dornier 17s of I/KG 2 took off to attack Hornchurch and III/KG 2 to attack Debden. Although Debden was bombed by a small number of Dornier 17s, the seven RAF squadrons that intercepted the formation succeeded in breaking up the attack. Six bombers were shot down and countless others damaged. Only four aircrew were killed but a further fifteen were taken prisoner, including *Maj* Martin Gutzmann, *Gruppen Kommandeur* of I/KG 2; a further seven were wounded including *Oblt* Gottfried Buchholz, *Staffel Kapitaen* of 3/KG 2. Meanwhile as this raid was returning to the Continent, to the west fifty-one Heinkel 111s of KG 55 were headed for Portsmouth Docks. Just four squadrons intercepted successfully, again preventing serious damage to the intended target and shooting down four bombers and damaging a number of others. To add insult to injury, a Heinkel 59 of *Seenotflugkommando* 2 flown by *Ofw* Herbert Eggers was shot down by Fg Off Paul Webb of 602 Squadron just before nightfall, having been engaged in picking up those bomber and fighter crews fortunate to have survived ditching – the four man crew were all killed.

The attack on Portsmouth was the last major daylight attack by *Luftflotte* 3 until the end of September 1940. Robbed of all its fighter aircraft, which had moved to the Pas de Calais, its bombers concentrated on relatively less dangerous night time operations and, as a result, losses were reduced dramatically, albeit for the time being.

The Do 17Z which contained Maj *Gutzmann,* Gr Kdr *I/KG 2, lies in a field near Eastchurch.*

27 August 1940 was another one of those days punctuated by drizzle and low cloud and the occasional German incursion and loss. However, 28 August saw the start of concerted efforts by the *Luftwaffe* solely against airfields in the south east of England. The chosen targets were Eastchurch and Rochford in the morning and the massive German fighter escort inflicted serious casualties amongst the intercepting fighters especially the Defiants of 264 Squadron who lost three of their number to JG 26, with at least another four damaged; the Defiant played no further part in the Battle of Britain after this day. In the early afternoon, Dornier 17s of KG 3 again attacked Rochford, 6/KG 3 losing the only German bomber shot down as a direct result of attacks by RAF fighters on this day:

Gefreiter Willy Gailer, 6/KG 3

I joined KG 3 in June or July 1940 together with pilot Krug [*Lt* Peter Krug], *Beobachter* Reinhardt [*Gefr* Robert Reinhardt][12] and gunner Brueckmann [*Flg* Anton Brueckmann] at Schweinfurt where we learned to fly the Do 17 and we were shot down on our second or third war flight against England.

I remember we were ordered to attack an airbase – I do not know where exactly – and whilst flying over England in formation, we were hit by anti-aircraft fire and our aircraft lost speed and fell back. After a

---

[12] Reinhardt was wounded in action on 15 August 1940 and was replaced by *Gefr* Artur Burghardt.

Left to right Gefr *Reinhard,* Gefr *Burghardt,* Gefr *Brueckmann.*
(Krug)

while, we were far behind our *Staffel* and were attacked by two Spitfires. Being the *Bordfunker,* I had to handle the upper rear machine guns so I tried to keep the attacking fighters away from us as did my comrade Brueckmann who fired the bottom rear gun. I am sure that one of the fighters was hit by our gunfire because he did not carry out further attacks against us. The other Spitfire continued to attack us and I became seriously wounded with the result that I was unable to shoot back any more. Anton Brueckmann suffered the same. I remember the pilot, *Lt* Krug, tried to escape by flying the plane at low level straight back to our base at Antwerp but he had no chance. As far as I still remember, we finally ditched in the Channel and the plane sank immediately. We were then picked up by fishermen and taken to a hospital in Margate.

Lt Krug's Do 17 Z, June 1940. (Krug)

Leutnant Peter Krug, *Staffel Fuehrer* 6/KG 3

It was a normal take off, after briefing about the target to be attacked. When we reached the coast near Folkestone, the anti-aircraft guns began to fire but did no harm to us. Reaching the Thames Estuary short of Southend, we were hit in the port engine which began to burn. The fire was put out by the extinguisher but from then on the engine was out of action. This forced me to dive down and turn out to sea to get home but we were intercepted by fighters and shot down.

Lt *Peter Krug.* (Krug)

Squadron Leader James Leathart, 54 Squadron

I sighted twenty-four Do 17s at 16,000ft over Manston. I dived to make a head on attack on the leader but couldn't get him in my sights. Pulling up again, I found a single Do 17 going home. I gave it a quarter attack from starboard and enemy aircraft crashed into the sea off North Foreland.

For the bombers, the day finished there. In the late afternoon, *Freie Jagd* carried out by a number of *Jagdgeschwadern* resulted in the destruction of eight RAF fighters. This was the sort of thing that the RAF wanted to avoid – heavy losses themselves with minimal casualties inflicted on the enemy. Trouble was, exactly the same occurred the following day. Apparently using a few bombers as bait, in excess of 500 German fighters sprung a trap on the thirteen intercepting RAF squadrons and this and a later *Freie Jagd* cost

Lt *Krug is brought ashore at Margate.*

the RAF nine fighters. The only German bombers lost that day were due to the inevitable accidents. However, during the night a Heinkel 111 of 3/KG 27 was shot down by a Spitfire of 92 Squadron flown by Plt Off Alan Wright and a Dornier 17 of 6/KG 2 was so badly damaged by an unidentified night fighter that it was written off on its return to France.

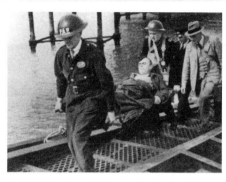

Gefr *Willy Gailer had the luxury of a stretcher.* (Fright)

August 1940 had indeed been a dark month for Great Britain and especially the RAF. With just two days of the month remaining and the weather forecast for those two days predicted fine conditions, it was to be expected that Fighter Command would still get no rest. With the German fighter units previously based to the west of France now established in the Pas de Calais, the German bomber crews must have felt confident as they lifted off from their airfields on the morning of 30 August 1940. The pattern of raids on that day is confused but it is believed that the first attack was by KG 1 which was briefed to attack Farnborough. The formation was broken up in a concerted attack by a number of fighter squadrons. The German unit lost five Heinkel 111s, including that flown by the *Staffel Kapitaen* of 5/KG 1, *Hptm* Rudi Baess, which was rammed by a Hurricane flown by Plt Off Edward Morris of 79 Squadron. Close on the heels of this attack was another by Dornier 17s of II/KG 76 against Biggin Hill. Immediately after lunch, more attacks materialised, one of the later attacks causing serious damage to Biggin Hill. This was carried out by the fighter-bombers of *Erprobungsgruppe* 210. However, the largest attack of the afternoon was against the Vauxhall Factory at Luton and the Handley Page Factory at Radlett:

Leutnant Ernst Fischbach, 7/KG 53

The weather that day was good. The briefing for the crew was about half an hour before take off which was scheduled for 1600 hrs. Twenty-seven He 111s took part in that raid to Radlett. I was the leader of the right *Kette* – the *Staffel Kapitaen* was *Hptm* Heinz Zorn.

After take off, all the planes met up and climbed to 9,000ft en route for Calais. Over Calais the fighters came to protect us. They did this but could

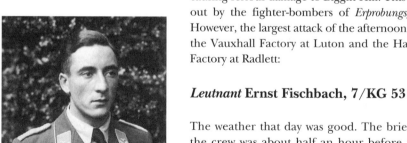

Lt *Ernst Fischbach, July 1940.*
(Fischbach)

not prevent us from being attacked. The RAF fighters came relatively late when our fighters, low on fuel, had turned back for base. The bombers, now alone, tried to go on and shortly after Maidstone, the first attack was under way. About seven or eight Hurricanes came slanting up from underneath and the opposite direction, spraying machine gun bullets into the bombers. After the third attack, my starboard engine was hit and it was impossible to keep up with the formation so I tried to get out towards the North Sea (in the direction of Blackwater Estuary) but three fighters caught me again and I had to change my mind. My crew were severely injured – two had been killed and two were so badly injured that they would have been unable to bale out and I couldn't leave the cockpit to help them. After belly landing, I got all out of the burning plane apart from *Gefr* Stilp.

The Gruppen Kommandeur *of III/KG 53,* Maj *Friedrich Edler von Braun, inspects* Lt *Fischbach and his crew.* (Fischbach)

Many of the bombers made it to the target only to get shot down on the way home:

Leutnant Wulff Roessler, 3/KG 53

We started (*Uffz* Gall, *Uffz* von Kuenheim and myself) from Vitry en Artois with our He 111 H-3 coded A1+CL and landed a short time later at Lille to change the aircraft because we had engine trouble. We shifted over to A1+IL with her *Bordmechaniker Uffz* Saam and gunner *Ogefr* Fischer.

KG 53 assembled over St Omer and picked up the fighters and headed towards the target north of London. Our position was on the right side of our *Gruppe*. Later on some British fighters appeared some 3,000ft above us and dived square into us, firing with all guns. We got one or more hits in the cooling system of our starboard engine and four minutes later had to stop the engine and feather the propellers. *Uffz* Gall was a good pilot and he easily trimmed the aircraft for single-engined flight. We

Lt *Wulff Roessler (left).* (Roessler)

overcharged the other engine and were able to hold our position in the *Gruppe*. We dropped our bombs at the same time as the others and turned for home.[13]

The *Gruppe* increased its speed to keep up with our fighters but we could not keep up with them and fell more and more behind. We could not dive to keep up with them so climbed to 14,000ft. Then an attack by fighters set the right wing on fire and killed or wounded von Kuenheim, Saam and Fischer. It was impossible for me to remove them from their seats to man their guns.

Some time later, a Bf 110 flown by *Lt* Walter Manhard with his wounded rear gunner flew under our aircraft to be protected by us, allowing him to escape from RAF fighters. I met Manhard later and he told me the full story.[14]

A few minutes later, bullets from a Hurricane destroyed our elevators and Gall and I both had to bail out...

Sergeant Henry Merchant, 'A' Flight, 1 Squadron

I was Number 2 of Red Section and upon sighting the enemy, followed my Section Leader into line astern. After attacking a Do 17 [sic] which was in company with another enemy aircraft, an Me 110 dived on me from astern. Breaking away, I shook him off and then saw ahead a single He 111. Climbing and going ahead, I attacked from the beam. On the second attack, the port engine stopped. At this moment,

a Hurricane from another squadron dived from the rear of the He 111 and got in a burst. Again, by attacking from the front, I got in a long burst and a man jumped by parachute. A further two parachutists jumped after about a minute as I put in another burst. The aircraft dived and crashed in the middle of a road near a cemetery to the east of Southend.

The remains of Wulff Roessler's He 111 strewn over a Southend road. (via Cornwell)

[13] The Vauxhall Works were badly damaged – over fifty were killed and over 100 injured.
[14] *Lt* Manhard was from 6/ZG 26; his *Bordfunker*, *Uffz* Franz Lechmann, had been wounded by RAF fighters north of Sudbury. On 3 September 1940 and with a new *Bordfunker*, Manhard was shot down and taken prisoner.

Leutnant Wulff Roessler

Gall, as a pilot, had an automatic parachute and because I opened my parachute by hand, he hung above me. This was the last I saw of him until we met on a ship on the way to Canada in January 1941. Then I talked with him for ten minutes – this was the first and last time we met after the crash. Twelve minutes later I landed on the shore of the Thames, between many people in swimming costumes. Nobody said a word and I was picked up by Home Guardsmen. In silence, I was taken by lorry to a training camp. There, a friendly Scottish sergeant put me with a German fighter pilot.[15] The next evening, I was interrogated by an RAF flight lieutenant together with two other officers. I only gave my rank and name and did not answer any other questions. The investigator became more and more angry then he said "Well, you did your duty and I did mine. It was not necessary to answer my questions because I know more than you do!" He then told me all about my *Staffel* and Vitry and so on.

A few more minor attacks took place before dark. II/KG 76, for example, attacked Detling without any noticeable results before the darkness allowed those units who had not been in action during the day to set forth. Amongst others, KGr 100 launched fifteen Heinkel 111s against Liverpool and Birkenhead that night with a further two attacking Plymouth.

He 111s of 3/KGr 100 set forth on another mission. (Schick)

---

[15] This was *Oblt* Helmut Rau, *Staffel Kapitaen* of 3/JG 3. However, Rau had been shot down twenty-four hours later so it is believed that the two officers actually met up the next day.

The RAF had been put under terrible pressure throughout the first full day of attacks in this new phase and the intensity of the attacks in the south east had needed at least twenty-two squadrons to be committed. Of those, many were in action more than once during the day. In addition to the daylight attacks, the RAF was almost powerless to counter the attacks by night. 30 August 1940 had seen the RAF flying its largest number of sorties so far during the Battle for the loss of twenty-one aircraft in combat and nine pilots killed. The *Luftwaffe*, in their biggest effort for two weeks, lost forty aircraft.

31 August 1940 started where the previous day had left off with 'rolling' attacks taking place from first until last light. The first bombers did not appear until 0945 hrs when the Dornier 17s of II and III/KG 2 crossed the Essex coast headed for the airfields at Debden and Duxford. Other airfields were targeted throughout the day included North Weald, Eastchurch, Croydon, Biggin Hill and Hornchurch; the latter two airfields were attacked twice during the afternoon and early evening. The second attack on Hornchurch was undertaken by the Dornier 17s of I and II/KG 76. They fared better than KG 3 which had lost three Dornier 17s in the earlier attack and only one bomber was lost:

Unteroffizier Albert Bloss, 2/KG 76

On 1 September 1939, the campaign against Poland started. During that time I flew eighteen missions. From 10 May 1940, we flew thirty-eight missions against France. During my tenth mission against Great Britain, I was shot down on 31 August 1940.

Over Hornchurch, our Dornier was attacked by anti-aircraft whereby the right engine stopped and so we were forced to leave the bomber formation. *Ofw* Lang was so badly wounded in the left leg that later on it was amputated in hospital.

Later on, we were attacked by five Spitfires. One of them approached our aircraft from the back in the so-called 'dead angle' of my machine gun. Some moments later I was badly wounded in the crown of the head which gave me cerebral damage and a total paralysis except in the left arm. The pilot and *Beobachter* were not wounded.

*The Do 17Z of 2/KG 76
shot down on 31 August 1940.*

Sketches made by Fw *Harald Pfaehler depict the combat on 31 August 1940.*
(Pfaehler)

After the crash-landing, we were captured by British soldiers and taken to a local hospital. On arriving there, I lost consciousness for a week…

Sergeant Maurice Pocock, Blue 4, 72 Squadron

I took off from Biggin Hill at 1745 hrs as Blue 4. We climbed to 17,000ft. The Sqn Ldr led us at enemy aircraft. As I was doing rearguard, I saw one Do 215 [sic] away from the rest of the formation with starboard engine smoking, losing height slowly. I carried out a Number 1 attack. I fired 240 rounds but had to break away owing to fire from behind. I dived to 10,000ft then climbed back to the scene of the engagement and searched around for the enemy aircraft. As I could not see any after a five minute search, I returned to Biggin Hill.

It sounds as if I selected a 'lame duck' and this does not show me up in a good light! However, perhaps he was a legitimate target anyway.

As darkness fell, the RAF pilots must have been relieved that the day was over, even if they were unable to defend against the German bombers which were about to take off to bomb targets under the cover of darkness. Thirty-eight of their fighters had been shot down and eight pilots killed; a further twenty-two pilots were wounded whilst the *Luftwaffe* had lost about thirty-eight aircraft. A change in *Luftwaffe* tactics now meant that it concentrated on one part of the United Kingdom which included Fighter Command airfields and aircraft production. It used rolling attacks escorted by a considerable and aggressive fighter force. RAF losses were increasing and they could not continue to replace losses inflicted by German fighters over the past two days if this trend continued. The Germans would continue to adopt the current tactics but only for a week after which fortunes were destined to change for both sides.

Sgt Maurice Pocock in belligerent mood.
(Lamberton)

CHAPTER 3

The Beginning of the End, September 1940

September 1940 started exactly where August left off with the first bombers arriving over Kent mid-morning making for Biggin Hill, Detling and Eastchurch airfields and London Docks (the Docks apparently being retaliation for the RAF attacks on Berlin). After lunch, it was Biggin Hill again as well as Kenley and Gravesend. German losses were light – only one bomber was shot down during the whole day, thanks mainly to the massive German fighter escort. This loss was a Dornier 17 of 9/KG 76 in whose crew was *Lt* Wilhelm Illg. Two weeks before on 18 August 1940, *Ofw* Illg had been a *Beobachter* in one of the Dornier 17s of 9/KG 76 briefed to carry out the low level attack on Kenley. His pilot, *Oblt* Hermann Magin had been mortally wounded and Illg had flown the damaged bomber back to France. This time, he and two of the crew of four were captured; Illg was later to receive the *Ritterkreuz* for his bravery on 18 August.

Again the day had been a bad one for the RAF, losing twelve aircraft in combat. Four of these came from 85 Squadron with Sgt (soon to be Plt Off) Geoffrey Allard being the pilot responsible for shooting down *Lt* Illg's bomber. The Operations Record Book entry for the afternoon of 1 September shows how the Squadron was suffering:

F540 Operations Record Book – 85 Squadron

Squadron again airborne at 1350 hrs to intercept enemy formation approaching Tunbridge Wells/Kenley area. At about 1355 hrs, about 150–200 aircraft (Do 17, Me 109 and Me 110) were sighted near Biggin Hill at 15,000ft. When sighted, the Squadron was still about 5,000ft lower and while climbing, were attacked continuously by 109s and 110s. Sgt Allard attacked a straggling Do 17 whose rear gunner baled out and whose pilot attempted a forced landing near the railway line at Lydd. Allard's oil pressure dropped and so he switched off and landed at Lympne but while the aircraft was being serviced, the airfield was bombed and his aircraft hit. Plt Off English carried out two quarter attacks on a Do 17 [sic] stopping its starboard engine; the enemy aircraft landed between Ham Street and Hythe and two of the crew were seen to emerge.[1] Sgt Evans attacked and destroyed an Me 109 with a seven second burst and an Me 110 with a five second burst but was unable to identify location of crashes. Sgt Howes attacked and shot down a Do 17 just south of Tunbridge Wells, two crew members baling out. He also damaged an Me 109. Fg Off Gowers was hit by a cannon shell and baled out with severe burns on hands and wounds in hands and foot; his Hurricane crashed at Oxted. Sgt Booth's aircraft was hit by cannon shells; he baled out near Purley and his aircraft crashed at Sanderstead. His parachute did not open properly and he suffered a broken back, leg and arm. Fg Off Woods-Scawen was posted missing and his body was found near Kenley on 6 September – his parachute unopened. Sgt Ellis was also killed in this fight. Six Hurricanes – all that remained of the Squadron – landed at Croydon between 1430 hrs and 1500 hrs and Plt Off Lewis had to land wheels up.

After a relatively quiet night for the German bombers, the attacks on 2 September 1940 followed a similar pattern to the previous day but this time started much earlier in the morning and lasted into the early evening. Similar targets were chosen and, yet again, only one German bomber was shot down by RAF fighters although two more Dornier 17s from the same unit, 9/KG 3, were written off on their return to France. The pattern looked to be the same for 3 September but the early morning attack by KG 2 on North Weald turned out to be the only major one of the day. The majority of German losses were fighters and, yet again, just one Dornier 17 (from 5/KG 2) was lost. That night the nocturnal bombers were again roaming all over the United Kingdom which forced one Hurricane squadron to take action:

87 Squadron Diary Entry – 3 September 1940

It was decided that 87 Squadron would start night flying again so 'B' Flight moved off to Bibury. The weather was about as good as possible for night flying and on the first night, Plt Off Beamont engaged an enemy aircraft south east of Bristol. He hit it but could not see the results.

No damage was reported to any German aircraft. For the moment, the German bombers were still relatively safe.

4 September saw no let up in the German bomber offensive. The first raid (by Dornier 17s of KG 76 against the airfields of Rochford, Eastchurch and Lympne) had no perceivable results but it is believed that this raid also hit the Shorts Aircraft Factory at Rochester, causing minor damage to the production line. However, the most noteworthy attack was by *Erprobungsgruppe* 210 against the air-

---

[1] This was in fact a Messerschmitt 110 of 13/LG1- *Ofw* Rudolf Kobert and *Fw* Werner Meinig were both captured.

field at Brooklands near Weybridge, the airfield being the home of the Vickers Aircraft factory. The attack was in two phases – as a larger formation headed towards targets in Kent, the fighter-bombers headed towards their target, reaching it for the loss of just one aircraft (that flown by its new *Gruppen Kommandeur Hptm* Hans von Boltenstern). They succeeded in stopping production for a number of days and causing the deaths of eighty-eight workers with countless others injured. This attack was particularly fortuitous for the *Luftwaffe* as Hitler was now becoming increasingly infuriated by the RAF's bombing attacks on the German homeland, particularly Berlin which had been bombed following the *Luftwaffe*'s bombing of London on the night of 24/25 August. Hitler now declared that the time for reprisals had come and this heralded the start of the *Luftwaffe*'s major nocturnal attacks against London – the London Blitz was about to start.

That night saw an increase in German night attacks and, at last, RAF night fighters started to meet with success:

A He 111 lifts off to bomb Britain.

Oberleutnant **Peter Biebrach,** *Gruppen Technischer Offizier,* *Stab* **I/KG** **1**

By August 1940, we had moved forward to the airfield at Montdidier for attacks against targets in England, partly large scale day raids but mostly night raids by individual aircraft. Targets were chosen in a some-what unsystematic manner or so it seemed. One night we might attack an industrial complex such as the Rolls Royce Works, another day an air-field or a Navy installation might be picked.

On 4 September, a report came in from Headquarters that two or three warships, thought to be destroyers, had pulled into Tilbury Docks and that we had to attack the Docks that night. Our crew was selected and in the usual pre-flight briefings we heard that the target might be protected by balloons in addition to anti-aircraft batteries. The weather was said to be fair with light cloud cover over the target area and with a light wind. It seemed logical that any defence would be aimed towards the south therefore it was decided to fly past the target and attack on the way back, flying as low as possible. This was easier said than done as there was no moon to help us in seeing what was ahead of the aircraft. Also, it was decided to fly on a course which would take us mid-way between Tilbury and the City of London (I would have preferred to have flown further east). We were to fly at 6,000m and night fighters were not expected. This was my fortieth war flight and I had flown by night against England many times before and hadn't once been opposed by night fighters, *Flak* or been picked up by searchlights.

We were scheduled to be over the target at 0100 hrs but, just before take off, *Ofw* Stockert (the upper gunner) reported that his gun would not move and was jammed. The *Gruppen Kommandeur* [*Maj* Ludwig Maier] and I thought about this for a moment and then decided that as it was unlikely that we would need the gun, we would continue. As will be seen, we were to regret this decision.

Contrary to our weather reports, the sky was cloudless over England, offering us no protection in case of trouble. Also, the westerly wind seemed to be somewhat stronger that anticipated. We tried to correct our course but not in time to avoid the defences around London. Our aircraft, in particular the underside of the fuselage and wings, had been painted with a water-based paint so as to offer no reflection. However, our aircraft were parked outside away from the airfield and prior to take off passed over tall patches of weeds and I assume that on that evening, some of this paint had been washed or worn away. Therefore, much to our surprise, we were suddenly picked up by two or three searchlights and in seconds were firmly held by many others which made it almost impossible to see anything in the cockpit. Seconds later, we were the target of a great number of anti-aircraft guns with well aimed salvoes.

We could smell the gunpowder from the exploding shells and the noise was incredible. However, we received no direct hits and there was no vital damage to the aircraft, as far as we could determine.

Black distemper applied to both a He 111 and its bomb load.
(Hoehler)

After a few minutes, the guns fell silent which was a relief to us but should have alerted us to some other trouble since we were still illuminated. A minute or so later, *Ofw* Stockert called that he could see something approaching. I reacted by taking the aircraft into a sharp right-hand turn. Almost simultaneously, I saw a great number of tracers fly past my port side followed by the attacking aircraft which I identified as a Blenheim. This surprised us as the Blenheim was thought to be slower than the Heinkel 111 and I surmised that he must have attacked from a higher altitude and it followed that he would not be able to repeat the attack as he was now below us. We therefore went back on course and continued our mission. However, without warning we were attacked again – the oxygen bottles exploded, leaving me temporarily unconscious due to the lack of oxygen. The port engine had partly sheared off and was spewing oil and wreckage – I managed to feather the propeller before the engine seized with a thud. Again, I made a sharp turn to starboard and pushed the nose down so as to escape the fighter...

Pilot Officer Michael Herrick, 25 Squadron

At about 0020 hrs, I took off from Martlesham to patrol a patrol line. I received a vector and then the wireless became unserviceable. After about ten minutes, I sighted an enemy aircraft ahead in searchlights but was unable to close and it drew away out of sight. Then at about 500ft above me, I sighted an enemy aircraft in a searchlight and attacked after five minutes. I opened fire at about 300 to 400 yards with a five second burst. Then the enemy aircraft disappeared. Immediately afterwards, another enemy aircraft was illuminated and after chasing for about ten minutes, I got within range and opened fire at about 400 yards. I then fired several short bursts with the range decreasing and obtained a good defection shot. The enemy aircraft seemed to halt and wave in the air and I overshot as I had used all my remaining ammunition. The searchlights turned on me and I was unable to see any more. As I overtook enemy aircraft, I noticed that it was falling to pieces and both engines were smoking badly. My rear gunner, Sgt Pugh, fired in both actions.

Oberleutnant Peter Biebrach

...We came out of the range of the searchlights but had lost some 2,000m altitude. The starboard engine was starting to overheat and was idling so as to give us enough electricity to light the instrument panel and give power for the landing lights. *Maj* Maier had gone to the rear of the aircraft and had established that both men there [*Ofw* Erwin Stockert and *Uffz* Horst Bendig] were dead and that there was considerable damage. However, the aircraft responded to all controls.

A large white 'stream' was seen further ahead and both the *Gruppen Kommandeur* and the *Beobachter* [*Oblt* Job-Wilhelm Graf von Rittberg] were of the opinion that this was the River Thames. I knew that this was impossible as we were still heading north-east and had passed the Thames a long time ago. I advised that we should leave the aircraft and had a brief argument over this whilst still losing altitude. When the decision to bale out was reached, Graf von Rittberg could not find his parachute until I remembered that the *Gruppen Kommandeur* had been sitting on it. With the parachute then in place, the starboard exit door was jettisoned and Graf von Rittberg flung himself out followed by *Maj* Maier. They had approximately 1,400m to drop. In the meantime, I had opened the door above my seat and climbed onto my seat squatting there ready to get out whilst holding the aircraft level. I left at an altitude of approximately 400m, pushed myself off the top of the fuselage (the aircraft was climbing suddenly and slowing accordingly) and I fell counting to three rather fast, pulled the rip cord and the parachute opened instantly. A few seconds later, I found myself on the ground in the middle of a fairly large clearing. It was shortly after 0130 hrs on 5 September 1940. I did not know it then but the war for me was over and it would be another six years and two months before I saw Germany again.

At about 0600 hrs, I attempted to orientate myself and to find a way out of the forest. As I had a severely sprained ankle and a sore back, this was a difficult task at first. I managed to find a country road and was unsuccessful at stopping a man on his bike and I arrived after about an hour in a little village and I tried to find some signs pointing to places that I might know. A blacksmith probably mistook me for a British pilot and

The fuselage of Peter Biebrach's He 111. (via Cornwell)

asked me into his house and his equally friendly wife served me a tremendous and most welcome English breakfast – I have sported her recipe ever since! I was then found standing in the yard by two policemen who had been alerted by the man on the bike. Both sported infantry guns with the bayonets in place. They carried out a perfect pincer movement towards me and I could not help but laugh. I was then placed in the rear of their little Austin and we drove off. First to the families of the policemen where I was given two more breakfasts, a bandage for my foot and new socks. Then we drove off to Ipswich where I was handed over to Police Headquarters. Shortly before getting to the town, one of the policemen remembered that they should have searched me so I was told to get out and their search produced my fully loaded Walther automatic. Having never seen one before, they handed it back to me so that I could unload it for them. I obliged.

For the next two days of September 1940, destined to be the last two days of this phase of the Battle of Britain, Fighter Command was again put under extreme pressure with a series of 'rolling' attacks against airfields. However, on the night of 5 September, the new die was cast when *Luftflotte* 2 launched its first major night attack against London, using bombers from four different *Geschwadern*. Then, on 7 September 1940, German tactics changed again.

Pressure from Hitler, and a realisation that all-out attacks on RAF fighter airfields had not destroyed the RAF, resulted in the *Luftwaffe* throwing its might against the British capital. It was hoped that the British will to fight, on seeing London being pounded day and night by German bombs, would falter and the RAF would be forced to commit all of its remaining fighters in defence of the Nation's capital; German fighters would then destroy the remaining Spitfires and Hurricanes. History has now shown that this was yet another German misjudgement.

There was scarce German air activity until about 1600 hrs on 7 September when radar screens detected in the region of 1,000 bombers and fighters spread between altitudes of 14,000ft and 23,000ft. By 1630 hrs, more than twenty RAF fighter squadrons were either airborne or at readiness and then thrown against the attackers. The target soon became clear when the German bombers droned onwards towards London, dropping their bombs on London's Dockland and setting much of it ablaze. The attack had lasted just under an hour and the RAF succeeded in shooting down forty-one German aircraft. Just over half of those lost were escorting fighters which had enabled the bombers to reach their target. The RAF lost twenty-two fighters but only ten pilots lost their lives.

Night came early to London on 7 September, brought about by the palls of smoke drifting from its Dockland. The *Luftwaffe* bombers came again that night on what now has been called the official first night of the Blitz and more civilian lives were lost. However, the start of the final phase of the Battle of Britain, with the *Luftwaffe* bombing commercial and civilian targets in addition to military ones, gave Fighter Command the break they needed. It is now thought that Fighter Command could not have sustained the pressure and losses experienced during the week prior to 7 September 1940 and if that phase had not changed, the outcome of the Battle of Britain could have been very different. Relieved Fighter Command's pilots might well have been, but the Battle of Britain was destined to continue for another fifty-four days.

The German bombers came again on 8 September when II and III/KG 2 headed for two separate targets in London. Two II/KG 2 Dornier 17s from the same *Kette* were simultaneously shot down by anti-aircraft fire whilst another exploded when attacked by a Hurricane of 46 Squadron. A III/KG 2 aircraft returned damaged after apparently colliding with an unidentified British fighter. That night, London received yet another pounding – it was just the second in what would transpire to be fifty-seven consecutive nights of pounding by the *Luftwaffe*.

9 September again saw the *Luftwaffe* making another major attack on London but not until the early evening. This was a relief for Plt Offs George Forrester and Jim Humphreys of 605 Squadron. They had spent the night of 8 September in London with their 'B' Flight Commander, Flt Lt Archie McKellar, and the two were glad of the rest, not going into action that day until the Germans made their appearance:

Pilot Officer Jim Humphreys, 'B' Flight, 605 Squadron

The Squadron was ordered off at about 1700 hrs and after some fifteen minutes, 'B' Flight was detached and vectored onto this raid. We made contact at about 1725 hrs. There were some twenty to twenty-five He 111s with Me 109s as close and high escort. Our vector placed us awkwardly at the rear of the formation and slightly below and it seemed that we were climbing for ages to get into the attacking position. All this was complicated by the odd peck from the close escorts.

As the high escorts were starting to show a little too much interest, I moved Green Section [Humphreys, Plt Off Cyril Passy and Plt Off Edward Watson] outwards, drawing them with us. Blue Section [Flt Lt Archie McKellar, Sgt Jan Budzinski and Plt Off George Forrester] then managed to attack, breaking up the bomber formation, and I turned Green Section in to pick off any of the scattered Heinkels. At this point, we were bounced by the Me 110s which I had not seen. Probably they were on free range.

My aircraft was hit three or four times, one being a 20mm high explosive right beside the throttle quadrant. I went down in an aileron turn for 2,000ft to 3,000ft and took stock. There was a sizeable hole in the cockpit wall, the throttle quadrant was gone, the cockpit was full of smoke and petrol fumes and I was feeling mighty sick. It seemed that she was about to burn so I baled out. This would be about 12,000ft.

I did not want to stay in that area so I did a free fall down to cloud level (about 3,000ft) and opened my 'chute. My hand was a mess – blood, flesh, bone and glove all mixed up together – so for the rest of the descent, I was hanging grimly onto the pressure point.

I came out of cloud over a Canadian Army camp at Bordon and drifted across it with the breeze. The natives were most unfriendly and treated me as a one-man invasion force. One feels so helpless listening to stuff going past from a Lewis gun! I was lucky – six holes in the canopy, one rigging line cut and one through the left breast pocket of my tunic which left a weal on my side. Come to think of it, I was lucky that day.

I landed just outside the camp in a copse just beside a railway line, was picked up by the Canadians and, having been relieved of my buttons, maps, flying boots, etc, I was taken into Aldershot. There I was put in the Cambridge Military Hospital and remained there for about four weeks.

Although Jim Humphreys thought he was a victim of the German escort, crew from one of the German bombers that 605 Squadron was attacking thought differently only then to be confronted by another one of the 605 Squadron pilots who had been 'on the town' the night before:

Oberfeldwebel Oskar Broderix, *Stab* III/KG 53

On the afternoon of 9 September 1940, about thirty aircraft from III/KG 53 took off from Lille–Roubaix to bomb the Queen Elizabeth Docks in London. I was flying in the lead aircraft of the *Stabskette* instead of *Hptm* Heinz Zorn, *Staffel Kapitaen* of 7/KG 53. Another aircraft in the *Kette* was flown by *Oblt* Barth. This was my fiftieth war flight – I didn't think it would be any different to the others so I had brought my Leica camera to photograph London.

Ofw *Oskar Broderix (right).* (Broderix)

In front of the He 111 H-2 they were flying in on 9 September 1940 are, left to right, Fw *Ernst Wendorff*, Fw *Willi Wenninger*, Oblt *Kurt Meinecke* and Ofw *Oskar Broderix*. (Broderix)

My *Beobachter* was different for this trip – usually it was *Oberst* Erich Stahl, the *Geschwader Kommodore*, but today it was my old *Beobachter Oblt* Kurt Meinecke. *Fw* Ernst Wendorff and *Fw* Wilhelm Wenninger had flown with me many times before but for *Fw* Willi Doering, this was his first trip.

We flew at an altitude of 3,000m and waited for our escort.

Then all of us flew towards London. Soon after crossing the coast, the RAF fighters attacked us and I saw many aircraft going down in flames. I cannot remember whether we were to do two passes or one over the target but we did drop some bombs and flew on west.

We were then attacked by Hurricanes which seemed to pick on the *Stabskette*. I heard Ernst Wendorff shout with joy – he had just shot down a Hurricane and we saw it go down.[2] Then another Hurricane attacked us. I heard Willi Wenninger say over the intercom "I've got him!" and then there was a crash and the controls went slack. The burning Hurricane had rammed us! I looked back and saw that the tail had been torn away and that the Heinkel was starting to break up. I remember pushing *Oblt*

---

[2] Believed to be the Hurricane flown by Plt Off Jim Humphreys.

A He 111 drops its deadly cargo.

Meinecke out of the cockpit and then lost consciousness. I awoke swinging on my parachute. I landed in a field and was captured quickly by soldiers who were brought by two girls. Later on I was taken to where my aircraft had crashed – all that I saw was a pall of oily black smoke.

Three Germans were killed in the crash just south of Alton in Hampshire; Plt Off George Forrester was killed when his Hurricane crashed just to the north of the town. It is believed that he had been mortally wounded or killed and it is conjecture as to whether he deliberately rammed the German bomber or not.

10 September saw a dramatic reduction in German air operations, bad weather being the reason for this. However, two German bombers did fall victim to Fighter Command aircraft in the evening. That night saw London, as well as Berlin and other targets in Germany, being bombed, the German bombers faring better than the RAF who lost two bombers in an attack on Bremen. Similar damage was inflicted on both capital cities.

The bad weather was still hanging around much of the United Kingdom the following day and it was not until mid-afternoon that a raid of "300+" was plotted heading towards London:

Armstrong Whitworth Whitley serial T4134 of 58 Sqn lies in the sea off Schleswig–Holstein after being shot down by flak attacking Bremen on the night of 10/11 September 1940.

Gefreiter Wilhelm Zimmer, *Stab* II/KG 26

Gefr *Wilhelm Zimmer keeping a look out for trouble.*
(Zimmer)

On 11 September 1940, we had been scheduled a day of rest. We were sitting in the canteen having our meal and a few beers looking forward to the rest. Then the warning came and we rushed to our accommodation to get parachutes, map cases and flying suits and then ran to our briefing. Our *Gruppen Kommandeur, Maj* Eckhard Christian announced the target as London and the flying formation.

At first we assembled over Belgium and Holland at an altitude of 5,000m and then the formation crossed the coast in the direction of London – it was then that we had a slight mishap. Because we were a crew of five and the *Kommandeurbesatzung*, there was additional oxygen for *Maj* Christian. It turned out that this had not been filled up so the *Major* and I had to share the same oxygen point!

We flew on through the *Flak* barrage. The weather was magnificent – above us a cloudless sky and at about 3,000m below us there were only a few drifting clouds. I think it was about 1600 hrs when London lay before us.

Now I heard someone yelling on the radio "Enemy fighters attacking behind us!" – this report came from our *Bordfunker* [*Ofw* Ziermann]. These fighters were Spitfires. I had already lowered my *Lotfe* bombsight and had in my sights our target – the docks along the River Thames. I leaned back a bit, looked up and saw that our fighters were involved in dogfights with British fighters about 1,000–2,000m above us. Now we were without fighter escort.

Then we heard a groaning – it was the *Bordmechaniker* [*Fw* Richard Herrmann] who had been wounded in the thigh by four bullets. The pilot [*Fw* Krothe] shouted "Drop the bombs – I cannot keep the plane under control as the engine is damaged!" Only now I noticed that I had been slightly wounded – grazes caused by splinters of perspex.

The pilot jettisoned the bombs which fell on the suburbs. The engine was switched off and we flew on with the remaining engine running fine. The British fighters flew attack after attack. The aircraft on our right flown by *Oblt* Gustav-Otto Bertram went into a spin and dropped away. All I could say was "Bertram is shot down." *Maj* Christian and I changed places. I went to the rear of the plane and took the *Bordmechaniker*'s position – when I wanted to dress his wounds, he refused and said that he had to fend off attacks.

Well, this afternoon, the RAF used really good tactics and we were not expecting that. The attacks were carried out in three waves – one from below, then one attack came horizontally and the third one involved our fighters high above us. We defended ourselves to the last cartridge – I was able to fend off some attacks from below. What happened next will always be a mystery to me. We had exhausted all our ammunition and were at the enemy's mercy. When our adversary noticed that we did not defend ourselves any more, he flew over our aircraft, wobbled his wings and dived away. After that there were no more attacks.

With our *Kette*, we curved around over London. In the place of *Oblt* Bertram, *Oblt* Ernst Haller, *Staffel Kapitaen* of 4/KG 26, now flew. My best friend *Gefr* Rudi Endrich was a member of the Bertram crew and on this day he was shot down a second time. The first time he was shot down over Narvik in Norway on 22 May 1940 but was released from captivity when the British troops retreated. I am happy to say that the Bertram crew were taken prisoner and survived.[3]

In fear and trembling, we crossed the Channel wondering how long we could stay in the air. It all went quite well until we approached our base at Gilze–Rijen in Holland. The undercarriage was lowered – it was a joy to see that it had worked and from my place in the cockpit, I checked if it was locked. I said "Everything all right!" but the last shock was to come. *Fw* Krothe came in to land and bumping and crashing, the plane turned round and round – all tyres had been shot to pieces.

Nobody had been wounded except the *Bordmechaniker* – immediately after our landing, he was transported to a hospital in Breda. Everybody was happy that we had come home safely but I still regard 11 September 1940 as a bitter defeat and a pointless waste of lives and material.

Gefr *Rudi Endrich, POW on 11 September 1940.* (Zimmer)

Despite a heavy fighter escort, the Heinkel 111s of KG 1 and especially KG 26 suffered heavy losses. KG 1 lost three bombers over England with a further two returning damaged whilst KG 26 lost seven with a further ten returning with varying degrees of damage. The majority of the losses were suffered by I/KG 26. From the *Stabskette*, one aircraft was shot down and the other two damaged whilst 1/KG 26 lost two aircraft and two damaged out of six flying that day. One 1 *Staffel* pilot, *Fw* Wilhelm Jabusch, even baled out over London and was captured,

Fg Off Brian van Mentz (centre) of 222 Sqn who was credited with shooting down Gefr Endrich and his crew (with Sqn Ldr R C Love, Fg Off G G A Davies, Plt Off J M V Carpenter and Plt Off C Stewart).

leaving his un-named *Beobachter* to fly the plane home, wrecking it in the ensuing crash-landing near Dieppe. The *Staffel Kapitaen* of 1/KG 26 would not have been impressed by this but as he too was shot down, he was not to know this:

---

[3] Three of the crew were captured; *Lt* Ferdinand Cramer, the fourth crew member, was killed.

Hauptmann Wolfgang Kuenstler, *Staffel Kapitaen* 1/KG 26

Our *Gruppe* had been at Courtrai in Belgium since 1 September 1940. On 11 September, we were briefed to attack Woolwich Arsenal. My *Gruppen Kommandeur Maj* Hermann Busch together with his *Stabskette* took command of my *Staffel* because we only had six aircraft ready for action on this day. We took off at about 1430 hrs Central European Time and had to climb and turn to meet our escort, Bf 110s of II/ZG 26. However, they were soon engaged in dogfights as soon as we crossed the coast so we had to go on by ourselves. At about 1630–1645 hrs, we were attacked by five Hurricanes coming from the front right. My *Kette* was attacked twice and after the second attack, my port engine seized and the other one caught fire. That did it! We turned away out of formation and after another attack from behind, we made an emergency landing south of Sevenoaks. Two of my crew had been killed but we succeeded in blowing the plane up with an incendiary bomb just as the good old Home Guard arrived!

Reichsmarschall *Goering visits Courtrai, 10 September 1940 – standing to his right is* Hptm *Wolfgang Kuenstler.* (Kuenstler)

The next three days were quieter, poor weather again being the reason. However, German bombers did continue to attack with relative impunity by night although losses were starting to occur, two of them indirectly as a result of the weather:

Uffz Alwin Machalett (POW 15 August 1940) and Uffz Erich Schmidt (POW with Hptm Kuenstler, 10 September 1940). (Machalett)

Oberleutnant Harry Wappler, 8/KG 27

I became a prisoner of war in the early hours of Friday 13 September 1940 between 0200 hrs and 0300 hrs. My plane hit part of a barrage balloon at Newport, South Wales.

The flight above ground was about 1,200ft. Very low I know but it was very bad weather and I was eager to know whether my last two 50

The remains of Harry Wappler's He 111 in a Newport street. (via Cornwell)

kilogram bombs were on target that night. It all then happened very quickly. The cockpit disintegrated and the same second I found myself out of the plane, feeling a blow to my right arm. I never flew with the safety belt done up and this must have saved me. Before falling unconscious, probably because my right arm had been broken in three places, I managed to open my parachute. I then suffered a blackout until about 1000 hrs the next morning when I awoke in the Royal Monmouthshire Hospital in Newport. The other three members of my crew were killed.[4]

RAF night fighters were also continuing to improve their effectiveness. Plt Off Michael Herrick of 25 Squadron had already shot down one Heinkel 111 at night and on the night of the 13/14 September 1940 would repeat this feat for which he was later awarded the Distinguished Flying Cross. At 0025 hrs on 14 September, he and his gunner Plt Off Archibald Brown took off from Martlesham Heath for a patrol over London. Over an hour later, he spotted a Heinkel 111 held in the beams of ten searchlights:

Oberleutnant Hermann Kell, *Staffel Fuehrer* 3/KG 4

By September 1940, we were stationed at Soesterberg in Holland. On the afternoon of 13 September, we were ordered to attack London during the night. By late afternoon, the weather had become very bad and it became obvious that a number of the crews didn't have the experience to handle this weather at night.

Officers of 3/KG 4. Front (l to r): Hptm *Karl-Gerd Roth* (St Kap), Lt *Hoehne,* Oblt *Hermann Kell,* Oblt *Klaus Born. Back:* Oblt *Fritz Bredemeier,* Lt *Hans Kalcher,* Lt *Helmut Furcht.* (Koch)

IX *Fliegerkorps* altered the order. Only one plane was to fly a nuisance mission that night. Target: Victoria Railway Station in London. I volunteered. The weather at take off was rain and wind with cloud at 100m. I decided to climb above the cloud where I encountered turbulence and lightning like I had never encountered before. At 5,000m I pierced the cloud ceiling – it was a wonderful moonlit night with no clouds. Ahead I saw the mouth of the Thames

---

[4] Harry Wappler's later claim to fame is that he and *Lt* Heinz Schnabel, a Messerschmitt 109 pilot from 1/JG 3, managed to escape and stole an RAF training aircraft. They succeeded in getting from Carlisle to Norfolk before running out of fuel and were soon recaptured.

– my interim target. I also noticed that the heavy rain had washed off the night camouflage paint of my He 111 – the 'Lady' was shining like a waxed apple!

When I reached the Thames Estuary, I was surprised how fast the searchlights caught me in their beams. I put it down to the 'apple skin' of my He 111. It was easy to get rid of the searchlights but it was apparently equally easy for them to catch me again as soon as I was flying straight and level. The appearance of my flight to London must have resembled the tracks of a rabbit pursued by a dog. At that time, we did not know that the era of radar had begun!

Over London, I could clearly see the railway tracks leading to Victoria Station. On the approach, I stopped the evasive movements, the bomb bay was opened and the *Beobachter Fw* Walter Hobe directed me to the target; even then we were held by many searchlights. I hoped that no night fighter would be in position until I had finished but I did not know that we already had a bug on our tail despite our efforts at evading.

Suddenly, a closely packed, never ending stream of tracer bullets came from the rear and engulfed the cockpit on both sides. There was no doubt that we had received many hits. The bombs were jettisoned and I turned the plane on its port wing tip. When we were level again, I noticed that the temperature in the port engine was rising so I shut it down to give us a chance of getting back to the Continent on one engine. This idea was short-lived as the port engine then burst into flames.

I informed the crew of my intention to glide northwards and to try to reach open country to bale out. I received no answer from the rear. *Fw* Hobe went back with a torch to tell them but returned with the report that *Uffz* Hermann Toepfer (*Bordmechaniker*) and the *Bordfunker Ogefr* Werner Mueller Wernscheidt, both fine men, were dead.

We glided, burning, from 6,000m to 2,000m with *Fw* Hobe standing beside me at the ready. At 2,000m I assumed I was over open fields, trimmed the plane for the last time, we shook hands and left the plane through the emergency exit above the pilot's head. We both landed separately in open fields. We met again in the cells at Chelmsford. For both of us the experience of six and a half years behind barbed wire had begun.

What is now regarded as the climax of the Battle of Britain took place on Sunday

He 111s of I/KG 4 taxi out on a daylight mission; a member of the crew sits in the emergency escape hatch above the pilot's head. (Koch)

15 September 1940 and what happened that day has been related in many books and journals. In an attempt to ensure that the planned invasion of Great Britain could take place, the *Luftwaffe* threw its might against London, the first attack manifesting itself at 1100 hrs when fighter bombers of II/LG 2 attacked the capital for the first but not last time. Twenty minutes later, Dornier 17s of II and III/KG 76 appeared over London's suburbs:

Feldwebel Rolf Heitsch, 8/KG 76

The attack height was about 6,000m, our target a factory to the east of London, close to the Thames.[5] On the return flight as the right-hand *Kettenhund*, I was the aircraft the enemy would target. Whilst in a left hand turn, we found ourselves at the rear of the formation and it was then that the fighters attacked.[6] As the slowest Do 17, they attacked us from behind. Trying to take evasive action by flying up and down, they hit us with three bursts with the result that we only had 4/5ths power from the engines. The right engine was totally destroyed and the left engine was just idling. We managed to get between two cumulus clouds and had to force-land in a field which sloped uphill and was occupied by cows at their midday rest. When the plane came to a halt, we could not get out because the exits had been so badly damaged by gunfire.

Because there was a strong north-westerly wind, our escort had turned back for home early so we were alone over the target. We had already delayed take off by half an hour but this was not passed to the escort so we were attacked and easily shot down.

A few minutes after we had crash-landed, the Home Guard turned up and took us prisoner. My wounded crew were taken away by car and I was taken away to a police station. I was destined to be a prisoner of war until 12 May 1948.

Whilst the RAF Spitfires had gone after the fighters, the bombers were initially attacked by Hurricanes which succeeded in splitting up the formation. Shortly afterwards, the Duxford Wing, consisting of a further five fighter squadrons, joined the attack on the helpless bombers and even though KG 76 reached London, the damage they inflicted was slight and then German casualties began to rise as their Dornier 17s tried to flee for France. KG 76 lost six bombers and a further two badly damaged; the cost in human terms was twelve killed, ten prisoners of war and three wounded.

The RAF fighters landed and rearmed and were ready for the next onslaught which was this time by Dornier 17s of II and III/KG 2 and II/KG 3

---

[5] It is believed that the intended target was actually the railway lines at Latchmere Junction.

[6] Eventual destruction of *Fw* Heitsch's Dornier 17 was credited to Fg Off John Dundas and Plt Off Eugene 'Red' Tobin of 609 Squadron.

A wounded crewman is taken away from Fw *Heitsch's Dornier 17.* (via Cornwell)

The same Dornier being dismantled prior to its final journey to the scrap heap. (via Cornwell)

The pilots responsible for the Dornier's demise – Fg Off John Dundas (left)...

...and Plt Off 'Red' Tobin (right seen with Plt Off Keith Ogilvie who also claimed a Do 17 on 15 September 1940).

and Heinkel 111s of I and II/KG 53 and I and II/KG 26. The total force of 114 bombers flew in three parallel columns three miles apart and together with its substantial escort, the whole formation stretched for some thirty miles. The targets this time were the Royal Victoria, West India and Surrey Commercial Docks in eastern London.

The RAF fighters threw themselves at the German formation and one of the greatest air battles ever seen took place over much of Kent, London and its suburbs, East Sussex and parts of Essex. However, London was spared serious damage because of the weather for when the German bombers arrived over London, they found their targets obscured by cloud. Unable to find their primary targets, their bombs were dropped on the south-eastern outskirts of the capital as they turned for home, all the time being attacked mercilessly by Spitfires and Hurricanes.

The German bombers suffered badly. KG 2 lost eight Dornier 17s and a further seven returned with varying degrees of damage; nineteen aircrew were killed, nine taken prisoner and ten wounded. KG 3 fared a little better – six aircraft destroyed and four damaged with fifteen of its II *Gruppe* aircrew killed, ten prisoners of war and four wounded. The Heinkel 111s did not suffer as badly as the Dornier 17s – KG 26 lost just one of its bombers with its crew of four being taken prisoner; a further three of its aircraft were damaged and just two crew members were wounded. KG 53 lost six aircraft with another two damaged; twelve aircrew were killed, eighteen taken prisoner (including *Maj* Max Gruber, the *Gruppen Kommandeur* of II/KG 53 and most senior German officer lost that day) and four wounded.

As this attack disappeared off the radar screens, twenty-six unescorted Heinkel 111s of I and III/KG 55 attacked Royal Navy installations at Portland and then, two hours later, *Erprobungsgruppe* 210 attacked the Supermarine Factory at Southampton. Both raids were ineffective and Plt Off Arthur Watson of 152 Squadron shot down a 9/KG 55 Heinkel 111 resulting in the deaths of three of its crew with the fourth being taken prisoner. Any further daylight attacks were cancelled because of the deteriorating weather conditions and it was again left to the German bombers to continue the onslaught against London under the cover of darkness.

The *Luftwaffe* had flown over 1,000 sorties on what is now called Battle of Britain Sunday for the loss of fifty-six of its bombers and fighters. The RAF lost twenty-eight fighters with twelve pilots killed, twelve wounded and one being taken prisoner of war. The German bombers had managed to get through to London but at a terrible cost. They did cause damage to the railway lines (but rail traffic was only disrupted for three days) whilst the Docks had got away unscathed. The day from the German viewpoint was a failure, having failed to achieve any of their primary aims whilst suffering a great cost in human lives and aircraft lost. The RAF had proven yet again it was not a spent force and had succeeded in thwarting the major German daylight attack of the Battle of Britain. German bombing raids by daylight were failing and increasingly the bombing switched to attacks by night; four days later, Adolf Hitler postponed the invasion of the United Kingdom indefinitely. However, despite the experiences of 15 September 1940, the Battle of Britain was still not regarded as over.

Understandably, the days that followed 15 September 1940 were much quieter for the German bombers which did not appear in force over Great Britain until 18 September. However, German reconnaissance aircraft were as active as usual, whilst to the north German seaplanes were particularly active and suffered two losses during 16 September:

Leutnant Clemens Lucas, 3/*Kue.Fl.Gr* 506

We were based at Stavanger–Sola seadrome. We had been briefed to torpedo a tanker of 8,000–10,000 GRT sailing south from the Moray Firth, escorted by two small destroyers. The reconnaissance plane had reported a speed of 10-knots.

At about 2300 hrs [on 15 September] we saw the tanker north of the Isle of May. Very low, we flew a wide turn and waited until the ship was in front of the Isle. Then it turned into the southern entrance and soon the full moon was seen to the north-west. In case of anti-aircraft fire, we attacked at low level. About 500m ahead of the ship, I climbed to 50m, aimed at the middle of the ship using my night sights as well as an angle of allowance, pressed the button on the right of my control column and released the torpedo. Now I had to fly straight ahead for thirty seconds so that our slipstream would not affect the torpedo. The tanker's speed had been about 3 or 4 knots – not much wake could be seen. The depth of the torpedo was set at 6m. After dropping the torpedo, I immediately went down to 10m altitude and saw that the tanker had been hit amidships.

However, both destroyer's pom-poms had already fired their first salvoes. Both of our engines were hit and stopped working. I was able to land on the sea without any problems – it was 0035 hrs in the morning of 16 September. Our *Bordfunker* [*Fw* Erich Kalinowski] fixed a drogue anchor to both floats to stabilise the plane. When two small grey fishing boats appeared at about 0400 hrs, we scuttled our aircraft. How? After we had set off two incendiary bombs, we took to our dinghy and ten minutes later the plane sank. The British fishermen took us on board and we gave them our dinghy as a present. Then they put us ashore at a small fishing port.

The He 115 of Lt Lucas is brought ashore despite sinking. (via Watkins)

At about 0800 hrs, we were picked up by two Jeeps commanded by an officer of a Scottish Regiment based in Edinburgh. We were treated very well and at the Officers' Mess, we got a rich breakfast. After two days we were transported to an interrogation centre at Cockfosters near London. In Germany we had been told already that there would be questioning so we remained silent. We only had our private identity cards with us on which were our parents' addresses. After three days, my parents got the information via the Swiss Consulate that we were alive.

The second Heinkel 115 to be lost fell victim not as a result of enemy action but, and not for the first time during the summer of 1940, the weather:

Leutnant zur See Hans Otto Aldus, *1/Kue.Fl.Gr* 906

Our mission began at the seadrome of Norderney and our task was an armed reconnaissance of the Scottish east coast. The outward and return flight would have lasted five hours which allowed us to stay for a good two hours on the reconnaissance, including a necessary safety factor. Enough time in good weather, even at night.

The weather proved to be crucial. Because of sketchy meteorological reports from the west, the forecast was inaccurate. We were caught in deteriorating weather – rain showers, low cloud and bad visibility. A fast approaching depression. Because it was approaching so quickly, we believed that it was a local, temporary depression and that the weather over our reconnaissance area would possibly be better.

Left to right Uffz *Meissner,* LtzS *Aldus and their usual pilot named Rethage.* (Aldus)

We did not abort the flight, particularly because from time to time the moon broke through the clouds and was reflected in the water. However, as we approached the coast near to Peterhead (by dead reck-

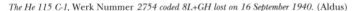

The He 115 C-1, Werk Nummer *2754 coded 8L+GH lost on 16 September 1940.* (Aldus)

A He 115 of 1/906 is brought back on land after another mission, Rugen, early 1940. (Aldus)

oning and radio direction finding) there was no visibility at all. I think that I can still remember that we saw some lights and we were shot at. In these poor conditions, we could not carry out our orders and so we turned back towards the sea. During this turn, one wing tip touched the ground resulting in an unintentional forced-landing! For me it meant serious injuries and I still suffer the after effects. For all three of us it meant captivity.

As far as I can remember, we stayed at a farmhouse for the rest of the night. I was then taken to a hospital in Aberdeen and after a month to a military hospital at Edinburgh. After five months I had recovered from my injuries and was taken to the prisoner of war camp at Shap Wells. I was eventually released in November 1946 when I returned to my home country.

The weather improved sufficiently on 18 September 1940 which allowed the Germans to commit one of its bomber units recently brought into action in the Battle of Britain. Originally a Dornier 17 unit, KG 77 was converting to the Junkers 88 for much of August and early September 1940. Unfortunately,

on its first major daylight attack in the afternoon of
18 September, the RAF taught III/KG 77 a severe lesson. Briefed to attack London and Tilbury Docks,
nine Junkers 88s were shot down, including that of
the *Gruppen Kommandeur Maj* Max Kless.

Again, the days that followed 18 September 1940
were hampered by poor weather and a lack (or
unwillingness?) of German bombers in daylight and
it must be said that the remainder of September,
and October for that matter, were an anti-climax
compared to 15 September. On the 21st of the
month, a rare German aircraft, a Dornier 215, fell
victim to a Spitfire pilot ostensibly on rest with his
Squadron near Liverpool:

*The badge of KG 77, a unit regarded by
many as an unlucky Geschwader.*

Believed to be Ju 88 A-1, Werk Nummer *7092 coded 9K+MR of 7/KG 51 after its crash-landing at Lille–Nord,
20 September 1940.* (Hoehler)

Plt Off Dennis Adams, 611 Sqn, November 1939.
(Adams)

Pilot Officer Dennis Adams, Green 2, 'B' Flight, 611 Squadron

I was ordered off from Ringway at 1630 hrs to investigate a Bogey at 20,000ft over Liverpool. I scrambled to this height and was then ordered to 25,000ft. On reaching this height, anti-aircraft fire started to burst around me and chase me and on looking up, I saw the enemy aircraft directly above me travelling east at about 220mph. On sighting me climbing up behind, the enemy aircraft turned west into the sun. On reaching a position approximately 450 yards astern, the enemy aircraft opened fire at me. I swung out to the right and did a beam attack on his starboard side, firing a five second burst. Immediately, a stream of coolant or petrol came from the starboard engine and the rear gunner ceased firing (enemy fire ineffective). I then went astern of the enemy aircraft and fired a longish burst at 250 yards closing to approximately 150 yards. The port engine then emitted brown smoke or oil vapour and stopped. The enemy aircraft continued in a westerly direction, losing height, and finally crashed in a field...

Leutnant Rolf Book, *Aufkl.Gr.Ob.dL.*

We took off from Caen that 21 September 1940. We entered British airspace at altitude of approximately 27,000ft near Plymouth on our way to Liverpool. The sky was cloudy and I had my doubts whether we could be able to take pictures over Liverpool. However, the sky cleared and we were able to take pictures for about twelve minutes. Apparently we entered British airspace without being identified by radar. I take this from the fact that we got no warning from our side which usually monitored communications between British fighters and the ground stations. On our way back from Liverpool, we suddenly noticed the fighter behind and above us, approaching very fast. Unfortunately (for us!) we couldn't do very much as our guns 'went on strike' after a few shots and the rest was inevitable. We couldn't bale out as *Uffz* Pelzer had been mortally wounded after the first attack and so we made a forced-landing – not too bad I think. As a result, I was guest of His Majesty for six years and two months.

The days that followed saw an increase in aggressive sweeps by Messer-schmitt 109s and the occasional fighter bomber attack against London. Bomber operations were very much limited to the occasional daylight nuisance attack against specific targets or mainly night attacks. Surviving logbooks from this period bear this out. For example, *Oblt* Erwin Moll, a pilot with 4/KG 76 flew his last daylight mission against Great Britain on 15 September 1940 and from then until the end of the Battle of Britain flew nine night-time attacks purely against London. *Uffz* Herbert Schick, a *Bordfunker* with 3/KGr 100 first flew against England on the night of the 13/14 August 1940 and flew a total of sixteen bombing missions, all of them by night, before he and his crew were returned to Germany at the end of September 1940. After 8 September 1940, all of his flights (nine in total) were against London. Both Moll and Schick were shot down and taken prisoners of war in 1941 during night attacks against London.

24 September 1940 would see another minor change in tactics by the Germans. A few bombers were briefed to attack London early that morning but turned back, either because of weather or the threat of fighters, before reaching the target. Then, just after lunch, the fighter bombers of *Erprobungsgruppe* 210 carried out the first of two attacks against the Supermarine Factory near Southampton. The first attack, which took place at 1330 hrs, succeeded in damaging the factory, not badly enough to stop production of the Spitfire but

Uffz *Herbert Schick*. (Schick)

resulting in the deaths of forty-two, most of whom worked at the factory. Another attack was carried out three hours later but was ineffectual. This time one of the fighter bombers was lost in addition to two of the escorting fighters; reports state that the German losses were attributable to anti-aircraft fire but it now seems likely that Spitfires of 609 Squadron were to blame:

Pilot Officer David Crook, 609 Squadron

As we were climbing over the Isle of Wight at about 25,000ft, we sighted the German bombers some distance away to the south, a great mass of machines coming steadily on in very good formation. Above them, ranging up to about 35,000ft, the Me 109s were circling round and round so that every now and then I could see a quick flash as their wings caught the sun. They were watching us like cats, just waiting to attack the bombers and then the fun would start and it would be the usual hair-raising competition to see if we could get the bombers before the 109s got to us.

The CO swung 'B' Flight into echelon starboard and prepared to do a beam attack. God, I thought, now for it. In that instant somebody shouted "Look out, 109s!" and I whipped round just as a whole pack of Messerschmitts tore over our heads not more than 30ft above us. They came down at a terrific speed out of the sun and we never saw them at all until they were on us. We split up in all directions, diving and turning to avoid them. I went down about 2,000ft and then looked round and saw a few Spitfires forming up again and chasing some Dorniers [sic] over the Isle of Wight. I went after them as hard as I could but was about half a mile behind and as we were all going flat out I didn't seem to get much nearer.

One Dornier was rather behind the rest of the Hun formation and two black streaks of smoke from his engines showed that he realised his danger and was doing everything he could to catch up. A moment later the leading Spitfire (I learned later that it was Sgt Feary) opened fire on the Dornier and gave him a long burst. The bomber flew steadily on for a moment and then he turned slowly over on his back and started to spin down. We all watched him; it was rather a shaking sight. Down he went, spinning faster and faster at an incredible rate for such a big machine

and then suddenly a wing was wrenched off. The Dornier gave a lurch and continued to dive but now turning crazily over and over. The crew must have all been dead inside the cabin for nobody got out. I saw the other wing and tail break away and the fuselage then went straight down like a stone and disappeared from sight. A moment later, looking down, I saw a patch of foam appear on the sea over 20,000ft below showing where he had dropped...[7]

Sgt Alan Feary (left) relates the combat to the Squadron Intelligence Officer.

---

[7] As normally happened, Messerschmitt 110s were mistaken for Dornier 17s and no Dornier 17s took part in this attack. Claims should therefore have been filed for three Messerschmitt 110s by Plt Off John Curchin, Plt Off Mike Staples and Sgt Alan Feary.

On 25 September 1940, London again had a brief rest from the daylight attention of the German bombers. Whether the Germans thought that the RAF fighters were concentrated around London thus leaving other potential targets relatively undefended is not known but the only major attack of the day was by the Heinkel 111s of KG 55 against the Bristol Aircraft Factory at Filton near Bristol (with *Erprobungsgruppe* 210 carrying out a diversionary attack against Portland).

Because of an error by the RAF controllers, the German bombers made it to their target unmolested. They succeeded in stopping aircraft production at the factory and causing in excess of 350 casualties but then the RAF fighters managed to intercept, shooting down four bombers and one of the Messerschmitt 110 escorts:

He 111 of 3/KG 55. (Kaufhold)

Unteroffizier Rudolf Weisbach, 1/KG 55

We were based at Villacoublay near Paris and the order was to attack the Bristol Aircraft Factory. In the morning, at about 1000 hrs, another *Geschwader* flew a light attack against London which hopefully would draw off the British fighters. At 1100 hrs, we took off, headed for Cherbourg and across the Channel for Bristol. Our escort was a *Geschwader* of Bf 109s which after an hour was replaced by a Bf 110 *Geschwader*.

Initially, we met with little opposition – as we approached the target, we encountered fierce *Flak* but then, after we had dropped our bombs, we saw the first Spitfire [sic] and they attacked immediately. During one of the attacks, we lost an engine (the oil supply was hit) and then could not set the pitch of the propeller. We were flying in formation at 5,000m and could not keep up so we dropped as much ballast as possible in the hope that we could reach the French coast on one engine. We then became the target of three to five Spitfires; I cannot say if there were any Hurricanes.

THIS AND NEXT PAGE *The 1/KG 55 He 111 at Studland, 25 September 1940.* (via Cornwell)

The Channel was very close just as another attack hit the second engine. At the height we were, there was no option but to ditch near Studland but because *Uffz* Altrichter was wounded, our pilot carried out a comparatively good crash-landing on land.[8]

After landing, we tried to get the wounded Altrichter out of the aircraft. Then, as the aircraft was relatively undamaged despite the crash-landing, we planned to set the aircraft on fire. However, we were approached by some civilians from a house 500m away. They were

[8] The destruction of this aircraft was jointly credited to Plt Offs John Wigglesworth of 238 Squadron and John Curchin of 609 Squadron.

armed and took away our pistols. Some ten minutes later, a lady brought some tea for the wounded – the pilot [*Fw* Fritz Juerges] and the gunner [*Uffz* Otto Mueller] had been slightly injured in the landing but Altrichter had been badly wounded in the thigh. After ten minutes, a military vehicle approached and we were all taken away but it was too late for Altrichter; he had bled to death.

A He 111 of KG 55 shows the after effects of an RAF fighter attack.

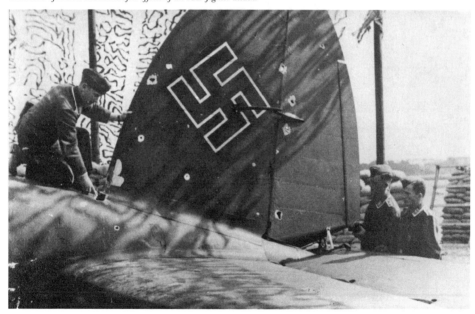

Whether the Germans were encouraged by the attack on Bristol is not known but the following day KG 55 and *Erprobungsgruppe* 210 attacked the Supermarine Factory again. This attack was also successful, succeeding in stopping the production of Spitfires and causing over 100 casualties. German losses were light – just one of the bombers and two of the Messerschmitt 110 escorts; a reconnaissance Messerschmitt 110 of 4(F)/14 was shot down by Flt Lt William Blackadder of 607 Squadron just after the attack, presumably tasked with assessing the effectiveness of the earlier attack. The RAF claimed to have shot down thirty-three German aircraft – a clear case of over optimism and over claiming, especially as five of their fighters were either shot down or written off (twelve of them being claimed by JG 2 who were escorting the bombers).

The German tactics changed again on 27 September when the Germans returned to their 'rolling' attacks. Preceded by a *Freie Jagd*, eighty or so heavily escorted Junkers 88s of I and II/KG 77 headed towards London only to receive the same punishment meted out to III/KG 77 on 18 September 1940. Four Junkers 88s were shot down (and a further eight were lost in a similar attack later in the afternoon) and the Messerschmitt 110 escort was similarly mauled.

Meanwhile, back to the west another attack was about to take place against the Parnall Aircraft Factory at Yate near Bristol by the apparently indefatigable *Erprobungsgruppe* 210. This time the RAF fighters were in the right place at the right time in great numbers. The attack was broken up and four fighter bombers, including those flown by the *Gruppen Kommandeur Hptm* Martin Lutz and the *Staffel Kapitaen* of 2 *Staffel*, *Oblt* Wilhelm-Richard Roessiger, were shot down; both of these officers were posthumously awarded the *Ritterkreuz*.

28 September was a day of relative rest for the bomber crews. They had been active during the hours of darkness but only a few Junkers 88s were committed to daylight attacks on London under a very heavy escort. The German fighters did particularly well on what was a very costly day for Fighter Command, accounting for seventeen British fighters; only two German aircraft (both of them Messerschmitt 109s) were lost in combat throughout the hours of daylight. 29 September was similarly quiet for the Germans and a better day for Fighter Command. The only incident of note took place during the early evening when Heinkel 111s from all three *Staffeln* of III/KG 55 attacked Liverpool Docks. Wary of what had happened to the *Geschwader* and other units over the west of Great Britain during the past week, the formation scouted around the coast up the Irish Sea, close to neutral Eire. Eleven Hurricanes from 79 Squadron based at Pembrey in South Wales were scrambled to intercept and as the sun began to set, they spotted the German bombers. Aircraft from 7 and 8 *Staffeln* had managed to slip past undetected but 9/KG 55 was unfortunate enough to be attacked. One Heinkel 111 flown by *Oblt* Hans Kohler was shot down and another two returned damaged, one aircraft having all of its crew wounded. The German gunners did well though, shooting down the Hurricanes of Plt Off George Nelson-Edwards and Fg Off George Peters,

the latter being killed; a third Hurricane, flown by Fg Off Paul Mayhew, landed in Eire and was impounded.

On 30 September 1940, it appeared that the Germans threw all caution to the wind; it was also destined to be the day which saw the last major daylight bombing attacks on Great Britain during the Battle of Britain and, for that matter, the remainder of the war.

Using their tried and tested 'rolling' attacks, the first major attack did not materialise until early in the afternoon when a large, heavily escorted formation was plotted heading for London. This was successfully intercepted and, although few German bombers were shot down, the remainder were turned back:

Oberleutnant Fritz Oeser, 2/KG 77

That morning, I received [the gift of] an ashtray which I took to be a bad omen. Before the mission to London, I had to instruct *Uffz* Klasing, the stand-in *Bordmechaniker*, how to handle the job of a *Bordmechaniker* and gunner because every pilot had to fly on this day and we were short of *Bordmechanikers*. Finally, flying in formation to the target, I was not happy when one engine cut out at 6,000ft over the Channel and I had to break away from the formation and leave my seat to see what the trouble was. I quickly found out that a switch was set incorrectly in the *Bordmechaniker*'s area – the engine ran again and I caught up again abeam the British south coast.

According to our information, we were sure that the mission would be one of the last as we had been told that "riots in London against the continuation of the war were at such a state that the police and Army could not keep control any longer." However, about 20 miles from London at 18,000ft, the British fighters were diving from 30,000ft into our formation, opening fire and continuing downwards. They managed to break up the formation. The result for me was one engine cooler out, oxygen bottles damaged, the greenhouse front left side without perspex, the rear upper machine gun out of action and the *Bordmechaniker* seriously wounded. I got an explosive bullet in the left shoulder and another caused a wide wound above my right eye.

Veering away from the formation, I ordered the bombs be dropped and we dived to ground level in the hope of escaping. Some minutes later, two fighters intercepted and tried to shoot us down. My only chance was to watch the attackers and by turning towards them when they were in an attacking position. Finally, one of the fighters turned off but the other one carried out another two attacks and obviously ran out of ammunition. He then began flying very closely in formation with me to see what had happened in the cockpit. Then he too disappeared. Suddenly, near the ground, another fighter appeared and attacked – we were only flying at 100ft at this time. My aircraft was scarcely manoeuvrable and flying at 100-

knot and then the second engine was hit and began burning. My only chance was a 30° turn to right to search for a field for a forced-landing. Before that, I had to fly over a large tree but failed – it smashed into the belly but I was still able to touch down in an almost perfect belly landing on Gatwick Racecourse…

Sergeant Paul Farnes, Yellow 3, 'A' Flight, 501 Squadron

I was on patrol with the Squadron who were ordered to climb to 20,000ft. I stayed with the Squadron to 14,000ft but then I was so cold that I decided to leave; the reason for this was the fact that my hood had jammed fully open. I came down through clouds about five miles west-south-west of Gatwick and commenced to return to base. I got to about eight miles north of Gatwick when I sighted a Ju 88, diving rapidly but not steeply, which was emitting a thin trail of white smoke so I assumed it had been damaged in a previous attack. The enemy aircraft was heading south so I turned through 180°, pulled the plug and commenced to chase him. We were then at 4,000ft. I overhauled him at Gatwick and was about to attack him when he turned towards me. I continued my attack from slightly head on, continuing to fire until I broke away 20 yards behind his tail. I turned to make another attack but could not see him. At that moment, I saw several vehicles driving across Gatwick aerodrome and looking at the direction they were going, I saw that the enemy aircraft had crash-landed on Gatwick Racecourse. After I had landed at Gatwick, I was informed by eye witnesses that after my attack, both engines had caught fire, emitting black smoke, and enemy aircraft had force-landed immediately after.

Oberleutnant Fritz Oeser

…I ordered the crew to leave the aircraft and to activate the incendiary bomb under my seat. At that moment, one of the crew at the front of the aircraft stopped this intention, stating that the hood couldn't be moved. However, when the cockpit cleared of smoke, I saw about thirty soldiers about 200 yards away. After about five minutes, they fired three warning shots into the aircraft to try and make us come out, not knowing that we were not able to do that. Maybe they assumed we were daredevils! However, shortly after that, we were taken prisoner and taken away.

A final attack in the east on that day occurred just after 1600 hrs when another formation of Junkers 88s again headed for London together with a heavy escort of Messerschmitt 109s. The formation was broken up and the resultant combats ranged from Kent almost into eastern Hampshire. However, no bombers were shot down and the losses were suffered just by the fighters.

Fritz Oeser's Ju 88 on display after its crash-landing. (via Cornwell)

As that attack in the east was coming to a close, another was developing in the west when forty-three Heinkel 111s of I and II/KG 55 tried to attack the Westland Factory at Yeovil in Somerset whilst eleven Junkers 88s of I/KG 51 carried out a diversionary attack on Southampton. A similar situation to what had happened on 27 September and in the east of Britain earlier on 30 September occurred when the formation, hampered by bad weather, was intercepted and turned back. Sadly, the Heinkel 111s unknowingly dropping their bombs on the helpless town of Shaftesbury. German bomber losses were predictable – KG 55 lost four bombers with twelve aircrew killed and six wounded. Four of the wounded, which included *Maj Dr* Ernst Kuhl, Operations Officer of KG 55, were picked up from the Channel; Kuhl would later become *Geschwader Kommodore* of KG 55 and was destined to receive the *Ritterkreuz mit Eichenlaub.* Even the diversionary attack by I/KG 51 lost an aircraft when the Junkers 88 of *Fw* Fritz Paczinski of 1 *Staffel* was shot down into the sea off Selsey Bill by Red Section of 602 Squadron; there were no survivors from the crew of four.

The deciding month of the Battle of Britain was over as far as daylight bombing operations were concerned and the RAF had emerged the victor, not just on the final day of the month but on almost each of the preceding twenty-nine days. The *Luftwaffe* still had the might but had failed to press home any advantage that it had won. Furthermore, weather, bad luck, tactical errors, the sheer guts of the RAF fighter pilots and the hard work of the supporting ground crews had very much influenced the outcome. It was true that the German fighters had managed to wrest air superiority from Fighter Command for much of the first six days of the month but then their tactics and aims changed. Air superiority was then lost by the Germans which allowed the RAF's vengeance to be wreaked on many of the bomber crews and their aircraft for the rest of the month.

After 15 September 1940, German bombers flew more and more operations by night which gave greater protection to the bombers and their crews, especially the Dornier 17 and Heinkel 111 which had proved to be very vulnerable against day fighters. It had been hoped that the newer and faster Junkers 88 could rely on its greater speed and manoeuvrability but was still no match for Spitfires and Hurricanes unless heavily protected by the Messerschmitt 109. However, the problem with the Messerschmitt 109 was its limited range and the Messerschmitt 110 had been proved to be woefully inadequate as a long-range fighter.

The last ten days of September 1940 had seen a sudden increase in fighter-bomber operations by single-seat fighters which was ironic as the premier German fighter-bomber unit, *Erprobungsgruppe* 210, had on 27 September 1940 suffered badly at the hands of the RAF. The final month of the Battle of Britain would now see a dramatic reduction in German daylight bombing operations and a greater switch to night time operations and much of the death and glory would be experienced by the German day-fighter and fighter-bomber pilots.

CHAPTER 4

Anti-Climax, October 1940

After the carnage of the previous three months, October 1940 was very much a let down and relief for the German bomber crews. Because of the switch to night operations and the onset of winter with its associated poor weather, major daylight attacks only took place on two days during October 1940 with the German bombers preferring to carry out single nuisance attacks. Even then, they were vulnerable:

Oberleutnant **Hans Langer,** *Staffel Kapitaen Stab/***KG 2**

After trying hard, I managed to get the permission from my *Kommodore, Oberst* Johannes Fink, to attack targets by single aircraft in daylight. On 2 October 1940, there was a 6/10ths layer of cloud over Great Britain. This type of weather, using the cloud banks as cover, suited single-aircraft attacks so we took off, the crew consisting of myself as pilot, *Oblt* Erich Eitze as *Beobachter, Uffz* Robert Seidel as *Bordfunker* and *Uffz* Hellmut Bellmann as *Bordmechaniker.* The target was the Handley Page Aircraft Factory near London. We set course and climbed just above the broken cloud layer at an altitude of about 2,000m. Just before 1000 hrs, we reached the southern suburbs of London – the enormous city was lying under a layer of haze but only a few small clouds disrupted the blue of the sky. I thought it would be senseless to carry on so I changed course back for the Channel.

Oblt *Erich Eitze,* Oblt *Hans Langer and* Lt *Heinrich Hunger; Hunger was later awarded the* Ritterkreuz *only to be killed in action over Russia on 14 August 1941.* (Langer)

After a few minutes, the *Bordfunker* shouted over the intercom "Fighters from starboard and behind!" – the height of the cloud base had decreased as well as the number of clouds so it was difficult for me to find somewhere to shelter from the attacking British fighters – three

Hurricanes. The first hits struck my plane. The *Beobachter* and *Bordfunker* tried to fend off the attacking fighters with their machine guns. It was difficult to aim at the fighters and then they attacked head on. By then it was hopeless to try and find shelter in the clouds and I was forced to descend and fly at low level. Then a salvo hit the instrument panel and the port engine began to emit black smoke, slight at first but then becoming thicker. Now there were only two Hurricanes left – the third one must have broken off due to lack of fuel. There was no hope of escaping so I gave the order to bale out. I unfastened my seat belt but I was touched on the shoulder and heard the *Bordmechaniker* say "My parachute has been torn." In the meantime, we were only at 80m altitude, the plane was losing speed and I could only control the plane by gliding. I withdrew the order to bale out.

Only one fighter was now circling close above the Dornier 17. With frightening speed, the ground got closer and closer and we could just make out an almost rectangular field. Suddenly, the *Beobachter* heard me shout "I'm not strapped in!" – the plane would crash-land in the next few minutes. Nevertheless, Erich Eitze unfastened his belt and fastened mine. At the last second, we were all ready and moments later the Do 17 touched the ground, sliding along on its belly, undercarriage retracted. I succeeded in side-slipping past a large pylon and no sooner had the plane come to a halt than the *Bordfunker* rushed out to destroy papers detailing call signs and radio frequencies.[1] Everybody feared that the plane would explode – in great haste, I struggled to get my flying helmet and microphone off but heard Erich Eitze's calm voice saying "Just a moment, I will do it" and cut through the cord with his utility knife saying "Now we can get out as we are guests of the English King!" Quickly, we left the immediate vicinity of our good 'kite', completely astonished and relieved that we had survived. It was 1028 hrs; the dogfight had lasted twenty-eight minutes – an eternity for those involved...

The lone Dornier 17 had the misfortune to be spotted by five pilots from 17 Squadron who were returning from patrol, low on fuel. Plt Off Frantisek Fajtl, Fg Off Howard 'Cowboy' Blatchford, Plt Off Jack Ross, Plt Off Leonard Stevens and Flt Lt Alfred Bayne were all credited with the kill:

Flight Lieutenant Alfred Bayne, Blue 1, 'B' Flight, 17 Squadron

I was leading 17 Squadron when we were vectored to intercept bandits as we were returning from patrol. I first sighted the Do 17 eight miles north-east of Colchester at 4,000–5,000ft in and out of 8/10ths cloud. I

---

[1] *Uffz* Seidel had experienced being shot down before (on 27 May 1940 south of Dunkirk) so was well versed in what to do this time.

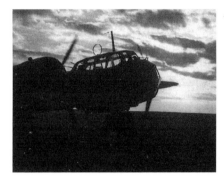

Hans Langer's Do 17 before…

…and after the crash-landing. (Langer)

eventually engaged just over Harwich with a rear attack in a break in cloud, opening at 300 yards and diving to 200 yards giving a ten second burst. Return fire was noticed from the rear top gun which stopped after a big flash from the port side of the fuselage near the cockpit. Enemy aircraft then went into cloud and I found him again over Ipswich and gave him the rest of my ammunition in another Number 1 attack at the same range. I then returned to base to rearm and refuel having been airborne for two hours. My Numbers 2 and 3 also attacked the enemy aircraft after separating from me.

The other pilots witnessed the crash-landing and headed for base very low on fuel. Both Fg Off Blatchford and Plt Off Fajtl force-landed in fields near Pulham; Plt Off Jack Ross didn't get much further than the field next to the crash-landed German bomber:

Oberleutnant **Hans Langer**

…Suddenly, we noticed a Hurricane which landed in the field a few metres away. A very young *Leutnant* climbed down from his plane, approached us, stood to attention in front of me, saluted and said "Congratulations Sir; you have given me a good fight. I've only got minutes of fuel left. Let's shake hands!" Still confused and angry, I replied "Three against one is not a fair combat!" to which he turned his back on me and walked back to his plane.

A few minutes later, some armed Home Guard appeared at the edge of the field. With the words "Hands up!" they told us to surrender. In the middle of enemy territory, resistance would be insane so we handed over our pistols. It wasn't long before a lorry with regular troops appeared and we were taken to a nearby village and put into a barrack-like building. There, us officers were separated from the NCOs – unfortunately we heard nothing further from them for the rest of our captivity.

Towards the evening, we were eventually taken to a dark, garage-like room where some time later, we got something to eat – two dried fish on a metal plate. We ate using our hands and slowly our fear and excitement faded away. We managed a sound, dreamless sleep, not waking until the next morning. Then we were given a cup of tea and some biscuits and soon we were sitting on a lorry again which took us to the train station. There the escorting officer, a Lieutenant, turned to me and said "You take my coat." I said that I would not wear the coat of my enemy to which he said "You will see." As soon as we entered the station, a large crowd recognised us as Germans and shouted "German baby killers!" Cold shivers ran through both of us but an escorting soldier wielding his rifle in a semi-circle and a Bobby, with his truncheon, fended off the more aggressive civilians and the officer followed with pistol drawn. Finally, we got into a First Class carriage where we were pushed in and the door locked. At the windows, people were shaking their fists at us but we could not hear their raging yells any more.

With unspeakable relief, both of us sank into the upholstered seats. The fear of the last few minutes had been harder to endure than the strain of the half hour dogfight. Eventually the train left the station and we suddenly got another fright when the escorting officer sitting directly opposite draws his pistol. In bewilderment, we feared the worse but he said "Being armed myself, I do not want to be faced by unarmed men." Whilst saying this, he removed the bullets from his revolver and put them into his pocket. A true, knightly gesture.

Hans Langer photographed at Euston Station, 3 October 1940. (Langer)

The first major daylight raid of the month by conventional bombers (as opposed to fighter-bombers) took place on 7 October when II/KG 51 attacked the Westland Aircraft Factory at Yeovil. The bombers succeeded in reaching the target, harried all the way by RAF fighters but the damage caused was not that severe, even though there were over 100 casualties. The Germans lost seven of the escorting Messerschmitt 110s, this aircraft making its last appearance over Great Britain en masse for the remainder of the war during this attack. The fighter losses could have been higher if it was not for the intervention of JG 2 which claimed at least eight RAF fighters. Nevertheless, just one bomber was shot down:

Oberleutnant Sigurd Hey, 5/KG 51

I had flown twelve missions against England, all of them but this one being flown by night. On this day, we took off from the normal II/KG 51 base at Orly; most of the night missions took off from Villeroche where we had installed an artificial horizon to help night take-offs.

Being a former instrument flying instructor, I was normally selected for night raids. I volunteered to fly this day as one of the pilots had been taken ill and as the wings of my aircraft were being modified by a Junkers Field Service team at Villacoublay, I took his plane and called for my crew in a hurry. We got airborne as one of the last of about twenty-five Junkers 88s and got a position on the edge of the formation.

Oblt *Sigurd Hey*. (Hey)

We arrived over Cherbourg where the Bf 109s had already been waiting for us for half an hour. They escorted us to the British coast and had to return because they were all low on fuel. Thus our only fighter escort from now on was made up from Bf 110s – no protection against thirty or forty Spitfires and Hurricanes now coming from all directions.

I was hit in the radiator on my starboard engine. Although I dropped my 500 kilogram bomb immediately and I feathered the damaged engine, I could not hold my position in the formation and began to lag behind. I therefore turned southwards, diving a few thousand feet and tried to reach the French coast on only one engine.

Then three Spitfires came, attacking from all angles. At first a hit in the controls forced me to hold the aircraft straight and level just by using the trim wheel. Next, the fuselage tank was hit and the aircraft caught fire. It was then that I gave the order to bale out but I received no reply because the three of them had already left because of the dense smoke. When the aircraft went into a flat spin, I was lucky to get out and landed safely by parachute where I was quickly taken prisoner by two old men with shotguns.

A number of RAF fighters, both Spitfires and Hurricanes, claimed to have shot down this bomber but the following, given by a Hurricane pilot, gives a good account of what happened:

Pilot Officer Robert Doe, Yellow 1, 'A' Flight, 238 Squadron

...At 20,000ft over Warmwell, Me 109s carried out a head on attack. The Squadron split up. I dived straight for the lower bombers which were straggling considerably and attacked a Ju 88 from astern, opening fire at 300 yards. The first burst stopped the starboard engine. Overtaking speed was very high so I half-rolled upwards and attacked the enemy aircraft from above with a short burst at 100 yards. I broke away and carried out a beam attack from the port side from 300 yards. Enemy aircraft turned away and started diving. As it dived, a burst of fire appeared in front of the tail which flew off. Three people baled out and the enemy aircraft crashed in flames 6 miles north of Maiden Newton.

As the month continued, despite many bitter air battles between fighters and fighter-bombers, no further major daylight raids took place. The pendulum of battle had clearly swung to night time operations with the German bombers being further aided by precision Very High Frequency radio beam navigation and bombing systems such as *Knickebein* and the Very High

A He 111 of KGr 100 – clearly visible on the fuselage are the three aerial masts associated with X-Verfahren. (Schick)

Frequency multi-beam and single beam precision bombing systems known as *X-Verfahren* and *Y-Verfahren* respectively. As yet, the RAF had no answer to this and the first airborne radar-assisted kill was still over a month off. Nevertheless, a number of German bombers were being lost at night as a result of anti-aircraft fire. However, for the moment losses were very light.

There was still the occasional daylight battle with the occasional surprising result. For instance, 92 Squadron definitely came off the loser in a combat with a Dornier 17 of 1/KG 2 on the morning of 10 October 1940. The Spitfires of Plt Offs John Drummond and Desmond Williams collided during what appeared to be a one-sided combat and both pilots were killed. Then one of the Dornier 17s gunners damaged the Spitfire flown by Sgt Walter Ellis forcing him to force-land and writing off his Spitfire in the process. The Dornier 17 returned safely albeit its pilot, *Lt* Walter Dilcher was killed.

This Ju 88 A-1 coded 9K+HS of 8/KG 51 was shot down by AA fire in the early hours of 10 October 1940 whilst bombing London; Uffz Richard Metschuldt and his crew were taken prisoner. (Wildermuth)

Another daylight combat took place over the Irish Sea on 11 October 1940. Three Dornier 17s of *Kuestenfliegergruppe* 606 were part of a force briefed to attack Liverpool Docks. Two Squadrons were scrambled to intercept the German bombers. It is believed that the Hurricanes of 312 Squadron damaged one of the bombers, two of its crew baling out whilst the bomber continued back to France where it crash-landed badly damaged. Two other Dornier 17s were shot down by Spitfires of 611 Squadron:

Leutnant zur See Juergen Von Krause, 1/Kue.Fl.Gr 606

On 11 October 1940, our target was again Liverpool Docks. Flying height was 4,000–5,000m and the size of our formation in between *Staffel* and *Gruppe*. We were attacked by RAF fighters (Spitfires) just before and after the target.

My Dornier 17 had dropped back a little behind the formation and logically was the first aircraft to be attacked. I can remember a series of hits caused problems with one engine. Consequently, we lost contact with the rest of the formation, turned further out to sea to the

Lt zS Juergen von Krause. (von Krause)

west and dived. However, two Spitfires stayed close. We hit one of them and perhaps it was shot down but the other one finished us off. After the second engine had seized up, we had to ditch. The aircraft sank immediately and we were lucky to get out in time and inflate our life jackets. After some time, I found our dinghy – I was able to inflate it using the compressed air and after a few hours, we were picked up by a Dutch patrol boat which took us to Holyhead...

Again, the RAF did not come away from these combats without incident. The Hurricane flown by Plt Off Josef Jaske of 312 Squadron was badly damaged by exploding bullets in the fabric and spars of the main and tail planes, elevators and aileron. Sgt Ken Pattison of 611 Squadron is thought to have got lost and was killed whilst trying to force-land near Kidderminster whilst *Lt zS* Krause was correct in saying he thought that they had damaged one of the Spitfires that attacked them:

Pilot Officer Thomas Draper Williams, Yellow Section, 611 Squadron

The Germans had started night bombing Merseyside and they used to send in a few aircraft just before evening to lay incendiaries and markers at last light. Our function was to intercept these aircraft by making a sweep out to Anglesey and back and then landing after last light anywhere we could. One of the more hair-raising experiences was to land at Penrhos near Criccieth.

We were always ordered to take off by telephone or Verey pistol. We were fitted with a Very High Frequency radio which was excellent but did not come into operation until we were about 11,000ft. We used to park down a slope near the guardroom at Ternhill and take off was a little exciting, weaving through the training aircraft doing circuits and bumps.

On 11 October 1940, we were about to take off at about 1800 hrs when we received a telephone message saying that a plot had been received on three-plus aircraft near the Scillies. The message said that if these aircraft continued on their present course, height and speed, they would be over Holyhead at 1830 hrs at 14,000ft.

We had heard this story often before and had been disappointed but we were up sun of Holyhead at 1815 hrs and to our surprise, three Dorniers arrived dead on time. My recollection was that we were six Spitfires and that it was six Dorniers but the entry in my logbook is inconsistent with this and indicates that there were three Dorniers and two of us, Fg Off Ian Hay having returned with engine trouble earlier on.

Fg Off Douglas Watkins (for some reason known as 'Dirty') attacked one Dornier and I followed in behind him. In retrospect, it would have been better if I had attacked a separate aircraft. My hazy recollection was that all the German aircraft were shot down but this seems to be inconsistent with my logbook. Anyway, the aircraft which we attacked immediately turned west, presumably heading for Ireland and we each made two more attacks from the rear.

I had been trained in the Fighter Command Number 1 Attack (an attack from the rear by a single aircraft) to break away by slipping down sideways so as to show the minimum aspect of one's own aircraft to the opposing rear gunner. This I did correctly but Douglas Watkins just got moving quickly by pulling up and to the right, showing the whole belly of his aircraft. In the event, he was not hit at all and I was hit on each of the two attacks. As I was breaking away from the second attack, there was an explosion in the cockpit and it subsequently appeared that I had been hit by an explosive bullet on the underside of the rudder bar. I started to bail out but then realised that the engine was still working and so I got back in and opened up the engine to maximum to obtain the maximum height before it failed, on the assumption that I had been hit either in the oil cooler or in the radiator. However, the aircraft continued to function and on looking around, I saw a ship between Holyhead and Ireland. I flew towards it and circled it at height for some time so that I could, if the engine failed, land beside it or bail out near it.

The engine continued to work with no sign of abnormal temperatures and so I set off for Anglesey. When I reached Anglesey, I looked for somewhere to land and found what appeared to be a suitable field at the south east corner of Anglesey–Bodorgan. I made a dummy approach but found that it was completely obstructed as a defence measure.

I knew that the only flare path in the north west was at Ternhill. I also thought that I would almost certainly crash on landing and it would be unfair to obstruct the flare path whilst other aircraft were in the air. Moreover, it was clear that the aircraft was not handling properly and I did not want to fly over the Welsh mountains at dusk. I accordingly followed the coastline to the Point of Ayr at Prestatyn by which time the plane seemed quite safe, although handling badly. I decided to try and land at Sealand. I knew that there would be no flare path but I knew the district and aerodrome well. My fiancée, later my first wife, was living at Hoylake and accordingly I crossed the River Dee and flew low over her house so that she might guess I might see her later. This caused some concern in the district as they had not had the all clear!

I then flew to Sealand and crossed the aerodrome waggling my wings as best I could as a sign of distress and then did a circuit prior to landing. I selected undercarriage down but it did not work. I then operated the CO2 bottle which is the emergency undercarriage system. I felt some difference in trim but did not get a green light. I then came in to land towards the north-west coming in over the embankment and bridge. Fortunately, the landing was perfectly normal and the undercarriage locked down. I then taxied back to the Duty Pilot's office by which time it was dark. The Duty Pilot was a Flt Lt and I am afraid I asked him in forceful tones where the ambulance and fire tender had been. He explained that they had followed behind on my landing run and had turned back when they saw I was alright. The atmosphere improved and he ended up lending me a Triumph Roadster, a pair of silk pyjamas and a five-gallon coupon for petrol and I duly spent the night at Hoylake.

In retrospect, I think I must have been hit by more than two bullets. The explosive one had broken the main undercarriage and shattered the emergency system and a number of electrical connections. Another one had shot the pitot head away and I was therefore without an airspeed indicator. The third went through the rear spar, splaying it out and jamming the left aileron. Fortunately it also severed the control cable between the ailerons, otherwise they would have both jammed. I was therefore able to partly use the right aileron.

The following day I returned to Ternhill but I gather the aeroplane remained at Sealand for many months before it was repaired.[2] The Dornier, by the way, went into the sea and the three crew were picked up. I hope the rear gunner survived as he continued to fire accurately throughout.

Apart from the odd daylight attack predominantly by Junkers 88s, the rest of the month saw the night offensive continuing. By now, the RAF was trying hard to counter the German night bombers and saw the Boulton Paul Defiant withdrawn from daylight operations at the end of August 1940, being used subsequently as a night fighter. The first Defiant kill by night had occurred on 17/18 September 1940 when Sgts George Laurence and Wilfred Chard of 141 Squadron shot down a Junkers 88 of 3/KG 54. Two days short of a month later, on the night of 15/16 October 1940, a night which saw particularly heavy raids on London and Birmingham, Plt Off Desmond Hughes and Sgt Fred Gash of 264 Squadron shot down a Heinkel 111 of 2/KGr 126 only to overshoot on landing at Luton, damaging their fighter in the process. However, civilian casualties were beginning to rise – the night of 14 October 1940 saw nearly 600 civilian deaths; the night after a further 500 were killed. The Blitz was intensifying and the RAF were helpless for the time being to prevent it from getting even worse.

German reconnaissance aircraft continued to be active in and around Great Britain during October 1940, assessing targets and damage. German losses had been relatively light but on 25 October 1940 RAF fighters met with unusual success:

---

[2] The repairs to his Spitfire serial P7356 were not completed until 23 February 1941 when the fighter was returned to 611 Squadron. It was eventually written off in an accident on 2 October 1943 whilst with 61 Operational Training Unit.

Plt Off Desmond Hughes (seen here as a Wg Cdr later in the War).

Leutnant **Konrad Wacker, 2(F)/122**

I flew the Bf 110 which was actually a 'destroyer' or heavy fighter. However, our unit used it as a reconnaissance aircraft. An automatic camera had been installed vertically in the fuselage which took a photo every few seconds. The engines had a special supercharger so that we were able to fly at 11,000m.

The problem with the Bf 110 was the short range and that is why I had jettison-able fuel tanks under each wing. Because of these, we could only get to 9,000m before dropping them. So, this was my undoing. During a reconnaissance flight to the Rolls

Lt Konrad Wacker (in flying helmet) beside the Bf 110 he was flying on 25 October 1940. (Wacker)

Oblt *Schwartz* (St Kap), Lt *Wacker, unidentified medical officer,* Gefr *Heinrich Gneist.* (Wacker)

Royce Factory at Derby, two Spitfires came down on me from a greater height (and out of the sun of course!) and I was handed to them on a plate. By the time I had dropped my tanks (one after the other), one of the engines had been hit. Being a good target for two fighters, the other engine's time soon came and I had no choice but to ditch. My *Bordfunker*, Heinrich Gneist, drowned – I think he had been hit and his life jacket damaged.

Pilot Officer Norman Norfolk, Blue 1, 'B' Flight, 72 Squadron

I was leading Blue Section [Norfolk, Sgt Maurice Pocock and Sgt John White]…I was vectored on 090°, climbing to 25,000ft. Blue 2 sighted enemy aircraft at 1427 hrs flying at 25,000ft due north. I climbed up into the sun to attack but enemy aircraft sighted me and turned to starboard to attack me. His attack was ineffective and I saw no fire. He passed over my head about 20ft above – I then saw the black crosses on the underside of a light blue wing. The upper surface was camouflaged similar to standard markings. After delivering attack, enemy aircraft dived towards the sea, flying south east. I chased enemy aircraft to about 6,000ft, opening fire at 300 yards; from there I closed to 200 yards and after a short burst, an explosion took place in the region of the starboard engine, giving out a long white cloud of smoke which I flew through. I was then too close to enemy aircraft to attack so I broke away to port to avoid collision. Enemy aircraft then went into cloud and after a short search, I returned to base.

Enemy aircraft fired on me at 300 yards but I saw no return fire after my second burst. Only one thing was observed – just before enemy aircraft turned to attack me, he jettisoned an object. To me it seemed square and flat in shape, about five inches in diameter and four foot long. It turned over and over endways, leaving behind a trail of white smoke.

The day after, an armed reconnaissance by a Fw 200 *Condor* of 2/KG 40 flown by *Oblt* Bernhard Jope, had spectacular results. He discovered, bombed and set on fire the liner *Empress of Great Britain*, resulting in the deaths of forty-five passengers. This was the sort of bad news that the British people could do without.

Two days later, it was the turn of a German pilot to be shot down for the second time during the Battle of Britain. Damaged by a British fighter on 28 July 1940, *Oblt* Friedrich-Franz Podbielski, *Staffel Fuehrer* of 9/KG 4, had crash-landed his severely damaged Junkers 88 at Schiphol in Holland. All four crew were wounded, one severely, and Podbielski did not return to duty until 1 October 1940. Even then, he was not allowed to fly.

Later that month, *Reichsmarschall* Goering visited III/KG 4 at Schiphol. A conference followed lunch after which the *Gruppen Kommandeur* of III/KG 4, *Hptm* Erich Bloedorn was appointed *Kommodore* of KG 30 and III/KG 4 was transferred to III/KG 30:

Oberleutnant Friedrich-Franz Podbielski, *Staffel Fuehrer* 7/KG 30

During the conference, I asked Goering if I could fly again and was given command of 7/KG 30.[3] My flight on 27 October 1940 would be my first as *Staffel Fuehrer* and the first after being wounded in July 1940.

On 27 October 1940, we were given the order to carry out Operation OPERNBALL, low level attacks on airfields in England at dusk, using three aircraft from each *Staffel*. After briefing, we flew from Schiphol over the North Sea towards Flamborough Head, low level over Scarborough towards the airfield at Linton-on-Ouse…

RAF Linton-on-Ouse Record Book, 27 October 1940

Linton had its first experience of attack by enemy aircraft. At 1815 hrs, three Junkers 88s approached from the north-west and dropped twenty (?) bombs, most 100 kilogram, from 2,000ft. One aircraft then turned and flew low over the Station with machine guns blazing but met with such a hot reception that it veered off to the north. This may have been the one which was afterwards brought down some 25 miles east-by-north of Linton. There were no casualties to personnel but a certain amount of damage was done to the aerodrome itself, the gas chamber was demolished and a few windows broken in the Transport Section.

Oberleutnant Friedrich-Franz Podbielski

After we had dropped our bombs, our starboard engine was hit and stopped. We lost height quickly and had to crash in a field behind a wood. We were quickly captured by armed civilians and then by police.

---

[3] He replaced *Oblt* Hajo Herrmann, later to become a highly decorated bomber and fighter pilot, who was injured in an accident on 18 October 1940.

The *Bordmechaniker Uffz* Otto Piontek was mortally injured in the crash and died that night. The same night I was taken by the police to York and interrogated.

Friedrich Podbielski's Ju 88 after its crash-landing. (via Cornwell)

Two more German bombers were lost during attacks on airfields on 27 October 1940 and a number damaged by ground fire; the effects of these attacks were negligible.[4] The remaining days of October 1940 were uneventful as far as the German bombers were concerned, the last loss being a Heinkel 111 of 9/KG 53 which became lost during an attack on Gravesend airfield on the night of 28/29 October, its crew all being taken prisoner. The Battle of Britain had ended but the battles over Britain had many more months and years to run.

Dornier 17Z of 5/KG 2 coded U5+AN which had taxied into a bomb crater at Cambrai–Sud after returning from an attack on London on the night of 27 October 1940; left to right Uffz *Ernst Frohlich,* Lt *Karl Manowarda,* Ofw *Helmut Petraschke,* Uffz *Ernst Geselle.*

[4] Some records state that *Oblt* Podbielski's Junkers 88 was shot down after attacking Driffield airfield but German records and Podbielski clearly state that Linton-on-Ouse was the target. It is therefore probable that *Oblt* Dietrich Marwitz, *Staffel Kapitaen* of 8/KG 30, was involved in the Driffield attack; he and his crew were reported to have been shot down by *Flak* and ditched off the Humber Estuary – there were no survivors.

Epilogue

1 November 1940 saw no real change in German tactics and air activity. A Dornier 17 of 4/KG 3 was apparently shot down by Hurricanes of 17 Squadron near a convoy sailing off the East Anglian coast. Spitfires of 64 Squadron then chased off an unidentified Heinkel 115 just before the fighter-bombers made their first appearance of the month over London. As this attack withdrew, a Messerschmitt 110 of 1(F)/22, probably assessing the effectiveness of the fighter-bomber attack, was damaged by Spitfires of 92 Squadron. For the next four hours, air activity was almost non-existent before a fighter sweep preceded an attack on a convoy off The Nore and shipping off Dover. The bombers in this case were Junkers 87 *Stukas* of StG 1, the *Stuka* being used offensively for the first time since 18 August 1940. They were heavily escorted and succeeded in sinking three ships for the loss of one *Stuka*. Then a few hours later, bombers and fighters of the *Regia Aeronautica* carried out an ineffectual foray over south-east Britain. The last daylight bomber incident occurred during the evening when a Junkers 88 of 8/KG 30 engaged on another attack on airfields in Yorkshire flew into a hillside near Whitby, killing all the crew. That night was a repeat of many previous nights with London, and this time Birmingham, receiving the attention of the German bombers. Two bombers fell victim to anti-aircraft fire.

A Stuka of III/StG 1. The pilot who took this photo, Oblt Otto Blumers of 9/StG 1, was himself shot down and taken prisoner on 14 November 1940. (Blumers)

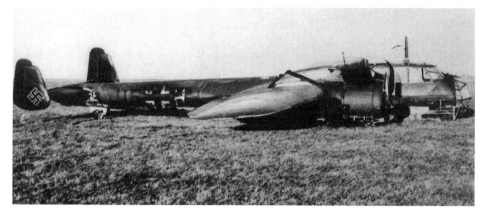

Another casualty – this Do 17 of 1/KG 2 crash-landed at Vitry-en-Artois on returning from London on the night of 13 November 1940. (Hoehler)

The two months that followed the official Battle of Britain saw no let up in the German offensive, albeit daytime attacks by bombers, because of the painful lessons learned in the summer of 1940, had become few and far between. Bolstered by night time successes and fewer losses, the night offensive took precedence. However, on the night of 19/20 November 1940 a very significant combat took place when the first successful airborne radar-assisted night interception occurred; but at that time, the full significance was not apparent:

Night Combat Report for Flight Lieutenant John C Cunningham, 604 Squadron

One aircraft, a 604 Squadron Beaufighter [callsign] non-Cockerel Blazer 24 (Flt Lt Cunningham), up 2221 hrs down 2259 hrs, engaged four-engined enemy aircraft type uncertain (Fw *Condor*?) near Brize Norton at 18,000ft at nearly same level and about 200 yards astern and at about same speed. Enemy aircraft returned fire almost immediately and appeared to slow down suddenly and turn to starboard. This enemy aircraft had no navigation lights and was intercepted by aid of: (a) Wallop control (b) Searchlight concentration on cloud (c) Airborne Interception (AI) Operator (d) Exhaust flames of enemy aircraft (e) Further instructions from AI Operator. Result inconclusive. Our casualties nil. Prior to this interception Blazer 24 sighted a smoke trail and two twin-engined enemy aircraft with navigation lights (believed formation of three twin-engined aircraft: six red lights were fired in pairs).

Later the following day, the wreckage of a Junkers 88 of 3/KG 54 was found at East Wittering in West Sussex; credit of its destruction went to John 'Cat's

Eyes' Cunningham. It was the first of his twenty confirmed night kills and many hundreds more for the RAF's night fighter force.

The 'official' Battle of Britain is today recognised as being fought between 10 July and 31 October 1940. Nevertheless, this book has shown that the first major attack against Great Britain during World War Two by German bombers took place not on 10 July 1940 but some three weeks prior to that on the night of 18/19 June 1940. Furthermore, even though the 'official' Battle of Britain ended on 31 October 1940, the months that followed saw no let up in the *Luftwaffe*'s offensive, leading some historians to ask why we do not regard the Battle of Britain as ending on 18 May 1941 when the majority of German bomber and fighter units were withdrawn to the east for the invasion of the Soviet Union.

The night war was also intensifying for RAF Bomber Command and losses were increasing. Here Wellington T2501 of 99 Sqn shares Vitry-en-Artois airfield with a He 111 of KG 53 after force-landing on the night of 4 December 1940. (Hoehler)

It must be accepted that the 'official' Battle of Britain saw the fiercest air battles and greatest loss of life for both opposing air forces and if it were not for Fighter Command's men and women, the course of the war would have been totally different. Nevertheless, the battles over Britain continued for another four and a half years, not by day but the vast majority being at night. These battles could not be directly compared to those fought during the summer of 1940 but for those on the receiving end, they were just as dramatic as these final accounts show:

Combat Report for Pilot Officer Richard Stevens DFC, 151 Squadron

Plt Off Stevens, callsign Steeple 3, left RAF Wittering at 0032 hrs in a Hurricane with orders to orbit Coventry… At about 0140 hrs, he sighted another He 111 about 1,000ft above him also travelling westerly. He 'tailed' this and at about 200 yards range, the enemy started firing from the lower gun position. The Hurricane dived, came up underneath and fired a deflection burst from about 100 yards at nose and centre section. To evade the return fire from lower gun, he pulled up sharply on the port side and gave another burst upon which the enemy gunner ceased firing. The top gunner of the enemy aircraft was firing accurately and the Hurricane was hit several times. He then made another quarter attack from below and saw starboard motor on fire and leaving a stream of glycol which obscured his windscreen. He dropped back to wipe the windscreen with his glove and returned to the attack and noticed port motor on fire. A further burst from astern and below from 100 yards caused bits of enemy aircraft to fall away and then it dived steeply into a cloud layer. A further burst was fired and hit enemy aircraft which was not seen again although Plt Off Stevens followed it through the cloud. When last seen, both motors were on fire and inside the fuselage was also burning…[1]

Feldwebel Hans Kaufhold, 3/KG 55

On 9 April 1941 we took off from Le Bourget near Paris. It was my twenty-seventh operational flight. I had not flown during the summer of 1940 because I was recovering from wounds I received when I was shot down and taken prisoner on my fourteenth operational flight on 27 May 1940. I had started flying again on 28 November 1940 and had flown a number of night missions against Liverpool, London, Southampton, Glasgow, Bristol, Hull and Plymouth. Our target this night was Coventry.

Hans Kaufhold in the mid-upper position of a He 111. (Kaufhold)

---

[1] Richard Stevens was a successful single-seat night fighter pilot and had amassed fourteen and a half kills by the time of his death on 16 December 1941. It is possible that Sgt Alan Wagner and Sgt Stanislaw Seidengart flying a Defiant of 151 Squadron were also involved in this combat.

It was a clear night and the moon was shining. When we reached Portsmouth at a height of about 4,000m, we were shot at by *Flak*. Then, just over Coventry we were attacked by a Spitfire [sic]. The plane came out of the dark, the pilot must have seen us very well in the moonlight. He was in a good attacking position and during this attack, Herbert Link [the *Bordmechaniker*] was wounded in the upper arm.

After that, the Spitfire attacked from behind. Now it was my turn to shoot back. Everything happened so quickly and at that time I was not able to communicate with the rest of the crew as my intercom connection had been broken.

The Spitfire attacked again from where he had attacked first but, by that time, we could not fight back. Our plane was burning and in the meantime the bombs had been dropped. The last thing I heard was someone saying "Soellner! [*Ofw* Heinz Soellner, the pilot] At 1,000m there are some clouds so let's hide there!" After that, when I was watching the Spitfire, Herbert Link indicated that we should bale out – the order had come from the *Kommandeur* [*Hptm* Otto Bodemeyer, *Gruppen Kommandeur* of I/KG 55 and the *Beobachter*]. However, I misunderstood him and in the meantime, both in the cockpit jumped by parachute but we remained in the plane. Herbert had lost a lot of blood and was unconscious and we then were still in the plane when it crashed. I cannot describe what happened next because I lost consciousness.

Hans Kaufhold (left) stands by the He 111 in which he was flying on 9 April 1941. (Kaufhold)

I think that when the plane hit the ground, both of us were catapulted out. When I regained consciousness, I was lying in a meadow with my flying suit on fire. I jumped to my feet and put out the flames but my wrists, hands and face had been burned. I hurried to get away from the plane – the ammunition was exploding and later, the fuel tanks exploded.

I followed a small path along to a road heard footsteps approaching and I hid behind a bush. When I eventually reached the road, I jumped into a ditch. I was in great pain from my burns and my lips had become very thick. I heard shouting and dogs barking – soldiers were looking for us German airmen but they failed to find me. I sat as still as a rabbit in the ditch and the seekers passed me by.

Soon the Fire Brigade came but there was little that they could do. It became quieter and soon there was nobody around.

The same He 111 in pieces at a Leicestershire farm.

I wondered what to do – the road was empty so I came out of the ditch and marched or should I say limped along the road. After a while, a car came around a bend and stopped in front of me. An RAF officer stepped out, raised his revolver and shouted "Hands up!" and so I was captured for the second and last time during the War.

For Hans Kaufhold, his war was finally over. For many more German bomber crews, the war would drag on and their suffering at the hands of the RAF would continue.

The scene at a German airfield at the end of the war – He 111s are broken up for scrap by the victorious Allies. (Camp)

Dramatis Personae

1.	19 June 1940	*Stab*/KG 4	He 111 H-4 2894 5J+GA	*Oblt* Heinz-Georg Corpus (*B, Adj*) – + *Lt* Erich Simon (*F*) – POW *Ofw* Walter Gross (*BM*) – + *Fw* Walter Wick (*Bf*) – +	Shot down by Flt Lt A Malan, 74 Sqn and crashed at Bishop's Court Springfield Road, Writtle, Chelmsford, 0030 hrs
2.	19 June 1940	*Stab* II/KG 4	He 111 H-4 8747 5J+DM	*Maj* Dietrich Frhr Von Massenbach (*B, Gr Kdr*) – POW *Oblt* Ulrich Jordan (*F, TO*) – POW *Ofw* Max Leimer (*Bf*) – POW *Fw* Karl Amberger (*BM*) – POW	Shot down by Flt Lt R Duke-Wooley/AC D Bell and Sgt A Close/LAC L Karasek of 23 Sqn and crashed at Blakeney Creek, Cley, Norfolk, 0045 hrs. Aircraft flown by Sgt Close also shot down in the combat
3.	19 June 1940	4/KG 4	He 111P-2 5J+AM	*Oblt* Joachim Von Arnim (*B*) – POW *Fw* Willi Maier (*F*) – POW *Fw* Karl Hauck (*Bf*) – POW *Fw* Paul Gersch (*BM*) – +	Shot down by Sqn Ldr J O'Brien/Plt Off C King-Clark/Cpl D Little of 23 Sqn and Fg Off G W Petre of 19 Sqn and crashed at Six Mile Bottom, Great Wilbraham, Cambridgeshire, 0125 hrs; both RAF aircraft also shot down in the combat
4.	19 June 1940	6/KG 4	He 111 H 5J+FP	*Lt* Hansjuergen Backhaus (*F*) – POW *Fw* Alfred Reitzig (*B*) – + *Uffz* Theo Kuehn (*Bf*) – POW *Uffz* Fritz Boeck (*BM*) – POW	Shot down by Fg Off G E Ball, 19 Sqn and ditched at Palm Bay, Margate, 0210 hrs
5.	1 July 1940	*Seenotflugkdo* 3	He 59 C-2 D-ASAM	*Lt* Hans-Joachim Fehske (*B*) – POW *Uffz* Ernst-Otto Nielsen (*F*) – POW *Gefr* Erich Philipp (*Bf*) – POW *Uffz* Struckmann (*BM*) – POW	Shot down by Flt Lt E Graham, Fg Off E J Wilcox and Flt Sgt H Steere of 72 Sqn into the North Sea, 8 miles east of Sunderland, 0601 hrs
6.	1 July 1940	3/KG 4	He 111H-4 5J+EL	*Oblt* Friedrich-Wilhelm Koch (*B*) – POW *Ofw* Hermann Draisbach (*F*) – POW *Ofw* Rudolf Ernst (*BM*) – POW *Fw* Alfred Weber (*Bf*) – POW	Shot down by Flt Lt R R Miller, Plt Off J Brewster and Plt Off J Bell of 616 Sqn into the sea off Hull, 1750 hrs

Dramatis Personae continued

#	Date	Unit	Aircraft	Personnel	Remarks
7.	12 July 1940	*Stab*/KG 55	He 111 P G1+FA	*Oblt* Walter Kleinhans (*B*) – + *Fw* John Moehn (*F*) – POW *Ofw* Fritz Knecht (*BM*) – POW *Ofw* Philipp Mueller (*BS*) – POW *Fw* Heinz Kalina (*BF*) – POW	Shot down by Sqn Ldr J Badger, Sgt C A Ayling, Plt Off H C Upton, Flt Lt T Dalton-Morgan, Plt Off D G Gorrie and Plt Off R A de Mancha of 43 Sqn and crash-landed at Hipley, Hampshire, 1430 hrs
8.	15 July 1940	2/KG 26	He 111 H-3 1H+EK	*Oblt* Ottmar Hollmann (*F*) – POW *Uffz* Erich Walz (*B*) – POW *Ogefr* Heinrich Probst (*Bf*) – POW *Ogefr* Walter Reinhardt (*BM*) – + *Gefr* Josef Tretzger (*HS*) – POW	Shot down by Plt Off J S Morton and Plt Off D Stewart-Clarke of 603 Sqn and ditched 15 miles east of Peterhead, 1212 hrs
9.	21 July 1940	4(F)/14	Bf 110 C-5 2177 5F+CM	*Oblt* Friedrich-Karl Runde (*F*) – POW *Fw* Willi Baden (*Bf*) – POW	Shot down by Flt Lt D E Turner, Plt Off C T Davis and Plt Off J Wigglesworth, 238 Sqn and crash-landed at Home Farm, Goodwood, West Sussex, 1020 hrs
10.	21 July 1940	4(F)/14	Do 17 M-1 5F+OM	*Lt* Georg Thiel (*B*) – POW *Fw* Fritz Bohnen (*F*) – POW *Uffz* Alfred Werner (*Bf*) – POW	Shot down by Sqn Ldr H A Fenton, Flt Lt D E Turner, Plt Off J S Wigglesworth, Fg Off C T Davis and Sgt L G Batt of 238 Sqn and crash-landed at Nutford Farm, Blandford, Dorset, 1445 hrs
11.	24 July 1940	2/KG 40	FW 200 C F8+BH	*Hptm* Volkmar Zenker (*F*) – POW *Fw* Willi Andreas (*BM*) – + *Uffz* Rudolf Wagner (*F*) – + *Uffz* Heinz Hoecker (*Bf*) – POW *Gefr* Leo Hohmann (*BS*) – POW	Suffered engine failure and ditched 15 miles north-east of Belfast, 0340 hrs
12.	8 August 1940	8/StG 1	Ju 87 B J9+GK	*Oblt* Klaus Ostmann (*F*) – W *Ofw* Wuestner (*Bf*) – uninj	Possibly damaged by Sqn Ldr J R A Peel, 145 Sqn; landed at Theville with 60 percent damage

13. 8 August 1940	Stab II/StG 77 Ju 87 B	Hptm Waldemar Plewig (F, Gr Kdr) – POW Fw Kurt Schauer (BF) – +	Shot down off the Isle of Wight, 1720 hrs
14. 12 August 1940	Stab/KG 51 Ju 88 A-1 9K+AA	Oberst Dr Hans Fisser (Gesch Komm) – + Oblt Werner Luederitz (F) – POW Lt Franz Schad (B) – POW Sd Fhr Adam Nothelfer – POW	Shot down by a number of pilots including Sgt E Shepperd, 152 Sqn and crash-landed at Godshill Park, Isle of Wight, 1230 hrs
15. 12 August 1940	3/KG 51 Ju 88 A-1 9K+CL	Uffz Karl Zimmermann (F) – POW Ogefr Karl-Heinz Fahrenheim (BM) – POW Ogefr Oskar Hansmann (BF) – POW Gefr Theodor Dickel (B) – +	Shot down by fighters and crashed into the Solent, 1220 hrs
16. 12 August 1940	8/KG 51 Ju 88A-1 4078 9K+BS	Oblt Eberhard Wildermuth (F) – POW Oblt Otto Staerk (B) – POW Uffz Heinz Droese (BF) – POW Uffz Konrad Roesch (BM) – +	Tail shot off by AA fire and crashed into Portsmouth Harbour, 1230 hrs
17. 13 August 1940	Stab/KG 2 Do 17Z U5+KA	Oblt Heinz Schlegel (F) – POW Oblt Gerhard Osswald (B, St Kap) – POW Ofw Gustav Babbe (BF) – POW Ofw Ernst Holz (B) – POW	Possibly shot down by Plt Off J A Walker of 111 Sqn; crashed at Pherbec Bridge, Barham, Kent, 0830 hrs
18. 15 August 1940	10 (Staka) /LG1 Ju 87 B	Hptm Rolf Muenchenhagen (F) – POW Fw Herbert Heise (BF) – +	Shot down by Hurricanes of 501 Sqn into the sea off Folkestone, 1140 hrs
19. 15 August 1940	8/KG 26 He 111 H-4 1H+FS	Oblt Hermann Riedel (F) – uninj Ofw Paul Suessenbach (BF) – uninj Ofw Kalle Mueller (BM) – uninj Fw Willi Scholl (B) – uninj	Shot down into the North Sea, c.1300 hrs

Dramatis Personae continued

No. / Date	Unit	Aircraft	Crew	Notes
20. 15 August 1940	1/KG 26	He 111 H-4 1H+GH	*Oblt* Rudolf Roch (*B*) – POW *Uffz* Willi Zimmermann (*F*) – POW *Gefr* Erwin Kulick (*BF*) – POW *Gefr* Alwin Machalett (*BM*) – POW *Flg* Ernst Henrichsen (*HS*) – POW	Believed to have been shot down by Plt Off W Millington, 79 Sqn and ditched in Cresswell Bay, Blyth, 1300 hrs
21. 15 August 1940	7/KG 30	Ju 88 A-4 5648 4D+DR	*Oblt* Werner Bachmann (*F*) – POW *Fw* Georg Henneske (*BF*) – + *Uffz* Werner Evers (*B*) – POW *Flg* Robert Walther (*BM*) – POW	Shot down by Spitfire of 616 Sqn and crashed at Hornby near Bridlington, 1325 hrs
22. 15 August 1940	4/LG 1	Ju 88 A-1 L1+FM	*Uffz* Fritz Dieter (*F*) – POW *Uffz* Willi Rimek (*B*) – + *Uffz* Otto Rezeppa (*BF*) – POW *Gefr* Werner Hohbom (*BM*) – POW	Shot down by Flt Lt S D P Connors of 111 Sqn and crash-landed at Great Ham Farm, Earnley, West Sussex, 1830 hrs
23. 15 August 1940	*Stab* II/LG 1	Ju 88 A-1 L1+SC	*Oblt* Stephan Suin de Boutemard (*F*) – POW *Ofw* Heinz Grund (*B*) – POW *Fw* Kurt Weigang (*BF*) – POW *Fw* Willi Lueder (*BM*) – POW	Shot down by Flt Lt A Hope and Sgt L Guy of 601 Sqn and crash-landed at The Jumps, West Tisted, Hampshire, 1810 hrs
24. 15 August 1940	*Seenotstaffel* IV	He 59 C D-AFFK	*Lt zS* Siegfried Boerner (*B*) – + Rest of crew and crew of *Oblt* Riedel of 8/KG 26 uninj	Shot down by a Hudson of 206 Sqn into the North Sea, 2230 hrs
25. 16 August 1940	3/StG 2	Ju 87 B-1	*Uffz* Ernst Koenig (*F*) – POW *Uffz* Josef Schmid (*BF*) – POW	Shot down by fighters into the sea south of Selsey Bill, 1400 hrs
26. 18 August 1940	6/KG 76	Ju 88 A-1 F1+GP	*Fw* Karl Krebs (*F*) – + *Fw* Otto Watermann (*BF*) – POW *Uffz* Horst Loeffler (*BS*) – POW *Sd Fhr* Willi Perchemeier – POW	Probably shot down by Sgt P C P Farnes of 501 Sqn and crashed at Aylesford near West Malling, Kent, 1340 hrs

No.	Date	Unit	Aircraft	Crew	Details
27.	21 August 1940	2/KG 2	Do 17 Z-3 U5+FK	*Lt* Heinz Ermecke (*F*) – +; *Uffz* Goetz-Dieter Wolf (*B*) – POW; *Uffz* Heinz Hermsen (*Bf*) – POW; *Sd Fhr* Kurt Rasche – POW	Shot down by Flt Lt G Powell-Sheddon, Sub Lt R E Gardner and Plt Off J B Latta of 242 Sqn and crashed at Conifer Hill, Starston, Norfolk, 1252 hrs
28.	21 August 1940	6/KG 3	Do 17Z-3 5K+AP	*Oblt* Herbert Schwartz (*F, St Kap*) – POW; *Oblt* Ulrich Matschoss (*B*) – POW; *Ofw* Wilhelm Loos (*Bf*) – +; *Uffz* Helmut Lehmann (*Bf*) – +	Damaged by Sqn Ldr J McComb, Sgt A D Burt and Sgt A S Darling of 611 Sqn and then collided in cloud with Do 17 flown by *Uffz* Georg Pollmann of 6/KG 3; crashed at Alford, Lincolnshire, 1314 hrs
29.	21 August 1940	4/KG 54	Ju 88 A-1 B3+BM	*Hptm* Lothar Maiwald (*B, St Kap*) – POW; *Ofw* Heinz Apollony (*F*) – POW; *Uffz* Kurt Miethner (*Bf*) – POW; *Uffz* Helmut Hempel (*BM*) – POW	Shot down by Sqn Ldr C Williams, Plt Off H A Bird-Williams and Plt Off J Ross of 17 Sqn and crash-landed at Marsh Farm, Earnley, West Sussex, 1615 hrs
30.	23 August 1940	*Stab*/KG 2	Do 17 Z U5+EA	*Oblt* Joachim-Heinrich Hellmers (*B, St Kap*) – POW; *Ofw* Guenther Wagner (*F*) – POW; *Fw* Albert Dietel (*Bf*) – POW; *Uffz* Paul Seidel (*BM*) – POW	Damaged by AA fire and crash-landed at Lodge Farm, Wickhambrook, Suffolk, 0920 hrs
31.	28 August 1940	6/KG 3	Do 17 Z-3 4251 5K+LP	*Lt* Peter Krug (*F, St Fhr*) – POW; *Gefr* Artur Burghardt (*B*) – POW; *Gefr* Willi Gailer (*Bf*) – POW; *Flg* Anton Brueckmann (*BS*) – POW	Damaged by AA fire and then shot down by Sqn Ldr J Leathart, 54 Sqn off Palm Bay, Margate, 1245 hrs
32.	30 August 1940	7/KG 53	He 111 H-2 2624 A1+CR	*Lt* Ernst Fischbach (*F*) – POW; *Fw* Wilhelm Kusserow (*B*) – POW; *Fw* Georg Distler (*Bf*) – POW; *Gefr* Leo Stilp (*HS*) – +; *Gefr* Walter Reis (*HS*) – +	Shot down by Flt Lt W Rhodes-Moorhouse, Plt Off H T Gilbert, Sgt N Taylor and Fg Off T Grier of 601 Sqn and crashed at The Rectory, Hunsdon, Hertfordshire, 1630 hrs

Dramatis Personae continued

33. 30 August 1940	3/KG 53	He 111 H-2 5532	*Lt* Wulff Roessler (*B*) – POW *Uffz* Helmut Gall (*F*) – POW *Uffz* Ernst-Erhard von Kuehnheim (*BF*) – + *Uffz* Adolf Saam (*BM*) – + *Ogefr* Otto Fischer (*BS*) – +	Shot down by Sgt H J Merchant of 1 Sqn and crashed at Lifstan Way, Southend, Essex, 1715 hrs
		A1+IL		
34. 31 August 1940	2/KG 76	Do 17 Z 3316	*Lt* Josef Kleppmeier (*F*) – POW *Ofw* Heinrich Lang (*BM*) – POW *Fw* Harald Pfaehler (*B*) – POW *Uffz* Albert Bloss (*BF*) – POW	Damaged by AA fire and probably damaged further by Sgt M H Pocock of 72 Sqn and crash-landed at Newchurch, East Sussex, 1800 hrs
		F1+BK		
35. 5 September 1940	*Stab* I/KG 1	He 111 H-3 3324	*Maj* Ludwig Maier (*Gr Kdr*) – + *Oblt* Peter Biebrach (*F, TO*) – POW *Oblt* Graf Job-Wilhelm von Rittberg (*B*) – + *Ofw* Erwin Stockert (*BF*) – + *Uffz* Horst Bendig (*BM*) – +	Shot down by Plt Off M J Herrick/Sgt J S Pugh of 25 Sqn and crashed at Rendlesham, Suffolk, 0110 hrs
		V4+AB		
36. 9 September 1940	*Stab* III/KG 53	He 111 H-2 2630	*Oblt* Kurt Meinecke (*B*) – POW *Ofw* Oskar Broderix (*F*) – POW *Fw* Ernst Wendorff (*BF*) – + *Fw* Wilhelm Wenninger (*BM*) – + *Fw* Willi Doering (*BS*) – +	Collided with Hurricane flown by Plt Off G M Forrester of 605 Sqn and crashed at Southfield Farm, Chawton, Hampshire, 1800 hrs
		A1+ZD		
37. 11 September 1940	*Stab* II/KG 26	He 111H-3 6856	*Maj* Eckhard Christian (*Gr Kdr*) – uninj *Fw* Krothe (*F*) – uninj *Ofw* Ziermann (*BF*) – uninj *Fw* Richard Herrmann (*BM*) – W *Gefr* Wilhelm Zimmer (*B*) – uninj	Damaged in combat
		1H+AC		

	Aircraft	Crew	Outcome
38. 11 September 1940 1/KG 26	He 111 H 6962 1H+AH	*Hptm* Wolfgang Kuenstler (*F, St Kap*) – POW *Fw* Erich Buettner (*F*) – POW *Fw* Johannes Schaefer (*Bf*) – + *Uffz* Walter Schang (*B*) – + *Uffz* Erich Schmidt (*BM*) – POW	Believed shot down by Plt Off E S Lock of 41 Sqn and crashed at Cripps Corner, Sedlescombe, 1630 hrs
39. 13 September 1940 8/KG 27	He 111P 2670 1G+DS	*Oblt* Harry Wappler (*F*) – POW *Ofw* Johannes Elster (*Bf*) – + *Uffz* Fritz Bernd (*B*) – + *Uffz* Herbert Okuneck (*BM*) – +	Collided with barrage balloon cable and crashed at 32 Stow Park Avenue, Newport, Monmouthshire, 0330 hrs
40. 14 September 1940 3/KG 4	He 111 H-4 3294 5J+BL	*Oblt* Hermann Kell (*F, St Fhr*) – POW *Fw* Walter Hobe (*B*) – POW *Ogefr* Werner Mueller-Wernscheidt (*Bf*) – + *Uffz* Hermann Toepfer (*BM*) – +	Shot down by Plt Off M J Herrick/Plt Off A Brown of 25 Sqn and crashed at Newmans End, Sheering, Essex, 0155 hrs
41. 15 September 1940 8/KG 76	Do 17 Z 2555 F1+FS	*Fw* Rolf Heitsch (*F*) – POW *Fw* Stephan Schmid (*Bf*) – + *Fw* Hans Pfeiffer (*B*) – POW *Fw* Martin Sauter (*BM*) – POW	Shot down by Fg Off J Dundas and Plt Off E Tobin of 609 Sqn and crash-landed at Castle Farm, Shoreham, Kent, 1210 hrs
42. 16 September 1940 3/506	He 115 C 3261 S4+CL	*Hptm* Ernst-Wilhelm Bergemann (*St Kap*) – POW *Hptm* Hans Kriependorf (*B*) – POW *Lt* Clemens Lucas (*F*) – POW *Fw* Erich Kalinowski (*Bf*) – POW	Damaged by AA fire and ditched in North Sea 7.5 miles north-east of Eyemouth, 0035 hrs
43. 16 September 1940 1/906	He 115 C-1 2754 8L+GH	*Hptm* Heinrich Kothe (*F*) – POW *Lt zS* Hans-Otto Aldus (*B*) – POW *Uffz* Herbert Meissner (*Bf*) – POW	Became lost in poor weather and hit hillside at Rosehearty, Fraserburgh, 2200 hrs

Dramatis Personae continued

	Date / Unit	Aircraft	Crew	Notes
44.	21 September 1940 *Aufkl.ObdL*	Do 215 B 0023 VB+KK	*Lt* Rolf Book (*B*) – POW / *Fw* Kurt Jensen (*F*) – POW / *Fw* Hans Kuehl (*BF*) – POW / *Uffz* Gustav Pelzer (*BM*) – +	Shot down by Plt Off D Adams of 611 Sqn and crashed at Trawsfynydd, Merioneth, 1655 hrs
45.	25 September 1940 1/KG 55	He 111H 6305 G1+BH	*Hptm* Karl Koethke (*B*) – POW / *Fw* Fritz Juerges (*F*) – POW / *Uffz* Rudolf Weisbach (*BF*) – POW / *Uffz* Otto Mueller (*BS*) – POW / *Uffz* Josef Altrichter (*BM*) – +	Shot down by Plt Off J S Wigglesworth of 238 Sqn and Plt Off J Curchin of 609 Sqn and crash-landed at Westhill Farm, Studland, Dorset, 1200 hrs
46.	30 September 1940 2/KG 77	Ju 88 A-1 2142 3Z+DK	*Oblt* Friedrich Oeser (*F*) – POW / *Ofw* Gustav Gorke (*BF*) – POW / *Uffz* Georg Klasing (*BM*) – + / *Gefr* Rudi Hulsmann (*BS*) – POW	Shot down by Sgt P C Farnes of 501 Sqn and crash-landed on Gatwick Race Course, 1500 hrs
47.	2 October 1940 *Stab*/KG 2	Do 17 Z 3423 U5+FA	*Oblt* Hans Langer (*F, St Kap*) – POW / *Oblt* Erich Eitze (*B*) – POW / *Uffz* Robert Seidel (*BF*) – POW / *Uffz* Helmut Bellmann (*BM*) – POW	Shot down by Flt Lt A W A Bayne, Plt Off F Fajtl, Fg Off H P Blatchford, Plt Off J K Ross and Plt Off L W Stevens of 17 Sqn and crash-landed at Rookery Farm, Cretingham, Suffolk, 1020 hrs
48.	7 October 1940 5/KG 51	Ju 88 A-1 8064 9K+SN	*Oblt* Sigurd Hey (*F*) – POW / *Lt* Fritz Bein (*B*) – POW / *Ofw* Christian Koenig (*BF*) – POW / *Ofw* Josef Krell (*BM*) – POW	Shot down by a number of fighters including Plt Off R F T Doe of 238 Sqn and Sgt E E Shepperd of 152 Sqn and crashed at Sydling St Nicholas, Dorset, 1630 hrs
49.	11 October 1940 1/606	Do 17 Z-3 2772 7T+EH	*Lt zS* Juergen von Krause (*B*) – POW / *Fw* Josef Vetterl (*F*) – + / *Fw* Heinrich Arpert (*BM*) – POW / *Ogefr* Helmut Sundermann (*BF*) – POW	Shot down by Fg Off D H Watkins and Plt Off T Draper Williams of 611 Sqn and ditched off Bardsey Islands, 1830 hrs

50. 25 October 1940	2(F)/122	Bf 110 C 2257 F6+MK	*Lt* Konrad Wacker (*F*) – POW *Gefr* Heinrich Gneist (*BF*) – +	Shot down by Plt Off N R Norfolk, Sgt M Pocock and Sgt J White of 72 Sqn and crashed in the sea off Yarmouth, 1440 hrs
51. 27 October 1940	7/KG 30	Ju 88 A-5 6129 5J+ER	*Oblt* Friedrich-Franz Podbielski (*F, St Fhr*) – POW *Ofw* Karl von Kiedrowski (*BF*) – POW *Fw* Heinz Heier (*B*) – POW *Uffz* Oskar Piontek (*BS*) – +	Damaged by AA fire and crash-landed at Richmond Farm, Duggleby, Yorkshire, 1800 hrs
52. 9 April 1941	3/KG 55	He 111 P-4 2962 G1+DL	*Hptm* Otto Bodemeyer (*B, Gr Kdr*) – POW *Ofw* Heinz Soellner (*F*) – POW *Fw* Hans Kaufhold (*BF*) – POW *Fw* Herbert Link (*BM*) – POW	Shot down by Plt Off R P Stevens of 151 Sqn and crashed at Roes Rest Farm between Desford and Peckleton, Leicestershire, 0145 hrs

Select Bibliography

Balke, Ulf, *Der Luftkrieg in Europa 1939-41*, Bechtermuenz Verlag, Augsburg, 1997

Caldwell, Donald, *The JG 26 War Diary, Volume 1, 1939-42*, Grub Street, London, 1996

Collier, Richard, *Eagle Day*, Pan Books, London, 1968

Dierich, Wolfgang, *Kampfgeschwader 55 'Greif'*, Motorbuchverlag, Stuttgart, 1975

Dierich, Wolfgang, *Kampfgeschwader Edelweiss*, Ian Allan, Shepperton, 1975

Foreman, John, *Battle of Britain – The Forgotten Months*, Air Research Publications, Walton on Thames, 1988

Foreman, John, *Fighter Command War Diary Part 1*, Air Research Publications, Walton on Thames, 1996

Foreman, John, *Fighter Command War Diary Part 2*, Air Research Publications, Walton on Thames, 1998

Goss, Christopher, *Brothers in Arms*, Crécy Books, Bristol, 1994

Mason, Francis, *Battle over Britain*, McWhirter Twins, London, 1969

Norman, Bill, *Luftwaffe over the North*, Leo Cooper, London, 1993

Patzwall, Klaus, *Luftwaffe Rangliste 1945*, Militaer Verlag Klaus D Patzwall, Norderstedt, 1986

Price, Alfred, *The Hardest Day*, Macdonald & James, London, 1979

Price, Dr Alfred, *Battle of Britain Day 15 September 1940*, The RAF Air Power Review, Volume 2 No 2

Ramsey, Winston (Ed.), *The Battle of Britain Then and Now Mark III*, Battle of Britain Prints, London, 1985

Shores, Christopher & Williams, Clive, *Aces High*, Grub Street, London, 1994

Vasco, John, *Bombsights over England*, JAC Publications, Norwich, 1990

Wakefield, Ken, *The First Pathfinders*, Crécy Books, Bristol, 1992

Wynn, Kenneth, *Men of the Battle of Britain*, Gliddon Books, Norwich, 1989

Index

Page numbers in italics indicate illustrations

387

Real battles. Real soldiers. Real stories.

Stackpole Military History Series

Real battles. Real soldiers. Real stories.

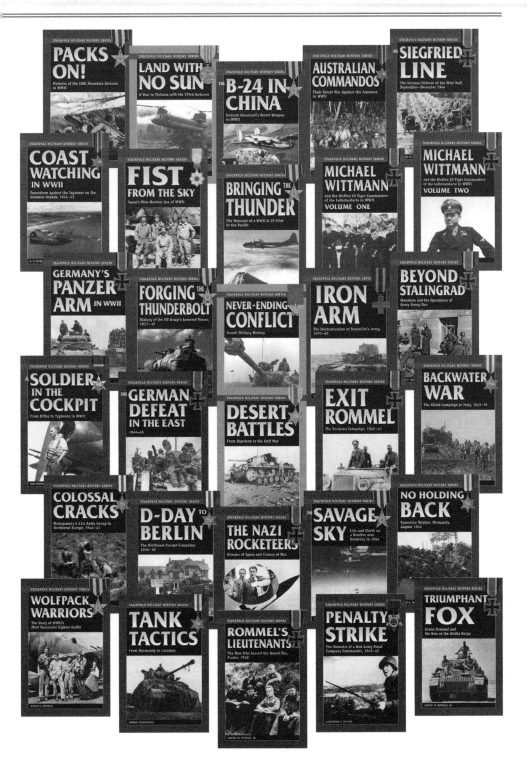

Stackpole Military History Series

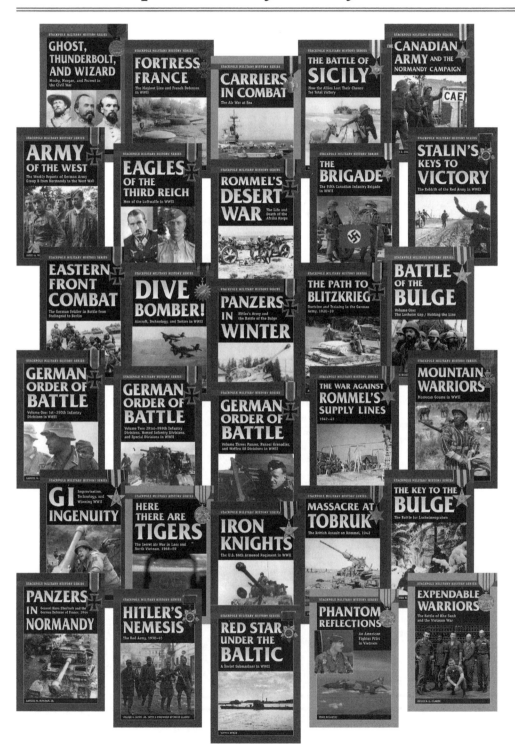

Real battles. Real soldiers. Real stories.

Stackpole Military History Series

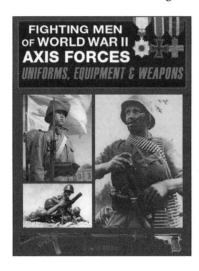
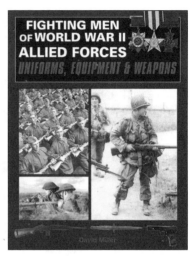